LIFELETTER

by Howard Newhard

xulon
PRESS

Copyright © 2008 by Howard Newhard

Lifeletter
by Howard Newhard

Printed in the United States of America

ISBN 978-1-60647-980-3
Library of Congress number TX u 369653

Book design by Christina Newhard.

www.xulonpress.com

FOREWARD

I t is often said that a person's life, however long or short, is a cycle of peaks and valleys. A mental picture arises out of this metaphor of a ride on an amusement park roller coaster, with its ups and downs, thrills and scares.

A more realistic analogy might be that most of our lives are like two cars traveling down parallel roads. One is plagued with potholes and obstacles popping up point blank without warning and the other presents a smoothly paved ribbon dotted with beautiful scenery and exhilarating oases.

This paradox gains complexity when one considers that there is one driver piloting both cars at the same time.

The measurement of the achievement and success of the driver's life clearly depends on his ability to maximize the sum balance of the physical, mental, emotional and moral attributes he possesses and is willing to expend. A personality displaying significant weakness in one or more of these fundamental values is destined for periods of depression or even tragedies during the drive. Imbalances of these values will inevitably result in regretful life events for themselves and their loved ones.

"Lifeletter" is a beautiful expose of one man's successful effort to balance the pace of both cars down his personal highways of a rich life filled with challenges through some very turbulent years.

Howard Newhard, with his seldom equaled recall of seventy plus years of life experiences, provides the reader with a stimulating "how-to" recipe that many can apply to their own journey. Regardless of the reader's choice of life goals, "Lifeletter" provides valuable reflections that will enrich their skill of balancing the high and lows that compound all human life.

A great writer once said, "We are a part of all we have met." I am greatly enriched by that part of me that was born out of the friendship and lessons gained from Brother in Christ, Howard Newhard.

Captain John Earl Klaas Sr. USN (ret)

Contents

Appendices

INTRODUCTION

This is my Lifeletter to my loving daughters Maria, Mariana, Michele and Christina. They have contributed much more to my life's journey than can be written. I also pay honor to Zeni, my dear wife, who overcame personal problems and disabilities to find true happiness in her last days here. She entered Eternal Life just before our 42nd wedding anniversary, having spent the previous 28 months in a nursing home, where I visited daily.

As I wrote this, I often felt I was telling it to you, my daughters, over coffee, lunch, or just sitting around; hence an extensive use of "writer's license," speaker's license, if you will, and "word-jiggling," ingredients in the natural flow of that situation and setting. This "speaking to you guys" mode also explains my jumping from the word "Mom" to "Zeni" intermittently, and mostly using "Nana" or "Pop-pop" rather than (my) Mom or Dad.

Realizing that one is not the same person from age to age, I tried to keep that in mind as I searched the memory bin and wrote the story.

When an old person dies, a library is lost; so if I act before I enter Eternal Life, not all, but something, will be preserved for those who are interested.

All events are true and "unglitzed." Some matters, dates, and exact places might be slightly askew chronologically and geographically, but close enough, and insignificant for the purpose of this Letter to you all.

I have written this at the urging of you guys. It was Michele who said seriously, "Dad, you never talk about yourself." It is the story of me, my experiences, and life. I will comment on historical, social, and political matters that I feel qualified to appraise, since they affected me and my generation, and those who have, and will, follow. I have written what is contained in my library of memory and intellect. These are historical recollections and representations learned by personal experience and other learning procedures. Occasionally, I have looked back at an old personal letter, but I have not done any outside research. In this regard, I have used that time-worn saying, "Ya gotta go with what ya got."

Writing the manuscript off and on through ages 78- 80, I surprised myself with the details of some memories I did not know I carried, until I raised the lid and rummaged deeply. Some I, of course, knew I had. Some, I suspected I had. Others didn't pop up until I thought on related matters. With others, I really didn't want to go there, a course I followed in a few cases without affecting the story. And so, today, all that I now am and hope to express, I owe to my Gingko Biloba.

When I was growing up I was too busy with school, studying, sports, working for cash, and working at home to think too far down the road. I was determined to go to college by some manner or means. Nana and Pop-pop could not send me, but I figured I could be an 8-year working student if necessary, or perhaps get an athletic scholarship.

I was that curled leaf out there on the lake moved by the shifting breeze, but internally guided by a faith, hope, and trust for the future. I did not "plan" my life but was taught to do my best and life would be okay. That, and an early introduction to praying, which led to thoughts of the Holy Trinity, gave substance to my "leaf on the lake" and not really worrying about the future.

Anyway, the short range daily and weekly challenges and goals absorbed my longer vision. My life in the overall has been a matter of "productive acceptance." Nana and Pop-pop influenced that in the way they lived their lives, and being taught by Benedictine monks in my high school days also enters into this self analysis.

While I sometimes think about it, and play some "if a," "would a," "could a," "should a," it is for fun without a desire now to have changed the outcome. That was not always the case.

Much is said today about planning your life: education, where to live, finances, the ideal spouse, how to get ahead, on and on. I am reminded: If you want to make God laugh, tell Him all your plans, and if you want to make Him smile, tell Him what you think He is thinking.

Now I am old, by age, living in south Florida for the past 23 years, and the tropics for the past 42 years. If someone tells me the dinner party is formal I will be sure to wear my black sneakers (made in Thailand) and put a crease in my black twill pants. And now it's time to talk.

It seems that most always I sought a variety of things to do and liked changing, challenging situations. When growing up I did not go back and take the same job two summers in a row. Volunteering for naval service during WWII at age 17, before completing high school, held that tack. Later on, the very nature of covert intelligence activity, with its variable, fluid, changing components, had a great appeal. Similarly living, working, and traveling in Asian countries for 26 years fit nicely into that aspect of my psyche. Even when selling annuities and insurance in Florida, age 58 to 71, I visited different kinds of companies and people in the state.

Married inter-culturally for 42 years, Mom and I developed broader perspectives because of it, and you gems, as I have said before, belong to the "bridge people" of the world, whose number is fortunately increasing, thereby providing needed understanding in this unstable, shrinking globe. People find your genetic tree to be interesting: Filipina (Malay), Spanish, Chinese, German, Polish, All-American.

I send kind thoughts of Peace and Love to relatives, friends, and other pilgrims who have shared a part of the journey with me.

Howard Newhard a.k.a.: Newy, Howie, Moose, Dad

1 | Nana and Pop-pop

Your "Pop-Pop," Howard D. Newhard, Sr., was born in Freeland, Pennsylvania in 1901. His dad was Andrew Newhardt, born in1866, and married to Katharine Herling Newhardt from the Cleveland, Ohio area. She was born in a German enclave and did not speak English until about age 12. Andrew was a railroader (brakeman, conductor, etc). The railroad was king at that time in Pennsylvania, the glue of the economy, as vital to the great coal and steel industries, as it was to the freight and passenger traffic. They had two sons: Roy and Howard Newhardt. Andrew died in a railroad accident when Roy and Howard were 7 and 5. Katherine's father-in-law was a man of some means, but had been against the marriage so much that he gave them no support whatever. Social Security, employee benefits, and family and children's services were yet to appear in our social structure.

So Katie had to deal with the grief and face the uncertain future. But she had a half-sister who gave her a job in a boarding house which she and her husband owned. At least this gave Gram a place to live, work, and raise the boys. She was so embittered by Andrew's father's rebuke, that she dropped the "t" from her married name and made it Newhard. Somewhere along the line Pop-Pop's name was similarly changed, but Roy and his eventual family kept the "t."

Back in Germany it was probably Niedhart (a name that is patronymic and traceable to the ancient personal name of Nithardt, which, in the High German, had to do with hatred and bravery, that old Hun warrior concept. As in the case of most German immigrants, the name was probably changed by the English captains of the ships running out of Bremen and Hamburg, as they phonetically wrote down the passenger's name; or on this side of the Atlantic, by the English speaking immigration officials.

It seems that the name was in eastern Pennsylvania early in the 1700's, since some Newharts (the most common spelling) were victims in the Fort Lehigh massacre of 1740; and it is a very common name on tombstones in the Lehighton area. I recall a large framed picture of Andrew's father, my great grandfather, and he had the distinguishable features of a Native American with high cheek bones, dark hair, an aquiline nose and a swarthy complexion. Ah, yes, Newharts were in Eastern Pennsylvania very early on. Pop-pop grew up in Lehighton until age 15 when he moved to Elizabeth, New Jersey, with his mom and brother. Howard and Roy then left school to work and earn wages, such was their situation.

The U.S. declared war against Germany in 1917. WWI had been raging in parts of Europe since Arch Duke Ferdinand was assassinated in Sarajevo in 1914. It was stalemated because defensive weapons, such as the machinegun, barbed wire entrenchments, and artillery pieces, were predominant. These weapons were killing the charging, or creeping and crawling, soldiers, who tried to follow the offensive plans assigned. The Battle of Verdun took months in the rain and mud. Nearly a million lives were lost there.

Dad was 16 in 1917, and he volunteered to join the Marines, lying about his age. This was discovered and he was rejected. He worked at various jobs and played semi-pro baseball around the county. His best friend was Frank Eilbacher, and they both played on the old Elizabeth Belmonts team. They sometimes played on Sundays on Staten Island, if they could find the right location so they would not be arrested by the police for breaking the New York Sunday "Blue Law" against playing baseball. Whether Jersey or Staten Island it was semi-pro, "pass- the-hat baseball." "Help the boys out!" a collector holding the collection hat would shout, as he made his way through the crowd. Worn-thin gloves, old spikes, and be-sure-to-count-the-bats-and-balls were common matters on the team. When a couple of new bats and several new balls were put in the mix, there were some smiles and the guys seemed to play better.

Pop-pop, with a tenth grade education, a lot of natural intelligence, good hand skills, and a nice gift of gab, was working in a shipyard in New Jersey when he was about 18-19. He was doing basic work, lifting and carrying material, and learning some riveting and welding. One day the foreman asked, "Can any of you guys read blue prints?"—silence—then Dad said he could handle it, not know-ing what "it" would turn out to be. "Well, take these home and study them and tomorrow we will discuss it," said the foreman. Dad was up most of the night studying the drawings and making notes. They talked about "it" early next morn-ing, and Dad was placed in charge of three other workers to do a small (not to him) specific task. He did okay, completed the job, and was starting to "get the beat." "Fake it 'til you make it," a mark of ambition.

One day he went to watch a local county league ball game at Warnaco Park in Elizabeth, but the real purpose was to roll dice with his buddy Frank and some other guys near the grandstand. Now Frank had met pretty Agnes Kress who was attending the game with her sister, Mary. After they finished throwing the cubes, Frank introduced Howard to Mary. They became friendly in a short period of time and started to date. After a while, Howard decided to ship out as an oiler on the freighter Cold Harbor, taking cargo port to port around North Africa and back. They were married shortly after he returned. And so the two best friends married the sisters Mary and Agnes. From time to time in the later years of the marriage Dad, in responding to the question "How did you two meet?" would reply that he won Mom in a crap game, and she would patiently smile and give him an "Oh, Howard." The same gentle and clement "Oh, Howard" she would say from time to time, such as: "Mary, there is no such thing as a bargain. It just means the store could not sell it any higher"—"Oh, Howard."

My mom, Mary, a cute blue-eyed strawberry blond, came from a poor, immi-grant family. Her father Ignatius Kress was born in Krakow, Austria (Poland after WWI, in accordance with the terms of the Versailles Treaty). He spoke 5 lan-guages and was very intelligent. Unfortunately, he was sickly, following an indus-trial accident in the Bayonne oil refinery. He was much older than his wife, Marcella Laurentz Kress, who was from Salesia, Poland. They raised 6 children. They also raised rabbits, pigeons and chickens for food, and Gram always had a vegetable garden every year. When we grew up a bit, Cousin Frank and I turned many shovels full of soil to prepare the garden in the spring. Shovel-shovel, rake-rake…good job.

Gram Kress always had a pot of coffee (with chicory) and a pot of chicken soup on the back of the old wrought iron coal stove in the kitchen. A small pot-bellied coal stove in the living room, and that cooking/baking coal stove in the kitchen, provided the only heat in the house. In mid-winter a trip to the out-house in the middle of the night was high adventure. But, later on, Howard ("Newt" to co-workers, team mates, and other friends) and Frank, both good with their hands, put a plumbing system in that little two-storied wooden house on Pearl St., near Bridge St. and the Elizabeth River. In those days the river water was clean and the fishing boats came all the way up to Bridge St. to sell their catch. Gone were the outhouse and the water hand pump in the kitchen sink. Surely they had a party since it was a real milestone, and Newt and Frank would not miss the opportunity to properly bless the occasion with a "nasdrovia" (Slavic drinking salutation).

Dad was a hard worker with plenty of energy. For most of his 45-year career with the Elizabethtown Water Co. he worked 5-1/2 days a week and rotated on emergency calls 24/7. In the summer he worked in his vegetable garden. He played industrial league softball until he was 40. He was a good bowler. He went to the ABC's several times with his team, and was in the money once or twice. Pocket change, but, hey, it's the ABC's!

Two of his "show-off" tricks for us children: Mom would be in the kitchen making mashed potatoes in a large aluminum pot. Dad would say, "Let me fluff them up a bit for you," and he would whip the masher around in the pot, get a rhythm going, and turn the whole pot upside down holding only the masher handle, spinning it around, with the mashing continuing and the potatoes staying in the pot by the centrifugal force. It was "show time" and we were delighted. His other one I remember was a one hand push-up. He would lie down on his stomach, put a small match stick between two fingers, push himself up into a push-up position, put the hand without the match behind his back and without touching the floor he would lower himself and take the match out with his teeth, raising himself back up with the one arm to the original position.

I can't remember that Dad said, "I love you, Howie." It was not the way of the day. Mom occasionally said it. But living in that loving environment where actions spoke louder than words, I never realized he didn't say those words until after he entered Eternal Life at age 76. None were needed.

Mom, the second child in her family, left school in the 7th grade to work in a commercial laundry and help Gram and the family. She also had chores around the house. Life was hard, but while the Kress family knew they were poor, they didn't know they were not supposed to be happy because of it.

2 | THE EARLY YEARS

Author with Nana and Marion, 1928

8 6 Third St. in Elizabeth, New Jersey, is down by the waterfront of that port city, which was named by the British in their colony days, and near a body of water, the Kill Van Kull, named by the Dutch long before that. I was born there on February 1, 1927, a cold wintry day. We lived on the third floor of a tenement house. Dad was working for the Elizabethtown Water Co., laying pipe, repairing mains etc. It was very hard physical work as was the way of the day, long before we had a machine for every job.

There was no doctor or prenatal program, but we did just fine with a midwife and advice from others who knew, especially "da momma" of the new momma. And so a healthy 10 lb. baby boy appeared. Two weeks before she entered Eternal Life at the age of 85, my loving mom smilingly told me I had given her a very difficult time. Oh, but that was only the beginning. When I was only eight months old, my sister, whom I love dearly to this day, pushed my baby carriage down the stairs with this writer in it. All the neighbors were astonished at my lung power. Marion, age four, probably figured "this kid is stealing all of my lines and scenes—I'll fix his wagon." Yes, Mom had her "off the wall" days long before the expression was in use. Of course my discourse of these early years comes from faint memory, plus a strong additive of family tales, told and retold among the members.

From age two to four, I played in the small back yard and on the side walk in front, along the cobblestone street. The peddlers made their rounds in horse-drawn wagons, and would pull up at my playground: "Hiya kid, watcha doin?" Then a big shout: "Hey, come and get your fresh vegetables! Good eggplant today, just five cents!" The ice man would pull up and cut a piece from large blocks of ice to carry up the stairs and put in the neighborhood ice boxes. I would try to pet the tethered horses but couldn't reach that high. "No, not on the legs kid, she gets nervous." The aroma from the horses was all in the mix of my sensual reception, which had a lot to work with, and gosh, those flies were big.

When three years old I climbed up some pipes above the old wash tubs, slipped, fell, and gashed my left eyebrow, which is scarred to this day. Mom responded to my screams and saw blood on my head and eye; poor Mom. But after some basic care, they, neighbors included, could tell I was okay and just needed some sponging, iodine, gauze and tape. At about the same age, I balance walked on the railing of a low porch, fell off, and broke my collar bone; and that wasn't okay, until I healed.

Down at the corner sundry store I was introduced to Eskimo pie, starting a true friendship which continues even now. Almost all transportation was by public trolley. There were very few cars. The Depression was upon us and most cars remained in garages. Walking was very popular, necessity being the motivator that it is.

An older kid named Vito was often called on to repair the outside lines and

Author with Marion at Warnaco Park, New Jersey, 1929

pulleys, used for drying the laundered clothes and attached to a large pole in the back yard for use at the first, second, and third floors. Vito would climb the pole and make the repairs. I thought he was pretty cool.

From 86 Third St. we moved to 157 Third St., which happened to be close to the Polish Falcons Social Club. It was an active family place, everyone welcome. I can still hear that special polka music. Mom and Dad liked to polka, and after a couple of "toots" on the beer mug, Dad was on falcon's wings dancing with Mom, the strawberry blonde.

Being big for my age, I usually played with older kids. At about 4, some of those kids would beat me up from time to time, though my "nose-punch" retaliations were commendable. Mom thought her boy had no future in this neighborhood. It would be many years before pre-kindergarten and learning to socialize nicely was a part of the social scene. She was determined to move out of the port area to a better neighborhood. But I'm ahead of the story.

Our neighborhood was mostly comprised of Polish, German, and Italian immigrants, with their first-generation children. The population density was much less than today. Starting when I was one-and-a-half years old, my gregarious dad, who liked a cool one after work, would occasionally take me to Mr. Krause's Saloon. Most of the men at the bar were neighbors and friends. There was a family room in the rear for women and children. Dad would plop me up on the bar, legs hanging over the side, a husky little blue-eyed, blond-haired tyke.

Mr. Krause would smile and say, "What'll you have?" I was taught to respond in German, "A schnifter," i.e., a shot. He would give me a shot glass with beer foam. Then around the bar we would all raise our glasses and shout "Prosit!"

The cars in those days had magneto starters and you had to insert the starter crank in a hole under the radiator and lean over in front of the car and crank it round and round until the magneto caught and the engine started. So sometimes for a laugh the men at the bar would tell me to crank up the car. I would then find Saucy, Mr. Krause's bloodhound, grab her tail and "crank up the car" to the laughter of all, except Saucy.

From the port area we were a walkable distance, a couple miles, to my Granma Kress' house. Granpa died when I was 2 or 3. I vaguely remember that he had a big red beard and would lovingly hug me, and I would squeal, not with joy. That beard was scary. We spent a lot of time at Gram Kress's place, especially in those earlier years. My cousin Frank Eilbacher Jr. is a year older and we grew up like brothers, as we remain to this day. We would play with the chickens, rabbits and pigeons. We would look for and find Granpa's double barrel shotgun and open the barrels, close them, and "click" the triggers. This was always done in a secret place because we knew we were not supposed to play with the gun. We did all the running around and exploring that kids are fond of doing. For sure our dads, the best of friends, smiled with pleasure and pride.

Mom finally got her way (not that Dad opposed it) and we moved to the Elmora section of Elizabeth. Dad was earning $30 a week, and I guess was helped again by his half aunt, Gram Newhard's half sister, Birdie. She and her husband owned a two-storied house at 830 Westfield Ave. (State Hwy. 28) which she rented to us for $30 a month. The property was about 60' by 150' deep with the highway in the front and the New Jersey Central Railroad running parallel in the back. The railroad embankment was about 12 ft. high and supported 4 pairs of railroad tracks. Our side of Westfield Ave. was all two-storied houses in a row. Across Westfield Ave. the houses were single family with relatively large grounds. From there, all the way to the school I would attend, about a mile away, and beyond, it was all suburbia, the nicest area of Elizabeth. We were as close as we could get. Mom was happy. There was a three-car detached garage on the property, which contained an Essex sedan, box-shaped with running boards, and a thermometer on top of the radiator that was readable from the driver's seat. It was a very heavy car and belonged to the Vans, upstairs. It was no longer used. The cost of running it was prohibitive in those Depression years. Another section of the garage was for storage for Aunt Birdie. In the other one Dad kept a box-shaped, red wheel, 1927 Chevy that the Water Co. provided so he could react to emergencies that might disrupt water pressure and service. He also had it for personal use.

We had a vegetable garden and, when old enough, I sometimes worked in it. Dad put in a home plate and a pitchers slab to the exact specifications in our yard. Back toward the railroad embankment he put up a basket and backboard, also to

Left to right: Marion, Frank Eilbacher Jr. (cousin), and author at Grandma Kress' house, 1929

Left to right: Marion, author and Nana at a park, 1929

specifications, always to specifications. By the great Zeus, he could read blue-prints. Dad and I had fun using the pitching mound and home plate. He taught me how to pitch. We were out there in the summer evenings, Sundays, or whenever, and later on we used the basketball hoop just shooting around or playing 2 on 2 or 3 on 3. There was a small drainage ditch that ran along the bottom of the railroad embankment, and I would spend a lot of time out there, winter and summer, damming up the water with a shovel. Then I would watch it fill up and break through the dam (Hydrology 301).

Mom and Dad got us a cute puppy from the pound. He grew fast. We called him Pal. He would follow me all over and he liked to tug at my winter garments when I was outside working on my water ditch/dam projects. I loved that little dog. One day Mom let him go outside to tinkle and he never came back. A year later, I was walking in front of the local White Castle hamburger shop and saw a dog that I believed was Pal. He was on a leash and the man who was holding the leash couldn't understand why I was calling the dog "Pal." I was so sure, so upset, that I immediately answered his question by loudly shouting, "You stole my dog!" Passers-by looked at the man as if he was an ogre, or stole the Fourth of July. "Give me my dog; I want my dog!" He said, "It's not your dog kid, no way, get out of here!" I grabbed for the leash and he pushed me away. I ran home crying and told Nana, whose concerned sympathy, while sincere, did not reach the level of "action." This was my first lesson in "Life Ain't Fair."

I lived at "830" from ages 4–12. In all those years I was outside much of the time with my neighborhood playmates, Sunny Mayor, the Kelleher brothers and others. Some of us "scrounged" the material to build a tree house that lasted a few years. Parental supervision was minimal when they knew where you were.

("That's nice, don't fight.") It was, of course, non-existent when they didn't know where you were. That was even nicer in a kid's mind.

The McGoverns were a family of 12. We played two-hand touch football on their street. A few of the McGoverns were much older than the rest of us but we always had balanced "choose-up" games. One of them, about 15, was a real big kid for his age. About a year ago in '06 the Associated Press carried a story that James McGovern was a distinguished fighter pilot in WWII and later became a legend in flying out in Asia. The story goes that an American bar owner in Hong Kong gave him the nickname Earthquake McGoon after the huge hillbilly comic character of Al Capp. He was shot down while flying a CIA air drop mission over Dien Bien Phu in the closing days of that French-Indo China war. The newspapers reported that his remains had been found in Laos, in '06, and identified, and so the "big kid" was finally coming home to an appropriate welcome and place of recognition.

We kids did a lot of "kooky" things. Sunny and I would collect pieces of glass and climb the railroad embankment to place the glass on a track. Which track? Well, you put your ear down on the different tracks and choose the one you can hear the train on. After the train roared by, we would race back to the spot and inspect the resultant white glass powder. Bottle caps, clothes pins, rubber bands, chewing gum and many other things were used in these advanced weight/pressure experiments, like Wow! We also liked to keep a small pile of throwing stones by the embankment, but not where Mom could see. We would then cut loose at the freight train cars when they thundered past. The engineer would see us and shake his fist, and I guess holler some bad words (we couldn't hear with all the noise), but he couldn't stop, and we kept throwing the stones at the big box cars.

The railroads around the country were, of course, the favorite transport for many of the hoboes during the Depression. It gave them a free way to get shelter in a box car, go to a warmer climate, go to an area with a better chance for work, or just walk the ties from time to time, waiting for the next freight to slow down for another free ride. My little bedroom was at the back of the house, its only window facing the railroad. On a summer night, with the window open, I would sometimes be frightened hearing a drunk, or sober, hobo singing in the night, or arguing about something, as he, or they, walked along the ties. At 5 years this was not good. Should I run for Mom and Dad? I was supposed to be brave. A perfect spot for the Japanese expression, "komata ne" (roughly, I'm in a fix). Putting the pillow over my ears didn't help either, but finally they would move on down the tracks. As time went by and the scene was repeated, my fears faded. "Hey you guys, shut up out there."

You, my dear daughters, know that I can't move on from this without repeating the words of that folk song, which was born out of the Depression, as so many were. I learned it by hearing Pop-pop sing it and you all heard me/we sing it often enough so that we still know it. I never heard it anywhere else but within the family:

"Oh, a bum, a bum, a jolly good bum, a bum I long to be,
To heck with the men who work all day while I sleep under the tree.
Asleeping in the icebox, tra-la-la la la,
We shoot the birds and the butterflies, tra la la la, la la.

"I met a man the other day, I never met before,
He asked me if I wanted to work ashovelin' iron ore.
I asked him what his wages were…a dollar n' half a ton,
Oh mister, I don't wanna work, I'd rather be a bum.

"While walking a western tank line, one summer's cooling day,
And in an open box car a dying hobo lay.
Beside him stood his partner with sad and dreary head,
And listen to the last word the dying hobo said:
Oh, I'm going to a better land, where everything is fine.
Hams grow on the bushes and it's summer all the time.
You don't have to work, not even change your socks,
And little drops of whiskey come rolling off the rocks!"

(Though for your sakes, "whiskey" became "ice cream.")

When about 5 or 6, I picked up a few wooden match sticks that Nana used to light the gas cooking stove. I guess I became fascinated watching Pop-pop light his cigarette or pipe with those three inch matches. I went out to the garage, to the half empty storage room, to have a secret place to see what it was like to light that match. I scrapped it on the concrete floor. It flared and burned my hand and I dropped it on some old crumpled newspapers on the floor. They started to burn. I didn't know what to do. I remember thinking: if I put that small 2x4 on the fire, then when I take it off there will be less fire. Ah, the logic of the pan-icked young mind, caught in the crisis. So I did that. It didn't work. The smoke and fire was rising. Better go into the house, fast. Nana took one look at my face and was shocked into realizing that something very bad was going on, big time. Fear froze my throat, resulting in a guttural: "Fire garage!" She hooked up the gar-den hose, called to Mrs. Van upstairs, and they hurriedly wet down the walls, sprayed the flames, and pushed out some of the burning material with rakes. It took a while. Some neighbors helped. Shaken by the experience and the thought of Dad's reaction, I went to my room and stayed there. Pop-pop came home from work and Nana told him the tale of the garage fire. He didn't punish me but made me aware of the gravity of the matter, and got my commitment to never, ever, ever, play with matches again. All of those two-family row houses were made of wood and wood-shingled walls and roofs. It was a close call that could have been a disaster. It was not brought up again in our family until the balm of time soothed the wounds of emotion.

But the story immediately made its rounds in the neighborhood and the extended family. "See that kid over there? Well, let me tell you…" "Did you hear about Junior?" Yes, a close call. Now, with age one is allowed some philosophical thought, and I conjecture: There are two kinds of close calls, good and bad. A "good close" is being near the coal stove on a cold winter's night, or nearest the wall when pitching pennies. A "bad close" experience requires imagination that you can still be in control and unafraid. Kids are good at that.

From the very early days to age 17, and off and on beyond that, I went to the beaches on the Jersey coast, crabbing in Barnegat Bay, picking dandelions in the country farms, and going to Green Pond in North Central New Jersey. This beautiful lake had very clear water. There were rocks and boulders throughout the region, a reminder of the Ice Age and the continual changes of Nature.

Parks and amusement parks were sometimes our free-time choice. When we went to pick dandelions we lived at "830." We would go far out of town, walk the farm fields carrying bushel baskets, and fill them with the dandelion flowers. No stems, please. Pop-pop would boil the flowers in huge pots of water with oranges, lemons, raisins, and other ingredients. Then he would let it cool and, I guess, "sit" (ferment) for a few days, before straining and pouring it into wooden barrels in the basement Home after work, he would go down into the basement, add a little sugar, and return to joyfully report: "It's 'cooking' and looks fine." Later in the process, he would bung the barrels and let the wine sit there. The uncles met often to play pinochle, and, of course, sip the wine. I hear it now, "This is great Newt, what's the secret?"

On the second floor lived the Van Schoik family: Mr. and Mrs. Howard Van Schoik, Howard, Robert, and Alvin. There were two Howards upstairs and two Howards in our family. So, to avoid confusion, my name around the house was Junior, for Heaven's sake, which I allowed until age twelve, when one starts to acquire some "voice" in the family. Thereafter it was Howie.

One day Sunny Mayer, the Kellehers and I were crawling around through the high grasses in an open lot, playing hide and seek, "bring in the bandit," cowboys and Indians, etc. Then Alvin, who was much older than us, showed up with a BB gun. Wow! What a great thing to have. We put some sticks up as targets and we each took a turn. Wow! Not satisfied with that, we got the idea to shoot a bird… yeah, now that's hunting! So we all crawled through the high grass along with Alvin…" Sshhh, be quiet." A sparrow landed in a bush in the clearing, Alvin took aim and Pow! We ran over to the fallen bird, which was definitely dead…and bloody. What had we done? This wasn't any fun. It was sad and bad and nobody spoke. Alvin, nonchalantly, went home. Then the four of us started putting Alvin down for killing the bird and we decided Alvin had to pay. One of us had to tell his mom and dad so that he would get a good "thumping." We solemnly drew grass shoots, these 7-8 year olds, to see which one of us would do it. Well, I drew the short one. I had to do it. My friends all went home to supper.

It was dusk. I went to the back of our house where there was a stairway going to the second floor. I started up the stairs, careful not to make noise, and reached the top. The doors leading into the pantry/laundry room and to the kitchen both had split windows. It was dark outside and I could see through both doors into the lighted house. All the Vans were eating at the kitchen table, ALL of them. Plan A was turning to Jello without a bowl. There was no plan B...until it came roaring into my mind. Now I had an Instant Plan B. I stood in the laundry room and shouted as loud as I could: "Alvin killed a bird!" Then I flew down the stairs like a frightened rabbit, hit the ground, took a big breath and walked around to the front door of our home for supper. "You're late, Junior, where have you been?" "Just playing, Mom." "Well, be here on time." "Yes, Mom." I never heard that anything ever happened to Alvin by way of punishment. The next day my friends asked me about it. I told them I fixed it. Alvin would surely get a good "thumping." "Did you tell his mom and dad?" "Yeah."

I started at Victor Maravlag School #21, the newest in the city, when I was 5. Marion was in 3rd grade and I went into kindergarten. This was a so-called Progressive School, as was the vogue in the early 1930's. The three "R"'s were still the basic emphasis, but music, singing, drawing, all kinds of games, and an indoor play area with a jungle gym made our days. In later years, the discipline of memorizing poetry, and historical documents such as the Preamble of the Constitution, the Gettysburg Address, Lincoln's Thanksgiving Proclamation, etc. had its value for the growing mind, and the meaning of the subject matter would work its way into the life of my generation, as it did my Dad's. That kind of knowledge was taught and repeated to us all through the school years. It provided the planks in the platform of patriotism which our generations needed to overcome their hardships in a unified way.

I walked the mile plus to school with Nana and Marion on that first day. After that Marion had the assignment to walk with and watch me, poor Marion. After a year or two I was going the route alone. Miss Galeckler was the kindergarten teacher and I liked it there. We had all kinds of games, the jungle gym, singing, drawing, playground, and later I played the triangle in the percussion band, and became friends with Carl Fenstemaker, Allan Watson, Harold Romano, Buddy Natelson and others. Ann Wafferage was cute: brown curly hair, brown eyes, and she was also my friend.

At the Halloween celebration that year we were all supposed to show up in costume at, say, 10 a.m. Nana and I were late getting me ready; then we walked the mile or so and arrived late. This bothered me. The party had already started and I really did not want to go in. I guess I was embarrassed. Miss Galeckler came out and she and Mom tried to get me to go in. It became a "pull him in" exercise; he'll like it once he is inside. Well, I didn't like it at all and I kicked Miss Galeckler in the knee. Nana was upset and I was a little sad over the matter as we walked home in silence. My older mind now says it really wasn't smart. I could have been partying with Ann Wafferage, "more root beer?" Miss Galeckler never showed any resentment, continuing to be pleasant and nice and a good teacher. That's Progressive education!

Soon after, they wanted to advance me to the first grade. Miss Galeckler and the first grade teacher came in and told me I was going to like first grade. We were into the third month of school and they sat me at a desk in first grade and gave me a reading book like See Spot Run, or something, and number exercise pads. Everyone knew the drills and, naturally, I wasn't up to speed. I was in "neutral." My classmates looked at me a bit dismayed. "Who's the new dumb kid?" I had not had adequate training at home to be prepared for this. With no headstart program of any kind, I was embarrassed and cried to go back to kindergarten, back to the jungle gym, finger painting, music, my buddies, and Ann Wafferage. No dumb boy, he. I'll never know if it was better or worse by not skipping "kinder" but my immediate concerns were covered as back I went.

From about 7 years old I occasionally walked to the butcher store for Nana. She would give me a list and the money, and I would give it to the butcher. We didn't have that many people around then, and most everyone in the neighborhood knew each other, at least by sight. The shop was in front of Bender's slaughterhouse, on Bender Lane off of Rt. 28, in Roselle Park. As soon as I walked in, one of the butchers would slice off a piece of bologna and hand it to me with a "Hiya, kid." I would eat it while he filled the order. He marked down the amounts on the paper bag and gave me the change. It was all very friendly. People had time to be nice. At the small grocery or vegetable store it was the same. "Hiya, kid. Here, have a cookie, I'll fill the order. Here's your change, it's all marked on the bag. Tell Mom I don't have Del Monte corn so I gave her Libby's. Say hello to Mom (or Marion)." Dad did not shop then. Then one day the first supermarket that any of us ever saw opened on Elmora Ave. To see that big sprawling store for the first time is truly memorable. This food marketing concept was being born then and would grow, for better or for worse, into a giant entity in our society.

Occasionally on a Sunday, Sunny and I, or Dad and I (Nana was a stay-at-home and Marion didn't care for baseball), would go to Warnaco Park to watch a baseball or football game. Sometimes I went alone. I would cross the railroad tracks behind the house into an open field next to the Borden Dairy bottling and distribution plant, past some houses, then into a wooded area, and finally to a street with houses and the entrance to the park. The park was attractive, with a nice lake for boating or ice skating. There were plenty of play fields, all well-maintained. This day I could not find anyone to go with me, so I started out the mile plus walk by myself. Mom gave me five cents for a Milky Way, which was my favorite. As I was walking the wide path through the wooded area a man came up beside me and started talking to me. I immediately sensed that behind his smiles and pleasant mannerism something was wrong. I walked a little faster, and he kept the pace, walking and talking. As we came toward the end of the wooded area, he said he would give me a quarter if I showed him the private thing. I started to run and shouted at him to "leave me alone" and he moved off in another direction through the woods. I continued on to the game, quite shaken. Watching the game helped. Buying a Milky Way and eating it surely helped. Then the voice of something I did not want around me, gently said, "You could have had five Milky Ways."

I was ashamed and angry about thinking such a thing (also, I could have been dead). This, and another similar incident when I was 15, must have left a subliminal impression on me, which was reflected many years later, when I was being screened and polygraphed for a top secret security clearance to work in the Office of Special Operations of the CIA.

Every year we had a neighborhood fireworks get-together for the 4th of July celebration. When I was about six, people were shooting off some fireworks one evening next door at the Kellehers. The fireworks were over and the kids were playing and the parents were chatting. I found a smoldering hand sparkler. I also found a small unexploded fire cracker which I promptly lit from the sparkler. It blew up while I was still holding it, followed by many "oh, no's," and "my Gods." Luckily it was a small one, and after rushing me to the doctor and being assured that my eye and minor burns would heal without effect, Pop-pop vowed, no more fireworks. Instead we would go to the 4th of July doubleheaders at Yankee Stadium. Now who said, "Life is a series of trade-offs?" Right on, dude.

Those trips to Yankee Stadium were PRECIOUS for this kid. Just going to the game was exciting, high adventure, for a little kid who lived near small woods, parks, empty lots, and suburbia. We would board the Jersey Central train in Elizabeth and go chugging through all of the factory districts on the way to the Jersey City terminal. July weather, no a/c, windows open, lots of breeze and some smoke and dust. Comparisons from another time are silly. That was the way it was, we knew no other; it was fun. Then we would walk onto the double deck ferry boat to cross the Hudson River to Canal St. in lower Manhattan. The first thing I would notice at the riverside was the smell of the salt air and the crying of the gulls. Oh, that ride across was superb with the skyline, the Statue of Liberty, and all of the big ships coming in and leaving. The docks, a long time quiet now, and some rotting away, were bustling with activity, and one time the Il de France passed right in front of us on its way to Europe. I never forgot, being just above the waterline, and looking up at that magnificent floating city, moving slowly down the channel.

At Canal St. we would take the old subway, with all of its noise and rattle, windows open, to 161st street and Yankee Stadium. Lou Gehrig was my special hero. A man of high virtue and morals, he was born in a German area in NYC. A great athlete, he graduated from Columbia University where he played football and baseball, a New Yorker through and through. We would go to the game very early to watch batting practice, pepper games, infield warm-ups, outfield practice (to the oohhhs and aahhhs of the crowd when an outfielder would throw strikes to home or third base).

Lou Gehrig made his famous speech at the Fourth of July double header in 1939…his farewell, "today I consider myself the luckiest man on the face of the earth." It was the beginning of his long goodbye, and we were there. I can still feel it. In 1989 I wrote a poem entitled "The Way It Was," in honor of Lou and the 50th anniversary of his announcement to retire, and about my disillusionment of today's industrial spectacle they call baseball (see Appendix A: The Way It Was).

On the way home as we waited for the train at the Jersey City terminal, Poppop and I would play various coin operated games, one-on-one, full of challenge, with no "let the kid win" gifts. I surely wasn't going to give him any chance to beat me. The glass-covered games involved hitting the ball past the opponent's positions to the hole-goal on the other side. He almost always won, but I would have my day. Similarly, I was playing my grandson Danny a game of checkers when he was about 8. I was winning. A friend who was watching whispered with a touch of curiosity, "Why don't you let him win?" No way! You earn your spurs honestly in this family.

About this time Marion and I went to live with Aunt Helen and Uncle Larry so the scene for the arrival of our brother Richard at home would be orderly, calm, and peaceful. A week later we excitedly went home and were so happy to see him there with Mom and enjoying all the fuss. Now our family was complete and he was the center of the family's attention.

I recall third grade (about 8 years old) pretty well. Miss Mahoney was the teacher and we did our basic math exercises and problem solving. Reading was going full blast and penmanship was taught, the Palmer method. We started to learn more about music and the boys were really into sports, baseball, basketball, football, and running. Often in the summertime at the school playground, we played softball, stickball, paddle tennis, "ring-a-levio" (hardly school-approved) and other games all day long. We prayed the Lord's Prayer or 23rd Psalm before class in that public school and pledged allegiance to flag, God, and country. When we started a choir, the songs ranged from children's ditties to Home on the Range, Red River Valley, etc. Some were songs of real substance and patriotism. I still remember the tune and words of two:

"Glory and love to the men of old, that their sons may copy their virtues bold. Courage in heart and sword in hand; ready to fight, ready to die for Fatherland. Who needs bidding to dare by the trumpets blown? Who lacks pity to spare when the field is won? Who would fly from the foe when alone or lost and boast he was true, as a coward might do when peril is past? Glory and love to the men of old!….." I know the tune. The music is like that of a triumphal march.

"The minstrel boy to the war has gone. In the ranks of death you'll find him. His father's sword he has girded on, With his wild harp slung behind him."

I only recall pieces of the rest. I believe it is an old Scottish ballad. It helped to prompt early thought on "What's it all about, Lord?"

Then there was "My Country 'Tis of Thee" started way back after the Revolutionary War, when our patriots wrote new words to the old tune of "God Save the King:"

"My country 'tis of thee, sweet land of liberty, of thee I sing. Land where our fathers died, land of the Pilgrim's pride, from every mountain side, let freedom ring. Our Father's God to thee, author of liberty, thy name be one. I love thy rocks and rills, thy woods and templed hills, my heart with rapture fills, like that above."

My school friends from kindergarten through grade six were Allan Watson, Tommy Cezslik, Carl Fenstemaker, Buddy Natelson, Harold Romano, Jack and Phil Karchman, George Williston, Lawrence Oxley, and others. When walking home from school, or on Saturdays, it was not unusual for us to find an empty lot and mark off a playing area with sticks and rocks and then play tackle football. In the street it was two-hand touch, but on regular ground it was tackle. We would draw plays on the ground while huddling…"You block, George, you go here and come back for a pass, and you two block Phil, Buddy, go long!" On Saturdays in the fall we would play until we couldn't. Long before Vince Lombardi said "Ya gotta leave it all on the field," that's what we were doing. In the summer it was softball and other activities at the playground. In winter it was football in the snow or sledding down a sloping street.

Carl Fenstemaker told me about this sundry store he would visit on Maggie Ave. and how he was able to swipe a candy bar when the "prop" wasn't looking. Hey, Milky Ways, I was listening. So he gave me the layout and we planned the heist for Saturday morning. No one was in the store when we walked in and the "prop" was off in the back room. So we split up and walked around looking. Carl picked up the loaf of bread his Mom had sent him for, and I stood in front of the candy counter. I deftly grabbed a Milky Way and slipped it into my jacket pocket, looked up, and there staring down on me from the other side of the counter, was a seeming giant of a man with smoldering eyes fixed into mine. Options flashed in my mind: Run for the door, or hold up the bar and say "How much is this?," or fake a big cry, with "I'll never do it again!" (That well worn "have mercy" Academy Award scene put on by children throughout the world.) But he then smiled and said, "Would you like a Hershey Bar?" Shakily, "No thanks, sir, I'm with Carl." That guy must have enjoyed watching those two eight year old imps working a heist on him, my first and last time in the business.

When I was ten it was 1937 and we had been in the Depression for eight years. It was always the topic of the day. It caused much suffering. There was no such thing as you must find a job that will make you happy. In point of fact you won't be happy unless you get a job, any job. Nobody ever said, "What kind of a job did you get at the factory?" They said, "Did you get a job?" Around town extended families might sit around the kitchen table and those who were working and had some payday cash might say, "What do you need? How much will make do this week?" Families were generally closer then. They closed ranks when the going got tough. The love and kind feelings often overcame some pettiness that had threatened their relations. Can ANYTHING good come out of a Depression? You bet!

We were fortunate that Pop-pop worked for a utility company where a layoff was unlikely. The company gave him a car and telephone with little cost so he could react to emergencies. I remember going to the store for Nana. It was common to ask the butcher for 10 cents' worth of bologna, or 10 cents' worth of stew meat, the same for vegetables. That way you lived within your means more easily. Sometimes the grocer in the neighborhood would give credit until payday. That was common. The local butchers had a lot of leftover bones with marrow and meat, a by-product of their cutting up carcasses. After two or three days they would be thrown away. If you asked for a dog bone, he would give you one or two of those free of charge. There was nothing wrong with them and it was not unusual to obtain an excellent soup bone in this manner.

I had many jobs while growing up, and later, while in college. But I vividly remember my first work-for-cash endeavor. I was ten and an elderly lady, four houses away, asked me to clean out and stack material in her empty two-car garage. So I worked a few hours on a Saturday morning, and after the inspection she gave me 25 cents and a grapefruit. Mom let me keep the quarter to go to a high school football game with my cousin Frank. The planned use of this cash flow was 10 cents roundtrip bus fare, 10 cents for the game, and 5 cents for a Milky Way. A great start, and no IRS hassle.

The sidewalks between the street and the row houses where we lived were made of large slabs of gray slate. They were a bit uneven and challenging for roller skating, which Marion and I did often. One day I was out skating on the side walk. I was passing an empty lot in the neighborhood when two kids I did not know jumped me and knocked me down into the lot which was a foot or more below the level of the sidewalk. We tumbled around, throwing punches when Agga! Ugga! Marion, who had seen it all, came flying through the air, knees, skates and elbows flailing away. She got one of them real good and they took off. That wasn't the last time she took care of me. She had come a long way since the baby carriage ride.

While thinking, gray slab sidewalks: Sunny and I would take an old wallet or coin purse and tighten the end of a long string around it. We would place the purse along the sidewalk, string covered in the slate separation, on into the grass behind a bush, where we lay "sshh-ing" each other while waiting for the victim of our prank to show up. When one did, and would stoop to enjoy their new found wealth, we would yank the cord and run like the wind, laughing all the way to the shouts from "ya rotten kids" to "That was fun; let's do it again!"

On the other side of the railroad tracks, going east a mile, into Elizabeth, was the Jerry O. Mahoney Co. They made diners and railroad dining cars. That whole New York, New Jersey and Pennsylvania area was filled with the old style diners in those days. New Jersey, they say, has the largest number of diners in the world. The history of the diner is as old as the railroads themselves, when a car would be specially outfitted to cook and serve food to the workers who were laying the ties and rails in the open country. I have always liked the original commercial ones along the roads, with no booths. Just a long counter with stools and the cooking equipment on the other side. Narrow, like an old railroad car, with a charm of its own, that made the "home cookin'" taste even better. Long since economically unviable, it has quietly passed, with honor, into the culinary history of certain parts of our country. If ever I drive by a long railroad car shaped diner, with a green neon sign hanging over it reading "EATS," that's where I will be for the next forty minutes.

Pop-pop played industrial league softball with the Colonials until he was 40. He quit when the younger guys started calling him "Pops." One evening, when I was about 10, he took me with him for a game at Continental field, in Petterstown, the Italian section of Elizabeth. I remember the whole playing field was smooth clay, like a tennis court. I wandered around in the crowd while the game was going on.

There were some seats in the grandstand but many people stood at ground level. In the middle of the game there was a big commotion right where I was standing. Some men with fistfuls of money were arguing about something, probably betting on the game. Pop-pop came running over from first base. Apparently he didn't want me to be close to the action if the arguing got worse. Many new words were flying. He led me to a friend in the stands and I sat with the man until the end of the game. Then Pop-pop and I and a few teammates headed for some food at a neighborhood bar. They wound up playing cards there and I fell asleep. We got home late and Nana was furious. "I was going crazy thinking of what might have happened. How could you keep him up so late?" and on and on. Now, Nana never raised her voice to Pop-pop or he to her. Well, almost never. It made me uneasy and unhappy, but only for a day and then all was back in order. Ah, yes, Order. St. Augustine said, "Peace is the tranquility of order." That's good material for a sign over every entrance door.

About this time Nana, who was always thinking her children should get into the arts, was able to find a cheap box piano so Marion, who was a motivated student, could learn and practice. I think the teacher came by a couple days a week. She tried to maneuver me into the enthusiasm that she and Marion had for the piano. It wasn't working, but Nana found an old guy who gave music lessons at his home. This man taught various string instruments including the mandolin. Aunt Helen, my godmother, had taken mandolin at an art school she had attended and she loaned me her mandolin. I didn't have the "vibes" for that and I struggled with it. I wanted to please Mom, but it wasn't working out. Then the teacher said if I would complete 8 lessons, he would give me a football. Although I did not find the string instrument to my liking, I pressed on, received the football, and quit the class. Sometime later I learned how to play the ocarina, the "clay sweet potato," on my own. It fit my musical aptitude.

Pop-pop bowled in a league at the Morris Ave. Billiard and Bowling Academy (real name) in Elizabeth with the Elizabethtown Water Co. team every Friday night. When I was about 11 I would usually go with him to set pins; this was before the automatic setters were developed. Sometimes I was the foul line judge for the match. I was paid either way, but I liked that "judge" job. That was before the electric foul eye, and, for formal competition, someone had to supervise the foul line. I would sit on a high seat off to the side and in-line with the foul line markers for, say, 6 alleys. I would blow the whistle when someone's toe touched the line in delivering the ball. Well, they all knew "Newt" and his kid, so they didn't grumble too much when I would blow the whistle on one of them, except in a close match. Then, in that smoke-filled, beer-scented room, I would catch some blazing eyes and strong words of rebuttal. But I always won, thinking, ha, this is great, having a whistle, a high stool, and the backing of the league and the owner of the Academy, a fleeting touch of enjoyed power. I received one dollar for my work of three hours. As usual I turned my earnings over to Mom, and I continued to do so until I joined the Navy. I guess none of us realized it then but Nana and Pop-pop had a good communal system working in the house…Contribute according to ability and receive according to needs (not wants, needs). I think that's right out of Marx's communist manifesto.

When we were in high school, my Union buddies Joe Koerner, Bob Teuscher, and Tom Jamison and I would go down to the Academy and shoot some pool on a Saturday afternoon. Years after college days, Joe from Columbia, Bob from Notre Dame, Tom from Seton Hall and I from Georgetown, occasionally re-connected. We always joked that we also graduated from "The Academy," no texts, but a lot of learning.

At around 10 years old my Uncle Jim, Mom's brother, and Uncle Larry, the husband of Mom's sister, Helen, stopped by one day to pick me up because we were going crabbing out on Barnegat Bay. It was common to fill a bushel basket with big blue claw crabs during a day on the water. We would use Moss Bunkers for bait, head, tail, or midsection, with a wire through them and tied to a string line. We would then lower the bait to the bottom and tie the string to the gunwale of the boat. Four well separated strings on each side of the boat would then set the scene for some action. When testing gently on a string you would feel if a crab was on there by the gentle tug because that rascal had the bait in his claws in front of his mouth and he did not want to let go. So you gently, slowly, drew up the string until you could vaguely see the crab hanging on to his lunch a couple of feet under the water. Then, using the hand net, while holding the string still with the other hand, in one quick motion you plunged the net off to the side of the crab, going down and under it, and then lifting the net straight up for the catch. We rented a wooden row boat. Jim had brought his outboard engine and we were off to a place across the bay that was the best guess for our purposes.

We had been crabbing half the day when a classical summer thunderstorm showed its ugly clouds and it became dark very quickly. The wind picked up. The waves were getting higher and the ensuing deluge was right out of a movie script. We set a course across the bay to the boat rental docks. That little outboard could only do a trawl speed and with the torrential rain and higher waves we started to take on water.

Jim was steering and Larry and I started to bail with some old tin cans. We had no life jackets. Bailing seemed a useless task as the waves continually came over the gunwales. It became darker as the sheets of rain enveloped us, and then the engine ran out of gas. Jim had a backup container but the trick was to refuel in that bouncing, pitching, inundated rowboat. The temperature had dropped and we were cold. "Bail, bail!" Larry set the beat while Jim cussed a streak trying to get the gas into the engine.

We all agreed that if we capsized we would look for each other and stay with the boat that would float, we hoped. I am writing it lightly, but we were scared. We kept bailing and the engine responded nicely to the pull on the magneto and we started our trawl again. With control of the boat, our chances improved and we didn't have to take broadside waves; but we kept bailing and it kept raining. We were colder, but getting there.

After a while we finally got to the rental dock area which was a bit protected and we tied up. The rain was less, but steady, as it was all the way back to Elizabeth. We stopped for burgers and hot coffee at the White Castle near our house, but I fell asleep in the car. Then we took the crabs home and shared them three ways. It seems we had a silent agreement not to tell Nana what happened. She said, "Oh, I was worried about you guys; we have had so much rain and wind here." "Nothing to worry about, Mary, we just had some rain, no problem." It was years later that Jim and Larry told the story of that day on Barnegat Bay when they thought we might not make it back to the docks. I didn't realize the true situation at the time. Kids don't think like that. For a kid, it was always going to be all right.

Grade five was Mrs. McClellan's class. She taught the usual subjects and mixed in some current events. But music was her forte. She sang and played the piano. Now I had always considered myself a fair singer. In the fourth grade I sang in the chorus. I also put on a cowboy outfit and sang a couple of appropriate solos. Then in the fifth grade, 10 to 12 of us tried out for a choir of only 8 voices. I was one of the cuts. Disappointment slipped its long sleazy tentacles gently around me and started to squeeze. Oh, the moment of Truth. Lesson 1 in Character Building, Lesson 2 in Life Ain't Fair. I always thought my buddy Allan Watson and I were equal in voice. My buddy, in whose house I would sometimes sleep and to whose dining table I was often invited, not only made the cut, but was even given some solos. It took me a couple of months to hear that voice inside, "Hey kid, you don't have it with the voice. Stick to the things you do best." Allan and I have not seen each other since the 6th grade and we were the best of friends. Later he went on to Princeton and had national ranking in tennis. I also recall the many times we would go to his grandmother's home on Shark River at Avon-By-The-Sea to swim and catch crabs and eels.

Allan's mom was a good tennis player and she also had a dancing school at the Elmora Country Club. Allan, the only child, couldn't get out of it of course, and he and his mom suggested that I attend also. I was silent. Word somehow got to Nana and she thought that would be a grand idea, her son dabbling in a bit of artful culture. I can't imagine Pop-pop approving that expense, but I can imagine Mrs. Watson giving Mom a break on the fee so her son's best buddy could also attend, thereby avoiding any change in Allan's attitude on the matter of ballroom dancing. I was in that class during 5th and 6th grades. My views changed a bit. Just a short while ago we guys were not supposed to have anything to do with girls. Now we danced with them; and while ballroom dancing was a bit stuffy, starting with the "two-step," fun kept creeping in.

I was going to the store on Elmora Ave. one day and I looked up into the blue sky and saw a beautiful airship, a zeppelin. It was flying low. It was the famous Hindenburg which had come from Germany and had just made a viewing pass over New York City before turning south to the Naval Station at Lakehurst, New Jersey where she would tie up and complete the voyage. A few hours later that beautiful dirigible exploded at the mooring site killing almost all the passengers, a terrible tragedy. The pictures and accompanying newsreels went on for weeks.

Moving on to the 6th grade at Public School 21 was a feeling of accomplishment. My grades were good and our teams were winning. "Newy" (my nickname at the time) was the captain of the basketball team.. Mr. Shallcross was the gym teacher and coach. He taught us teamwork. I do not remember the classroom teacher's name but she must have been good because I made good progress there so that when I left and went to the area junior high school I was placed in grade 7A1, the top grade. Naturally some of my classmates went into 7A1 also and I made a new friend there. Joe Koerner had attended PS 12. He was smart, humorous, a good athlete, and we hit it off. Going to Jr. High was fun and challenging. I walked 1-1/2 miles to school. We went from class to class from a home room base, like high school, wow! I remember walking to school those crisp September mornings, the change in the air, the end of summer. Life in the kids' world was good. I was keeping the beat.

3 | Growing Up

Newhard family, at home in Union, summer of 1943.
From left to right: Howard, Marion, Richie, Nana, Pop-pop.

Six weeks after I started at the Alexander Hamilton Jr. High School Pop-pop received a nice promotion. It involved our moving about 10 miles away to the town of Union, which was one step out of the farms. The Water Company had property there, about 500 by 1,500 yards. It contained a pumping station, a water well field, and a catch basin for water storage and treatment. The east side of the property was next to the Suburban Golf Club. The western boundary was at the cross roads of State 24 and U.S. 22, narrow roads in those days. We moved into an old, gabled house with a wrap-around porch, a cellar and an attic. That was a popular country style at the time it was built. Surprisingly, it was very similar in style and size to the modest Eisenhower house in Abilene, Kansas, which I visited decades later with my own family. The water company had built that house in Union for a man named Bond who had come down from New England to operate the old coal and steam-powered machinery used in running that pumping station. It was converted to electric power several years before the old man died. Pop-pop was taking his place, in addition to his regular maintenance and new projects work. Mr. Bond's son, Ernie, was the Fire Chief of Union, a good friend of Pop-pop's and later my coach in the "under 15" baseball league.

When we moved there, the old high, gray, wooden lap strake walled buildings, and the 60 ft. high smokestack for the outmoded coal /steam powered plant with the huge flywheels were our sleeping next-door neighbors. Directly behind the house was a stretch of lawn, and beyond that an open section of high grass, growth, and trees for a half mile or more, parallel to U.S. 22. I would find good use for those large old empty buildings, and all that acreage; some dry, some swampy, plus a pond, all of which I came to know so well. Many years later Dad would leave a lasting landmark on his career with the Water Company when he helped build the tallest hydrosphere in the world, at that time, right there along U.S. 22. We call it the "blue scallion" to this day, because of its color and shape. Dad's promotion included the house, water, electricity, telephone and car, nice "bennies" for sure. We lived at 1800 Morris Ave. (State 24). We had no nearby neighbors except a daytime gas station diagonally across the road at the entrance ramp of U.S. 22.

State 24 runs from Elizabeth through Union and Springfield to Morristown. It was a horse and coach road when General Washington used it coming out of the New York area, retreating from the British after they decided to get tough with those rebel colonists and "shut the lid" on them. He led his troops to Morristown where they encamped for a while before being forced by the pressing British to retreat to Valley Forge, Pennsylvania, and suffer the barest, meager rations, and the frozen Hell they were to endure with inadequate food, clothing and equipment. But they stayed. They held on. Honor, duty, country.

There is a mansion that was built just before that time. It is on Morris Ave. in Union and belonged to the old Kean family which had farmland there that was ceded to build Kean College in the 1960s. The mansion is a State Monument now, but when we lived in Union Capt. Kean, a WWI veteran, lived there. Pop-pop, working for the water company which the Keans owned, would stop there occasionally to fix some plumbing. He told me there were large cuts in the banisters from when the British had gone through, hacking with their swords. Capt. Kean never changed those markings, visible indications of the British frustration.

The Union school system had 8 grades of grammar school and 4 grades of high school. I attended Livingston School (named after William Livingston, a signatory of the *U.S. Constitution,* representing New Jersey), which was in a suburban setting, a mile plus from where we lived. Most of the walk to school was through open areas with no houses. Making friends came easily and in a short while I was comfortable there. The whole family was excited. Marion continued to attend school at Battan High in Elizabeth, the all-girls public school. Pop-pop drove her there on his way to work, or she took a bus on Morris Ave. Livingston had a uniformed football team that practiced several days a week. Joe Mente was the gym teacher and coach. He saw this tall string bean running around the playground playing touch football and said, "I have a uniform for you. You're going to play end." We played both ways in 1939, Urrah! We had a wood shop and Mr. Holtz, a polio victim, was a very skilled and good teacher. My stellar achievement there was a clothes tree which is now in Maria and Mike's apartment, built to last. I made friends quickly. Bob Teuscher would be a close and lasting friend along with Bob Bruno, Tom Jamison, Joe Koerner and others. Penny Taylor and Shirley Jacobs were also friends in my class. Penny's parties were much fun.

Miss Elizabeth Huntington was my home room and American History teacher in 7th grade, Social Studies/Civics in 8th grade. She was one of the finest educators, among the many, who influenced me along the way. She taught me how to study, write notes, draft an outline, and how to write an essay. The sincerity and friendliness she brought to the classroom, or in one-on-one matters, gave me a good perspective. But let me not deceive. She had a "crusty" side that was also beneficial for the students, for she was a disciplinarian and ran a tight ship. It was she who would most influence my going to St. Benedict's Prep in Newark. She was a meaningful influence in my life. Somewhat incapacitated from a severe hip injury, this middle-aged woman walked with a difficult limp and must have endured frequent pain.

My two years at Livingston School were truly formative. My grades were good and I played on the football, basketball and softball teams, as well as in summer baseball. The school had a large playground without fences which contained a softball field, basketball hoops, and an area where the teachers held summertime classes for small children. We put in a lot of time on those ball fields. As far back as I can remember, a group of kids coming together for a baseball or softball game would choose sides as follows: The whole group would choose the two best players and they would select their teams from the group. One would throw a bat to the other, handle up. It had to be caught below the label. Then, with the bat between them, the two captains would place hand over hand, alternately, until the very top of the bat was left. The last one who could grab the bat with a finger or two or the whole hand, then had to swing it around his head three times, which was very difficult to do if you only had room on the bat to hold it with one or two curled fingers. This is where the saying "he got the short end of the stick" comes from. If he was successful, he had the first choice of players. If he dropped the bat, his opponent had first choice, and they would alternate their choices until the group was selected.

As I mentioned, Union was one step out of the farm, with many still around. In fact the Union High School nickname was the Farmers. It was a wonderful area to grow up in. There was a pond on the property; the west branch of the Elizabeth River (a stream) ran through there. There were marshes around the pond and, at a higher level to the northwest, it was full of high, dry, grass, and many trees.

I recall going out on winter nights, ice skating on the pond, whether dark or moonlit. A few times I was joined by Mary Lou Olsen, whose father had a coal company in the area. She was a classmate and when the class gossips found out about that…WOW…Moonlight, snow, ice skating together, all alone, chatter, chatter, snicker, snicker…It was all so silly because we were just casual friends who liked to skate. Almost always I was out there alone at night in the moon-light, or darkness, with the ice expanding and splitting and making those sharp, loud, cracking noises because of the increasing cold. I was in another world and far away.

The situation in Europe was progressing toward war. In 1938, when I was 11, Hitler had invaded Czechoslovakia, without resistance, after Neville Chamberlain, the British Prime Minister, took a soft position of trust with Hitler. Peace at any price was the mode of the day in France and England and certain-ly the U.S. So our policy and lack of preparedness gave Hitler silent encourage-ment. And even in September 1939 when Hitler attacked a weak Poland with the "blitzkrieg"(lightning war), after signing a non-aggression pact with the Soviet Union, the U.S. stayed with its isolation policy, except for some supplies for Britain and others who had declared war on Germany. Had we stayed strong mil-itarily we could have declared war on Germany early and reached a rapid con-clusion. The U.S. military cemeteries around the world and in the U.S. attest to the foolishness of peace at any price. The longer you wait, the more will die when you are dealing with a tyrannous dictator; and finally you must go to war.

Our Philco brand radio was always tuned to the news. Pop-pop bought two newspapers a day, so we always knew the war's progress or regress. Pound for pound and oil can for oil can the professional military and scientists in Hitler's Germany developed the best fighting machine in the world up to that time. They had been training and motivating young people since 1934 and they knew how to effectively combine infantry, armored, and air power into the blitzkrieg tactic.

The French, living in the past, and thinking Defense, improved and strength-ened their Maginot Line, an elaborate, well-planned and expensive fortification system that they thought would repel the Germans. They changed their defensive plans many times but always with the Maginot Line as the anchor. But Germany, with its Von Schliffen plan developed by that skilled tactician who emphasized, "Keep the right wing strong," did an end run on the Maginot line and stormed through the lowlands of Belgium and Holland and into France.

The German submarine fleet was formidable and almost broke the Allied shipping lanes later on. With each new success, pride powered Germany's people and military; pride that blinded them from seeing the monster that was being created by Hitler. This pride extended abroad and the German Bunds in the U.S. and elsewhere were very active overtly and covertly. It was not only pride, but the sense of "pay-back time" for the hardships they had suffered as a result of the Versailles Treaty after WWI, which France loved, but I do not think the U.S. even ratified.

At 13, I started to work some Saturdays and sometimes after school at the gas station nearby. Brad owned the station with his brother, a non-active partner. Brad wanted me out the door and wiping the windshield before the driver could turn off the engine. Service, service; that's what he emphasized in his instructions. I would pump gas, put in some oil and water, and be polite. Sometimes I had the questionable privilege of changing a truck tire. Occasionally Brad left me there by myself while he ran errands. Here was a 13-year-old pumping gas, handling the cash, and selling soda, good management training.

Soon after, I added another source of income by going over to the Suburban Golf Club and caddying. Saturday was my day for that. The Caddy Master, Frank, was one tough dude. He had to be because he had to deal with the men caddies, some of whom were hard workers and knew the game; and then there were others, made up of drifters and drinkers, who followed the sun to work in the warm climes, caddying, clamming, fishing, boat-crewing etc. Frank gave the teenage caddies to the less fussy players, and certainly not to the players who bet big bucks on their games. When I was just starting and learning the ropes, I often had to wait until late in the day to carry a bag. As I picked up experience and became older, I would get out earlier. Some days there were not enough caddies and we would carry double bags. It was a hard job running back and forth between your players, but the money was good. The caddy fee was $1.50 for 18 holes and they usually tipped 25 cents. I could make $3.50 in four hours when the minimum wage was 25 cents an hour. I gave it all to Mom but was seldom turned down for a movie, or other expense.

I do not remember how the job really came about, but the summer I was 13 or 14 I worked 3 evenings a week in Elizabeth at a bicycle rental shop. A man who owned a pharmacy nearby there started that operation by renting out bicycles from a large commercial garage. So Pop-pop drove me from Union at about 5:30 and picked me up about 9. I ran the place by myself. The customer signed out for the bike on the punch time card, took the bike, and left their drivers license. The rental charge was 25 cents an hour which I collected when they returned the bike and retrieved their license. The pharmacist would come by at 9 or so to count the bikes and the cash against the time-punch tickets. I never had any problems except once. He told me he was going to a dinner party and so I was to lock up the bikes in the garage and take the cash home and give it to him the next time. Fine, except that at 9 p.m. I had a problem. There were only 31 bikes instead of 32. So I called the pharmacist. He always left me a phone number. He left the dinner party and came over. We were both surprised when we counted the bikes and there were 32. We also found a drivers license that I had not placed in the box but had left aside during a busy time. He wasn't angry, saying I did what I thought was best. He went back to his party and I locked up and the licensee stopped by the next evening. I guess this sticks with me because I thought I had made a mistake. I always tried to avoid a mistake because it seems Dad was a bit strict and mistakes did not sit too well.

In the 7th grade our English teacher was Miss Smith. Writing, composing, sentence structure and diagramming (do they do that anymore?) was her bag and she was good at it. But handling energetic, athletic, 13-year-old boys who thought the world was their apple was not taught in Education 306, or was it? Miss Huntington had no problem, and later the Benedictine monks certainly had no problem; but we would help Miss Smith gain some experience in this matter, and she would help us to learn classroom discipline.

One day five of us were sitting together in English class. It was Friday and the weekly test would be given soon. We disturbed the class by laughing at a comment one of us made, without permission, perhaps regarding another student or the teacher. Miss Smith took swift and angry action. "You five will stay in detention after school and will not be allowed to take the test, for which you will receive a zero." Well, the injustice of that hit me immediately. I passed the word that when the wall clock clicked to 10:15, we would get up and leave and go to see Mr. Smith (no relation) the principal. When we got up, she shouted, "Sit down!" When we walked out the door she bellowed, "Come back here!"

Mr. Smith was surprised to see us walk into his office in the middle of class time. He was more surprised to hear our story. We complained that punishment for bad conduct was okay but our grades should be based on what we know. He told us he agreed, but then he suspended us until we would give him a letter from our parents stating they knew the situation and agreed with the suspension while asking for reinstatement. In my small world, and in society at large, people of authority, teachers, policemen, etc. were considered to be guideposts for the young, and parents would automatically favor them, wanting to know what the child did wrong, not who wronged the child. There is a reason for that. Life was more simple. Officials did not have layer upon layer of laws to frighten them from being sensible, practical and doing their job. I think the zero test mark stayed in the record and Miss Smith won in a "blow out." But the injustice was there and she did not commit another one against the Zombies (to be explained). We students, teachers, and parents learned from that…all to the good I hope. But learn or not, in 8th grade I would have one more suspension from Mr. Smith.

The Zombies was the name of our make-up, non-school basketball and soft-ball team. We had gold on black uniforms with Zombies in script on the chest and a gold Z on black caps. We took a picture of the team after one of the soft-ball games. We all laughed at Bob Bruno's remark. "The message is we are all sleeping, ZZZZZZZZ."

We would find teams from other places in the area and arrange a game. On several occasions, my cousin Frank's team came over from Elizabeth to play us. We always had tough, close, games. We liked to compete. The playing fields were often a bit rough. The cheapest way to build a base for a playing field was to use coal stove ashes. Coal stoves heated boilers that provided hot water and steam for heating in the winter. Oil heating was yet to arrive. These coal stoves yielded ashes which were removed regularly from the stoves in the basement and shov-eled into large metal ash cans. "Don't forget to take out the ash can" was a com-mon cry around all the homes. The garbage and ashes were picked up at curb-side. So those fields were dusty and a little rough. No matter, we made all the plays, slid hard, and loved it.

The importance of coal ashes sticks in my mind. In that whole area in east-ern N.J around Elizabeth, Newark, and Secaucus, a broad area centered by U.S. 1, garbage and ashes fill went on for decades culminating in turning swampland into Newark Airport, The Meadowlands Complex and surrounding productive environs. I believe it all started back in the 1920s. Certainly they had filled in enough swamp to have a small airport at Newark prior to WWII. In fact, we had a small dump site on the north side of Morris Ave., across from the Suburban Golf Club property. It went north and eventually filled in Reds Pond where they built a large shopping center along U.S. 22 in the 1960s, and a single family hous-ing development along Morris Ave.

Along the north side of Morris Ave. there was an ash dump stretching along the open State 24 from where we lived to the Townley area and the school. There were very few houses or street lights. At night, cars seldom passed by on that sin-gle lane road. The people who ran the refill area had equipment and dump trucks which they parked near their office shack, deep inside the property, away from the road. They had five or six large dogs which they kept to guard the equipment. It was summer. I had been playing ball that evening until about 8 p.m. It was dark by the time I left the field down near the Lehigh Valley Railroad and started to walk home along Morris Ave. (Rt. 24). I was walking on the Suburban Golf Club side of the road about a half mile from home when I heard a dog bark, then another, then many, in a pack. They came flying across the road to me. I was alone and there was not a climbable tree in sight. I was scared, very scared. My little guy inside told me to "Walk straight, keep your hands at your sides, don't run, walk straight." And here they came, barking and snarling, and banging up against me. If one had started to bite, I guess I would have been torn to pieces. Hang on, walk straight, don't run, don't talk. How I kept control I don't know. After about 100 yards of barking, and growling, sniffing and bumping, we were getting farther away from their turf. A few cars blew their horns in passing but did not stop. The growling and snarling let up and then they left as quickly as they had arrived. I was shaking and arrived home with my blank stare and ghastly face on. Nana immediately knew "there was big trouble in River City." Pop-pop was out bowling. I told Nana the story and, exhausted, went to bed.

Nana told Pop-pop when he arrived home. The next morning, before going to work, and unknown to me, Pop-pop did not go to the police but he went to see the manager of the refill operation. In full control, he told the manager to lock up his dogs because, if he didn't, Pop-pop was going to shoot them. He told the guy the story of my close call. We never had a problem with those dogs again. They were removed from the property. Pop-pop had many good friends in the police and fire departments. My guess is the word got out about those semi-wild dogs and someone from the police department asked them to remove the dogs. To this day I have a mild problem with a strange large dog without a leash.

Late in the spring the usual City Field Day was scheduled for the grammar schools. I would play shortstop on the Livingston softball team. The track team was short one hurdler. A week before the meet Joe Mente set up some hurdles and had me practice the technique of clearing the bar. Pleased with my hurdling style, he added me to that event. In my first race I was ahead as I cleared the last hurdle. I stopped and jumped for joy. I had never run the hurdles before or practiced the whole routine and distance. I thought the finish line was the last hurdle. The little voice said, "Ya wanta get away?"

In the summer of 1939 the whole family went to New York World's Fair in Flushing Meadows Long Island. It was in full swing. I remember seeing the Trylon and Perisphere, which were the central buildings and futuristic symbols of the technological advancements to come. They had displays of television, laundry machines, cooking, heating, air conditioning etc. We all walked away with a nice disposition and the feeling that we were really coming out of the Depression and looking forward to the future.

That summer Pop-pop bought a 1937 Dodge sedan, long stick shift on the floor, the car with which I would later learn to drive. Uncle Jim was then living in East St. Louis and working for Phelps Dodge Copper and he invited us to come out and visit. So Nana packed whatever she thought we would need into several dresser drawers, and we loaded them into the trunk of the car. We did not own suitcases. I don't recall the route, but it was narrow roads and high adventure for us all the way.

I remember we stopped one night at a motel in Ohio, rolling hill countryside, narrow road, barns and farm houses all around. A low-cost, out-of-town motel in those days consisted of say five individual cabins plus an office cabin along the road. We were assigned our cabin, drove over to it and unloaded the dresser drawers. We then washed socks and underwear with bar soap, wrung it out and hung it somewhere to dry, a frugality not yet expired in the recovering from the economic depression. There were no shades on the screened windows, normal I guess in that rural setting since you should be sleeping after sundown. The only trouble was the farmers across the road was still running their produce stand with a big bare bulb light above it, and their voices seemed loud in the stillness of the night. But soon it was quiet, the heat of the day was gone, the big light was out and we all had a good night's sleep. I don't remember much else from that pleasant trip though St. Louis in August was not a recommended tourist spot. Of course it was always fun to see Jim. He was doing well and expecting to be assigned back to Phelps Dodge, Elizabeth.

Livingston had a pretty good football team. One afternoon when we had no practice, one of our great thinkers floated the hot idea to take our football uniforms from our lockers and carry them to Jamison's house and change there. Then we would go through the woods to the fairway and scrimmage on that marvelous manicured grass.

There would be few or no golfers out late in the afternoon on a weekday in October. It was a great idea. So we scrimmaged and ran plays, thought up plays, and were having a super time. Then, a big crunch, pile up, and George Boe let out a cry of pain. He had broken his collar bone. We carried him to Jamison's house and someone arranged to get him to the hospital where they diagnosed and made him a cast which he was in for about 8 weeks.

We took the uniforms back to the school knowing the word would be out. The next day Mr. Smith suspended everyone involved in taking school equipment off the property without permission. We were suspended until the parents wrote a letter asking for re-entry. I think Pop-pop was a little amused, but he didn't let on and gave me the responsibility talk. He wrote a letter to Mr. Smith and I was re-admitted and also allowed back on the football team. That would be my last school suspension. I would get probation much farther down the line, but no suspension. Oh, what a good boy.

I can't recall our football games clearly but I do remember one game we played at the Morris Ave. field. I was chasing after the opposition's ball carrier who was headed for a touchdown. We had no face masks then. I chased him down and dove at him, knowing it was going to be a great tackle. The heel of his flashing cleats whacked me across the bridge of my nose. I woke up with my face in the grass and a broken nose, which all future photos would pick up, an acceptable trade-off for the love of the game.

Miss Huntington was our home room teacher and taught us Civics. We all could recite The Gettysburg Address, Preamble of the Constitution Lincoln's Thanksgiving Proclamation, and others, building our base of patriotism,

The boys and girls were now much more aware of girls and boys. The small parties at Penny Taylor's included kissing games and lots of dancing. We were the "in crowd" of the class. Shirley Jacobs and I had a small "crush" going. That Spring the whole class of about sixty of us took a memorable ride on the Hudson River Day Line from NYC to West Point, a full day's outing. The day was perfect with the aroma of spring and the beautiful Hudson River Valley as our art gallery. We had music on board and all the joy and laughter you might expect from teenage friends and classmates. I spent a lot of time with Penny and Shirley. It was exciting. Miss Huntington must have been observing all of her home room students that day and enjoying herself. The next school day she had a little gift for everyone with a humorous note to be read aloud. I don't remember my present, but the note read, "Shirley or Jean, which do you mean?" A big laugh went up from the class, as I cleverly smiled to cast such silliness away. But my blush betrayed me.

The days moved rapidly now. The softball season was ending. Term papers and final exams were looming. With a "where did it all go?" graduation day was NOW and we graduated with many "keep in touch" promises and "see you soon"s.

At the end of the summer, just before starting at St. Benedict's Prep, Tom Jamison invited me to spend a week at his parents' cabin at Lake Wallkill, located in the mountains of Sussex County, the "ice box" region. The summers there were warm by day and cool at night. We were in or on the lake most of the day and welcomed nightfall. The smell of the pine, oak, and sycamore and flowers was invigorating. Mr. and Mrs. Jamison were nice people, and some of Tom's cousins were also there. One was 14-year-old Jean Price from East Orange. We liked each other. I dated her off and on until I was 17 and joined the Navy.

4 | ST. BENEDICT'S PREP

The Core Years

After graduating from Livingston School, being all of 14, the age at which Social Security cards were issued, I applied for a job at SE&M Vernon. It was a paper supply company in the old Durant automobile building on Frelinghuysen Ave. in Elizabeth. I worked in the shipping department, filling and packing orders. I had to be accurate and strong. Paper packed in boxes is a heavy item. I worked 8 hours a day, five days a week, at $0.25 per hour. I was there all summer and played baseball on Saturday and some evenings. I recall the boss of the shipping department, Leo, I think, telling me that he was working there at the bottom of the Depression, for a pittance. When he made a mistake, his gruff boss would call him over to the window overlooking Frelinghuysen Ave. and say, "Now Leo, you see all those guys standing around on the corner? They want to work. Now why the hell should I put up with your stupid mistakes when I can get one of them?" Leo would shudder and profusely apologize and make promises. He had four mouths to feed. Those were very bad times indeed.

Early that summer Nana and Pop-pop reached an important decision about finances. They would pay (probably monthly) my $120-a-year tuition at St. Benedict's plus the carfare, books, and other fees. My godfather, Uncle John Kress, took me over to Newark, to those red brick buildings stemming from the corner of High and William Sts. where the school, church and abbey were (and are) all together. Around 1865, the monks came from elsewhere to build and start the red brick abbey, church, and school, originally called St. Benedict's College. High St. was on the high ground rimming the inner city in those days. They were the same old standard red brick buildings that I went to in 1941. The students called it the Beehive after the school's nickname, the Gray Bees. That style of brick structure was common throughout the industrial and municipal areas of that region. Many are still around today. Some of my classmates affectionately called 520 High St. the "pickle factory" after we were there a while and into the routine of it all.

When Uncle John, Nana's brother, and I went to the school the first time, I was uneasy. Would they take me? My grades were okay. I guess my uneasiness came from not knowing what to expect. We talked to the Headmaster and I went through a preliminary interview. He gave us the papers for Mom and Dad to fill out. When we went back with the papers and the grammar school transcript, the Headmaster reviewed them and said, "What course do you want?" WOW! I was in! There was Scientific, Latin Scientific, Classical, and Business. Uncle John and the Headmaster agreed on Latin Scientific for me. It was a good solid college prep education. I was elated.

I started in early September. Dad drove me to the bus stop in Elizabeth, on his way to work, and I took the public service bus to Newark and walked to the school. My return was a bus to Union and a mile and a half walk from the drop off to home. Often I would hitch-hike from the bus stop. In later years I rode a bus over U.S. 22 to Newark.

A Benedictine abbey is independent from the diocese in which it is located, although, of course, there is liaison for matters of mutual interest. The abbey exists because the monks there are following the rules of St. Benedict. This teaching order was established about 504 A.D. and St. Benedict wrote down some 90 rules of conduct for spiritual communal living for the monks to follow. Various monastic orders have used the rules of St. Benedict throughout the ages. Vows of poverty, chastity, and obedience are included in the code. The monks also agree to stay at the same abbey to work, pray and help each other and the surrounding community in a lifelong commitment.

Of course there are exceptions for a variety of reasons. Assignments for missionary work, or military chaplaincy in time of war, come to mind. Each Benedictine monastery throughout the world is independent and does not report to a provincial head as do other orders. Each abbot reports to the Holy See in Rome.

The Abbot is chosen by vote from among the monks. Each monk has an equal vote without regard to longevity. The abbot is their father in the abbey family. The word Abbot comes from the Aramaic, abba, meaning father. In recent years I went on a closed retreat, with eight of my friends, to a Benedictine church and abbey here in Florida. We ate with the monks. After supper we walked through the kitchen, on our way to our rooms, and said good night to the Abbot who was washing the pots and pans: "For the one who will lead must serve the others," as Jesus taught.

The monk joins a monastery to raise his and others' levels of spirituality through prayer, work, and community service. When he enters Eternal Life it is a day for celebration, and the funeral mass will reflect that in the liturgy, homily and eulogy. All members of a Benedictine Abbey are monks who have taken vows. Some might be ordained priests, some brothers, but all are monks. The story of St. Benedict's Prep and Abbey in Newark needs telling in more detail than I know. It needs telling not only for what it is, but what it has done for the community of Newark in current history; from originally serving mostly German immigrants in the late 1860's to now serving mostly students and other people from the inner city, of which it is now a part.

About 2003 one of the monks, who had lived at the Abbey in the pre- and post-social turmoil of the 1960s and 70s, and taught at the school during that time, wrote a book called *Downtown Monks*. This is a book that tells the true story in the time covered. The school has become well-known by what it has accomplished after it closed down (and reopened) in the early 1970s, due to rioting in the city, fires, and students being robbed for money while walking to school from the bus stops. Many thought the closing was permanent and some of the monks moved to other monasteries. Those who stayed eventually voted to reopen the school and run it as before, but also to take deserving students from the inner city. High St. had become Martin Luther King Blvd. and it was time to move on. In fact the social justice reform that Dr. King advocated was from the earliest teachings of the Church and emphasized throughout the years in various papal encyclicals. Fr. Martin who became the Abbot in the late 50's or early 60's marched with Dr. King many times.

The school was reopened under the same tradition and system that was always there. The Alumni were made aware of the financial challenges arising from the plans for the future, and have responded over the years beyond the expectation of the planners. The monks of St. Benedict's today are part of a monastic tradition that marked its 1500th anniversary in recent times.

When I started there in September 1941, we formed the class of 1945. So many special friendships were to be established by becoming classmates and teammates and experiencing, together, that higher calling above self which that kind of education engenders. Discipline, the key to the system, was based on honor, reinforced by a demerit program, and "jug" (after school detention), teenagers being what they are. A coat and tie was required dress for the classroom. Being late for class was 5 demerits, cheating on a test was 25 demerits; insubordination was 25 demerits, disturbing the class, 10 demerits. Fifty demerits in one school year would result in expulsion. I probably didn't have 25 demerits in all the time I was there. Oh, what a good boy!

So many fine teachers and coaches influenced my development. Many of them had graduated from the Beehive themselves. There was Fr. Flynn who taught English. His accomplished hobby was derivations of words. He later became the Headmaster. He was efficient, kind and understanding. The oldest among his siblings, he worked until age 24 to help them get their higher education started, then went into the seminary. Fr. Mark Confroy taught religion and English. He helped me a lot in those subjects and in everyday matters. He was a friend. Fr. Martin was our freshman music teacher; much later he became the Abbot. Fr. James was the old Algebra disciplinarian. "This course is 80% repetition and drill," he would say. 80 year old Fr. Benedict taught religion. A great advocate for helping other people, he left a long-lasting note with more than one of us when he said, "If you ever have a chance to give up your life for another, do it. God will take you home right away." I guess the ever-prevalent thought about the war of that time had some influence there. Fr. Richard, the Athletic Director, was a good guide and counselor. Off and on, over the years, we were early arrivals each morning in the school cafeteria, talking of many "cabbages and kings" while having coffee and waiting for classes to start. There were others I will mention as I write along.

The first day was, of course, very exciting. No one knew anyone. After a general assembly and talks by the Abbot, Headmaster, Prefect of Discipline etc., we were assigned to our classes, about 20 to a class. I remember coming home that day with my Latin Book and some other homework. The first sentence in the Latin book was

"Hibernia est insula." (Ireland is an island.) I read it to Nana and told her what it meant. She was overjoyed (no doubt having visions of her first son becoming a priest).

In my freshman year I played intramural basketball and we were the top team in the freshman class. The school had two representative teams to play other schools. One was the high school team made up of four year students. The other was the prep school team made up of 19- and 20-year-old postgraduates, mostly from other schools. Harry Singleton, All Eastern from Seton Hall in the early 1930's, was the coach of the high school team and Ernest "Prof" Blood was the coach of the Prep team. Singleton saw me playing intramural ball and asked me to work out with the high school team. So I made the varsity squad in my first year. I played in my first game at St. Peters of Jersey City. Their playing area then was a large, deep stage, and the spectators sat in a theater seat arrangement. Weird, but not the unknown reason I played so badly, missing shots that I was making back in Livingston. Was it stage fright in the theater/gym? Maybe. I did better later on when Harry gave me other opportunities.

Pop-pop and Nana did not check my homework but would surely ask if I did it. On a few occasions Pop-pop and I would talk about an Algebra problem I was struggling with. He said, "I don't know the system they want you to learn, but I will give you the answer and perhaps you can work it backwards." What a guy. Yes, a tenth grade education back in 1915 was very, very, good. A big part of it was called Arithmetic, add, subtract, divide, and multiply, under the drill, drill, repetition, repetition umbrella of learning, so necessary in those formative years. I also recall him advising me, when I would speak or write with some incoherency by placing conditional remarks, or the subject, or the verb in the wrong places. His corrective remark was, "Gosh, that's like, throw me over the fence the horse some hay."

After the basketball season I took a part-time afternoon job at a pharmacy in Elizabeth. I was the soda and sundae maker in the luncheonette part of the store. The boss was practical. "Don't take anything from here. At the end of your shift you can have a soda or a sundae, but no helping yourself or giving anything away." I followed this strictly except that a few friends who came in occasionally enjoyed a generous serving. On Saturdays during my freshman year I caddied, or worked at the gas station. It was sort of seasonal. Did you know that some men were so crazy for golf they would play an orange colored ball when there was a light snow on the ground? I was usually pumping gas then.

On a Sunday afternoon early in December I was sitting home by myself, listening to the old Philco radio. A highly excited news announcer came on and said that Pearl Harbor had been attacked. They stayed on and kept updating the report. At that moment I really missed Nana, Pop-pop, Marion and Richie. I wanted to talk about this. From that moment on, I planned to volunteer as soon as I could. President Roosevelt declared war a couple of days later and from then on it was the issue of the day. It permeated the lives of all the citizens.

Many volunteered. The draft was increased. The rationing of many items began: meats, rubber, metals, some foods, building materials. Housewives began to save meat fats from cooking. This was systemically picked up separately from the garbage. The glycerin in the fat was used for explosives. By the next year or so everyone had relatives, friends, and neighbors in the armed forces. The spirit of the nation was geared toward winning the war, unconditionally. We did not have people in the media talking against the government's efforts, and we certainly did not have people clamoring for peace while our guys were being killed and calling for justice from their graves—just the opposite. The civilians loved the people in uniform and did many things to help them, from a few kind words to organizing clubs and groups to do things for them. The love and support was so obvious.

I recall one evening. I was waiting for the bus on Broad St. in Elizabeth to take me to Union. People were shopping, waiting for buses, along that very wide sidewalk. Three submarine sailors, with campaign ribbons on their chests, came along on cloud nine, with somewhat distorted visions, and a bottle of happy tonic between them. They were singing, and many of the people were cheering them on as they passed, a sound way to say thanks. With all the applause, and in the right frame of mind, they locked arms and did a few buck and wing steps as they moved by, singing the old drinking song, *"Oh, God made the Irish but he didn't make them much, but they're a hell of a lot better that the gosh darn Dutch. Sing glorious, glorious, one keg of beer for the four of us. Glory be to God, there are no more of us, so the four of us can drink it all alone!"* That is so clear in my mind to this day, even the exact location on Broad St. The people loved the "troops," let them have some fun; they earned it.

Fast forwarding over the many years right up to now, I was talking to a guy in the check-out line, "How old are you," he asked. I replied, "81." "Oh, you're just a kid," he jokingly replied. "Where did you serve, Europe or the Pacific?" I asked. "The Pacific; I was in the Navy," and we swapped Navy stories. Just a few days later I was doing my hospital ministry and was talking with a patient, whom I noted was 84. "Where did you serve?" I asked. "In Europe," he replied, "I was in armored reconnaissance in Patton's 3rd Army, in 4 major battles." The guys in my generation speak to each other this way. Where did you serve, not, did you serve? because almost every age-eligible male served in WWII.

American History and Civics was emphasized early on, as was reciting those important documents that I mentioned previously. This gave individual citizens a patriotism which fostered the discipline needed to organize to a higher calling than self, and win. Were we the greatest generation? Has there been a greatest generation in our short history of 8 generations?

The use of the superlative degree "greatest" implies that the myriad of conditions during each generation has been the same for comparison, and of course that's not true. The generation of Washington and the founding fathers was outstanding in achieving its goals and solving its problems, as was the generation of Lincoln. While I have always felt that each generation has met and solved the problems it has faced for the betterment of those to come, I must admit that I do have a concern that the nation, as a whole, might now lack the patriotism and resultant discipline to continue forward and meet its challenges, political, economic, social, and military (see Appendix B).

During my sophomore year at St. Benedict's the school built a basic-training type obstacle course for juniors and seniors on its property across High St., opposite the school. Joe Kasberger, the football and baseball coach, was in charge of the obstacle course training. Almost the entire graduating class of 1942 went into the service. Biology was taught by Fr. Damian, who had done missionary work in China. A fine educator, his class was alive. He gave a broad brush to how the biotic world works, and wove in the details of various plants, fish and mammals. He touched on human nutrition also. I recall him saying, "If you have a full day of hard physical work to do and I offer you a pound of nuts or a pound of steak, which will you choose?" Everyone said steak. Wrong. We all know that now, but red meat was king then and considered the healthiest way to sustain oneself. Later we learned the details of "nuts nutrition," which I have forgotten. I'd still go for the steak, medium rare. Food habits are so hard to break.

I got a part-time job after school at McCrory's 5&10 on Broad St. in Newark. I worked for the main cashier, carrying the money bag around when he checked the cash registers in the store. I also did whatever other jobs he assigned. Some of the young women who worked there full-time would giggle and make passes as I came around. They enjoyed themselves, having fun with the 15-year-old kid who was a bit bewildered (but liking it). I had that job until Christmas vacation started, at which time I worked out of the Union Post Office carrying and delivering the mail. We walked the whole route in all kinds of weather, living the motto "Neither sleet nor storm nor gloom of night shall keep these couriers from their assigned and routed tasks."

I can't think of those winter jobs without recalling Bubble's Diner at Union Center, where I would stop for a break and hot coffee. We all knew Bubble's place, police, truckers, townspeople, students, all came in to "jaw" with Bubbles, while he cooked and served the long tiled counter (no tables, my kind of diner). Coffee was 5 cents and the best hamburger ever was 10 cents. The homemade soup was great. The place had a dirt/gravel driveway. Big Bubbles, all 250 lbs of him, was an engaging talker and loved what he did. He stood there in his huge apron, laughing and chatting away, always with that oversize all-purpose knife in his huge hand. He used it to turn eggs, flip burgers, stir soup, cut cheese cake and chop the veggies. After each cooking or serving maneuver, he would wipe the knife on his apron and press on to the continual task of providing good food and making people happy. Had he known, Norman Rockwell would have added one more Americana painting to his collection.

In January, after Christmas vacation, I went back to playing basketball for Harry Singleton and his double post pattern of play. I liked the game very much and was fairly good at it. That spring, Pop-pop and I converted a large old tool shed into a chicken house with wood floor and roosts. We cut out an opening so the chickens could go out into a chicken yard that we fenced in. We bought 100 chicks then and yearly thereafter. We had plenty of eggs, and chicken every Sunday; enough to give to relatives from time to time, helping to offset the meat rationing. It was my job to keep the chicken house clean and provided with fresh straw. Soap, water, brushes, lime and clean straw were the basis for my Saturday morning "happy times." Twice a year I whitewashed the whole inside of the chicken house. I also worked in the large vegetable garden as needed, preparing soil, seeding, cultivating and harvesting. Pop-pop worked in the garden much more than I did. Nana jarred many of the vegetables which she stored in our pantry in the cellar.

My sophomore year moved to a close over the spring months and my friendships at St. Benedict's and in Union continued to grow. My grades were steady and I was a happy camper. That summer I had a job landscaping at the Suburban Golf Club. The care and maintenance of a golf course was interesting and I liked working outdoors all day. We reconstructed sand traps, planted trees, mowed, fertilized, improved drainage. Every morning very early I went around to all the greens with a long, thin-tapered bamboo pole and, with a "whippy" motion, I brushed the dew into the grass. The experts considered that to be downright therapeutic for the pampered greens. I played ball in my spare time or hung out with Teuscher, Jamison and Joe Koerner, my old buddy and classmate from 7A1 at Hamilton who had now moved to Union.

My junior year included a great physics course by Fr. Terrence. He made you think and solve and prove. The physics and chemistry labs were on the top floor. Occasionally the night air up there was filled with music coming from Fr. Terrence's trumpet and Fr. Michael's (chemistry prof) clarinet, sometimes with a backup recording of a big band. The latest Harry James (the best known trumpeter of the time) record was selling for fifty-nine cents and Fr. Terrence wanted it so he could "take a ride" with the great one. But he, like all of the monks, had no money. So he went to the Abbot and asked for the fifty-nine cents. Father Abbot gave him the money and the beat truly went on.

One afternoon, after getting off the bus from Newark, I was hitch-hiking home. A man of about 40 picked me up and we were having a pleasant conversation until he switched it to talking about girls and me and sex, as he was slowing down to let me out. Then he tried to put his hand on me. I could not get a full swing at him in the car so I drove my left elbow to the side of his head. Instant headache. I got out of the car rendering some choice words and walked to the house. At the start of my junior year in 1943 there were no PGs (postgraduates) around for the Prep School team; they were all in the service. So we had only one team in each sport and featured them as the Prep School teams. Prof Blood, the basketball legend, was the coach and had been for a long time. A fine gentleman and a great educator, he held the national record for the number of consecutive games won for a high school. He achieved this at Passaic High School in the 1920's: 158 straight wins and 212 out of 213. Much has been written about this great man who was a wrestler and a gymnast in his youth. He knew

Dr. Naismith, the inventor of basketball, from his early days at the Springfield Massachusetts YMCA. Fast break! Run, run; train yourself to know what you will do with the ball before you get it. Pass, pass, pass, move the ball fast, it's a team sport. He frowned on dribbling as a general pattern. Many full court, fast break drills were pass, pass, and lay it in. He would often blow the whistle for dribbling rather than passing. I played forward on the varsity in my junior year along with Bucky Connors, Jim Cavanaugh, Tim Shea, and Jack Dalton, who is a legend in his own time in the St. Benedict's community. He gave a life of teaching, coaching, and dedication to the Beehive. When you visit the St. Benedict's campus, you will see the Dalton Gymnasium.

The system Prof used that year was interesting. There was the "big" team I just mentioned, averaging about 6'3" and a small faster team with 6'5" Tim Shea remaining at center. Prof seldom used an individual substitution, but instead would change the whole team. It worked nicely. We had a good year.

The area where we lived on the Water Co. property was called the Hummocks (that high ridge of ground). Pop-pop put up a basket and backboard when we first moved there. It was out beyond the chicken yard and I spent much time out there winter and summer over the years. I also put up a basket in an old pumping station building so we could shoot baskets and play two on two during snow time. It was the Hummocks Coliseum complete with poor lighting and ancient dust. But, oh, what fun. I also used that large building to throw baseballs and practice pitching against some targets painted on the old wooden walls.

In my junior year many friendships continued to grow, Frank DiGiralamo, Red McEntee, Chud Reagan, John Downey, Frank Farrell, Bob Fay, Frank Noonan, Art Newman, and many other students. My friendships in Union also progressed without awareness, as is the case in those growing years. This was the year of Physics, Geometry, English, Religion, History, French and PT. Life at the Beehive was structured: 9 a.m. to 2:30 p.m. with half an hour for lunch and 10 minutes between classes. We had PT everyday in the standard gym uniform. Ten minutes to change from class clothes and be on the gym floor, and ten minutes to shower and change back. We did calisthenics, running, chin ups, tumbling, boxing drills, obstacle course, push ups etc. in the course of a week. As you can tell, I was busy all the time. I never noticed how busy I was as I increased my commitments.

But back to the junior year and the basketball squad. We played our home games at 8 p.m. in the old Stanley Gym. The junior varsity game was at 6:30. On game days, rather than go home and back to Newark, we would sometimes use the late time by going to the Branford to see the afternoon matinee which consisted of a movie, a newsreel, and the onstage highlight, one of the big bands such as Goodman, Dorsey, Ellington, or Glenn Miller. They all came through Newark as part of their East Coast tour. We always ate a light supper at a diner on Market St. and then walked over to the gym to watch the JV game before changing for our game. When Nana and Pop-pop did not come over to watch the game, I would take a bus home, arriving there about 10:30–11:00 p.m. When we played night games away from home court I had to make special arrangements to get home.

I recall one game we played against the Columbia University V-6 (Naval Training) team. Prof introduced me to their coach, whom he knew, in case I wanted to go there after the war and perhaps could get an athletic scholarship. It was nice of Prof to do that for me.

I was almost 15 when Pearl Harbor was attacked and I was determined to join the Marines after my 17th birthday and upon completing my junior year in June 1944. But as we practiced to go into the State Basketball Tournament in February 1944, I had a serious injury to my left foot and ankle. I missed the tournament. The doctor said it would have been better if I had broken it; then he could have set it for a quicker recovery. Although I pitched for the baseball team that spring, using a firm ankle wrap and tape, there was no way I was going to pass the preliminary examination at the recruiting station. "Take off your socks and shoes. Now roll back and forth on your heels. Walk on the balls of your feet. Now rock on your feet from side to side." But by November of my senior year, and again playing basketball, I was ready. I went to NYC and volunteered to join the Marines. I was too light at 6'2" and 155lbs. "Even a quart of water and three bananas won't make it," said the sergeant with the voice of experience.

As mentioned, as the injury started to heal I tried out for the baseball team. Pitchers and catchers were called first in March when we worked out in the gym. Joe Kasberger was the football and baseball coach. Another legend. From a ranching family in Oregon, he was the product of a Benedictine education and later went to U. of Oregon where he was an All Pacific halfback. He later coached at a small Benedictine college out there, and had a year of coaching under Knute Rockne at Notre Dame.

Then he came east and received his teaching degree at Columbia University. He came to St. Benedict's in the mid 1930's to coach and teach Business. A tough, rugged, individual, he was a driver, a disciplinarian and a builder of character. He coached football and baseball in a professional manner. He projected himself as a member of the squad and always wore the baseball uniform, pants, jacket, cleats and cap, the same at football practice and games. But there was no question as to who was in charge. At the school he wore a business suit, as did the other lay teachers. Always in great shape, he would put on the pads and show a lineman the right technique in blocking or tackling. "Now hit me," he would holler and the kid would bang into him. "Oh, you call that a hit? Try it again!" Or in baseball, he would pitch the batting practice (and he was good). He taught me a lot about pitching. I learned much more about pitching and fielding my position from him than from my college coach, who was a regular in the big leagues for 20 years. He also hit the fungo ground balls in infield practice, talking it up all the time. "Let's hear you out there. What, are you tired?"

Joe ran up outstanding records in football and baseball. It was drill, drill, practice, practice. "You play the way you practice," he always said. As an educator he, like Prof, wasn't just talking about the sport, but we would find that out later after the seeds took root. Benedict Field was a large parcel of land near Branch Brook Park in outer Newark. It had a football and baseball field, running track, field house with locker rooms and showers, storage and maintenance sheds. When the weather was warm enough, or almost warm enough, the whole baseball squad worked out there. We walked from the school to the subway (some trolley car lines ran underground in the city and elevated to the surface on the outskirts). It stopped 5 blocks from Benedict Field. At practice Joe would go over the basics time after time: sliding, cover first base, complete the double play, hit and run, pick off plays, throwing to the right base, batting, running bases etc.; we learned it all from Joe. He liked his pitchers to be in good shape so it was not unusual for him to keep three or four of us after practice to "shag" fungo fly balls. He would hit them almost out of your running reach, a skilled fungo stick hitter. Then I would shower, dress, take my books and walk back to the trolley, go into Newark, walk to the bus for Union and get home about 7 p.m. Then it was eat, study, sleep and up at 6:15 a.m. I never thought much about it being a tough schedule. That's what I was supposed to do and I liked it.

There was a hot dog and hamburger joint near Benedict Field call Ting-a-Ling's. On the occasional day when practice was short, we would stop there for a hot dog with lots of onions and relish. Ting-a-Ling cooked the hot dogs in a deep fry wire basket. The joke was that he changed the oil every 2,000 hot dogs. I had four wins and no losses that spring, pitching behind two good friends who were seniors, Bucky Connors (who played a while in the Phillies chain after his Navy time, and Bob Feeney, who had a great change-up and curve ball.

One game comes to mind. We had a rivalry with LaSalle Military Academy at Oakdale Long Island. It is run by the Christian Brothers (charities, teaching, hospitals, the brandy guys). It was spring of 1944. Jack Dalton was playing first base and a LaSalle runner spiked him and was called safe after Jack dropped the ball. It was a cheap shot; the runner had plenty of room. On the next play the batter grounded to the short stop who threw to Chick Myers, our second baseman, who was covering the bag to relay on to 1st base for the double play. But "the spiker" slid high into Chick with his cleats and Chick came down on the runner's chest with the ball still in his hand, and he rapped him "up-a-side the h'ad." Now Joe abhorred fighting on the field, and so did Prof. It was against the code of good discipline. Realizing that, we all ran out there to break it up. Bucky Connor, the captain, came running in from center field, shouting for Chick to stop, and he reached for the stunned guy to "help" him and in the same motion scooped up some infield dirt and rubbed it in his face. The base runner got up sputtering, stuttering, and complaining as the umpire threw him out of the game. We went on to win. Joe talked about the need for good conduct as we all showered and dressed in the locker room. We should not have left the bench; "Do your fighting on the score board" was the motto. But it was nice to see that life was fair in this case.

When school let out for the summer, I took a job with the Burry Biscuit Company doing a variety of manual activities. The operation was very large and was housed in a part of the old, long, Durant car manufacturing building. Durant was a contemporary of Henry Ford and he made cars called the Moon and Star. The operation went bankrupt. Over the years many companies bought, or rented, space in that long, long, former assembly line plant that was two-storied in some sections. But before I get to Burry Biscuit, I want to mention the Big Bear, which was a huge indoor regional market place also in the Durant Building. I went there with Nana and Pop-pop, off and on, since I had been six or so. The farmers, butchers, fisherman, and merchants of all kinds came from all over to display and sell their items. The smell of roasting coffee, chocolate blocks, freshly ground horseradish, dill pickles in barrels, spices and fresh baked goods stimulated the shoppers to buy, and left lasting memories.

The Burry Biscuit operation was centered around a 300 ft. conveyer oven. All day and night the different batches of cookies were placed in one end and slowly baked as they moved along the conveyer to come out the other end ready for packaging, boxing and shipping. Frank Noonan, my St. Benedict's and Union buddy, also worked there that summer. We were shifted around on a weekly basis. The operation of the mixing room on the second floor was interesting. All of the measurements for the ingredients to be baked were, of course, very large, considering my reference point for oatmeal cookies was Mom's 3 cups of this and 4 cups of that.

To fill an order for a certain batch of cookies, the chief baker would have us put the ingredients in several open, elliptical, heavy metal containers on wheels. They measured about 10' long, 4' wide and 3' deep. Three or four would make an order. The mixing was done with large mobile mixers. Then we moved the vats into a special room which would be kept at a precise temperature while the yeast did its work and the right consistency was reached. We would then wheel it out, grunt, grunt, and cut pieces out of the dough with a garden spade. It was shoveled onto a flat small platform that was floured for sliding. We flattened the dough by hand roller and then pushed it down a chute to the first floor, where it was picked up by a roller and cookie cutter before going for the slow ride in the oven. Another mixing room job was lifting, opening, and dumping 100 lb sacks of flour into a large sifter, all day.

I worked the various jobs more than once in the course of that summer. There was no air conditioning in those days. Working around that big oven in July and August was tiring but not difficult. I was in good condition and took my salt pills and water. The girls working at the end of the conveyer packaged the baked cookies by hand. Because of the heat, they wore shorts and cool tops. When I worked in the shipping room, boxing and steel banding the wooden crates (we sent a lot of cookies to the military), I was often among the gals picking up more boxes of cookies to crate. We all had fun talking about the "flirty" things that such an environment creates. If management had realized this fringe benefit, they would have reduced my 27 cents an hour pay.

But the best jobs in July and August were in the mixing room. That's where they kept the chill locker for chocolates, nuts and other perishables. Purposely lax on keeping the door locked, the "honcho" let us take a needed break from the heat in there from time to time. I must confess that Noonan and I occasionally bent his trust a little by adding some nuts and chocolate chips to our home made lunch. One day, toward the end of that summer, we bought some beer (no ID then), and put it in the cooler. At the end of the shift we sat in there and drank it and talked of many things, as friends do. Later on we would be at Georgetown when he was well into pre-med and I was just starting at Foreign Service. I introduced him to his wife Kay when I was back at Benedict's after my Navy stint. They married while he was at Georgetown Med School. Retired now, I have not seen him since our youth, but I know we are friends to this day.

One night that summer I was hitch-hiking home from a card game at Joe Koerner's. It was dark on Morris Ave. with occasional traffic. As I walked along, looking for a possible ride, I saw, there in the dark distance, a guy trotting along, heading toward me. As he came closer, I noticed he had work shoes, was disheveled and a bit dirty in his plain work clothes. A bit thin and hollow-eyed, when he was near me he said in a rough German accent, "Yunun Chersey ya nu vere?" (Union Jersey, you know where?)

I pointed up the road to Union Center, the middle of town. He grunted a thank you and continued his slow trot into the night. The war was a long way off and we did not have any kind of citizen alert system and no one was on edge. Oh, we had periodic blackout drills, more to help in our "pull together" attitude than to worry about air defense. So I didn't give that trotting German guy much thought. There were a lot of German immigrants in our area. But many years later I figured out that he was probably an escaped POW who jumped off a Lehigh Valley railroad train that ran above and over Morris Ave. heading west. When we were so safe at home we accepted everything without a thought of suspicion or an enemy in our midst. Obviously he was looking for someone he knew, or a friend of a friend, who lived in Union.

Senior year started and we were kings of the walk with a serious purpose. The war continued. Hitler's Fortress Europe was cracking and the Pacific War was in our favor. The Japanese Navy was smaller after the battles of Midway and the Coral Sea. The battles of Iwo Jima and Okinawa were yet to be fought. The Philippines had been liberated, Mc Arthur had returned as promised, and the Japanese General Homma was tried and convicted at the summer home of the U.S. Ambassador in Baguio, that beautiful mountain area at 5,000 ft., the City of Pines. Many years down the road I would enjoy many visits to that lovely place. Some crucial, and not so crucial, battles had been won on the Pacific islands by this time: Saipan, Guam, Tarawa, Guadalcanal, and Peleliu come to mind. Well, that's what was going on overseas but it would not disturb the fun of being a senior, loving this school, classmates and teachers. This was the year for Chemistry, English, French, Religion, Civics and PT.

The football team was good and the basketball tryouts started in November. My foot and ankle injury from my junior year was talked about. Some newspaper clips showed concern, but I was feeling better than the write-ups indicated. Good enough to quietly take and pass my Navy physical in November in NYC, the week after I visited the Marines, as mentioned. I took the parents' consent papers home. I had told no one about my plans except Frank DiGiralamo, "DiGi." "Oh, why do you want to do that," fretted Mom anxiously. She knew. So did Dad. I explained that many of my former fellow students and team mates were serving. Neighbors and relatives were in service and I had been waiting a long time. I pointed out that Dad had tried to join the Marines in 1917, but was too young. Cousin Frank had graduated school more than a year before and joined the Navy.

Quietly they approved. Mine was not an exceptional case. It was a common event of the time. Dad's generation and mine were much alike in values: honor, duty, country. About 1,500 ex-students from St. Benedicts were in service at that time, 35-40 had been killed in action.

Finally, I did tell the Headmaster, Prof., Joe, and Fr. Richard that I planned to drop the rest of my senior year and go into the Navy. They suggested that I sign up after I graduated, but all wished me well, when they realized I was determined and committed.

Then there was Fr. Martin, with a Ph.D. in music, who had taught us classical music. That good and holy monk went from the monastery and teaching into the Marine Corps as a chaplain. He made 3-4 major amphibious invasions in the Pacific, Guadalcanal and Bougainville come to mind. He returned to the monastery and his teaching in 1944, a man of God who had counseled thousands and blessed the dying on the battlefields, the quiet hero. Prior to my Navy departure, he counseled me and gave me a Benedictine medallion which had been made at the Monte Casino Abbey, the Citadel of the Order. He blessed it, and me. I was truly touched and inspired.

Digi and I went to a show at the Branford Theater while waiting to play a basketball game one night. The movie had a patriotic theme as did many during and right after WWII. This one used the old Army Air Corps as its theme. It had a good plot and lots of Army Air Corps "sizzle." Digi was really sold. He had been thinking about it. Now he was going to go in the Air Corps and wanted me to go with him. No, I was already committed to the Navy, but we were both "gung ho" to serve. And I'll bet we won the ball game that night.

Then the night of my final game, right after New Year 1945, we played Trenton Catholic in the old Stanley Gym. At half time Prof called for attention and announced that it was my final game and that I was leaving for the Navy soon. He wished me Godspeed and I got a standing "O." The players on both teams shook my hand. Nana, Pop-pop, Richie, and Marion were there. Although we lost, one Newark newspaper captioned the write-up "Newhard in Flashy Farewell." Happiness, thy name was Howie.

5   NAVY DAYS:

Growing Up Fast

I received my notice to report. I was to go to Grand Central Station in New York City on January 6, and bring the notice and a small bag of personal effects. Nana and Pop-pop drove me to the Station in the evening. We went inside and joined a large group of young men, milling around, carrying small tote bags. A petty officer appeared and told us we would board a train on track so and so and to start moving and bring our papers. Mom and Dad and I said our "will writes" and goodbyes, and off I went with 4-5 railroad coaches filled with young guys, all unknown to each other. "Where ya from?" was the most popular question to soften the edge of being strangers with an unknown future. We were told to sleep as much as we could (in sitting positions on the old hard straw woven seats) because tomorrow would be a very long day. We were going to Sampson Naval Training Station (boot camp) on Lake Seneca, New York.

The noisy, rattling train chugged through the night, the old coal and steam engine working hard. We arrived at Sampson, which was north of Elmira and south of Lake Ontario, early, early in the morning. A few of us had slept off and on, most had not, due to the excitement of it all and the general conditions. The train windows were iced over. It was below zero outside. This was not good and one might surmise it was not going to get any better very soon. "All right you guys, get off the train, take your gear with you and fall in line." Then they walked us to a nearby field house that served as a processing center. It was snowing heavily and it was deep. There were work crews of "boots" shoveling the train tracks in the rail yard.

Once inside the field house, each one of us stood in one of the squares painted on the floor. There was a cardboard box and crayon in each square. We all stood in our assigned squares, took off all of our clothes and shoes and put everything we were not going to need into the box. Wallets, watches, and personal items went into the small tote bag. We wrote our home address on the box (a rather ominous act and subtle reminder as to who owns you, baby). Then we all walked to one end of the field house where a few walkways were created by seven foot high temporary walls. Behind the walls and up on stepladders were several processors holding hoses. As we slowly walked past, one at a time, we were sprayed (showered) with the hoses. Cold water only. Save money. "Don't you know there's a war on?" After the walk-through showers, we were given a towel to dry off.

Now the medical exams would begin. The most memorable part of this was the drawing of blood. The pharmacist mates (PMs) came around and broke us into circles of about twenty, facing inward. Then a PM would come around to each "boot" and wrap a short rubber tube tightly around a bicep. He then put a needle attached to a test tube into the swollen vein and let it hang there. All the PMs would shout "Squeeze, squeeze your fist, give me some blood. Squeeze. Squeeze." We all were naked, on a cold day, in circles, with tubes filling with blood hanging out of our arms, to the beat of "squeeze, squeeze, squeeze." More than one guy got "jelly knees" and more than one thought he would drop. But everyone finally got through the physical process; cold, but with some sense of accomplishment. Then, still naked, they led us over to the haberdashery section, where the latest apparel of the season, and trends of the day, were being featured and fastidiously selected. "What size are you? Here, this will fit! This is your mattress cover. Don't carry it. Drag it! You will be given what you need. Put on the work uniform, socks, work shoes, skivvies, sweater and watch cap. Everything else goes inside the mattress cover."

We finally left the building and climbed into open trucks with our gear and headed for the big barber shop where a new crop of "skin heads" would be created with the din and hum of the electric clipper. Oh, the sad faces I saw. I didn't care. I already had a crew cut, so another inch or so was no problem. Then we climbed back into the trucks to go to our unit and company assignment, i.e., what bunk in what barracks? We all went to the Farragut Unit. The barracks were double-deckers. A company of 120 was assigned to each deck. It was a very long day, as advertised. After being assigned a bunk and a foot locker, we had to stencil all of our clothes. They said to be sure you stencil your black belt with the white ink. If the dog tags are blown off, the belt is the only way to identify the body. What a lovely way to end the day. Now, after all of that, we were told we had to wash the dirty mattress covers that we had dragged around the processing center. That was the last activity and we were in bed about midnight and up at 5a.m. the next day. Why did they tell us to drag the mattress cover? Why, just to make our stay there a little harder.

Over the ten-week period we had Physical Training (PT), obstacle course drills, gunnery, seamanship, close order drills, regimental guard duty, firefighting, navy regulations, military etiquette, and we ran the "grinder" every morning before breakfast. That was a circular paved roadway (when you could see it) about a half mile around. The new "boots" who had been sitting at desks and not working out before coming in had a tough time of it, until they became accustomed to the routine of boot camp. During the first two weeks there were some who ended up on the side of the track, in the snow, trying not to "barf." I went into boot camp during basketball season. When you played for Prof. Blood, you were in shape. So when we were up early to run the "grinder," I liked it. I was an athlete who spent his 18th birthday running the "grinder," doing close order drill, climbing cargo nets, and going to class. I put on about 15 lbs. in boot camp. I guess it was a lighter schedule than the one I previously pursued.

Our Company was scheduled to complete a fourteen-mile hike. The Chief Petty Officer in charge of our company, and responsible for our proficiency, hiked us about 5 miles out and 5 miles back. The snow was deep and it was falling again. He said it was too damn cold and put us all down for fourteen miles. Nobody complained. He was a good "boot pusher." He had played professional football on the west coast. His name was Frye, a cousin of Lonnie Frye who played second base for, I think, the Cincinnati Reds. He was tough, but fair, and when they added up all of our Company's progress criteria, plus the marching drill and inspection in front of the brass in a big field house, we won the Rooster Award and a one day liberty in the small town of Geneva on Lake Seneca.

I remember getting off the Navy bus in Geneva and seeing a gaudily dressed woman come running up to one of the older "boots" and kissing him; off they went arm in arm. I thought she was a relative who had come to meet him. I didn't really get it until some of her co-workers showed up and did likewise. But Fred Miller, my buddy from the heart of NYC, knew exactly what was going on, and he "got his jollies" from my naiveté. Miller and Dick Philo and I, all 18, went on to the USO and snacked on sodas and sweets, bought and mailed postcards, and walked around that quaint little town, a nice change of pace. Dick Philo was a big, strong, athlete from Glens Falls High, New York. I remember at PT they paired up everyone by height to put on the gloves and whack each other around, 60 pairings at once. Philo had me by 25 lbs. and since we were all supposed to really "mix it up," he enthusiastically rang my bell a couple of times… and the learning process went on.

Fred Miller and I became friends in boot camp, went to radar and radar countermeasure school together, volunteered for a dangerous mission, served on the same destroyer as radar and radar/counter measure operators, and were discharged on the same day at Lido Beach, Long Island. His Dad owned Miller and Sons Jewelry on Fifth Ave., NYC. Fred planned go to a jewelry design school. To this day we have not been in touch, and that is sad. Once, I tried to look up Fred Miller in the NYC telephone directory …oy vey!

The firefighting school at boot camp was very well run. It was serious business. It pulled us together as a team in a "help each other" frame of mind. The firefighting school basically consisted of several concrete buildings with variously shaped large rooms in them, simulating compartments aboard a ship. In those rooms they had the capacity to light fires of various intensity, oil or gasoline. It became very hot and it really got your attention. Our learning levels skyrocketed. We worked in groups, mainly using the fog nozzle extension on a fire hose. It was designed to spray, at high pressure, thin streams of water against each other, creating a water fog, a mist. This reduced the temperature around the fire to a level that would not support combustion, and it would go out. The "Christmas Tree" fire was the most difficult to extinguish. In one of the rooms there were some pipes connected in the rough outline of a Christmas tree. These pipes had tiny nozzles through which gasoline or oil was sprayed and ignited. Crouching low and supporting the pressure hose and fog nozzle, in a tight row, we had to go in there and put it out; and we did.

We also had gas mask drills at the fire school. During one of the classes, they put us in a large, sealed room. We put on our gas masks, as taught. They pumped the room full of tear gas. Then we were ordered to take off the gas masks and thought "what are you, nuts?" as we followed the order. Everybody started tearing, coughing and choking. Then they opened a door and let us out into the cold

Lake Seneca air. Oh, was that ever good. The purpose? I suppose you can't know or appreciate the pleasure without knowing the pain. In addition, it provided motivation to learn how to use your gas mask.

Boot camp was a fun study in human nature, although I did not realize it then. In that small, narrow environment little matters take on importance. "One-ups-man-ship" was prevalent. Being ahead chronologically was important to most "boots" in that 10 week program. For example, when the truckloads of "skin heads" pulled into the barracks area, others who may have been there only a week or two would holler "skin heads, skin heads!" In the third or fourth week, the dog tags were issued: name, serial number and religion. That was a happy moment for many, and they let the dog tags hang out of their shirts or jumpers while they were eating at the mess hall table. This showed the newer arrivals that the guys with the dog tags were "old salts."

In the fire school training almost everyone was blackened all over from the oil smoke and some of those "experienced" fire bugs would linger around, before showering, talking with the newer "boots" from the adjoining barracks. "Let me tell you all about it. Oh, yeah, it's dangerous. Sure you can get burned. Yeah, I've been here 8 weeks." "One-upsmanship" at its finest. Such an environment makes "one-upsmanship" important to some who are in need of applause.

The classification I asked for upon my first visit to the recruiting station was to be the gunner on a TBM, torpedo bomber, but that never materialized. Then, early in boot camp, I asked for submarine service and was turned down in a two-minute interview as I stood naked in front of two psychologists, one of whom said to the other that I was too high strung. Anyway there was a war on and the Navy was going to place us according to the needs of the time, correlated to our General Classification Test results. So the Navy chose me to become a radar man. I broke boot camp in March and went back to Union in my dress blues, carrying my duffel bag. I took trains and buses and hitch-hiked the last couple of miles. The people I met on the way home were all nice and talked to me and wished me well. When I hitchhiked I had a ride immediately. I felt good. I was a qualified Seaman 2/C, U.S. Navy.

Spring had sprung. Soon Pop-pop would prepare the garden soil. Smokey, our black lab, was happy to see me back. Nana, Pop-pop, Marion and Richie, who was 10, all had plenty of questions. We were a happy family. It was a very fast week. I visited St. Benedict's and saw my teachers and coaches. I visited my classmates and partied with some of them. Mom and Dad had some family parties for me, and I think my Uncle Frank had a party for me also. At the end of it all Nana and Pop-pop drove me to the local train station and I headed back to the OGU (Out Going Unit) at Sampson, where they told me I would be going to Radar School in Ft. Lauderdale, Florida. My Travel Orders were cut and after a few days some 15 of us, including Fred Miller, assembled to board a train to Florida.

The train out of NYC was a regular commercial train with a dining car. We also had beds in a Pullman car (pay a little more and go first class). The song

"Gonna Take a Sentimental Journey" was at the top of the list and they played it often. Jean Price and I liked that song. We sometimes "slow dragged" to it. I was a little lonely as we rolled and rumbled along through the night, in and out of sleep. At about 2 a.m. the train stopped for coal, or water, or whatever, and some middle-aged mothers and grandmothers came along knocking on our widows. "Hi, y'all, want some coffee, doughnuts?" I wearily opened my sliding window. The sign read Rocky Mount, North Carolina "Lady, it's 2 a.m." "Oh, ah know. You boys do so much fo' us, we don' mind comin' down here anytime to say thanks. Coffee? Doughnuts?" "Yes, but…" my little man inside said, "That's right Howie, go ahead and say something stupid about these nice Rocky Mount folks, hhmmm?"

"Hound Dog" Haile, a product of Rocky Mount, would be a radar shipmate in a future assignment, and many years later when my hometown buddy Bob Teuscher and I shared an apartment in Washington, we had occasion on many Saturday nights to party with some folks over in the Mt. Rainier area. They would take turns hosting. (Hosting? Put out the booze, chips, crackers, cold cuts and pickles and pump up the music.) We had some great parties there. The crowd included Jim, an Army major and his wife, Eddie Yost and Gil Coan of the old Washington Senators baseball team who showed up from time to time. It was a good mix of people including two gals from Rocky Mount, North Carolina who Haile would have termed "as purty as a speckled hound dog." The gal I liked had a boyfriend. His name was Lemuel. He watched her pretty well. He liked to hunt and ride horses. Ah yes, I knew by then it's a smart monkey, who doesn't monkey with another monkey's monkey. All this from thinking about "Rocky Mount;" that's nice, but back to the story.

At Ft. Lauderdale, the Trade Winds and the Ft. Lauderdale Beach hotels were side by side along the beach. The Navy had built one enclosure fence around them. One was the Radar School and the other was the Fire Control School, i.e., controlling gunfire with a specialized radar system. There were four students to a room in double bunks. We had about 40-45 in our radar class. We were up at 6 a.m. and ran the beach toward a nearby light house and back. Then we showered and had breakfast; classes started at 8 a.m. and lasted until 7 p.m. with the usual breaks.

Radar means Radio Detection and Ranging. A high frequency directional radio wave is sent out. Part of this wave bounces back off an object such as a shoreline, a ship or a plane and returns to the radar set, which processes and passes it to scopes of various types, making the waves "readable" as to the range and bearing and the size of contact or contacts. The course and speed of the contact(s) is determined after a few "fixes" or readings. There were several kinds of scopes. One was the "A" scope which showed the contact as a green, grassy triangle, the height and breadth of which the experienced operator could interpret to determine the size of the ship. Another was the Plan Position Indicator, which showed the distance and direction to a ship or coastline relative to the set. We studied the

GS, surface search, the SR air search, and the SP which did both and was state-of-the-art in its time. Each one was highly recognizable from outside the ship by the shape of the antennas. We had to know all of the knobs and switches, how to interpret a "pip," how to read ranges and bearings, how to plot courses and speeds, projecting relative positions one, two, five minutes hence. We learned to write upside down so officers on the other side of the plotting board could read it, and backwards if it was a transparent vertical board, for the same reason. It was a lot to learn in a short period. Very often an instructor would holler at someone, "You! Stand up and listen! There's no sleeping here!" The lighter side of it was that I had a beach front room in a fine Ft. Lauderdale Hotel and I ran the beach and swam in the surf.

I do not think the Navy had been at that location very long before we arrived. We had some of our plotting classes in what had been the main dining room. They had not even taken out the heavy, floral design, wall to wall carpeting, or the impressive chandeliers. It was not easy to visualize plotting in the CIC (Combat Information Center) of a carrier or battleship from this 5-star environment, but all the essentials we needed were there.

I recall that every day while we on our morning jog, a captured Italian submarine would leave the nearby Port Everglades and head out to sea, a mystery to me to this day. After we were there about three weeks we had a one day liberty. Four or five of us took the bus down U.S. 1 to Miami. There were wide open spaces along that stretch then, a lot of sand dunes and sea oats between Ft. Lauderdale and Hollywood and Miami. We had a good meal in Miami and took a boat tour on the waterways (what else would a sailor do?) This included a visit to a Seminole Indian Village where we looked down into a dry pit and watched one of the braves wrestle an alligator, a good show. He even rolled the gator over on its back and rubbed its stomach until it relaxed and he could remove his arm lock on the jaw, still rubbing the tummy. We were generous when they passed the collection can. We all had the standard $10,000 government life insurance. That poor daredevil surely didn't have any coverage. From there we probably took in a movie, had another meal and went back to Ft. Lauderdale before taps and lights out. The fourth and last week was hectic. The instructors kept testing us and running drills. They wanted to make sure we were ready for the Fleet.

After the short commencement ceremony, a few of us were assigned to the Special Projects School, Naval Research Labs in Washington D.C. for a six-week course to study radar countermeasures. This was the latest in jamming enemy radar. Miller and I and a few others proceeded to the Anacostia Naval Station in S.E. Washington to join up with others to form a class of about 25. Chief RdM Tony Flanak was in charge of our class. He had spent a lot of time in a PBY Catalina, flying on patrol missions in the Atlantic trying to make fixes on surfaced Nazi U-Boats (submarines). Chief Flanak was a great teacher and leader and sort of "mother-henned" us youngsters. "Now don't go in this place or that place when you get liberty tomorrow night," etc. There actually was a bar in that general area called The Bucket of Blood.

We were there to learn and practice how to jam enemy radar. We would pick up a radar or radio wave moving through our area, see it on an oscilloscope and hear it in our ear phones, radar having the higher pitch; the higher the frequency, the higher the pitch. Once we tuned in and knew the frequency (and could see it and hear it), we would then set the random noise jammer accordingly and hook it into a hollow guide wave trap. Our jamming transmission would not be going out to the target at this time, but would follow the hollow guide wave trap and show up on our scope as a large squared-off pip covering the target pip (enemy radar/radio transmission). Then you knew you were on target and, if in combat, you would change the hollow guide wave trap connector to the antennae for transmission and jam the target. The fact that you had the target pip covered on the scope showed that you had the right frequency and direction and the random noise jammer with the photo electric cell would do the rest. The photo electric cell changes noise into electrical energy. Naturally, we never proceeded beyond this point to actually jam any "make-believe" target in the DC area, heaven forbid!

We learned and practiced the basics and had problem-solving drills. In about the fourth week Chief Flanak asked for volunteers to take on a dangerous mission pertaining to Radar Counter Measures (RCM) after joining their ships. Miller and I raised our hands and so did four or five others. It was all top secret, as was the course, and no questions would be answered at that time.

Naturally Washington was a great liberty town and we spent many of our liberties sightseeing. Our pay was $66 a month so we were not going to be seen in the Shoreham, Mayflower, or Duke Zeibert's. However, the many tourist attractions were all bargains, as was the public dining room at the Capitol Building. We provided kudos to their renowned Navy Bean Soup. Who would know better? We went on to finish our RCM training, those who had volunteered did not get assigned to a ship, just yet; instead, about eight of us were flown to the Marine base at Cherry Point, North Carolina. This was my first flight ever. It was a C-47, "Gooney Bird," all aluminum, bucket seats along the walls, and absolutely no frills. "Save money. Don't you know there's a war on?" We climbed aboard, strapped in, and boy, was it noisy. I knew nothing about those airplanes, the changing pitches of the prop, how they maneuvered, and the "thump" of the landing gears raising and lowering. Who doesn't remember their first flight from those days? I tell you, this fella was wide-eyed and anxiously looked over his shoulder and out the window the whole way.

At Cherry Point we met up with about 10 more RCM operators, took a ferry boat to Ocracoke Island, 40 miles at sea, on the outer banks, near Cape Hatteras. They told us we would get our mail through the Cherry Point address that they would give us. We were not to tell pen pals or family where we were. We were not to talk with people in the small fishing village at the end of the island. The three weeks I was to spend there is not recorded in the service record which I was given upon discharge.

Ocracoke is about 20 miles long and about 2 miles wide. It was somewhat barren, with sand dunes, sea oats and various dry grasses. There were wild pony-sized horses roaming the island. It was right out of a pirate lore vision, in which it actually has a rightful historical place. The Navy had a small docking facility which had a few boats. The largest was a reconverted 104 ft. sub-chaser. It contained all of our RCM gear, plus an SG radar system, and some equipment for mechanical jamming, in addition to the electronic jamming which we had already been taught. That would be our practice station from the sea. But there was more, and the real reason we were here.

The facility was far from basic comfort level. It was spring. The small, ground-level, cement-block barracks that we lived in had torn and broken screens and the sand was wind-driven up against the walls. It was everywhere because it was a sand island with constant winds. The mosquitoes were big and ugly. Many nights I would take the mattress cover off my mattress and get inside of it, pull it over my head and lay on the uncovered mattress.

There was a main building where we had our meals, critiques, and the radar that we would jam electronically and mechanically. During the first week or so we boarded the sub-chaser every morning and stayed out most of the day, conducting exercises. That part of the Atlantic is famous for its normally high waves, and its storms. It was known as "the graveyard of ships" since the early days of the sailing ships. We would maneuver up and down the coast of the island and pick up the radar that was tracking us and then, in the manner described, we would jam it, taking notes chronologically for the 4 p.m. critique. It sounds so nice writing about it now, but that sea, even on a normal day, was big. That small, skinny, cigar shaped, 104 ft. sub-chaser just rolled and pitched and made life miserable One day the mechanism holding the directional antennae at the top of the short stubby mast, broke, and we had to take turns climbing up there and aiming the antennae by hand while we rolled and pitched. What a way to break in for sea duty. We were all seasick and just worked through it. That lasted for four or five days and then the "sun came out" and we were "old salts." When I later would go aboard a "tin can" destroyer as a crew member and see the troubled faces of those going through their seasickness adjustment, I was glad for the sub-chaser experience. Miller and I would give them a "What's all the fuss?" look. Salty, man; one-upsmanship? Of course.

Then we learned about mechanical jamming. We would go out, well off-shore, then head to the radar target on the beach and fire a rocket that would burst at a preset distance and height. The rocket was full of aluminum strips cut to one half of the wave length of the target radar. This was called "window" or chaff. On the target radar scope, the chaff would appear as a lot of reflection and clutter and would hide our ship behind it until it drifted down into the sea, during which time we would change course/speed, and try to confuse the trackers. Several well-placed, timely, bursts would conceal us so that we could not be fired upon in an actual situation. Another maneuver was to fire a couple of rockets and then release a weather balloon with 8 or 9 feet long aluminum streamers attached to the line hanging below it. On the PPI radar screen this would appear to be our ship coming out from behind the "window." A smart radar operator would always know the course and speed of the wind. The training was long and repetitive. We liked it. We wanted to "play" the way we practiced.

During the latter half of our stay at Ocracoke, we started to work with bicycle generators which provided the power to run a complete electronic jamming unit. It was an amphibious operation. We would go out to sea in a Higgins boat LCVP (Landing Craft Vehicle Personnel), a personnel landing boat with a front ramp that dropped down when you hit the beach. On the Higgins boat we had all that we would need for a successful mission. The generator was on wheels. We would come in, hit that heavy surf, drop the ramp, and pull and push the generator and the equipment ashore, across the sand and up onto a high sand dune. Then we would connect all the gear components, start up the generator, and proceed to jam the target radar. When we came off the boat with boots and gear and rifles, the instructors would shout, "Hold up those rifles, keep them dry." Not in this surf, buddy. But you know what? You can put a rifle in water, take it out, shake it a bit, put a round in the chamber, and it will still fire. It's the sand in the surf that can cause the trouble. Anyway we practiced over and over until we got the whole procedure down pat.

While we were at Ocracoke, Sunday was our day off. I recall one time some of us who liked clams went out on some sand bars on the west side of the island. The tide was out and we raked up cherry stone and chowder clams and had a feast. We also had fun body-surfing over on the Atlantic side. Those waves were big and it was fun. On dark, moonless nights the stars created a beautiful low ceiling over us. The waves with their characteristic crack/crash sound were a constant reminder that we were forty miles at sea. Nevertheless, as we adapted, it was music to sleep by.

One Sunday about ten of us got into a large, thick-boarded, heavy, open boat that would seat about twenty. It had two masts. The only problem was that none of this inspired group of sailors knew how to sail a boat. It was "hit or miss" all the way. Naturally we sailed on the western, bay side, and clumsily got the hang of a few of the basics. After a while we were several miles from the shore. That clear water beckoned and about four of us took off our clothes and jumped in and hollered, "Be sure to come back!" We knew it would take a while. So we swam around, floated, treaded, and swam some more. Finally they were able to turn the boat around and head our way.

Now the gunwales were high out of the water and you could not just grab the gunwale and pull yourself up and over as the boat came by. They had some thick ropes hanging down for us to grab, but they did not slow down much, didn't know how. Well, the other three grabbed a rope and were pulled up, but I missed my rope and they went on by with a "We'll be baacck!" Suddenly I felt a chill. For sure the water was cool. Here I was by myself, treading water, isolated, miles at sea. The boat seemed a long way off and had not yet turned. A subtle fear started its dance, which I tried to ignore. "Come on now," I said, "This is fun, float on your back, like they taught at boot camp." "Yeah," said my small voice, "It's called the Dead Man's Float." Now the dance got louder. I was coping with a bad situation, and I was cold. But here they came, full sail. My little inside guy said, "Don't miss it now, Howie, or you're screwed." Oh, boy, the adrenalin was pumping. I grabbed that rope, slammed against the boat as it splashed through the waves, and they pulled me in. "Are you okay?" "Sure, why did you come back so soon?"

We went back to the barracks, showered and changed, and then went for a walk that took us to the little village on the island. These people had their heritage steeped in that location for two hundred years. They were sea farers, fishermen, and they had their own style of life and way of talking. We had been told not to talk to them for security reasons, but we did not talk about us, we talked about them. "Hey old timer, ever been to the mainland?" "Nope, but I waas teh Philadellia once when I bruk ma leeg." "Sorry to hear that, sir. How many fish can you catch in one day?" "Jus 'bout enuff." "Oh. Well, nice talking to you, sir." "Yup."

We finished up our training and had our final classes, briefings, and "good lucks" to all. "Hey Chief, when do we get our diplomas?" "Get out of here!" We took the ferry back to Cherry Point and then a plane to Anacostia. When we returned, Tony Flanak told us we had 4 days leave before we went to our assigned ships. That Flanak was a fine guy. For some 6 years after I left his class he sent me a Christmas card, and I can just see him with a 3x5 card box keeping all the addresses of his ex-students up to date.

It so happened that my class was graduating at St. Benedict's while I was home on that short leave. They had made a diploma for me (even though I had not completed all of my credits), which they were going to mail. So I graduated in uniform with my class at a Mass in the Abbey Church. The comment next to my picture in the yearbook read: "It would take more than these few words to give a fitting description and show enough appreciation to this great fellow. Howie is undoubtedly our most outstanding athlete. He is an all-round fellow and a sterling example of fine and healthy living. In addition to his exceptional work both on the court and diamond, he has done equally well in his studies and has developed a personality that is unbeatable. We take our hats off to Howie." Sometimes a touch of TTH (Truth Trumps Humility) is okay.

We had a family party or two. I recall telling my good friend Tommy Jamison, while sharing a quiet time of reflection of our long friendship, that I didn't think I would be coming back. Long after I had shipped out, Tom, who was "family," told Nana, "Howie doesn't think he's coming back." Nana told me about this some ten year's later. Oh, she was a quiet one.

The next day, travel orders in hand, I took a train to Norfolk Navy Base to go aboard the USS Vesole DD878 as a Seaman 1/C RDM and RCM operator. I arrived at the Base, showed my orders, found the Vesole, walked up the gangplank, duffel bag on the left shoulder, turned and saluted the flag flying at the fantail, then saluted the Officer of the Deck (OD) and reported for duty. Yes, just like the movies. There was no compartment or bunk or footlocker for me to stow my gear. We were going to be a slightly over-complemented ship. I would live out of my duffel bag and store it in the RCM room next to the gyro compass on the first deck below. They gave me a hammock to string up at night, which I did, next to the gyro. The whole ship was dusty, dirty, and noisy with jack hammers and riveting guns dominating the scene and filling your brain. The Vesole and the other three destroyers of our squadron were brand new, built in Orange, Texas. They would now be made into state-of-the-art radar picket and radar countermeasure ships. To accomplish this they had to take off the torpedo tubes and replace that area with a tripod mast, some 35 feet high off the main deck, which would hold various countermeasure antennae. I would come to know all about that mast and its platform cap later in the voyage. Our radar section would consist of thirty enlisted men and three officers, including Bill Hulse, the well-known track miler from NYU.

The redesign completed, we left Norfolk, sailing alone, and took a course north to a radar school at Brigantine New Jersey, near Atlantic City. There we would pick up the final two radarmen (one of whom was "Hound Dog" Haile from Rocky Mount) to fill our roster. We moved to within 3 miles of the beach and idled, waiting for them to come out to us on a Navy launch. The Combat Information Center (CIC) or "radar shack" was right under the bridge. Those of us who were not on watch went up to the outside bridge, a few at a time, to use a pair of high-powered binoculars to watch the girls on the beach. The OD was a radar officer and he wanted his guys to be happy. "Hey, it's my turn" was a well-worn phrase until the launch arrived with the assigned crew members. We moved out to sea and headed south, past Norfolk, where we teamed up with the Borderline and two other destroyers to complete our squadron which joined with the new 40,000 ton aircraft carrier Boxer and set a course for Guantanamo Bay, Cuba, "Gitmo." It was a bright, sunny, July day. The swells were normal.

The Vesole was the flagship of the squadron. The Captain on board was known as COM DES RON 12 (Commander, Destroyer Squadron 12). En route to "Gitmo," we began to learn the routines of sea duty, and the basic exercises of general quarters i.e., battle stations, changing places and picking up new courses and speeds for carrier maneuvers, plane-launch positions, how to operate the IFF (Identification Friend or Foe) system, practice tracking aircraft, etc. Fred Miller and I were the only qualified RCM operators, and Bob Gallo was the only qualified RCM technician on board. He was also one of the volunteers from Tony Flanak's class in Washington. Two operators and a technician; how organized it all was.

The RCM gear was top secret and we had the keys to the RCM room, which was away from CIC down below the main deck. Not even the Chief Boatswain Mate, the usual "keeper of the keys" on such a ship, had a key to the RCM room. I guess the Radar Officer in Charge had one but when he came down to watch us operate we had to let him in. And so we continued practicing our newly acquired skills in electronic jamming, as described.

We arrived at Guantanamo, Cuba, and had 5-6 hour port and starboard liberty in the evenings, i.e. every other evening. We were not allowed off the Base so, whoopee! Play some ping pong, shoot some pool, or see a movie. Culture abounded, Spanish that is, but it was outside the gate. No matter, we were there six or seven days to practice our jobs, qualify in gunnery, surface, air, and shore bombardment, and get ready for battle. The last thing the skipper needed was for some crew members to forget the time and get in trouble in some manner that would affect our mission. We practiced working together as a four destroyer squadron, laying smoke screens, simulating submarine attacks, dropping depth charges, shooting at drone aircraft or towed air targets with our 5 inch-38 guns (3 double turrets) and quad 40 mm and twin 20mm guns. We shot at towed targets on the surface and did shore bombardment in designated areas. Now a destroyer was all steel, nicknamed a "tin can." The decks, bulkheads, and overhead superstructure were all steel. So when we started to check out our proficiency with the 5.38's, we started with shore bombardments. The heavy CRACK/BOOM of those guns firing from an all-steel, thin-hulled ship, floating in the water, is easily recalled to this day. This was the tin can Navy at its best, getting ready for the big game, scary, and challenging our imaginations of bravery and courage with a mix of fear. We were the Vesole DD878, COM DES RON 12.

CIC, the Combat Information Center, or "radar shack," monitored and acted upon voice messages, as appropriate. We had to learn proper voice and transmission procedures to accomplish this. The call name for COM DES RON 12 was "Weak Kneed" and the Borderline was "Chamberpot." One day we were practicing laying smokescreens for each other. The Borderline was going to lay a smokescreen for us in conjunction with our shore bombardment. She properly cut between us and the shore and let go with her smoke machines. I was at my battle station in CIC so I could not see outside, but the voice radio crackled. It was the flag commander on our bridge above us. "Hello Chamberpot, Chamberpot, this is Weak Kneed, over." "Weak Kneed, this is Chamberpot, send your message, over." "Chamberpot. Weak Kneed here. Charlie, that looks like a cheap cigar, what the hell's going on?" "Hello Weak Kneed, we'll get right on it." And of course they did.

All three hundred of us were getting to know each other, talking about common matters, playing "where ya from?" standing in the chow line and talking, and talking some more when eating together. Those who were in the same division such as gunnery, deck, radar, communication, or engineering naturally bonded faster. As I recall, sleeping compartments were assigned by division. I know my compartment assignment, when they got around to it, was just below the mess hall and combined radar, sonar and radio operators. It was right at the water line and the ship was 300 ft. long and about 40ft wide at midship, with a cutter type bow and tapered fantail. The top speed (flank speed) was 33 knots, about 38 miles per hour. When called on to do that, she would shake, rattle, and roll, living up to the nickname, "tin can."

The adjustment to the crowded conditions on that "tin can" was taken in stride, an accepted part of the assignment. We showered wherever there was space in that common area. The toilet rooms were designed with the limited space in mind. Walk through the "head" hatch at certain times of the day and there would be 8-10 guys in a row, sitting on toilet seats, talking, joking, smoking, reading the daily bulletin from the radio shack, and doing their thing over a large metal trough with continually flowing sea water. Almost everyone smoked and lighting up a cigarette was a common motion. So here were nine guys in a row, a perfect setup for a never overused practical joke. A sailor on the last seat at the top of the flow would cunningly ball up a large amount of toilet paper when he was leaving, fire it up with his Zippo lighter, and drop it onto the flowing water as he exited through the nearby hatch. In rapid quick order, the guys in the path of the flaming paper would pop up, one by one, like the contraptions in a carnival shooting gallery with a shout of choice words for the joker.

I slept in a hammock next to the gyro, or right on the steel deck, until we approached the Canal Zone, and they completed the project for sufficient bunks. In my compartment they were three-tiered. They were merely rectangular pipe frames with a piece of canvas strung on to it, and a thin mattress on the canvas. The piping was hinged to the bulkhead (wall) and chained from the overhead so that all three tiers could be taken up against the bulkhead when not in use. Obviously space was always a consideration. Three foot lockers were placed on the deck under the lower bunk. I had a middle bunk and the pipe rectangle that I slept on, and the pipe rectangle above me was, from my elbow to the first knuckle of my middle finger, about 18–20 inches. There were two huge laundry bags in the compartment. We threw our dirty clothes in there. It was picked up on a weekly basis and delivered back, at which time we distributed the stenciled clothes to each other's bunks. Later on we found an additional use for the bags that was a well-kept secret. There was just enough room to pass each other in the aisles between the bunks. Right up the ladder and through the hatch and you were in the mess hall...ah, location, location, location.

I liked being on board a destroyer in those blue tropical waters. The sparkling phosphorous-filled bow and prop wash put on a continual show at night, as the darkened ship, running with an easy roll, passed through a closed canopy of brilliant, small, white, gems set on their familiar black show cloth.

After five weeks of sailing on the long skinny tin can, we started to get the hang of leaning against the roll as we walked the decks. We were starting to feel "salty." As our team work improved our esprit de corps became obvious.

Friendships were starting to grow. The guys I remember from the radar group included Fred Miller and Bob Gallo. Our leading petty officer was a 1C RDM named Coyle. He had been on two destroyers that were sunk in battle and he was leery about this, his third voyage. I recall him describing the Kamikaze explosions and the scattered human debris all over the twisted metal and burning deck. He was a good, firm, kind, Christian man and knew his job well. The "Rock" was a 2CRDM on his second voyage. Lots of energy, fast-talking, a good leader with a sense of humor, he liked to call our group "Rock and his pebbles." The rest of us were RDM strikers who would normally be awarded a 3rd class petty officer rating. But with 28, count 'em, 28 RDM strikers on board, one should be prepared for another "Life Ain't Fair" reminder.

Allan Gustavson, 18, was from Iron Mountain, Michigan, and talked about ski jumping when anyone would listen. John "Bunky" Hack was from the Bronx: gregarious, a talker, good at give-and-take in the bull sessions. His nickname indicated his off-duty activity of choice. Lou Franz was a third class Quartermaster, often steering the ship at the helm on the bridge above CIC, or working in the nearby chart room, correcting geodetic charts from Navy reports. He played basketball at San Francisco U. before joining the Navy. There was a guy named Bozowski. We called him Bozo. He was a hard worker, serious and a good athlete. Then was Haile, that real country boy from Rocky Mount, North Carolina whose description of a good looking date was, "she was just as purty as a speckled hound dog." Jack Lenner was a very serious young man, very smart, and college bound someday, as were most RDM Strikers.

Our routine was around-the-clock, 4 hours duty, 8 hours off. Much time was spent out on deck in bull sessions. Sometimes it was a large group, sometimes small, or one on one. We talked of home, family, girlfriends, the war, politics, girls, "scuttlebutt" (rumors), girls, and hopes and dreams. We got to know each other pretty well. We had "jelled" into the crew of a fighting ship by the time we approached the Canal, heading for Pearl Harbor.

We went through the Panama Canal with the Boxer. It was a surprisingly awesome sight to watch the big gray 40,000 ton nautical airfield barely fit into the locks and then being raised about 30 feet before going into the next lock and repeating the process. Some history came to mind, which probably contributed to my amazement. I thought about the laborers, crews, technicians, and engineers who had to struggle with the tropical elements and the dreaded malaria, which took a great toll. Crossing the whole isthmus took a while. We passed through the large lake, were pulled along the canal by a special "donkey" engine, went through the locks, and ended up at the city facing the Pacific Ocean, Balboa or Panama. We would now begin a voyage to the Pacific coast, Pearl Harbor, Tokyo Bay, Yokosuka, Tokyo, Yokohama, Hakodate, Kure, Hiroshima, Guam, Saipan, Hong Kong, Shanghai, Tsingtao, Taku, and Guam. One of us would not return.

"No fumar" said the sign as we passed through the locks. "What's that say?" I asked, somehow surprised to see a foreign language sign used in this American setting. I was 18 and away from home for the first time. One of the older guys said, "It means no smoking. See, we are flying Baker (red flag) on top of the mast. That means danger and no smoking. The smoking lamp is out." Well, I knew about Baker and thanked him for my first Spanish lesson.

We left the Canal Zone and sailed to a point that put us well off of the California coast. We did practical exercises all the way, such as changing station on the Boxer, first up front, then behind, then port and starboard. We tracked and reported surface and air craft. Miller and I practiced our RCM techniques. I looked forward to the real thing, while the new ingredients of anxiety and apprehension mixed with honor, duty, country. We practiced and drilled, sailing toward Hawaii to later join the 3rd Fleet.

I knew and could use every switch, knob, lever and button on the complicated equipment in that CIC "shack" and the RCM "hut." I could plot, track, vector, interpret, project, and jam. I also knew how to get ashore with all the RCM equipment, set it up, and jam. I was a qualified special specialist in the United States Navy, and I was good (TTH at work again). I was eighteen years old.

6 | NAVY DAYS ... CONTINUED

Hiroshima, Japan, as it looked after an atomic bomb was dropped on it on August 6, 1945. The devastation from the blast site to 0.4 miles south can be seen.

The idea of using a radar picket destroyer developed as the war progressed. The picket would go many miles out, away from the carrier group, and pick up enemy targets and radio back their courses, speeds and numbers. In this manner we would see on our radar the "bogies" (enemy ships or planes) and related intelligence long before the enemy could make radar contact on our main Task Force. As radar pickets improved, they were of concern to the Japanese Navy, which responded with suicide kamikaze (wind of God) attacks. Many destroyers were sunk due to kamikaze attacks in the Battle of Okinawa, the last battle of WWII. We further improved our ability to attain early warning data when Radar Counter Measures (RCMs) were developed. Those picket destroyers that were equipped with RCM gear could go out away from the task force and would pick up the enemy's radar. In that manner, the picket DD would know the direction of the enemy ship (not distance) long before our radar or the enemy's made contact. As mentioned, the high frequency radio waves from the radar had to bounce back off the target and into the receivers to get a "pip" to determine direction and distance so we could plot a course and speed. But with the RCM gear, we received the enemy radar before they were close enough to generate a bounce strong enough to return to their ship where they could plot us. So we not only knew their direction on an early warning basis, but we could "jam" the radar we picked up, making it useless, as we closed in to track them.

As we cruised well off California, the famous ground swells were evident; not a rough sea, but the usual large rolling waves. Working parties were called for all over the ship for a general clean up drill. It was decided that the platform which capped the tripod mast, and supported the RCM antennas, needed painting. Since Newhard and Miller were the only two qualified RCM operators on board, imagine who had the privilege of drawing the paint and brushes from the paint locker to do the job? Right on. We proceeded to climb the steel rungs, which were welded to the tripod mast. We reached the platform, about 40 feet above the deck. It had no railing because that would interfere with the high frequency radar waves of the antennas. Our safety harness was whatever we could devise from a length of rope. Fred and I spent an hour or so up there while the California ground swells made life interesting and thoughtfully precious. That ship was not designed to carry a tripod mast, which raised its center of gravity. As mentioned, it was built with torpedo tubes and no tripod mast. At that height, with the rolling sea, we would be moved, say, 5 feet to starboard and 5 feet to port, all the while holding the paint cans and painting. Fred wanted to know, "Who is going to come up here and inspect our job?" smart lad. We climbed down to the deck with paint buckets, brushes, a lot of it on us, all to the delight and laughing comments of some shipmates to whom we sent artful hand signals of goodwill and love. Question: This was a new ship. That platform would not have needed painting for a couple of years. "Hey, Fred, why?" "Why, just to make it harder."

We left the California area and headed for Pearl Harbor, doing training exercises all the time, all the way. We did a maneuver that would become very familiar, re-fueling at sea. While underway, the destroyer pulls up near, not too near, the aircraft carrier. The carrier shoots a "lead line" over the "tin can." The re-fueling crew grabs that thin line which is attached to a hawser. They pull the hawser over and then comes the re-fueling hose attached to the hawser, which is hooked up and secured. Meanwhile the destroyer is pitching and rolling, even in a normal sea, and the skills of the re-fueling crew and the helmsman are honed some more. We are flying Baker and the smoking lamp is out. Before completing the exercise and taking in the lines, the carrier, that floating city with everything, would send us some ice cream or canned fruit. We all liked re-fueling.

Early on, we noticed tiny dead weevils in the bread. They came in the sacks of flour (it was a package deal). Following the behavioral pattern of most for the first month, I tried to pick them out before eating the bread. Then for a month or so I spread whatever was available on the bread to help relieve my mind, while answering my stomach's call for attention. After that, it was an "aw, the hell with it" mode, perhaps justified by the latest studies on protein.

We were a couple of days out of Pearl Harbor when Japan surrendered following the atomic blasts at Hiroshima and Nagasaki. I recall the happiness of Coyle and the other guys who had been in battle, and the similar response from others, although they had not seen action. I also remember some who felt suspended in time. They had trained and planned a long time for the championship game on a Saturday night. Then they arrived at the field and suited up. But suddenly, someone turned off the lights, closed the stadium, and called the game off. I was one of those, glad it was over, yet disappointed by an unfulfilled curiosity.

We pulled into Pearl and loaded ammo, re-stocked stores and cleaned up all around. When a loading party was called for, members of the crew were expected to volunteer. If there were not enough workers to handle the material and get it loaded and stacked in its proper place, then someone in authority would choose the necessary crew members to get the job done. That was not usually necessary, because some of us crew members would "play a fiddle" off of the supply line. Remember the large laundry bags down in our compartment under the mess hall? Here is the scenario: one volunteer carries two cases of canned peaches forward along the deck. As he passes a hatchway that leads to the mess hall, and, further below, to our compartment, he hands one case to a "co-worker" standing inside the vertical hatch, who hands it down to the next level, through the horizontal hatch, from where it is passed down into the compartment and placed in the bottom of the laundry bag. Next comes a case of pineapple juice and so on, but not too much. As I write this, I, and probably the reader, say, "So what?" Then some deeper reminiscence makes it as clear as this morning. In our little world those things had meaning, involving the pleasure of the palate, overcoming a minor deprivation, and beating the system, which we were a part of, without doing damage to it, or ourselves.

I had two days leave and went ashore with some friends. The Navy had taken over, and was running the Royal Hawaiian Hotel. Miller, Gallo, "Bunky" Hack and I shared a room. Double-bunk beds, facing the famous Waikiki Beach, 5-star atmosphere, for 50 cents a night. Oh, my. Over the years I have visited Honolulu many times, both with my family and before I had one. The old beach front, deluxe cottages that were at the location where the Hilton Village was born many years ago, and the Halekulani toward Diamond Head, and the Royal Hawaiian, generate many memories. But once thinking of Hawaii, my mind always goes to the first visit and we young "swabbies," who didn't even know we didn't know.

I checked out a surfboard from the recreation facility and paddled it alone, way out beyond the breakers, just past where some Liberty ships were anchored and waiting to go into the port. was a joy to be away, away, away from all the routine and structured life, out there on that beautiful water, quiet, peaceful, touching my soul. "What's it all about, God? I haven't learned much." All was silent except for the gentle waves lapping on the surfboard as I lay there at peace. It was a long, but enjoyable, afternoon and would bring the refreshing sleep that such a day promotes.

We left Pearl with the carriers Boxer, and, I think, the Intrepid, to conduct more exercises while en route to the Yokosuka Naval Base on Tokyo Bay. It was September. The unconditional surrender had been signed aboard the battleship Missouri. General Douglas MacArthur had assumed his office in the Dai-ichi Building, continuing as Supreme Commander Allied Forces Pacific (SCAP). I believe he had another title concerning his administration over Japan. The military occupation of Japan by the U.S. was probably the most peaceful occupation in history. The reason was that once the Emperor told his people over the radio (and that was the first time they ever heard the voice of their god-leader) to share his heart-wrenching embarrassment and shame and surrender completely to the Occupation Forces, the instruction was carried out as expected. Had he said Japan would not surrender, they would have continued to fight to the death, man, woman and child, such was the character of their insular culture. More on this later.

From the beginning on board the ship, as we all developed large, medium and small groups of friends, i.e., good, better, best, it was apparent one would open up more and share deeper feelings and ideas. There was little "one-upsmanship" in this environment, but lots of truth and understanding that such friendships create. Aside from standing watch and sleeping we had about 8 hours free time within every 24. We had no library, correspondence courses, cell phones, or e-mail, and mail call was "whenever." We naturally took to hanging out at various sections on the ship. It seems the psyche tries to develop a network that creates humor and laughter before succumbing to boredom, lethargy, and dull vibes. One by one almost all in my group had a nickname created and applied in the course of those bull sessions. In that tight, limited environment the psychological workshop produces ways to keep a level plane. Some of that mix was the humorous give-and-take jokes, kidding about appearance, ways of talking, characteristics, etc. It's the kind of give-and-take that is only at home and cherished among friends, but unnatural among strangers.

Most of our nicknames were hung on us as this garden of friendship grew. Bob Gallo, an Indiana corn farm boy, had taken one look at the Washington Monument and said with a Midwest twang: "My, that'll hold a lot of corn." Miller and I carried that from the RCM School to the ship where "corn boy" spread. "The Rock" hung it on himself, liking "the rock and his pebbles" idea. "Bozo" was supposed to be a little dumb. "Bunky" Hack provided a lot of "setups" for "ribbing" him about his frequent napping. Alan Gustafson was "Big Swede," and we would break into an appropriate accent to which he would respond, acting out the fun with ice fishing and ski jumping stories. One skinny, fair-skinned RDM, whose name I forget, was called "Tender Gear" by the "Rock," implying the tenderness of a gal. "Tender Gear" was popular with the gals when we hit port, but he sometimes gestured and made comments that implied a much different attitude, playing out his nickname, to the laughter of all. Haile, the guy from Rocky Mount, North Carolina spoke with a heavy southern drawl, and he, of course, was "Hound Dog." On one occasion I "grubbed" a cigarette from someone. I didn't get to Small Stores to buy a carton and I was out of cigarettes for a few days. I didn't smoke much, but I also scrounged a few the next day. Somebody said, "Hey Scrounge, why don't you buy your own?" It was a joke. At $1 a carton, no one ever said "no" to such a request. But from then on I was "Scrounge" and, in the spirit of our friendships and camaraderie, I too acted out my nickname by frequently asking someone for a cigarette, playing "straight man" for the comments to come. We all played our parts to keep the party going. Gallo, an RCM technician, was far from a "hayseed;" "Bozo," a smart RDM, played the dummy nicely, and "Rock?" He was really a "pussy cat."

At Yokosuka, on Tokyo Bay, there was a Japanese heavy cruiser that had been sunk right at the dockside, leaving only its superstructure showing above the water, an eerie sight. It was a reflection of, and a pay-back for, Pearl Harbor. Destruction was everywhere. Gasoline cars were gone. There were some charcoal powered ones. The driver would stop, run around to the trunk, open it and shovel on some more charcoal and proceed. That's ingenuity. The whole place was a mixture of grays, browns, and blacks. It was dirty, dusty, and all broken down. There was a lot of damage and open sewers. Rubble was everywhere, but some trains were already keeping a schedule. I recall that 3 or 4 of us bought a couple bottles of beer and some rice crackers and took a train to Kamakura, on Sagami Wan (Bay). The beautiful sitting Buddha of Kamakura was in the big park there, holding everyone's attention. Many years later while living in Japan I would visit that park a few times, and again view that huge copper green 30ft high Buddha, sitting there in the dark of the night, among the whispering trees, in contemplative detachment from the folly of Man.

Wherever we went, in our walking around, we naturally said hello, smiled, gave candy to the children and cigarettes to the men. The character of the Japanese helped to prompt these polite, friendly exchanges. I am sure that many of the older Japanese with whom we exchanged greetings, and who had been prepared to fight us to the death, said to themselves and others, "Why, they're just kids." At Yokosuka Naval Base, we had set up Headquarters for the Fleet. Right after that, of course, they put in the Officers and NCO Clubs. The Navy built a gymnasium in a reconstructed building. I was elated to play some basketball on a good hardwood floor. It was real happiness to be able to work out after the confining shipboard routine. We had some good players on the Vesole. Lou Franz had played guard at U. of San Francisco. One of the officers had played with the Whiz Kids at U. of Illinois. Elmo Tate was from Kentucky; he ran fast, and never saw a shot he didn't like. Big Allen Gustafson played a solid center. There were other experienced players, including me, who made up the squad. We were good, and won our share of games. We even beat the Boxer, later on, in another port. We had to play the game on their hangar deck. The steel plates, rivets and tie-down rings were a real test, not good for the knee caps and elbows.

From our ship at Yokosuka we had liberty in Tokyo and Yokohama several times. The incendiary and concussion bombings there left mostly rubble, except for those areas that were purposely not bombed such as The Emperor's Palace, The Imperial Hotel, The Dai-ichi Building and that whole area adjacent to Hibiya Park. The Japanese never lost their sense of organization, and went right to work and had some trains and trolleys running. Bicycles, pedicabs, and rickshaws were common. A few steel and concrete buildings partially survived and there was some resemblance of a retail section along the Ginza. Some of my shipmates would buy up their allotted cigarette ration for the month at $1 a carton and then get the ration of some non-smoking friends and head for the Ginza with four or five cartons. There they would make some good deals for silk, pearls or whatever; such is the selling power of short-supply materials, bolstered by underlying addictive habits. There were regulations against such conduct, and fraternization, which all melted reasonably into history, without much publicity, as soon as the Japanese surrender proved itself to be peaceful, the real thing. They were acting in true character by following the Emperor's wishes. Within a generation, Democracy would take roots from the Constitution and framework that was established in the post-war years.

When MacArthur and his entourage flew in the first time to set up their Headquarters, he insisted no one be armed. Some top staff members including his G-2, Col. Willoughby, had their reservations, but he was very sure that was the right thing to do, and time gave it the blessing of proof. A memorable example of a cultural difference took place when the people filled the sidewalks to see the American Commander go by the first time, on his way to his Headquarters, at which time they bowed. Members of the Japanese National Police lined up along the curb, facing the crowd with their back to the street and MacArthur. Some American news reporters mistakenly took exception to this "obvious" insult. But the Japanese culture at the time required a demonstration of shame and acceptance of their situation, and that was not to show their face to the representative of the Power that defeated them. The ultimate example of that was when Emperor Hirohito finally went out from his palace to visit MacArthur, an unheard-of move, thereby contributing support to what MacArthur was about to do. MacArthur had thoughtfully and diplomatically waited for this to happen.

He then moved quickly. He had some major problems, all interwoven, to address and solve. At the top of the list was to break up the zaibatsues which were commercial seats of power, conglomerates that fully supported, and profited from the war effort under the Emperor. Banking, industry, fishing and farming were all controlled through zaibatsues, which managed about 75% of the wealth. One you know, in a modified form in the current day, was Mitsubishi, which means three diamonds, as shown in the logo. They built one hell of a fighter plane called the Zero, which had an edge over us until Grumman designed and built the Hell Cat and Corsair for the Navy.

The next matter was Land Reform. It was most important to get the land into the hands of tenant farmers who had passed along their debts, owed to the landlords, from father to son, for centuries. Third was to write a democratic constitution, creating a representative government with equality for all. Now women would vote for the first time.

The rapid recovery that Japan made after such a catastrophic defeat, involving a huge toll in life and property, say, 1945 to 1958, is often over-simplified by attributing it to a disciplined, educated society, with the ability to copy and adapt material and systems that were necessary for competitive progress. Those elements are certainly in the mix, but the three changes mentioned above provided Japan with a base to lift it out of its pre-war feudal system and into the global economic/political arena. To understand the effects of what took place, compare the Japanese post-war geopolitical/economic situation to, say, the Philippines, also a democratic nation, a founding signatory of the United Nations and strategic in world geopolitical thought.

Without its vast import/export system, Japan is a mediocre country. Raw materials, a broad range of farm products, and natural resources are minimal. With land reform, the tenant farmer became a debt free landowner and from his awarded section of land sent his products to market. Now, for the first time, he could rub a few coins together, and they were increasing. He wanted to buy farm implements, a small radio, a bicycle, and later a washing machine! So a domestic market, a large one, had its beginning. Housing materials also came into demand.

Money started to flow through more hands and at a greater speed. With the expansion and development of the domestic market, Japan naturally ventured abroad. It started sometime around the Korean War. By then their products were good enough to compete with selected items abroad. Radios, cameras, motor scooters, and home appliances come to mind. If untested items failed abroad, they would be brought home to the protected domestic market, which was screened from foreign competition. The rest is well-known history, and much of that success started with land reform.

The Philippines was provided its independence from the U.S. in July of 1946, as promised "at the right time" by every president from the time of the Spanish American War, after which it became a U.S, Territory. World War II had left Manila badly beaten up after the Japanese Navy and Marines refused to declare it an open city. While their Army left and retreated north, the rest "holed up" and made our 1st Cavalry Division and others, military and civilian, pay heavily to reclaim the city. The Philippines is a naturally rich country with timber, gold, 8 billion coconuts a year, hemp, tropical fruits of all kinds, sugar, coffee, cocoa, abundant fishing, and rice and corn production. Blessed with sunshine, rainfall and nutritious soil, they can "grow cucumbers out of the rocks." It sounds like a tropical paradise, and it could be, but not without land reform. That is why a domestic market, in which to test new manufactured products, was never developed. About 5% of the people own 80% of the wealth. What a shame. Under that crippling system, engrained into the culture which evolved from 3 centuries of Spanish rule, the Philippines has regressed relative to the average and below average wage earner, and continues to do so, thereby providing a ripe grain named "revolution," waiting to be harvested by experienced recruiters, agitators, terrorists, faithful loyalists to the Communist or radical Muslim causes.

The Communists have been active in the Philippines since the 1930's. Luis Taruc was a leader for the Soviet's ambitions there, prior to WWII, and then the leader of the Communist Hukbalahap, which attempted an uprising in Central Luzon around 1954 and was defeated. In the late 1960's, Communist China was making good inroads there. Today Communist China is very active there and sees the Philippines as a prime target in its over-all plan for control of the East Asia shipping lanes and other strategic planning purposes. But I digress from the time of the tale, and will cover the Philippine matter later.

We went to Yokohama. Oh, the devastation of what had been a heavily industrialized and populated area! Yokohama had been hit with tremendous incendiary raids. The air became so hot that thousands would jump into the water. But the city-wide inferno took the oxygen out of the air, killing as many as the heat, smoke and bombs combined. The sights, colors and smells labeled those unpleasant memories "unforgettable." In November, our squadron sailed north to Hakodate, an industrial port on the southern peninsula extending from Hokkaido. There was a light snow and it was cold as we passed through the

Tsugaru Straits. Later I would spend four years in that area of vivid seasons, long winters, heavy woods, and a charm of its own. Hokkaido was about 20% of the land area of Japan and 5% of the population. Hakodate had partial damage from the war. The trains, dock terminals, and ferry boats to Honshu were back in limited service. The snow was "crunchy" as we walked around the city, wearing our pea jackets with our dress blue uniforms. We probably had some steamed crabs and yakisoba, and of course some Sapporo beer, Hokkaido's own. The difference is in the water.

From Hakodate we sailed back to Yokosuka and shortly after departed for Kure and the former Japanese Submarine Headquarters on the Inland Sea, now quite deserted and asleep. It was incomprehensible that these tranquil settings once bustled with activity that carried on the Bushido warrior code and helped give rise to that powerful navy that took a long time to conquer. Bushido, the way of the warrior, exists on the concept of the importance of warfare in the human spirit, adherence to which had been installed in the Emperor Hirohito at an early age by his mentors, themselves adherents and military careerists. This idea, warfare as an integral part of the human spirit, has had the limelight on the postings of milestones along the road of human history. The great Roman Empire, Genghis Khan, the Spanish Empire, the British Empire and its military glue, and many others, religious and political, are examples, focused and controlled by a minority in power, all using their own particular justifications for their actions.

But I am in that global majority that contends that Love is the overriding force in the human spirit, since God is Love (John1:4-16). Those minorities who are in power and have been in power, have the "drive" to stay in power and have naturally used their military arm to continue their way—Hirohito, Genghis Khan, Hitler, Stalin, Castro, the Chinese Communist Politburo, on and on. But Democracy looks better all the time, doesn't it?

As we moved through the Inland Sea, we became aware its islands were full of coastal gun emplacements in heavy fortified concrete bunkers. The Japanese were experts in such defenses. Iwo Jima was a good example. Years later, on a deserted island off the coast of South Korea, I would use an empty, dismantled, two-story Japanese coastal gun bunker as a secret classroom to train a North Korean agent for infiltration into his homeland. I know the Japanese built very good gun emplacements and, had the war not ended and if our invasion plans included the Inland Sea, it would have been the second Red Sea, a real turkey shoot.

From Kure we boarded some open trucks and proceeded on a country road to Hiroshima. It was a chilly December day. As we approached the general area, we saw a farm house or two with slight damage to the thatched roofs. A little farther and the next few farm houses had slightly more damage. Then a bit farther and one of the roofs was off. Then a wall was missing and so on, increasing damage as Hiroshima, or its remains, came into view. As we approached the first river to cross, we could see the whole city was rubble. There were three or four rivers to cross to get into the city. The bridges we went over on the way in were intact because they were at ground level and the blast waves traveled over and alongside them, rather than against them perpendicularly.

It was a shock to see so much destruction and suffering. Those who had survived the blast were coping on the periphery of the city in whatever makeshift way they could. People were dying. Walking, standing, lying down or sitting, they were dying. Boards, tin sheets, cardboard, paper, rocks and cloth, whatever, made up the shelters. Very little organized help was yet apparent. They were dying. Little kids with wet sores on faces and arms were in shock and inside, dying. The radiation effect would last for years. The city had lost 100,000 people up to then. The atom bomb was dropped with a proximity fuse that went off at 150 ft. in the air to achieve a wide dispersion. The area directly below the bomb blast probably contained buildings. That area was now shaped like a sandy saucer. There was nothing there. Many people were vaporized. Many years later, while living in Japan, I met a Japanese woman who was fifteen years old when the blast went off. She was in her high school locker room two stories below the ground. She completely survived. She never found anyone she knew except those few classmates who were with her. Family, friends, and city were all gone. Did I write "completely survived?"

We all found it difficult to smile or say nice things as we gave out candy, cigarettes or whatever, but we stayed with it, driven by our compassion. Going back to Kure that night on the trucks, we were all quiet (unusual for that crew), lost in our inner thoughts. I don't think we got back "into gear" until we were well underway and headed for Guam a day or so later, doing battle exercises all the way. Hey, but the war is over. Yeah, for now, but train anyway. We would all carry the Hiroshima memory with us forever. Back in my bunk, I thought, "What's it all about, Lord? I don't know anything."

While a faith existed, that is, a belief in God, much was by rote, a repetitious base that formed the roots for the watering and nourishment that was to come later. If there was an answer to my question, I never heard it, as a troublesome sleep enveloped me.

Beaten up from the fighting, Guam was filled with tents and Quonset huts. The Japanese soldiers' "no surrender" code persisted for many years after the war, in small, isolated, circumstances. About 1972 I was living in the Philippines and making business trips in the region, including Guam. They found two Japanese soldiers living near the Telefofo Falls in the interior of the island. They had survived off the land, streams, and jungle for those 27 years. Old and weary, they reluctantly surrendered. Similar scenes took place on many islands in the Pacific over those years, indicating the determination and mind-set of our former foe. Surrender was a sin, disgrace, and brought enduring shame on self and family. The Marine's silent "take no prisoners" motto resulted from the many bitter battles and gruesome treatment they received from the Japanese if held as prisoners, and so accommodated that Japanese code.

I was anxious to get to Guam because I had heard that my St. Benedict's team mate and best friend, Digi, was in an Air Force unit on Guam. After we dropped anchor (Apra Harbor was not yet built, the sea wall was half-finished), I got permission to go ashore for 24 hours. We would be there a week before going to Saipan and then head to the China coast. I had his address but no AF people could help me. I walked and hitch-hiked all around and finally saw a Red Cross hut. They could not help me either. Post-war Guam was a hodge-podge of Navy, Marine and Air Force activity, helping to rebuild the regional center for homeward bound personnel, incoming personnel, military training, etc. and it was overloaded. I was dejectedly leaving the Red Cross hut to hitch a ride back to my ship, I had tried my best. I got to the gravel and sand dusty road, and from a distance I saw four Air Force guys barreling along in a weapons carrier, the driver in a concentrated forward hunch, no cap, hair flying. Yeah! I shouted, "Hey Digi!" and he slowed down, looking back, thinking some "swabby" wanted a lift. As soon as he saw me start to run, he recognized who this guy was. "Howie!" he shouted and a mini reunion ensued. Imagine, in the middle of the Pacific Ocean, 1,500 miles from the Philippines, and a "jillion" miles from New Jersey, the two best friends met. I went to his barracks where I met his AF buddies, drank some rationed beer, and talked about Benedict's, classmates, "remember whens," politics, and home. We both planned to return to St. Benedict's to pick up the necessary credits for college and play some postgraduate ball. They drove me back to the ship late at night as they had an early morning take-off on their B-29.

We went out on more exercises and drills with the carrier Boxer and some other ships, doing a 4 on, 8 off routine, except for calls to general quarters drills, fire drills, air launch drills, changing station drills, gunnery with surface and air targets, drills, drills. We were at sea quite a while, probably three weeks. It was decided that the crews needed a break so we anchored off of a small deserted island in the warm tropics. We went ashore in some Higgins boats from the Boxer. We had softball equipment, footballs, checkers, cards, and some good old American 3.2 "soda pop." We played some softball with a high level of "ribbing," swam in the surf, and had some serious discussions prompted by the warm 3.2 beer. But hey, it was the only bar in town and we were grateful. One of the discussions we got into was "Why are we having such heavy maneuvers and drills. You would think the war was still going on." Actually the Pentagon planners were concerned about the Soviet Union which was in the process of occupying Eastern Europe and North Korea, and would support communism in many places globally. Nevertheless, we did not let those heavily weighted world affairs get in the way of our day of games and fun, and even the LCVP Coxswain (driver) had a little buzz on as he steered the craft through the gentle waves and back to the anchored ships.

After that we went back to the Marianas. We anchored at Saipan, where we went ashore on liberty. We walked around and talked to the people. The place, like Guam, was beaten up from the war. A few of us walked into the heavy undergrowth to visualize what it must have been like to fight in that environment. In one area, sharp coral crevices and small ravines were everywhere with heavy growth coming right out of the jagged coral. Our Marines lost many there and had a tough time taking the island. Many young men were never brought home from those battles in the Pacific, lost in the jungle's density, or in the sea. I never forget them. Honor, duty, country, lives always in the memory of their deaths.

We went back to Guam and anchored again offshore. The next day the call came over the loudspeaker for a working party. "Now hear this, all available hands lay down to the fantail for a loading supply party." I went along and there were about seven of us. We boarded two 6 wheeler trucks, the "deuce and a half," and went to the water front warehouses where we started to load supplies. Soon an officer with a hand speaker came riding up in a jeep and said there was an earthquake in the floor of the Pacific, near Alaska, and we were ordered to drop everything and head for the highest ground we could find because a tidal wave was expected. He said the ships were already underway and leaving the area and would come back for us when it was clear. In driving for higher ground we found a small mountain plateau with a cluster of abandoned tents, left over from the war. We stayed in those broken tents for two days, enduring the bugs and mosquitoes and staring out at the eastern horizon, looking for that tidal wave. At least we had some canned goods and juices. After a couple of days, we saw some ships coming back to Guam and we cheerfully left our raggedy tent city and returned to the Vesole. They called for another loading party and allowed us the day off. The tidal wave did hit land, but it went the other way to the Alaska coast.

Somewhere during that time frame there was another call for a loading party, for which Miller and I did not care to volunteer. We locked ourselves into the RCM hut. It was a "short-handed" call, and the Chief Boatswain's mate started to select "volunteers" for the job. Well, the Chief had seen us go into that compartment and he banged on the door: "I know you are in there, come on out, I need you for loading supplies and gear." Silence prevailed (we did not believe he knew we were in there, he was just fishing for "volunteers." He left. We took a nap and later when the "coast was clear" went back to our routines. A week later, while at sea, we were formally notified and directed over the captain's signature to report for a Captain's Mast in dress blue uniforms. When we did so, the Captain read the charge and the Chief testified as to what happened. In our individual responses Miller and I admitted the Chief was correct and pleaded guilty. For punishment we each received ten hours of work in the engine room, cleaning the inner workings of the machines, the hottest ugliest job on board, especially in the tropics.

I reported to a Chief Motor Machinist Mate who would assign me the tasks and keep the time record. After my third or fourth work detail I was up to about six hours. I guess the Chief figured this kid is not accustomed to the heat down here so I'll give him a break, and he said to me, "You have done six hours. I am going to mark you down for ten, but if you ever tell anyone, I will make sure you get twenty." What a nice guy. I didn't even tell Miller.

Of course the radar was all shut down while in port, but we did stand radio watch on voice circuits. The next day I had the mid watch, 12 midnight to 4 a.m. When finished, I went on deck for a smoke and then went down into my compartment to sleep. It was dark, as usual, with just enough light from the small red nightlights. Jack Lenner, who slept directly across the narrow aisle from me, was standing next to his bunk, adjusting something by his pillow. I said "hi" and climbed into my bunk and went to sleep. I was in a deep sleep for maybe an hour when I "dreamed" I heard a gunshot far away. In my subconscious I thought it was a guard up on the main deck shooting a warning shot at an unauthorized approach to the ship. Then I started to wake up as I heard a moaning sound, a painful moaning. I thought it was Haile having a nightmare. So I reached down and shook him. "Hound Dog, wake up." "I am awake." "Well, who is it then?" "I think it's Jack." Someone snapped on the over head lights. "Oh, my God." There were gasps and groans and signs of the cross. Jack had shot himself through the head with the Colt .45 that he used for mail duty. He was still alive, moaning from the soul, and feebly touching at his brains, especially a large deep blue artery that was hanging over his face. Blood was all over the bed, sheets, pillow, and the bulkhead near his bunk. The smell and sight hit me heavily, as it did the others. That gut-wrenching scene was emblazoned in the memories of all who were there. We called the medics and they carried him out. We had tied up next to the Boxer and they took him on board. Surprisingly, he lived another 5 minutes or so, the bullet having gone between the lobes of his brain.. Apparently with all the crew members, mattresses, laundry bags, pillows, bunks, and the rest taking up so much space in that crowded compartment, the sound waves had been muffled and distorted. In addition, he shot himself from back to front so the gun had to be between his pillow and his head.

At best, we could tell he had been depressed. He was very bothered by the lack of promotion. He was a good radar man but there were no third-class slots to fill. That was very important to him. The routine in the postwar days aboard a ship such as ours probably affected him. We really don't know. Anyway they put him in a simple wooden coffin and put the coffin in a small compartment up on the boat deck and we, the USS Vesole, headed for the International Cemetery at Yokohama, Japan. Some of us volunteered to stand watch at the door of that solitary compartment on the boat deck to accompany Jack. I stood mine in the middle of the night, with the underway breeze, the sound of the wash, and the roll and pitch of the ship. "What's it all about, Lord?" I asked. No answer in the wind, or anywhere else. I had not yet learned how to listen. We sailed on into the night. It was a rainy day when we docked in Yokohama. They unloaded the casket, put it in a truck, and headed for the cemetery. I did not go. Jack was not there. I prayed for him.

The next day we sailed back to Guam and joined up with our destroyer squadron, the Boxer, and some other ships. We then set course for Hong Kong. I have been to Hong Kong many times over the years, but that "old Hong Kong," with the beautiful, peaceful natural harbor, before the Kai Tak runway and sky-scrapers changed the symmetry, is a pleasing memory. Chief Moody, our Chief Radio Man, had 17 years of destroyer duty at that time, all in Asia, and going into Hong Kong Harbor he would say "Now back in 1934 that building wasn't there, the Harbor command was over there," etc.

There were many ships in the harbor and sampans were all over the place. In the middle of the city were the large soccer and cricket fields, well maintained with a touch of the British gardening know-how. There were step-streets going up, away from the downtown area. I recall seeing wealthy Chinese being carried up and down the steps in veiled sedan chairs. This is a beautiful natural harbor and gateway to Canton Province and the British had been there for a hundred years or more; and their presence in administration, architecture, rules and regu-lations, banking and business, military police, and right down to some retail stores was obvious. We went up to Victoria Peak and took in the beauty of it all. We tried a pub or two, drank some good beer, and chatted with some of the cute Chinese gals wearing those attractive high-collar dresses with the split skirts. Some of the guys seemed to disappear for a while but they came back and regrouped with us in time to catch the last launch from the pier to our ship, anchored in the harbor.

We were in port three or four days. The first time I had the harbor watch radio circuit duty for our ship in Hong Kong, a call came in from someone, the Harbor Commander, the Boxer captain—I don't remember. It was an invitation to our Division flag commander for lunch a day hence. I took the message down, misplaced it, and so it was not routed by the messenger. When there was no response, the sender queried our ship a day later and our commander upbraided Lieutenant Bill Hulse who was the responsible Officer. He restricted him to the ship on our last day in Hong Kong. Hulse did not punish me, but we all knew the story. I apologized to him and my respect for him went higher. He had my attention and loyalty the rest of the voyage.

We went on to Shanghai, practicing and drilling along the way. We anchored there in the famous Yangtze River. Many business-minded Chinese came out to our ships in sampans and wanted to come aboard to sell their goods, silks, pearls, and robes. We allowed two or three women to come aboard and sew uniforms, make silk jackets with dragons, embroidered robes and the like, but we did not allow sampans to idle near or next to our ships. We posted forecastle and fantail guards 24 hours. There were times at night when it was necessary to fire some warning shots. On board our anchored ship, some of us took turns accessing the big swivel binoculars on the outer bridge. We would scan the city for various points of interest. Out on the balconies of a few places were brightly clad women who were waving at the ships. They knew most of the binoculars in the task force were probably looking their way. Marketing 201, good advertising based on good information.

Shanghai was the great international port, queen of the China coast, a fine natural harbor. It had an interesting "beat" and character. There was a French and Russian section. Why French, I do not know, perhaps a protectorate arrangement from the old days, similar to the former German mandate of Tsingtao (our next port of call). The Russian section was there because of the Russian emigrants who came out, particularly from the Maritime Province, during the Communist Revolution from 1917–1922. Rickshaws were all over the place. Opium dens were scattered around like the bars in Manhattan. Rickshaw runners with muscular legs and emaciated torsos would take a break from running to have a "fix," squatting by the side of the dusty road sucking on their opium pipes.

Going ashore involved some gastronomical delights and adventures. One day we would be in the French Quarters dining on Soupe A' L'oignon, Souffle Fromage, and Shrimp Quiche. Then another time might find us in the Russian Quarter eating perogies, borscht, roast pig and Russian pastries. At another time, it would be a one-dish Chinese meal, a big bowl of noodle soup with seafood and vegetables with white rice, and a pot of tea. Did I go first class? You bet. Did I spend a month's pay in Shanghai? You bet. There were no money exchange procedures; we just paid in U.S. green backs. Chinese currency after the war was so highly inflated it was the last choice of receipt, even after barter. The Japanese had been out of there only 7 months. The Nationalists were trying to hold China together and establish order while the followers of Mao Tse Tung wanted Communism to be established and throw out the Nationalists. Chang Kai Chek, spoiled by President Roosevelt, and now overestimating his U.S. backing, thought he could appease Mao and still keep the country under his rule.

Years later I would learn that Whittaker Chambers, Algier Hiss, Elizabeth Bentley, Harry Hopkins, Judy Coplon and others were Soviet agents of influence and/or espionage. The communists in the U.S. from the early 1930's had made good progress in the media. They publicized events and editorials and convinced many that what was going on in China 1945-50 was agrarian reform, spontaneously started by the people. Actually, it was the Soviet Union and Stalin supporting Mao's efforts to destroy the shaky Kuomintang Group led by Chang Kai Sheik and establish communism.

Today, the Peoples Republic of China has become immensely wealthy as it continues to peg its currency in the world market place, thus establishing huge favorable trade balances which it is using to build itself into a super power while ravenously purchasing natural resources from around the world. From outside it seems to some that it is veering toward capitalism. Inside, it reeks with the abuse of human rights as all power, plans, and privileges are directed by the Communist Politburo, as always.

We said farewell to that intriguing city and headed out for more exercises and an eventual stop at Tsingtao to the north. One night we were sailing far out in front of the task group which was small and well-scattered now, just COM DES RON 12 and the Boxer. Our units and all other U.S. Navy ships in the area, no outside lights showing while underway, an extended wartime procedure. I had a mid watch and was on the GS surface search radar. I picked up a contact and called the range and bearing to the plot room and tracking was started. I called off other contacts and ranges and bearings and all were being plotted. After a few more "fixes," it appeared that one of them was on a collision course with us, a "head to head" situation. That pip on my A scope had my attention for sure. That "two ships passing in the night" is for poets. I wanted a lot of distance between us at the closest point. After a few more fixes and plots a collision course was confirmed and we had it about 30 miles out with each ship doing about 15 knots. The bridge above us was notified and responded. "What kind of ship?" From my A scope interpretation I replied, "An LST, or destroyer."

If you were going to change course in that situation you have to notify the Captain who set the course before he retired. The same for the closing ship, if it was a U.S. Navy ship. Well, the OD on the bridge was not eager to do that, and the contact was not changing either. It was an average sea with about a mile or so of sea return on the scope. The bridge called down "What is it now?" We replied, "Still the same, 5 miles and closing." Well, it's up to the OD to take care of these matters, but I guess nothing was done. Then the bridge called down excitedly, "What is it now?" I quickly started to "fix" on it but the "pip" was inside the sea return. "It's zero," I shouted for all in the "shack" to hear, as I grabbed handles on each side of the SG and braced for the shock. But nothing happened, and a minute later I was picking up the pip opening aft from us. The forecastle watchman told us later that an LST (it was an LST) passed close enough for him to spit on. Strange how many accidents are based on dumb decisions; why wouldn't you wake the Captain if in doubt of the ship's safety?

We proceeded north, well out from the China coast. At daybreak the lookouts began to spot mines floating in the water. There were many scattered over a large area, floating, but mostly fully submerged. They could not be picked up by radar and were not easy to spot visually. When a mine was spotted we would blow it up with the Quad 40 millimeter guns. Why they were there, how they got there, we never knew, but we saw many of them and destroyed many of them as we proceeded to Tsingtao. We were all uneasy about the mines and some crew members did not sleep in their compartments but dragged their mattress up on deck and slept there.

Tsingtao was a natural port. It had been a German mandate in the old days, and some German cultural influence still prevailed. The famous Tsingtao beer was very good and continued to be brewed by German brew masters. There was a good German restaurant called the Dutch Villa high up the side of a hill, overlooking the harbor. We went on half-day rickshaw tours and got a good look at the town. Now opportunities to share the pleasure of the ages with a woman were always there, but Miller and I and some of the other younger guys stayed away from that. Many were lovely and while the immorality of it all touched my conscience, it was the fear of disease that also calmed the leaping hormones.

We were in Tsingtao about 8 months after the Japanese surrender. A U.S. Marine garrison had been posted. The Japanese had gone home. China was in turmoil. Up in that northern area, the Chinese Communist military infiltrators were starting to make their move. The Japanese Army previously had a major command and large number of troops in strategic Tsingtao. One day we were walking around and came upon a large three-storied building. Picture a military school with a large, three-story barracks, circular, with a garden in the middle and the inside walkways overlooking the garden. This building was made of stone and concrete. It was a huge brothel started by the Japanese Army, probably the only one in town to keep good control on the matter. In their typical systematic fashion they had a complete procedure worked out for the troops. A soldier would pay his yen for a brass coin. Embossed on the large coin were four different positions regarding sex. The soldier would give the coin to the prostitute and point to the position of choice. She would obtain payment in cash when she turned in the coin to the right authority. A few of us wound up sitting outside by the big front door waiting for some of our shipmates. The Chinese girls there thought we were very unusual. Not so, but fear is a great motivator. The health movies left a strong impression and I wanted to be sure I went back to the ship alone.

A few of us were sitting in a large bar one night listening to some music. Sailors and Marines were scattered around in a large, nicely furnished room. Out of nowhere, a big Chinese gal shouted at a Marine, in English, "If we go to war with the Americans, we will kill them all!" The Marine knocked her back over a sofa and it was a "punch palace," sailors, Marines, Chinese, all mixing it up. We, a few shipmates, looked at each other, looked at the side door, and walked on down the road in time to point out to the mobile Shore Patrol where their emergency call came from. Oh, such good boys!

As mentioned, the Communists, led by Mao and his troops had gained strength, and were starting to move down from the north. The U.S. put the word out to all American citizens living in those northern areas (they were mostly missionaries) to come out if they wished. We put a group of Marines from the carrier ashore at Taku, north of Tsingtao to bring out anyone who wanted to come. We were well off the beach and not close to the limited action. I remember the long, low tide, mud/sand flats in that area. Those areas of the China coast and across the Yellow Sea to the Korea west coast have similar highly fluctuating tides, as I would find out years later.

After a few days, we headed toward the area between Okinawa and Guam and conducted more exercises. While we practiced the drills, we were told a typhoon was in the area and we could not avoid it. There were no satellites and computer modules in those days. It started to get dark and rough late in the afternoon.

As it worked out, that was the worst typhoon to hit Okinawa in many years and it is still very high in their record book. We battened down all outside hatches and secured all moveable gear with special attention to depth charges and ammunition. We turned off all of the radar equipment because of increasing sea return on the screens. Sea return is caused by the radar beam hitting the sea waves near the ship and bouncing back. The larger the waves, the more sea return, which renders the radar useless in a heavy storm. Still, we stood our regular watches in the CIC radar shack to be aware of any damage. The times I was in the shack we rolled so much that we had to secure the chairs and stand up during the watch. As the typhoon increased, the smashing and crashing noise of it was all-powerful. As the ship pitched up and down and rolled from side to side, she shuddered and creaked. The power of water in the open sea viewed from a "tin can" is a sight to behold. The wind was 110 mph. The waves were 40 to 50 ft. high. The Boxer's flight deck was about 100 ft. above the water line in a calm sea. She was taking some wave wash on the flight deck during the height of the storm. If you were in its bow it was like riding an elevator 10 floors up and down very fast and repeatedly; but our destroyer, which normally rode about 14 feet above the water at mid-ship, took water over the whole ship. A joke circulated that we should receive bonus pay just like a submarine crew; another note on the human nature of the crew of a ship, living together, sharing the good and the bad. One could not plan to wring some humor out of such a dangerous situation, but it just rises to the surface to help.

At the height of it all that our "tin can" did a 47-degree roll and we feared we would not get through the night, much less the next roll. Off-duty crewmen were in their quarters, or anywhere they wanted to be. A few broken arms; bruises and contusions, were common. It was a long night of hanging on. Some were tossed out of their bunks by the power generated. Not that they planned to sleep, but many laid down, on their stomachs, spread-eagled, as the best choice to "ride it out" and not get hurt. Finally, when the black, ugly, stormy sky of night showed the dimmest glow of a rotten day to come, we cracked open an outside hatch for a peek. The waves were still very high, but we could discern a decline toward a friendlier sea. The Borderline lost one man, swept overboard. We had cracked expansion joints and the steel, welded gun tubs on the fantail were torn up and smashed into the quad 40mm gun mounts like a crushed beer can. Later on, some guys from the Boxer told us that when they had enough sky light to see, we would often just disappear from their view as we went down in the trough of those giant waves.

The antennae of the SR radar (shaped like a huge bed spring) had its connection to the drive motor broken by the rolling power. They asked for a couple of volunteers to climb up the mainmast and tie it down. It was swinging out of control. Miller and I gave it the "frowning clam" look. There were no volunteers. Hell, it was a shook up crew and anyway the radar was useless. It was repaired when we were in Guam a few days later. The low-high-low curve of the storm cycle lasted about 18 hours. Those cooks, bless them, wanted to be sure we ate something, even if they would not and could not cook. Baloney sandwiches were the answer, hundreds of bread, baloney and mustard sandwiches. We just passed them around. Mmmm, good.

We set course for the Mariana Islands. When we arrived at Guam, some of us were notified to draw our pay, sign off the ship, report to a holding area, and await a transport that would take us to the U.S. Then we would take a troop train to the East Coast and be discharged. Miller and I and some of the other crewmen thought that was a splendid idea. Nevertheless I left the USS Vesole DD 878, my home for a year, with a touch of sadness that I did not want to show. I suspect others felt the same. For centuries sailors had referred to their ship-home as "she." Now I knew why. But we all covered up our feelings. "Boy, I'll be glad to get off this bucket." "Yeah, this ol' tin can needs a real scrubbing." Now, at this writing, thinking back, I still know the feeling. We went to the holding area, carrying our duffel bags and papers and were assigned our barracks. I went outside and looked for the mess hall. I fell into the long line and there in front of me was Frankie Farrell. So again, two St. Benedict's classmates and friends met on Guam about 7,000 miles from New Jersey. We had a good time exchanging Navy stories and talking about the future.

A few days later we all boarded a very large ship. It was converted from a captured Italian luxury liner to a troop ship and held about 5,000 troops. Miller, Farrell, "Bunky" Hack, a couple others from the Vesole and I, hung out together on the 9-day sail to San Francisco, actually, the Treasure Island Navy Base. At TI we were processed, received our travel orders and had three days liberty before getting the assigned troop train to cross the country to Lido Beach, Long Island. An old chief petty officer of the Shore Patrol gave us a lecture as to conduct and staying out of trouble. "You guys have not had anything to drink for a long time. You have a one-shot capacity, a one-fifth imagination and two shots will knock you right on your ass. So be careful and don't give me any trouble." We stayed at a good Navy-run hotel, the Drake, I think, and had a great three days touring San Francisco, visiting the bars with dance floors, and getting some good meals. After that we boarded a filled-up troop train, and 6 days later we were on the East Coast ready to shift gears into our futures.

What was the dangerous mission that Chief Flanak recruited for, and Miller, Gallo, and I teamed up for? The Navy never told us. It was Secret. The war ended. There was no need to know. Many years later I researched and found that the War Department began planning for the invasion of Japan in April 1945. The invasion would take place November 1. It would be the largest invasion ever. Bigger than Normandy. The planners estimated that we would suffer one million KIA (Killed in Action)'s to completely subdue the Japanese. About one and a half million Japanese military would be lost and about two and a half million civilians would also die. Code name Olympic designated the invasion of Kyushu, and Coronet designated the invasion of Honshu, directed to the Kanto plains and

Tokyo. As I recall, there were some 40 landing beach areas in total, each with the name of an automobile. Yes, we had that many, even then.

Considering the training we had after we volunteered that day at the Naval Research Labs, we would have gone in early, probably with some kind of pathfinder team, got up into the high ground with our equipment and jammed any Japanese radar that was operating. Research also revealed that the Japanese side had a sizeable army at home, a large number of kamikazes waiting to attack, and a prepared civilian population. The Japanese overall plan was to defend against the Americans coming ashore and continue fighting street by street, house by house, inflicting sufficient damage to try to effect a ceasefire and peace negotiation. If the atomic bombs had not been dropped, my intuition about not returning, as expressed to Tom Jamison, foretold the truth.

GOODBYE, NAVY

Hello Again, Monks

Author (player #12) is returning captain of St. Benedicts' basketball team. Digi is player #5.

The troop train environment going across country was, oh, so much different than that troop train overnight to the Sampson boot camp. Then, we were very young, untested, untrained, unknowing, and among strangers. On the homebound troop train we were friends by mutual association and training, and had a common immediate future, the discharge process to return to civilian life. The atmosphere was congenial. Talking was loud and happy and dice games were abundant. Our individual adjustments to civilian life were yet to be experienced. Often overlooked and undervalued, the adjustments, while painful to some and affecting many, were seldom discussed among the veterans and their families. Except for severe cases, counseling and similar care was just not available. But my adjustment quirks were normal for the day, and it was nice to know I was returning to St. Benedict's … my core years.

I was discharged at Lido Beach, Long Island in July 1946. In the exit processing, a Chief Petty Officer addressed our group on the advantages of a Navy career. He said that we will be going to war with the Soviet Union in the future and any of us in Radar, Sonar, or Radio who wanted to re-up for 3 years would receive an immediate promotion. Ah, at last I could have my 3/c RDM rate. My mind told me if I was going for 3, I was going for 30. I figured I could make Chief by age 28-30. I could take college courses along the way in my career, achieve a degree or two and then, at age 47 (thirty years), I could coach and teach in some small college. It was tempting. I liked the Navy. But the trend of the time was to get out, and I was not without that influence. Also Digi, Farrell, and Downey, and others were going back to St. Benedict's to accumulate credits for college, playing ball all the way.

So I processed out of the Navy, received a small amount of money from "pay due." I signed up for the Veteran Administration's 52-20 club, which provided discharged veterans $20 a week for 52 weeks, to help them along while they were getting adjusted and finding work or going on to school. I said my goodbyes and "keep in touches" with the few shipmates in that group. It is so sad that I never got back in touch with Fred Miller. Then in dress blues, and with a full sea bag, I took the necessary trains and buses toward Union. The war had long since ended. The people, in general, had lost their outward support of the military. Noticeably there was a change from outward friendliness to a general acceptance, and a casual hello. It caused me to wonder.

The change from military to civilian life was a bit confusing. It was not a breaking away from the past to change into something different. Our past experiences and environments are a part of us forever. There is no leaving them to history. When our country is at war and in danger, almost everyone becomes patriotic and outward expressions abound. When we are not in danger, it's ho-hum, another soldier. Why is the thankful attitude toward the military not constant? Why does the level of patriotism go up and down with world conditions? It reminds me of Kipling's poem, Tommy: "Oh, it's Tommy this and Tommy that, and it's Tommy, stay behind. But it's thank you Mr. Atkins when the troop ship's on the line." As I sit here writing, we are in a war in the Middle East that will have a widening scope. It will be a long war. But most of the citizens, perhaps misinformed, don't recognize the situation. They are indifferent to it all. Therein lies the enemies' pleasure and our handicap for survival.

I did not tell Nana and Pop-pop I was in the U.S. but they knew I expected to be home in the summer. That nice old house on the large plot of ground with an abundance of trees, the chicken yard, vegetable garden, and the fields beyond, looked better than ever on that early July day, and orchestrated into a happy, thankful, homecoming. Smokey, over in his house under the apple tree, gave a knowing bark. I went up the steps, rang the bell, the door opened. Mom gave a happy "yelp," and Gram Newhard, hearing the excitement, came down the stairs, talking all the way. Mom, Gram, and I hugged, sat down at the kitchen table and poured some readily available iced tea. It was summer. The windows were all open. The iced tea was great. We kept talking over each other until we calmed down after a few sips. We talked a long time. Each one had many things to say.

In a while Richie came home from working in the nearby gas station that I had worked in years before. He was doing well at Livingston School and liked to go out with Dad on emergency calls. He was glad to see me and jumped into the conversation, but I am sure he was thinking, "Oh boy, I have to share the bedroom with him for a year until he leaves for college. I hope he learned many tidy habits in the Navy." Rich is eight years younger than I. In our "growing up" days, the difference in age did not allow us a common ground for doing things together, except working around the house. I recall one time when I was about 17 and Rich about 9, Dad had told me to cut the grass (using the old no-engine "push" mower). It was Saturday. I had planned to play a "choose-up-sides" game at the playground. I told Rich that Dad wanted the lawn cut and I would cut it when I returned from the playground (knowing how he loved to please Dad and would cut the whole lawn which took about 2 hours). When Dad came home, we both told him how Richie moved right in and cut the grass while I was away, that rascal! Time and circumstances have not allowed Rich and I to be close over the years, but there has always been a special place in my heart for him.

Dad came home around 5 p.m., as usual (out at 6:30 or 7 and home around 5). He was very happy that I was home, and we talked and shared, including some cold beer. Dad knew I was now a man, at 19. Marion came home from work a short while thereafter. She was her usual cheerful self, loving, and full of news, and I soon sat down to my first family dinner in a long time. The family dinner was an important ingredient in our home, from the earliest of times. I never realized its synergistic, anchoring, and belonging value until I looked back when my own family was developing and Zeni naturally shared my views on the value of the family dinner.

Shortly after my return, I headed for St. Benedict's to sign up for the fall semester. The empty halls during the summer vacation eerily contrasted with the heavy activity of the school year. The Dean of Studies welcomed me back. I signed up for the full program, English, Math, Chemistry, French and Religion. Then I went home, got in touch with Cousin Frank, and the next day we went to the beach for the weekend. That Jersey coast, in season, is marvelous for body surfing, and we had a great time, two "old salts." A week or so later…yup, back to the shore with another "ol' salt," classmate "Fox" Farrell. While there, we struck up a conversation on the beach with two pretty gals who were in the School of Nursing at the Jersey City Medical Center. We were two well-traveled, suave, "smoothies"…probably opened up with, "Pardon me, but is that a yellow swim-suit you are wearing?" or, "Excuse please, but do you know there will be a hur-ricane coming?" Whatever, it all fell into place and the four of us enjoyed dinner that night and met on the beach the next day. "Dottie" (Dorothy) was a blue-eyed blond with a dental poster smile, and she and I dated as our studies and time allowed. A Saturday night date was a real adventure (especially in winter), driving the old family Dodge from Union to Jersey City, U.S. 22 and the old Pulaski Skyway (a marvelous engineering work in its day, over the New Jersey meadows and swamps). Fox would often join me to see Kay, pretty, with a quick wit, like Dottie.

School started and it was different than before. Getting back to academic dis-ciplines took some time. I recall one friend, also a returning vet, was asked to read a page, making a point in the lecture, and he bumbled through it. After the class, he left the building. I followed him knowing we both had a math class with Fr. Richards next. I found him sitting in his car, mad at himself and crying and say-ing he was going to quit school and go to work. We had a real heart-to-heart talk, but he would not go back into the school, saying he needed the day off. I told Fr. Richards about the absence and he picked up on it the next day and was a big help. My friend stayed in school right on through college. I too had a situa-tion. Just before the basketball season started, Prof chose me to captain the team again, and at general assembly the Headmaster asked me to say a few words to the students as sort of a welcome back gesture. Well I clutched the mike and "ohm, uba, ahhed" my way through a terribly stilted talk. It was embarrassing, and it took me a while as I worked at the adjustment.

About this time Dad asked me if I wanted to go to Annapolis, saying that he would ask Capt. Kean if he could get me an appointment. I always liked the Navy, but the timing was bad. There was that psychosocial adjustment thing going on and I knew I was not the same solid student or athlete due to less con-ditioning, self-discipline, and overall interest. But I did slowly get back into stride and by the end of the first semester I was truly home.

We were now the postgraduates (PGs) starting at age 19 in the fall and leav-ing at 20 in the spring. Dick Haesler, Billy Conn, Mike Kerwin, Joe Grum, Leroy O'Neil and other top athletes were in the class of '47 and we PGs joined them— Downey, Farrell, Digi, Sam Cavallero, and others. These, plus the ability of Coach Joe Kasberger, gave us the best prep school football team that I have ever seen. They went 8–0. Haesler played fullback and Conn was a running back. Herman

Hickman, the assistant coach at West Point under the famous Red Blaik, saw them play and said they were the closest thing to the great Blanchard and Davis combo All-Americans that he had seen at the pre- college level. Joe was delighted with that team, and he deserved much of the credit. "Hit me! You call that a hit?" He continued to put on the pads and mix it up, and did so for many more years.

That winter and spring were full of activities, slowly helping a slightly better me to surface. We had a good basketball team, but I really didn't reach my best and it was noticeable. There was too much going out with the guys, dating the gals, and playing with the debilitation twins, smoking and drinking. Moderation, "shmoderation," that's a cop-out. Prof knew there was something different. He invited me to his home in Passaic where he showed me many pictures of his life, wife and family, the old Passaic Wonder teams, Prof with his wrestling and gymnastic trophies and, of course, his basketball feats and trophies. He also showed me the pictures and write ups about the pet black bear he trained and played with and took on exhibitions in his younger days. He was an amazing man. Above all he was an educator. In the gym classes and the basketball practices he always taught, "Whatever is your biggest problem/concern/fear at any time in your life is the thing you attack first, head on." Well Prof, I haven't passed at 100%, but those words filled my memory guide path and I have always carried them.

Dottie and I were serious. I recall many dates. One Saturday I took a train to Jersey City and we planned to meet and stay over at her guardian aunt and uncle's in Weehawken. A record snow storm ensued. There was no transportation to Weehawken, so we walked those many miles up Hudson Blvd. and arrived exhausted but happy. Another time St. Benedict's was playing some New York team at the 69th Regiment Armory court in NYC. Dottie, Kay, "Fox" and I went over together and afterward went to dinner. I had played well and my companions let me know it. I needed that. Another time I drove Dottie and Kay to my home in Union for some ice skating on the pond. She met my family and it was noticeable that everyone liked each other. From time to time I would drive to Jersey City, pick up Dottie, go over to Marion and Bob's in Hillside and baby sit Carol, my baby niece, so they could go out, while we had a cozy evening.

In late February, Joe called for pitchers and catchers to start working out in the gym. He also asked Digi, Downey and me if we wanted to help him get the field and bleachers ready for the season. Of course. We would have done that even if we didn't get paid. We loved that school. Joe, then about 50, was in such great shape that he out-worked us, especially when it came to carrying long bleacher boards. "You guys want to take a break?" (smiling) "Nah, we're okay" (puff puff).

When the season started, Doc Dougherty, a big lefty, and I were the mainstays of the staff and Jack Feehan was the back up; a good "chucker," he could throw that circle change-up which Joe liked. This was the first of several seasons that set the State record for consecutive wins, about 63. All those drills at each position over and over paid off. "You play the way you practice." That spring of 1947 Doc was in the rotation to start against La Salle Military in Oakdale Long Island. Joe "talked it up" all the time, but was really ratcheted up for this one. I think he was sensing a no-loss season. Anyway Doc had two men on and one or two out in about the 7th inning. Joe told me to go down to the open bull pen and warm up. I got warmed up, so I stopped. I was ready.

From the players' bench, Joe looked down to the bull pen and, seeing me not throwing, hollered at me for all to hear, "Are you ready down there? cause if he walks him, you are in there." Doc walked the batter and loaded the bases and I was in. I took my warm-up pitches and Joe came out to the mound and excitedly grabbed my arm with a look of grave concern, "Can you get the curve ball in there for the first pitch?" "Sure I'll get it in, Joe." So Leroy showed the deuce for the curve and I threw it. Outside. "Ball one." "Yeah, yeah," barked Joe, "you'll get it in there." He really wanted this game. A lot of coaching philosophy today calls for a mix of discipline and some "touchy feely" fatherly love. Not so in the old school of the day. Oh, the love was there, but it was quiet, unstated, like the morning mist in the mountains, sometimes seen, and then gone. I got the side out and held them the rest of the game while we scored a run or two. It was a happy bus ride back to New Jersey with Joe doing most of the talking. What a man.

At another time I pitched a full game against Admiral Farragut Naval Academy and won. Here I am again, hard pressed to be humble in the face of truth. I never lost at St. Benedict's. I began to realize I was a pretty good "chucker." This team had it all and Joe was to get a no-loss season for the school and go on to win about 60 or so straight over the next few seasons. A true educator, coach, and teacher, Joe had left it all on the field and among his players when he entered eternal life many years later.

Unknown to me, in April, 1947, Frank Geiger, a Newark businessman, Georgetown graduate, and scout for G'town athletics was looking for two pitchers and contacted his friend Joe Kasberger, who recommended Doc and me. He introduced us to Geiger who was also arranging for Haesler, Conn, and Cavallero to play football at Georgetown. Geiger contacted the GU Athletic department and all was arranged. Before this I had planned to look into a Physical Education program and have a career in coaching. The first thing I asked Frank Geiger was, "Do they have a Phys Ed program?" "Oh, no, there's a liberal arts college and a Foreign Service School." I chose the international business course in the Foreign Service School. I had been in Japan and China and I had an interest in going abroad again some time…no real plans, as mentioned.

Joe Judge, the Georgetown baseball coach, wanted one of us to start summer school in July to obtain two semesters of eligibility to play varsity ball in the spring of 1948. Doc and I agreed that I would go in July.

The season ended, all were happy. We cleaned out our lockers at Benedict's Field and Joe gave a nice talk and said, "If anyone wants to write to me during the summer, just send it to The Dales, Oregon; they all know me there."

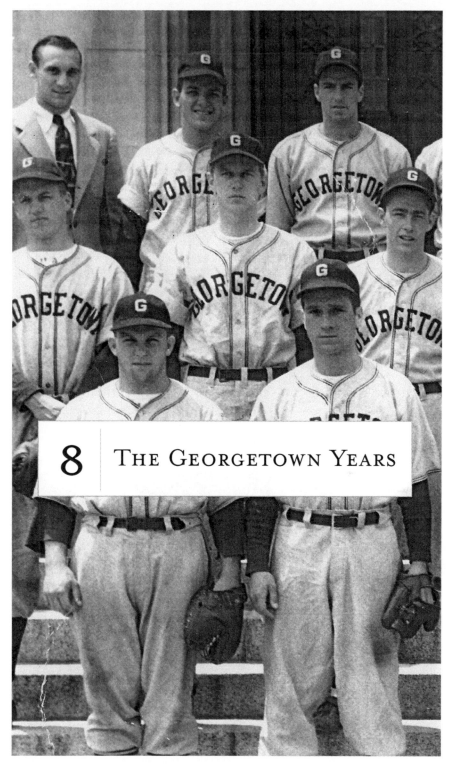

8 | THE GEORGETOWN YEARS

Author (second from left, second row) in Georgetown baseball team uniform

After the 4th of July in 1947, Nana and Pop-pop drove me down old U.S. 1 in that big '37 Dodge to Washington DC and the Georgetown campus, the Hilltop, at N.W. 37th and O Sts., overlooking the Potomac. It had grown out of a tiny missionary house in the earlier 1700's, expanded over the years, and was formally established in 1789 by John Carroll, the Bishop of Baltimore, using the same establishment date, and an almost identical seal of our beloved country. A little trivia…what area did that first Diocese of Baltimore cover?…Answer…From the Mississippi to the Atlantic and from the Canadian border to the Gulf of Mexico, and not a fax or cell phone in sight. The communication and transportation implement in those days was called a horse.

We arrived and went into the Healy Building with its Gothic roof, Flemish towers, Roman arches in the basement halls, and the huge tower with a giant clock that kept the time for the whole neighborhood. It was Saturday. I checked in to get a room assignment. The official registration would be on Monday. We went out to an early dinner so Nana and Pop-pop would have a timely start for their return trip home. They were happy. This son's second departure from home was a feel-good time compared to the first departure, two and a half years ago.

The room assigned to me on the third floor of Healy was right under that huge clock (snuggly close). Bong-Bong every fifteen minutes and then the

Pop-pop, Nana and Howard Jr. on the Georgetown University campus, August 14, 1949

hourly tolling bong, particularly enjoyed at 11 and 12 midnight. That lasted for the summer semesters and then I transferred to the Old North Dorm. There were not many students coming onto the campus for the summer semester. We were told that the Sunday Mass would be in the Dahlgren Chapel at 8 a.m. and breakfast in the senior dining room at 9:30. The next morning, after some "hiya"s and "where ya from"s we went to the chapel. There were some words of informative greeting, then the celebration of the Mass, after which we proceeded to the senior dining room. Wow! It had large circular tables with linen table cloths and napkins, silverware and good china. Uniformed waiters, down to white gloves, served us lamb chops and scrambled eggs and home fries, all served on platters family style, fruit, biscuits, milk, and coffee, I kid you not. Oh my, I was going to like it here. Thank you Miss Huntington, Mom and Dad, St. Benedict's, Joe, Prof and Fr Richard, Frank Geiger, and above all, thank you God. I was on a full scholarship: room (with maid and linen service), board, books, tuition, and laundry, I still kid you not.

The Georgetown School of Foreign Service contained the business program with an international flavor. There was no business school per se, as yet. A curriculum of eight subjects a semester was set, with no electives, except one in the senior year. In addition to Accounting, Economics, Money and Banking, Business Finance, Business Law, Insurance, etc., we took Constitutional Law, Maritime Law, Marine Insurance, Geography, Political Science, a philosophy package (Logic, Ethics, Metaphysics, Epistemology), English, a History course every semester, and more, planned into about 17 hours per week. Oh, this was not going to be easy.

For that summer schedule I had The Development of Civilization, and Accounting 101. Dr. Carrol Quigley, that noted historian, taught a most interesting course on the Rise and Fall of Civilizations. He gave us a text on ancient history to read on schedule, but he never touched on it in his lectures. The "tie-ins" were up to the student. The accounting course was just plain vanilla. The instructor didn't know where to find the fruit, nuts, or whipped cream. I recall the lengthy assignments, working with the large, desk-covering, sticky, accounting sheets in the summer humidity with no air conditioning under that Bong-Bong of a clock (oh, poor baby).

Late in July the football team checked in to start practice. Our freshman team that year went 8-0, beating Maryland, Navy, and other "heavies" of that day. Haesler, Conn and Cavallero were a part of that performance. Joe was surely pleased. I sometimes watched those summer practices. Washington in July and August is hot. Today in such circumstances players are encouraged to drink plenty of water, rightly so. But in 1947 the shouts would go up from coaches to "stay away from that water." Seems the physical trainers thought a sweating "big ugly" would lose his extra off-season weight and be better off with less water. Perhaps those generally accepted practices received some validity from the stories of the War, such as Merrill's Marauders, a Marine battalion that took long treks in the Southeast Asia jungles while fighting the Japanese Army. They had trained on minimal water to meet the conditions they would face.

The Jesuit Order, founded by St. Ignatius of Loyola, is a teaching and missionary order. A Jesuit priest is 10 years in the seminary before being ordained. There were degrees all over the place, seldom mentioned. The Order was strict, and so reflected on those who would live on the campus. You had to follow the rules, some of which were:

- Attend Mass on assigned days 3 times a week.
- In your room by 10 p.m., lights out by 11.
- If you are out overnight you must get permission first and cannot come back in until 7 a.m.
- All students had to wear a coat and tie to class or no admission.
- There was a graduate school student prefect on each dormitory floor who was required to visit each room, for a bed check, starting at 11 p.m.

Now many of the on-campus students were military veterans who preferred to set their own hours. Some interesting situations evolved, as we will see.

That summer I met Joe Judge, our baseball coach, the twenty-year Washington Senator first baseman, .298 lifetime batting average, and one of the best fielding first basemen ever. He was a contemporary of Walter Johnson, Ty Cobb, Lou Gehrig, Babe Ruth and many others. A personal friend of J. Edgar Hoover of the FBI, he sometimes gave a recommendation for one of his players who qualified to enter the FBI agent training program. Joe asked some guys he knew to take me along with them to play a ball game in Culpepper, Virginia. It was good ol' country hard ball, except I never got a chance to pitch; but the trip made for a nice summer Sunday.

Washington was a great place to go to college. A beautiful city, steeped in history, the politicos' stomping ground, "where the action is," all muting the fact that it was a unique college town. However, taking one year of accounting and one year of The Development of Civilizations in a two-month summer stretch, diminished the college catalog's enthusiastic rhetoric.

Dr. Quigley, one of the best profs I ever had, lectured on social, political, religious, military and other matters that interactively have influenced the rise and fall of civilizations. He gave only one test per semester and that was the Final, which was made up of three broad essay-type questions. When I took it, I read each question carefully and proceeded to write on the ones I knew best. But the third one was from a footnote, a large footnote in the text (ah, now he refers to the text). It had to do with the Northwest Quadrant and contained the answer I needed, but I had disregarded that footnote with the tiny-size print. When I saw the question: "Explain the historical meaning of the Northwest Quadrant," it was, duh! A clueless, blank and empty mind. My inability to define the term naturally negated any reply. Double Duh! I must have "aced" the other two because I received a grade of 66. Regardless, that meant I failed the course and so was on probation, a beautiful start.

For a change, I then planned more than a year ahead. I would go to summer school at George Washington University in D.C., or Seton Hall in New Jersey the next two years with pre-approval to transfer the credits. That would lighten the load all the way through. My scholarship did not include summer school at G.U. except for that initial year, so I would use my G.I. Bill for the summer school tuitions. A thought comes to mind regarding tests. Except for the U.S. Navy General Classification Test, and sometimes in grammar school, I do not recall having multiple choice questions mixed into my tests.

The fall came and the campus filled up to about 1,000 students. Many lived off campus. Friends were easily made. My roommate, Harry Wheeler, was also a Navy vet and played tackle on the freshman football team. He survived the mass exodus when 50% of that freshmen team flunked out at the end of the fall semester. No easy rides for the "jocks" in those days.

Gym rat that I was, I often worked out at the old Ryan gym. Al Remole who had played at Trenton Catholic, and his roommate Randy, were putting together an intramural basketball team, the Ran-Moles and asked me to join. It included Al, Bill Resch, All-City Philadelphia, Denny Owens, who could shoot the lights out, Miggs Reilly, then in law school, who was with the outstanding Hoya squads in earlier years, and some others who were "all" something. We won the school intramural tourney, and went on to win the D.C. Tournament, playing all the other schools' champions, American U., Catholic U., Howard U., George Washington, Gallaudet, and Maryland. In the course of all this the basketball coach, Elmer Ripley, an original Celtic, saw me playing in the gym, and asked me if I would like to work out with the varsity squad. Well, considering The Northwest Quadrant, and the rest of the academic work to come, and the fact that if I played basketball and baseball I would miss Christmas and Easter vacation time, and the fact that I already had a scholarship, I had to thank that grand old man of the game politely, but a no thank you was in place. Some guys, like Dick Falvey, the basketball captain and fine third baseman, studying pre-med to become a dentist, could handle that academic/athletic challenge, but I had not learned the drill.

I mentioned the disciplines involved in living on campus, and how some of the veterans, young by age, but quite mature, were not the typical college student. The Prefect of Discipline was a red-haired priest, a good-natured person, but he had a job to do and he made sure the rules were kept or the appropriate penalties applied. The students called him the Red Rider. He was known to be out roaming the campus at 2 a.m. on a Sunday morning looking for those

Three "Jersey-ites" at Georgetown. From left to right: Doc Dougherty, author, and Joe Deleo

few who had been out on the town and now were trying to get back to their rooms. Of course they could not come through the front gate and say "good morning" to the guard. They would usually filter in back by the med school and baseball field.

A dormitory neighbor, who knew the intricacies of campus infiltration in the early morning hours, was out one Saturday night and became as drunk as a rummy who found a free and extended happy hour. The tale goes that he was making his unsteady way back to our dorm through the dark fields and bushes on the outer rim of the campus, when the Red Rider hollered "Who's there?" Where upon my dorm mate shouted, "Yah, Yah, Father, you can't caaatch meee." And the hide-and-seek race was on in the middle of the night. It went on a long time with a taunting call and then a run to another location, with the Red Rider coming up empty as the elusive target won each "round." He obviously won some others, since he graduated, and later became the successful CEO of a very large corporation.

Dottie and I corresponded using that ancient letter writing system with the "yucky" envelope flaps and stamps, and when I went home that Christmas we dated often. I worked out of the Union Post Office again and renewed acquaintances at Bubble's place. Bob, Joe, Tom, and I got together for some pinochle and visits to the Academy. At the end of the semester, I was removed from probation, but I would bbeee bbaack!

Pitchers and catchers started to work out in February, and in March it was the full squad. The northern teams came south early in the season and our early games were at home. Later on we would travel to Philly, New Jersey and New York to play. We had a good team and the spirit was high. A lot of ribbing went on among us and against the opposition, our brand of humor, and laughter was common. I recall Johnny Moskal, our super-energetic catcher, running off to the side of the first base line to retrieve a possible bad throw by an infielder, and hollering to the base runner, "I bet I beat you down there!" Or someone shouting at the opposing pitcher, after he throws his best fastball, "Hey banana nose, is that all you got?" or, "Hey rag arm, throw that ball right"…on and on, oh, we had fun.

We played at Princeton that spring and Nana and Pop-pop came over to watch. Also watching was the coach at Fordham who was putting a team together to play for Proctor, Vermont in the Northern League that summer. He had been in touch with Ray Corley, our left-fielder transfer from Notre Dame, and a couple other guys, and they had mentioned me to him and would introduce me after the game. It was a tie game when I went in as relief pitcher in the 7th inning. The bases were full and we had the infield drawn in. They put on the squeeze play, bunting the ball straight out from the plate. I had practiced for this one multiple times. You go straight in toward the ball and home plate, don't straighten up, but catch the ball in your bare hand and in a bowling motion throw it knee high to the catcher in front of the plate. No problem. I came charging off the mound in line with the ball and Moskal, but it was not a normal-shaped mound. It was flat, disc-shaped; about 14 ft. in diameter and the whole thing was elevated about 10 inches above the infield grass. So I started to run in on that flat surface, hit the drop off, and "kafluey" I was on my stomach, looking at the ball, as the runner crossed home plate. I finished up okay, but we did not score anymore and lost. I met the Fordham coach before going off with Nana and Pop-pop. We laughed about my grass-stained uniform. He said he would like to have me play at Proctor that summer, but I told him that I had plans to go to GWU summer school in D.C. (Smart Howie, following the plan)

That summer at GWU I took Taxes, Statistics, and European History. There was no room for a part-time job. That was going to be a tough ten-week academic stint. My GI Bill took care of the tuition and $75 a month cash, and Pop-pop and Nana sent a small amount from time to time. I teamed up with Danny Pace, Joe Cardillo, both from Port Chester, New York, and a guy from Catholic U, who had been in the Air Force. We were all low on funds so we got a ground floor apartment (row house type) on 1st St. N.W. near Rhode

Island Ave. (low rent, very low rent, in the natural economic flow, no municipal rent control needed). We learned to eat cheap. Potatoes, spinach, collard greens, and pasta became our staples. We got to know some gals at Catholic U who were studying theater. They threw a party from time to time and we never missed a one.

We lived in a low-rent, tough neighborhood. One night Joe was walking home and some guy was sitting on the low wall in front by the sidewalk. "How ya doin' bro?" said Joe. No answer. He looked down, and the guy is holding his stomach and a little blood was visible. "Let me help you, man." "No, I'm okay, just restin'." Joe went inside, looked out the window before going to bed, and the guy was gone.

Danny Pace, football center and ex-marine, and I became friends as neighbors in Old North Dorm. He and Wheeler, another "big ugly" would joke about my tall, thin, wiry build and say that was the kind of target they liked to hit on the field, so they got to calling me "Rocky" in jest. Somewhere, somehow, Dan or Joe got to talking to a "Blackie" D'Ambrosio in a local store. He came over to the apartment. a few times. Dan introduced me as "Rocky," which got a raised eyebrow. Seems he really knew his way around the back streets and stairs of D.C., was friendly with the cops, talked about the "after hours" clubs, and was obviously street smart. He never showed us any other side except being a real nice guy. He said he had been in the Marine Corps and fought at Guadalcanal. He would stop by with some baked goods, stay a while, and then be on his way.

A bit older, Blackie liked being around these college types who would talk economics, history, and other interesting matters, in addition to sports and the latest scandal and lock-ups that he knew. He arranged for us to go to an after hours club one Saturday night. It was right out of central casting with a standard script. We got to the place about midnight ("commercial" D.C. folded around 11 p.m.). Blackie knocks on the door, peep slide opens, no words, the guy sees Blackie, door opens, and all five of us walk through. Two big "greeters" give a "hi" to Blackie and look us over. Blackie makes the introductions. "Bruno, this is 'Rock'," another raised eyebrow, we "shake." He puts his left hand on my right bicep to look for muscle, and a pat in each arm pit to check if I'm "packing." A little smile, shake of the head, and he finishes the intros. The place is packed. The band is good. We all have some drinks and take a table and eat. Off in the back rooms, the cards and dice are hot; a true illegal money maker. We stayed a while, met the owner, then thanked Blackie and went back to the books, or to bed, (aw, c'mon) for the summer had a way to go.

I finished my courses, which transferred to G'town, and got ready for the sophomore year. Harry Wheeler and I started off as roommates in New North Dorm, but shortly thereafter he decided to leave school to go to work for his uncle in his home town in Connecticut. The school found me a roommate in

Copley Hall, a sophomore, non-vet, who was a very dedicated student, English major, with no athletic interests whatsoever. He was a nice guy, always talking about his latest reading or writing project, and there I was going to classes, studying a bit, talking sports, gym ratting around, doing my morning calisthenics, and working an occasional job. I think the school was trying to raise me toward my academic potential by placing me with a highly dedicated student, but it just didn't come about at that time.

I got a job as a short-order breakfast cook in a luncheonette up on Wisconsin Ave., 6:30 a.m. to 10 a.m. M-F. I scheduled my courses in afternoon and evening sessions. The boss, a pharmacist, had a 40-seat luncheonette in his drug store, not unusual in that time frame of history. I was to prepare cereals, pancakes, eggs, bacon, ham, toast, home fries, coffee etc. "Think you can handle it?" "No problem," sez I, thinking Bubbles, (and fake it 'til you make it). "Okay," said the boss, "see you tomorrow, early." I got there extra early because the broad answer to cooking for 40 seats, at rush hour time, was in the preparation. Pancake mix and oatmeal in advance, home fries done and warming, bacon/ham fried and warming, two eggs in 10-15 cups ready for "spill and fry" action. A waitress took care of the tables and I cooked the food and served the 4-5 counter seats. It all worked fine and I left, ready for my classes.

As time wore on, so did I. I had the job, school, studying, and working out and playing with the Ran-Moles again in the intramural league. In early December I was thinking of telling the boss I was retiring to write a short-order cookbook, hah, no, just kidding, but quitting. The matter took care of itself. Toward the slower end of the shift a guy came in, sat at the counter, ordered something, and coffee. I reached around and took the metal coffee pot and poured him a cup, and then was returning the pot. "Fill it up, damn it," came the strong sullen voice, "I've been coming in here every day and I never take cream and I want a full cup of coffee." My pressure gauge was going up. I turned with the metal coffee pot in hand to completely fill his cup. With hard, resentful eyes, he kept up his tirade about bad service. In my wisdom of age today, I know he was sick, but this young in-shape athlete in a split-second thought almost whacked him with the coffee pot. I was a bit shaken, thinking what might have been. He must have sensed it for he did not speak all through his breakfast, poor kook. After the shift, I gave the boss notice and left in about a week, none the worse for wear.

That Christmas it was the usual family fun, and more trudging the "assigned and routed tasks" of Uncle's Post Office. Dottie's and my correspondence had fallen off. I went to see her, sensing a goodbye, which was right. She was going to be finishing her training, getting her degree and had met a young dentist and they were going to marry. It hurt, more a matter of pride than losing something that I had not had for a while anyway. That was one lucky dentist, and with her smile, he didn't have to pay for advertising.

Early that spring I threw good games against Fordham and another school. Two scouts living in New Jersey and representing the Tigers and Red Sox introduced themselves after one of the games. The Tiger's guy knew my Uncle Frank from the Elizabeth area. No one was throwing money at me, but you took that to mean "when you get your degree, or if you want to now, we can give you a little something, put you in B or A ball, and you ride the bus from town to town and see how far up the professional ladder you can go. After two years you will know if you can make the "bigs" or not. The talk was light: "How ya feelin'? How's the arm? Ya doin' your wind sprints? You're looking good; we'll keep in touch." Gee, I was a pretty good "chucker."

Later that year I started the North Carolina State game at home. I was pitching a three or four hitter in the fifth inning, and we were rolling. Dean Cassell from Union, a former team mate in the under 15 league, was on the mound for North Carolina State. Moskal was calling a good game. My usual pitching style was to throw almost all pitches; fastball, curve and change-up halfway between overhand and side arm, that is, about a 40-45 degree angle, measuring from directly above my head. I threw side arm on one pitch and Joe Judge hollered, "Where did you get that pitch from? Stay over hand, stay over hand, out there." I had never heard that from him before, but I followed his instruction and threw the fastball and curve ball both with a straight-up overhand motion. It didn't feel right but I could do it. Later I got into a tight spot and needed the out, and I was going to throw my best fastball ever, over hand, and get the third strike. Whoosh! I exploded from straight-up over hand, everything I had went into that pitch, right over the top, and I popped a sizzler right on the outside corner. "Strike three." "Now that one had something on it," yelled Joe, "way to go." I walked into the dugout holding my arm. It hurt. I had "thrown it out." I went out there the next inning, fighting the pain, and got pummeled. "For God's sake get in shape," shouted Joe, not knowing the truth, and he took me out, saving the game. Joe had the experience and other qualities of a good coach and I in no way blamed him for my arm problem. How and why it happened may or may not have been because of a change in the angle of delivery.

The arm never came around for the rest of the year. Whirl pools, massaging, electrical therapies, etc…zilch! It never came around to pitch at that level, period. Dr. Herling Jones, Pop-pop's cousin, Birdie's son, had successfully operated on some pitcher from the Rochester Red Wings who had a similar condition, a badly stretched tendon from the armpit to the elbow. But talking to him after the school year, I decided not to bother. Nobody, including me, thought I could make the "bigs" and without that it didn't seem worth the trip. Many, many years later, I found out from Nana that Pop-pop thought I could make it, but he never told me. If he had asked me to try, I would have tried. If he had asked, or told, me to go to Annapolis, I would have. But he always left my future up to me. It's that age-old parent-child matter that never gets settled, with the pros and cons both being valid.

I kept working out and trying to throw without any pain. Sometime I was almost there but it would not go away. On game day I was now the third base coach. We went up to Jersey to play Seton Hall. Nana and Pop-pop and Cousin Frank sat in the stands behind third base. Frank, whom I love like my brother, was not going to miss this opportunity. We had competed since we were toddlers, and here he was in his last year at Seton Hall. With a nice booming, for-all-to-hear-voice he would shout, "Hey 22, what are they saving you for, the senior prom?" or "Hey, coach, put on the bunt sign, that's all you'll get from this pitcher." The game was always fun. I think we won that one.

Home that summer, I worked the midnight shift 5 nights a week at The Ballantine Brewery in Newark. Nearby was the Seton Hall downtown extension program where I took two courses with Digi, who was doing fine at Miami U. After class I went over to Ballantine Brewery, and worked from 11:30 p.m. to 7:30 a.m. The routine was that Teuscher, Koerner and I played pinochle late afternoon on most dates I had class, then I would get the bus to Newark, go to class, have some time for study, and go to the brewery It was all manual work, bottling plant, clean up detail, load freight cars, load trucks, feed conveyers, take off from conveyors. I was loading a conveyor with four other men one night and the shop steward union boss told me not to work so fast because he was trying to put another person on this crew. I really had trouble with that one and was happy to move on to the next weekly job.

I stayed home a lot that summer and was with Mom, Dad, and Richie, who was starting St. Benedict's. We did not have to go places. Just staying in the same home, seeing each other, talking, and sharing meals were very important to us. Marion and Bob were nearby and the same holds true there. We were all very close.

Starting my junior year, I became friends with Ed McGrath, an Air Force vet who was also in the Foreign Service School. We had many good discussions about classes we took, politics, the Church, on and on. Another friendship that developed more was with Dick "Horse" Haesler, best fullback St. Benedict's ever had. We took a similar program in the F.S. School and had some classes at the same time. More than a few nights we stayed up late, pumped up on coffee, studying and cross-testing for a Final ("I'll bet he will ask about…because …") Cell phone and e mail friends to this day, that "Dr. Horse," ex-Marine, is a winner.

I moved off campus and took a job as a night desk clerk at the Blackstone Hotel, on 16th St. across from the YWCA. Owned by the (Admiral) King family, it was first class and had 72 units, the Old Fashion Room (a restaurant), and the usual support services. Don Lawrence was a fine manager. There were four clerks. We lived there, ate our evening meal in the restaurant, had maid service, free laundry, and $50 a month. Such a deal. One of the clerks worked there three years while going to Georgetown Dental School.

My job as night desk clerk 11 to 7 was to meet and greet, register new occupants, handle general questions, bring the position sheet up to date for the manger in the morning, answer the switchboard and run the elevator after midnight. I had all the keys and was the only one on duty during the night. As mentioned, D.C. was an early to bed town and it was very quiet around there after midnight. I had plenty of time to study.

From the clerk's counter I could see into a small part of the Old Fashion Room just off the lobby. One night I was on duty just before it closed. There was a man, about 40, well-dressed, dining, and enjoying a cheerful conversation with one of our waitresses, obviously friends. I went through the routines of my work; quiet time ensued by about 12:30. Around 1 a.m. that same guy walks in and says he's a TWA pilot on a layover and is in a card game around the corner and needs forty dollars to "keep the kettle boilin'," and he showed me his TWA and other ID, which read G.W. Tucker. Nice guy, easy talker, $40? Why sure. I took his check and gave him the money and that was that. About 3 a.m. he came back in, just a little tipsy. "Hey buddy, I got those rascals runnin' and I'm about to clean up, but I need your help for $70. You give me back my check and I will make one for the whole amount, or I'll just write one for $70, which is best for you?" So he wrote out one for $70 and I paid it out and wished him well.

About a week later Don Lawrence called me in. "Howie, did you cash these checks for G.W. Tucker? They are no good. No such account at Riggs Bank." I was shocked and apologetic. "I will go out to that local address he gave and talk to him, Don; be right back." The address was an empty lot out in the N.E. section. I went to the TWA office and they put out a world wide ticker inquiry to locate G.W. Tucker. Negative. I talked to the waitress, presumably his friend, and she said no, she never met him before and didn't even know his name. I told Don to please take it out of my salary, a little at a time, but being the fine person he was he said no, but what did you learn to protect the hotel's interest in the future? We talked it over and established a rule. No check cashing unless approved by the manager (another first).

Years later, having had more life experience and CIA's case officer work and training, I would realize that G.W. Tucker was a pro. He sat at the right place in the Old Fashion Room so that I would notice him having fun with his waitress "friend" (he pre-established himself in my mind). Then he came in friendly, never pushy, asking for help, using good-looking ID backup. Then he came back, friendly, never pushy, and used a "presumed close," as they say in sales, offering me choices on what was best for me in helping him. G.W. was a pro.

Another Blackstone memory: I always had a pot of coffee "at the ready" in the kitchen. One wintry night the local cop on the beat came in to get warm. I offered him some coffee. We talked sports and whatever, friendly. This was repeated whenever he had the beat in our neighborhood. One night he was sipping his coffee and asked me, "Anybody ever come in here asking for a girl?" "No, it's not that kind of a place." "Oh I know that, but look, the guest doesn't know that, so if someone should ask you, all you have to do is give him this phone number to call, that's all. And you will get $5 for each one. How about it?" My little guy inside said, "Watch out!" I found it insulting that he would ask me to step into the gutter with him, but I had to be careful. The cop on the beat can always make trouble if he wants to. "Gee, Tom, that's really against my basic beliefs and I really couldn't do that. But, hey, that doesn't mean we can't be friends. I enjoy your visits and like our talks. You really know about sports." Well, he did come around some more, but not as often, and then I did not see him anymore.

After a while another cop, younger than Tom, would stop by, have coffee, and make happy talk. We got along fine. One night he said, "Hey, a few of us (cops) are going out Saturday night to a party. Want to come along?" "Sure," says the adventurous one. So they picked me up in front of the hotel, talked about getting a couple of bottles to take to the party, and we drove somewhere up 9th St. to a fairly rough neighborhood. We stopped at a darkened corner. A man came out from the shadows beside the building holding something under his coat. He asked, "Whatcha want?" "Two bourbons." "Got 'em right here. That's $15." As the bottles were handed through the window, the cop showed his badge instead of the money and said, "Thanks." "No, no!" hollered the bootlegger and tried to get it back, but we drove off, while their laughter on a job well done filled the car. We went on to the party in another part of town. It was mostly police officers and their wives, girlfriends, a nice time as far as that went.

I left a bit early and was thinking over the whole matter of police, prostitution, bootlegging, and after-hours joints. That liquor bootlegger had objected strongly and wanted his money because he was paying for his protection in that illegal activity. His "right" was being violated. It was interesting to me because I had just done a paper for my Political Science class on New York City in the 1890s, when one Rev. Dr. Parkhurst, a very effective reform advocate, built an organization, which joined forces with Teddy Roosevelt, the new chief of the NYC police department, and together with their choice for mayor beat the incumbent who had been well entrenched in the corrupt Tammany Hall system of government. Roosevelt went on to become governor of New York as that century drew to a close.

One thing I carried away from that research was how long-term corruption develops its own system for survival. For example, a police reporter named Lincoln Stephens, who later wrote a book entitled *The Muck Rakers,* received his weekly cash-pay envelope one Friday afternoon, met his wife, and they took the street car to where they would have dinner. After dinner, he reached into his inside pocket for the envelope and it was not there. He went to see his friend, a police captain, and told him the story. The captain said not to worry and to come back Monday for his money, which he did. The captain merely put out the word to tell the pickpocket who was working that trolley (and paying the cops for the privilege) that he "picked" the captain's friend and to give it back. One time a well-known pickpocket, who, by mutual agreement, had been barred from practicing his trade when he visited the City, started to "lift" a watch from the watch chain they wore on the vest in those days. The "paying" pickpocket who saw him in action in his "protected" territory hollered, "Pickpocket!" and called for the police. The intruder apologized saying the watch had a safeguard that he had never seen and he could not help having a go at it. They told him goodbye and he never came back.

The houses, or apartments, of prostitution had the protection of the cops on the beat to keep things quiet and orderly, and the cops received periodic payments, a part of which went up the line of command. Then there was the case of the German immigrant lad, coming to NYC when he was 5 years old. At 18 he was a big, good-looking kid and someone suggested he join the police force, which he did. He was, of course, trained in the system that existed, wherein the police came to rely on the graft machinations to help solve crime. Informants were plentiful, as cops and crooks were business partners. The young German lad worked hard and became a Captain about the time of the grand reform when Teddy R flipped over their apple cart, and the Tammany clock was cleaned. Many policemen lost their jobs. The Captain was demoted to a foot patrolman on the waterfront. One night there was a big robbery there and a barge full of expensive furs was pilfered. When the police reporter, Lincoln Stephens, a friend, asked him what gang did it, he responded, "I don't know. We don't know who is working the waterfront any more."

Since power corrupts and absolute power corrupts absolutely, it follows that the longer it goes on, the more difficult it is to establish reform with law and order for the good of all. By extension of thought, one then sees the necessity to have term limits in all three branches of federal, state, and local governments. Well, no large city is squeaky clean but NYC of today has come a long way, even with the crushing influence of drugs on today's society. But D.C.? That is a study unto itself, and in dire need of a Teddy Roosevelt.

Some 25 years after my "hotel career," we were in the U.S. on vacation. I was showing ya'll the sights of D.C. including where Daddy went to school and worked off and on, and I wanted to show you the old Blackstone Hotel. We all went down to K St. NW. I was excited. As we turned the corner onto 16th St. NW, surprise!! There was a three- or four-storied, block-long, government building, and I wound up trying to explain the small town mode and what it all looked like on that section of 16th St. when the Blackstone had been there, some twenty five years before. There was almost nothing there that I could relate to, and that caused a touch of emptiness.

As our junior year spring semester was closing, Horse and I planned to make our way (train, bus, hitch-hike) to Atlantic City for a long Memorial Day weekend meeting with class mates before heading home. I told Ed McGrath our plan. He was staying in D.C. that summer and suggested that he sell me his car, a heavy, old, roadside oddity with an engine and wheels. "What's your rock-bottom price?" "Twenty five," he said. "Is there a warranty?" "Yeah, sure, I'll mail it to you." "Sold." My first auto. Knowing all about business law in our imagination, we drew up a bill of sale. "That'll work," said barrister McGrath, and I drove off to park and tell Horse we would be going straight on to Atlantic City.

When the last day came we checked out of the dorm, loaded the car, and off we went, reaching Rhode Island Ave. and heading north on U.S. 1. Then the car gave a bit of a cough and sputter, slowed down (I pushed on the gas), and it stopped. We smelled gas. "It's flooded," said the two master mechanics at the same time. "Hey, Horse, just push it a little ways and I'll release the clutch, and that should do it." After about twenty yards it kicked right in and off we went, happy and anticipating the weekend to come. A few miles further and that ugly rascal gave a sputter and a cough, sloowweed down (as I fed more gas) and stopped, amid the honks, "get off the road" shouts, and air mail messages by hand.

"It's flooded," said the engineers. We were now at the city line. Horse got out and started to push, and push, and ppuusshh. I looked in the rear view and he was getting that far away look that exhaustion prompts. "C'mon Horse, let's get this started or we'll miss all the fun in Jersey." "Fun? What fun? Why aren't YOU pushing?" "Because I have to steer." "Well, I can steer." "Yeah, but I steer better and it's my car." Puussh...and pppuuussshh, man, he was some fullback, but the car would not start, RIP. We pushed it well off of the road, parked it, took out our luggage and hitchhiked. We managed to flag down two trucks and two cars on our way to Atlantic City and had a great weekend at the planned get-together.

Home for the summer, I took a good paying union job at The Metals Disintegrating Co, alongside the Lehigh Valley Railroad in Union. They melted copper and aluminum ingots, then shot the liquid through a large atomizer out into a huge metal skin sphere, 4 stories high. The spray then cooled into dust, settled, and was shoveled into 55 gallon steel drums and shipped to paint companies. Around the blast furnaces the temperature was about 140 degrees. We worked in shorts, no tops, and oiled ourselves and wore goggles as we fed the ingots into the roaring monsters. Breaks for water and salt were mandatory. There was just enough copper mist in the air to turn us a pale green without the oil protection.

Inside the sphere we wore a respirator, protective clothing and footwear as we shoveled the dust into the drums. At another time we would cart the drums to a sealing area and then place them on the platform for loading, which was the last part of the process. It was very heavy "grunt" work and I sure stayed in good shape. There was always the danger of static electricity or a spark from some origin igniting the dust in the sphere (the answer to, "why good pay for 'grunt' work?"). Some years later, when I was off in Korea, Pop-pop sent me a newspaper clipping saying the sphere was completely destroyed by an explosion.

That summer cousin Frank's wife, Lillian, introduced me to her cousin, Connie Hines, who was about 19, very cute and attractive in features and personality, and she liked to play softball. After a few dates it was obvious to both of us that this relationship was going to blossom and get serious. She was of a Protestant denomination, and her brother was a minister. As our early serious conversation moved along, I was sorry to see the course of it all. She was saying that she could never subscribe to Catholicism and its belief in the body and blood of Christ being present in the bread and wine in the celebration of the Mass. I explained the doctrine based on biblical writing and knowing that our faith is a gift from God. We surely were apart on this crucial matter and that was the reason our friendship stayed as friendship. At the time I had wished it were otherwise. She sure was a fine young woman.

I saw Bob Teuscher. He was going to start at Georgetown Law School and suggested we be roommates. We found an apartment near Du Ponte Circle, not a "signature" address in those days. I signed up for the few courses I had remaining and took them in the evening. I then found a full-time job at the Office of Alien Property in the Justice Dept. I was a file clerk/courier. When some attorney needed a file to review, we had a procedure to follow to be sure he received what he wanted. Some files were ordinary, some were classified. Mrs. Gray, who was close to retirement, was our boss, kind and sweet, but with a touch of the persona of my DI in boot camp. I worked with a few guys who were also students. We got along well and sometimes, during a slow day, we would go and read some of the more interesting cases involving alien property.

The last year started well and I liked my classes, especially the continuation of business law. I graduated in early June 1951. I was 24 and a veteran. If it was not for Nana and Pop-pop attending the graduation, I would have been comfortable receiving my diploma by mail, such was my mindset, which will be understandable early in the next chapter. Besides, my education was just starting.

9 | C.I.A.
Charlie–Item–Able

Author in Korea, 1952

Ed McGrath, he of used-car skills, graduated from Georgetown Foreign Service School in May 1950. In November he came over to the Hilltop campus to see me and related he had received his top secret security clearance and was working in the Security Division of the (hardly known) CIA, which had been established in 1947. He thought I would find the Agency interesting and meaningful as a career, a place where one could help to make a difference. We talked some more and I became more enthusiastic as he answered my questions. He made the arrangements and introduced me to some people, including the Chief of Security, who would become the legendary "mole hunter," a Mr. Englehardt, I believe. Someone gave me a preliminary interview. The degree I would receive in May 1951, my experiences in the Navy, and my athletic background were plusses. I submitted the written, formal application and a month or so later I was contacted and told to report to an unmarked office on G St. N.W., where I was placed in a personnel pool of about twelve who were waiting for the investigations to be completed for their possible security clearances. I resigned from my job at Alien Property. I told Mrs. Gray I was going to work at the Pentagon. She wished me well: "I always knew you would be okay and could make something of yourself." It sounded as if she had wrestled with that one.

I reported at G St. every day. We did a lot of non-sensitive work: organizing papers, filing, making signs, etc. Coffee-drinking was very popular, with intervals of lectures about historical events, music, international news, and whatever else might be of general interest.

Ed George was living in a house with a few guys out in Chevy Chase. They had just come back from jump school and were waiting for assignments, and Ed was waiting for his clearance. We became good friends. I reported to the pool 9 to 5 M–F and went to class at night to finish the remaining 6 or 8 credit hours for my degree. Another friendship that started in the pool was John O'Brien. "O.B." was from Boston, had quit college, and had been recruited for some mission he knew nothing about, yet. (Another one hoping to make a difference.)

In February I was notified that my investigation results were in. Then I went for two long sessions of psychological testing and interviews. ("Oh, what am I doing here?") "Am I in yet?" I asked myself, to which my little guy inside responded, "Not yet; you think it's that easy?" After that I went back for the polygraph exam. You answer yes or no to the questions asked. It took quite a while. When it was over, the polygraph interviewer said, "I got a reaction on the questions about Communism and homosexuality, please explain." I told him I would avoid anyone who was homosexual, that I had a strong dislike for such people and distrusted them. This was undoubtedly a lasting reaction from the incidents I mentioned in Chapters 3 and 5.

Regarding Communism, I told him I had read about Marx and Lenin in my studies of Russian History and I hated Communism for its aggressive atheism and enslavement of the people. Then, in the usual procedure, he said, "Other than what you have told me, is there any other reason for those two reactions?" Answer: "No." The test was over. "How do you think I did?" He replied, "Someone will tell you officially, but it looks okay." After a week or so someone did tell me that I had received my top secret security clearance and I was to start my first assignment, a courier/messenger, sort of a mark-time job until I graduated.

I reported to the Chief of Administration, Joe(?). He and his secretary Helen had come over from the General Services Administration to help get the fledgling Agency up and running administratively. They were very dedicated and worked tirelessly. I was given that courier job, reporting to Helen (to show how small CIA was then). I worked out of the headquarters which was composed of five or six temporary, two-storied, wooden buildings that had been constructed during WWII to handle the space needs of that time. They were along the Reflecting Pool, near the Lincoln Memorial. I drove a car around Washington D.C., stopping at the Pentagon, Justice, Navy, FBI, Commerce, etc., delivering and picking up classified and unclassified documents for routing to addressees. I was on the move all the time. I worked from early morning to 5 p.m., continuing with my classes in the evening, and partying on Saturday night until I graduated in May 1951. The "until" applies to my class schedule and not the Saturday night fun. Then, I was given a promotion and started on some basic training toward becoming a career intelligence officer.

The Korean War had started in June 1950, and it would last three years. During that time the U.S. had about 100,000 wounded and 50,000 killed in action. Some 2 million Koreans, military and civilian on both sides, lost their lives. The Agency had started a mission presence there with a handful of people. It was a small headquarters under military cover called the Joint Advisory Commission Korea (JACK), located in On Chong Ni, near Tongnae, about 10 miles from Pusan. I did not know about this at the time. I was just taking some basic training in the Office of Special Operations (OSO).

One day I received a request from some guy in the Asia Division to come in and talk about a possible assignment. I went to his office and we had a lengthy chat about me, and about him. He had been with the OSS in WWII and talked of parachuting into North Africa and operating resistance units behind the German lines. War stories followed. Then he turned the conversation to me in some detail, following my education, athletics, and Navy service.

He asked, "Do you like to live outdoors for long periods of time?" (What do I look like, nature boy?) "Sure," I said (now what "kook" would say yes to that?) He went on, "Would you like to do something really important? Do you really want to make a difference?" "Why, what do you have in mind?" I feigned, knowing what was coming. "Korea," he said, "ha, ha, ha, I know you're full of the ol' piss and vinegar." Well, I hadn't exactly thought about it in those terms, but I did like the idea of duty, honor, country, and trying to make a difference against the Communist monster that wanted to impose its will around the world, and I committed myself in those terms. He was elated, and called in another official. We chatted some more and later they introduced me to the Chief of the Korean Desk. The train was getting ready to leave the station and, strangely or not, I still remembered having the lights turned off just before the "big game." It wasn't going to happen this time.

The Chief was friendly and happy to get another warm body with a security clearance that was willing to go and do a job. The ranks in JACK were thin then, and he had slots to fill. He took me to meet a couple of others working at the Korean Desk and then arranged for me to take some leave prior to departing for Korea.

It was now mid-October, 1951. I called Nana and Pop-pop and told them I would be home for five days. I invited Ed George to come along with me. We had built up a friendship. I often stopped by his house in Chevy Chase. A tall, good-looking gal with black hair and eyes lived next door and was around Ed's often, as was her mom who baked pies for him and the other guys living there. "Chickie" Bement was young, as was her mom. They will be back later.

Well, I went home and stayed at the old house on Morris Ave. and visited relatives, friends, former classmates, and probably visited the Beehive to see Fr. Martin, Joe, Prof, and others there.. We had a few parties and it was a good feeling to be back home with Nana and Pop-pop, Uncle Richie, Aunt Marion and Uncle Bob and your cousin Carol. Even Smokey liked my being there.

I gave my future APO address to everyone. Dad had earlier said that he thought after graduating I would come back to our home area to live. He was a bit disappointed. I had told one and all that I had taken a job with the Dept. of Defense working with the supply section and going to Korea, but not to worry as it was very safe way back at the supply headquarters. I guess Dad figured, well at least he has a job and will probably come home to work when he gets back. Finally we said all the "I love you"s and "will write"s and it was time to go. Ed drove as I waved goodbye to all standing by the house as we rolled down Morris Ave. toward Elizabeth and U.S.1, the main highway to Washington. I cried a while. Who wants to displease a loving dad, or cause concern to a loving mom? But a higher purpose was involved and I wanted to be there when the roll was called.

We drove along U.S. 1 and with the miles, and Ed's lengthy and cheery prognostication, I was coming back to where I should be. We crossed the Delaware River on the time-worn Cape May ferry, drove through old Baltimore with its red brick row houses and the many crab shops and restaurants, through College Park past Maryland U., and finally Rhode Island Ave. in DC, U.S. 1 all the way, almost to the door. I reported back to the Chief of the Korea Desk, finished up some training over the next few weeks and started to process out for the Korea assignment. A few days later Ed drove me to the airport (I sure was going to miss having a driver). En route he gave me a going away present, a book, *The Prophet* by Kahlil Gibran. He had underlined a passage:"and when your friend leaves you grieve not, as the mountain is seen clearer from the plains."That was very friendly, nice, touching, but an ominous note to contrast the cheery prognostication about my future. Nah! Ed was an optimist and one of the most humorous guys I have ever known. He could have made a prominent living as a humor columnist.

I was booked first class from Washington to Tokyo, which improved my attitude toward flying. Quite a difference from the first and last ride in the ol' bucket seat "gooney bird," to which I would soon be reintroduced. From San Francisco I took a Pan Am Strato Cruiser, the Queen of the Sky. With four prop engines she cruised about 300 mph. The first-class passengers enjoyed beds, 5-star meals, and a cocktail lounge that was reached by going down stairs into a very large plexiglass bubble under the belly of the plane. The technology undoubtedly came from developing the various gun turrets for the bombers of WWII. What a view! out over the Pacific at sunset. What a way to enjoy your pre-dinner cocktail. What a way to go to war.

It took about twenty hours to cross the Pacific. I recall that it was a while before I sank into a deep sleep. During that time the hum-noise of the engines contained symphony music which was very clear to me. It was not that I was programming and anticipating, forcing the notes, rather they came to me as if I were at a concert. I had no control over it, unless I did not want to hear it and changed to a new thought mode. I mention this because it was the first of many times over the years that I heard beautiful music before sinking into sleep on a long range aircraft with the engine drone in the background. All inquisitive "shrinks" please apply for an appointment. I must keep this orderly.

We took the northern Pacific route with a ground stop at Shimya, Alaska. My seat partner was a Dutchman with large interests in Indonesia, such as oil, copra, jute, lumber and tobacco. He was interesting and we talked "a world of matters" during the long trip. When we parted at Tokyo, he gave me his card (which noted that he was the Chief Mucky Muck of a large corporation) and said that after I finished with my Army supply job I should contact him if I wanted to have a profitable career in Southeast Asia (ifa, woulda, coulda, shoulda, hhmmm.)

I was met at the Haneda Airport in Tokyo and driven to the Yokosuka Naval Base. What a change had taken place since I was there six years before. The old Japanese cruiser was still soaking in its watery grave, but all else was much brighter and cleaner. The charcoal cars were gone and the gasoline engine was back in vogue. New buildings were up and there was scaffolding everywhere. I spent a few days at Yokosuka where I had some briefings regarding our Korea Mission. I drew my immediate needs: army gear, boots, clothes, parka, etc. and left my civilian clothes in a locker. I was driven out to Tachikawa Air Base where I boarded a bucket seat C-47, took off, flew over the Tsushima Straits and landed on the metal matted runway at K-9 airfield just outside of Pusan. I went to the Quonset hut terminal building where I was met by someone from JACK. We drove the 10 miles in the ever-present, essential, universal jeep over the old dirt and dusty roads, past the dry rice fields and the villages with mud or wood walls and thatched roofs to our small headquarters in On Chon Ni.

As a military unit we had commandeered several wooden buildings there for which, I understand, we compensated the owners. The building that contained our quarters and mess hall was an old Japanese style two-storey wooden hotel with tatami mat floors upstairs and wood floors on the ground level. There were hot springs in the area, and this hotel had been built around a garden that had a hot stream with smooth rocks running through a natural pool in the middle of it. It was not elaborate. A travel brochure might note it as "country-rustic." We slept on army cots in a large, open room upstairs. The Chief of Mission and his small staff had individual rooms on the ground level. Our offices and communication section was in another building nearby, under 24 hour guard on the outside. Inside, we rotated taking night duty, bedding down on a cot, with a carbine, next to the locked filing cabinets in Registry. In another section of that small village we had a warehouse and a motor pool compound. All the streets were dirt and created endless dust or mud depending on the season. At one end of the village was a small mountain with a historical park and a few monuments. There was also a Korean Army field hospital.

As soon as I settled in, the chief of the OSO told me that Andy Brown's operations had a priority for me and that I would gain a lot of experience quickly by working for Andy. He was one of the most interesting persons I would ever meet. Andy and I would become good friends until his demise from ALS in San Francisco in 1975. Somehow, we still are. Arsney Yankovsky, Andy Brown at first introduction, was born in the Maritime Province of Russia around 1910. He was Polish and Russian and part-Chinese. He spoke and dreamed in four languages, Russian, Japanese, Korean and English (heavy accent, great vocabulary). When the communist revolution moved across Russia, through some 16 time zones, it did not get to the eastern sector until about 1922. Andy, his dad, and two brothers moved into Manchuria. They had to leave Russia. They were kulaks (land owners); and, therefore, enemies of the state in the Marxist lexicon.

Their business was herding and penning wild deer for meat, skins, and cutting off the horns periodically to grind into a powder which men of that expansive region consumed for aphrodisiac purposes, the Viagra of its day. They also trapped and hunted. I have seen pictures of their hunting camps in the snow, showing many kinds of game, including the Siberian snow tiger, the largest in the world. They also took organizations on naturalist expeditions, including National Geographic.

Korean civilization had its nascent stage over 4,000 years ago, becoming the "Hermit Kingdom" around Kanghwa-do (island) with its own language, writing system (Hangul), and its own music and art. I recall seeing ancient ceramics, beautiful glazed grays and greens, made from a mysterious process that appeared to be cracks, like spider webbing, only the cracks could not be felt by rubbing the fingers over the smooth surface. I also recall the centuries old, beautiful love song about a broken boy/girl relationship, named Ari-Rang. China and Japan have influenced Korea over the centuries for sure, but it is neither one of those cultures. It has its own. It is Korean.

In modern times, Japan conquered and occupied Korea about 1905. This had to do with overall Japanese regional strategy at that time in history, including the Russian-Japanese war, wherein Japan showed itself to be a real power in the region. Japan took the Kurile Islands from Russia and thus became a strategic threat to Russia on into WWII.

From Manchuria, Andy and family moved into northern Korea and established a more permanent setting, continuing the business they knew best. When the Russians occupied North Korea at the end of WWII, for the agreed-upon purpose of disarming the Japanese troops there, and then going home, as the U.S. military had agreed to do in the South, Andy was under surveillance and he had a hard time of it. With his language fluency and engineering degree (he studied civil engineering and English in Shanghai) the Russians took him into analytical intelligence and used his talents. Now he had a long-time close friend, a Korean, call him Bear, whom he knew in the Manchuria days and who was back in his home area in Korea. Bear had been a Master Sergeant in the Japanese Kempe Tai, (thought police, or secret police). Andy had been planning for a long time to escape to South Korea with his wife Olga and his daughter Anne. He involved Bear who wanted to escape with his family also. And so they did, with Bear implementing the plan and obtaining (or stealing) a boat. It was 1950. They were picked up by a U.S. patrol ship and Andy wound up in the 24th Corps, G-2. After interrogations and reviews, he started to work for G-2. Subsequently he was transferred to JACK, where he started to build intelligence nets into North Korea.

Our commanding officer, the Chief of Mission at JACK, was Col. Ben Vandervort, a West Point graduate. A hero in WWII, he had been with the 101st Airborne under General Gavin. The 101st jumped into France in the dark early morning of D-Day. In the movie "The Longest Day" actor John Wayne plays the part of Ben Vandervort who broke his leg and was pushed around in a cart so he could stay in the action and command. After his leg healed, he did another command jump, this time in Holland, and he had an eye blown out in the fighting. This ended his military career, but he went into the Agency at some appropriate time. He was the best Chief of Mission of the three we had while I was there. He had a full range of leadership qualities and was reasonable and used his advisors. Sometimes when he was "chewing someone out" in his office, he would take out his glass eye and polish it in his handkerchief while he made his point. That was a real "attention grabber." I liked him and worked hard in that mission.

At different times and places, Andy took me with him to meet several of his compartmentalized PA's (principal agents). Bear, a large, 50-year-old Korean, I have already mentioned. "Dosty," who Andy nick-named after Dostoyevski, the great Russian writer, because of his high-minded approach to life, had been a major in the Japanese Army, and was a man of great enthusiasm and creativity. He was always cheerful and ready to start the victory march through Pyongyang. Chon, another PA, had also been an officer in the Japanese army. His efficiency more than made up for his dull personality.

Our little office there consisted of Andy, me, and Carroll Harver. Only 21, Carroll did the required office work, files, records, reports typing etc. I understand he had a full career and finished at a high level in the Inspector General's Office. Soon after, Nestor Sanchez, "Chico," ROTC, Capt.'s uniform, trained in armored warfare, masters degree in Political Science, arrived in the mission. He too was assigned to Andy's shop and we became very good friends which, I am sure, lasts to this day.

One of the operational nets Andy had set up in the northeast area of Korea was above Chongjin. It needed some re-supplies to be dropped (parachuted) at a designated, isolated (we hoped) point in the mountains. North Korean money, a radio, hand generator, rice flour, ammunition, clothing, and other material would get the ride. Nestor and I wanted to do the job together, and Andy and the mission OSO chief approved.

We sent out a radio message instructing the team to mark out a drop zone by lighting three fires in a triangle on top of a designated mountain at a specific date and time (about 1 am). They radioed their agreement. That afternoon I took a nap, anticipating the long night that was to come. When I awoke, I dressed in heavy winter gear with lots of pockets for extra ammo clips and chocolate bars (with nuts, of course). Thermal wear was not available yet, but woolen "long johns" and socks, leather jump boots and woolen shirts and pants would do the job. Art Biereman, our medic, came in and asked me if I wanted to take a couple "L" (lethal) pills along with me. The gruesome treatment the North Koreans gave their prisoners was well known. Only a small percentage would come home. In my case there would be no chance of that and at best I would end up dying in a Soviet Siberian gulag, after all the interrogations were finished. I thanked Art for his concern, but suicide was never in my lexicon. If capture was imminent, I envisioned going down in a shootout. Oh my, how idealistically noble. I never thought that all they would have to do was wait until I fell asleep in the snow.

With my wisdom of the years and my firm faith in a merciful God, I am not sure a "turn-back-the-clock" decision would be the same. Whatever, we headed for the airport, picking up two Korean team mates from Dosty's group to work with us. We briefed the pilots as to the drop zone on those three dimensional 250,000 inches to1 new maps*, and to go in low and slow (900 ft. at 90-100 mph). We went to our storage shed at K-9 and proceeded to load the plane, a C-47 ol' "Gooney Bird." We strapped on our parachutes over all of that winter gear which was topped by a parka, feeling like 600 lb. gorillas. We left the cargo door

---

*The new 250,000 inches to one inch maps were plastic, and molded to actually show the precise contours, gradings, and elevations of the land and mountains at 250.000" to 1'. One inch equaled about 3.2 miles. Colored in the normal graphic map hues of greens, tans, and brown, they were very helpful in understanding and developing a plan.

at the airport, and took off down the steel matted runway. It was about 20 degrees around K-9 and 40 degrees below zero in the region of the airdrop. There was no heat in the plane except in the small, two-seated pilots' cockpit. It was all aluminum, wings, floors, fuselage, and bucket seats, all metal. The overall descriptive word is COLD.

It was a clear, half-moon night just before Christmas and snow covered all of Korea. The DZ was about 3 hours away up near the Manchurian border. Some of the time Nestor and I stood in the open cargo doorway, hanging on to the static line and watching the snow covered landscape. It was natural to do this. Watching the terrain and talking with someone, or just being alone, was better than sitting in a bucket seat with an "inside only" view while the tension built. As we moved well into North Korea, and with good visibility, the pilot would try to follow valleys running north/south. That way they could fly a bit lower in trying to avoid enemy radar, if there was any. As we flew along in such a manner, I, standing in the open doorway, would see small clusters of light coming from a house or a small, very small village in the valley. As we moved on, the lights, slightly ahead, would go off until the sound of our motors disappeared.

As we approached the DZ, we started to haul the cargo into the large, open doorway. There were 3 Navy A-10 containers (long cylinders about 7'x 2' with a cushion on the bottom, a secure lid on the top, and a place to hook the parachutes on the sides) and one large cargo net bundle. We placed two A-10 containers on the deck to the rear edge of the door, side-by-side, with the third on top of them, and all the cushion ends slightly protruding into the slip stream. The cargo net was in the middle of the door, edging the doorway so it could be rolled out when the light went on. We had parachutes on all the equipment and hooked them up to the static line. I was sitting on the metal deck steadying the Navy A-10's. The triangle fires had been spotted and we would wait for the pilot to turn on the "go" light.

We were bouncing around a bit, as you expect in mountain country, and the A-10 underneath, against the back edge of the door, was moving out a little more. Some more bouncing in the wind and it moved out yet again, at which time I put my right foot against the bulkhead at the edge of the doorway, grabbed the lines on the side of the cylinder, and pulled to keep the cylinder in. Nothing happened and we continued to bounce. With the roar of the engines, that wind in the doorway, and the 40 below zero temperature I reached around for the lines again to pull the cylinder to a better set-up position, but somehow in grabbing the lines, I also pulled the parachute line which popped the chute in the doorway.

We immediately started to pull down the billowing chute and dragged it to the very back of the aircraft where we secured it away from harm. Had any part of it gotten out into the slip stream it would have billowed toward the tail and then pulled out the heavy A-10 and hooked on the tail. We pulled in the chuteless, non-deliverable, A-10 and secured that also. The light came on and we pushed out the other two A-10s without a problem, but the cargo net bundle got caught on one of the cargo door locking levers that were built into the floor. The pilot made a large circle to give us time to free the large bundle and drop it on the return pass, but it was too difficult working in the open doorway in that temperature, with our 600 lb gorilla outfits, and the plane rockin' an' rollin'. So we lashed it down to keep it in and headed for home, three hours away.

I had been pulling and pushing and working in the windy, 40 below doorway for quite a while. I had lost a glove. The saliva in my mouth was coagulating and breathing was difficult. I was cold to the bone and my body was shutting down. I lay down on my back on the aluminum deck and just breathed. After heading south for a couple of hours, I was still cold but breathing a bit better. I did not get any worse and soon I got up off the deck and sat in an aluminum bucket seat. Cold? What cold? Soon that nice feeling arrived, the one that tells you it's getting better.

We landed back at K-9 and unloaded the un-dropped cargo in a warehouse which we controlled at the airbase. We then dropped off our two Korean teammates and Nestor and I proceeded on the 10-mile, dark, dusty, dirt road to our Headquarters. Before sleeping, Nestor and I reported to Andy, who slept on the second floor in the back of the building. We called his name as we went up the stairs, as he told us to do. He always slept with a gun under his pillow and was aware of night noises. Well, we told him of the partial results. He was glad we were okay, thanked us, and said we could finish it later in the next new moon cycle. I slept until midday, finally feeling normal, thanks to sleep and a well-conditioned young body.

Dosty had recruited a group of refugee North Koreans (he probably said "Do you want to really make a difference?") to be trained, motivated, and dropped into a mountain area to set up a net and recruit, and infiltrate designated targets. In fact, about 90% of the Koreans I ever worked with were from North Korea. They knew the evils of Communism and were motivated. Not so surprising that the ROK Capitol Division, the best one in the South Korean Army, was mostly manned by North Koreans.

To start, we needed a training camp, on the outskirts of Pusan, with a classroom, dormitory, kitchen, mess hall, large courtyard, and a high fence all the way around. Building materials were scarce around Pusan. However, we knew the big ships, particularly the ammunition ships, left some lumber on the docks after unloading. Good lumber was required in the loading and shipping of ammunition.

The Pusan dock area for U.S. shipping was secured by the U.S. Army Provost Marshall, Military Police (MPs). I went into that area with appropriate "ID" and looked for the master sergeant in charge of stocking and controlling the lumber. Bingo! "Hey Sarge, I have my own truck and I need a lot of lumber to build a large, decent place for refugees and orphans" (now that's a good "grabber," right?) "Sorry sir, we are not allowed to release lumber. They ship it back on the empties." (Not so; only some of it.) "Sarge," I said, "You can help me put this lumber to the best humanitarian use. It's for children. I know you have kids, or you are an uncle and love the kids." "Yes, sir, but the regulations…" "Sarge, here's a fifth of Old Crow to show you I'm sincere and understand your situation. Next week, if I can pick up the first load, there will be a case of Johnny Walker scotch for you and your guys. With the last load there will be a case of very good bourbon." His smile lit up the dock area. "Oh that's great, sir, real thoughtful. You can have all the lumber you need. I'll sign the control papers." Gee, what a nice guy. "Operational" booze closes another deal.

There were some good carpenters and construction guys in that first class of 12 or so, and they finished the training compound quickly as I kept driving that "deuce and a half" and delivering the lumber in-between other activities. Dosty, ever the energizer bunny, assigned two or three of his staff to make sure the construction was completed as soon as possible. He himself was there much of the time, directing, instructing, and making it happen.

Everyone on Andy's team worked all day, seven days a week, planning, writing reports, studying information, meeting with PA's, supplying a couple of 25-ton wooden fishing boats at Pusan Harbor, planning ops for the spring, taking care of families of agents we had put into NK. What exactly were we doing? We were trying to run positive intelligence operations against the Communist North Korean Government.

Some guys who came to the JACK station I already knew. Big John O'Brien showed up at JACK. We laughed and joked about our days in the "pool" on G St. He was in OPC, the paramilitary section, and spent most of his time at a training island off the coast nearby. I stopped by the mess hall one morning for breakfast and there was Joe Hitzelberg. He was also OPC and had recently arrived. Joe was a good football player at Georgetown, where we were classmates and friends, along with Joe MacManus, who was trained in psychological warfare.

In our mission headquarters in On Chon Ni village we had a little bamboo bar and any member who was at JACK Hq. on any given night might stop in and have a "toot," a little frosting on the cake of friendship. Earl Evans was flying pretty high one night, and not alone. In good humor, with a touch of truth, I told him he looked like a catfish. This proficient observation was promptly agreed to by all the imbibers concerned with this profound and enlightening conversation. "Oh yeah?" he retorted, "You look like a damn moose to me." "Yeah. You bet. Hear, hear!" came the affirmations of the gifted. All chimed in and repeated the new nicknames in the give and take that followed. At early mess the next day the names were repeated, spread, and stuck, just like peanut butter. From then on I was "Moose." Even today, if I am in touch with one of those old friends, the name is Moose. Later, when I would sometimes write up and emboss my own travel orders to go some place in Korea, I wrote them out "Signed, Lawrence Fielding Moose, Capt. Infantry."

O.B. was scheduled to do an air drop to a paramilitary group in the general area of the "botched" drop in December. We did a double-drop mission and had two Korean helpers. The C-47, without the cargo door, as usual, roared down the K-9 runway as O.B. and I straddled over the large cargo net bundle laughing and joking as we took off. Surely our Korean team mates, properly buckled into their bucket seats along the wall, figured us as happy, or brave, or stupid. How about a pinch of each? The missions went smoothly and were completed about 2 a.m. We headed home without incident. From time to time we held on to the static line in the open cargo doorway and talked and watched the ever-changing terrain clothed in that beautiful white blanket of snow illuminated by the half moon.

One time I was scheduled to do a drop with three North Korean teammates. We flew out of K-16 airfield near Seoul heading north. After we had crossed the bomb line, one of the pilots said "Our Loran gear is out, we have to turn back." Loran was a navigational aid. I said no, that we could read the terrain by the moon. It was true. The snow covered the ground. The visibility was very good. It was easy to see a mountain target with a 250,000:1 3D relief map on your lap for reference. I had done it before, watching and helping out the pilot. But, no, the pilot's word is law in flight, so we "scrubbed" the mission and returned to K-16 where we stored the drop material in a room in a large building which JACK secured and controlled.

A few weeks later I ran that same mission again, using civilian American pilots from CAT (Civil Air Transport). This was an offspring of the old days in China in WWII. Gen. Clare Chennault had developed the independent Flying Tigers, freelancers who flew combat against the Japanese for cash. That was before we had declared war on Japan. Gen Chiang Kai-shek had a good relationship with Chennault who remained in China with his Chinese wife after the war. When they had to leave the mainland and move to Taiwan in 1949 in the wake of the Communist advance and take-over, Chennault was allowed to start CAT, the forerunner of the current China Airlines.

The DZ (drop zone) was up in the northeast corner of Korea. We flew out of K-9, Pusan. It was a clear, cold night. The heavy snows had fallen all over, beautiful, and dangerous. I briefed the pilots as to the DZ, winds, speed, altitude, etc, same as usual. I also told them to set a course/line for the target well before we got there, and to stay on the same course for a good distance after the drop, so it would be difficult for the enemy to ascertain the place of the drop, if they were tracking us. When complete, we would head for the Sea of Japan and swing south for home.

We approached the general area from the south, of course, but flew right over Chongjin City, the pilots assuming the city had no AA guns. I was holding on to the static line and looking out the open cargo doorway. Unexpectedly, Boomp! Boomp! Boomp! I saw the explosions of the AA shells in the sky. Boomp! Boomp! "Hey, they're shooting at us!" I hollered, more surprised than afraid. We didn't expect it. The pilot "zig-zagged" the lumbering C-46 and we were out of it 20-25 starbursts later.

He adjusted to the planned course to the DZ and went in low at 100mph. My Korean teammates and I waited for the green light and pushed the cargo out smoothly, thanks to only moderate air turbulence. We continued on course and elevation as planned. I stayed in the open door way after the drop, enjoying the beautiful winter scenery in the partial moon. An unmeasured time lapse rolled on as I watched, mesmerized by the moonlight on the undulating quilt of snow. Then I saw a wide stretch of ice, a very wide stretch of ice, a river, a wide river, all iced over. Hey, that has to be the Tumen River! We had flown into the Soviet Union! As I ran to the cockpit, the pilots, having realized it also, banked the plane toward the Sea of Japan and hopefully home. We got lucky again. I should have played the Irish Sweeps. Before long we were well out into the Sea of Japan, steering south, and "headin' for the barn."

Those CAT pilots were a cool, laid-back group, a mix of nonchalance and confidence. I recall coming back from an R&R in Japan on our CAT charter (C-46, bucket seats) flying over the Sea of Japan. Only about six of us JACK members were on the flight, which was also bringing supplies and equipment. I went up to chat with the pilots and opened the door. They had it on automatic pilot. One was sleeping; the other was reading a comic book. Were they good pilots? Absolutely. Just free spirits and loving it.

It had been a long, cold, trip and we landed at K-9 about 4 a.m. My three Korean teammates and I were tired and cold. Before driving them to their quarters and heading for On Chon Ni, I stopped at the Red Cross service building, open 24 hours, for coffee and doughnuts. The four of us walked in dressed in boots, winter gear, armed, and looking a little raggedy. No one was around except for the Red Cross attendant, an American. "Four coffees and some doughnuts please. Oh, that hot coffee will be great." "I'm sorry," she said. "It's against the rules to serve Koreans." Now I knew the reason was that they didn't want every Korean worker on the base stuffing away the free goodies with a quart of coffee every day. It made sense, but it was 4 am, the place was deserted, and I was in no mood for anything that sounded like discrimination against my guys who had just risked it all with me. "Look," I said, "We are very cold and hungry and I want some coffee for my men." "No," she said, glaring, "I can't do that." I bristled. "You give me that coffee or I am coming over this counter and get it myself."

Way over in a darkened corner was an Air Policeman, an AP sergeant. He came toward me. "Sir," he ordered, "your men will have to leave." I was "ringing." "We are not going anywhere, Sergeant. Who is the commanding officer of this base? I want to see him! Wake him up! What's his number? Where are his quarters? I want to see him! This is disgraceful! These people are friends and allies." He slowly acquired that "who is this guy?" look. He paused for time, and, I guess, not wanting to be involved in anything that might upset his commanding officer, he murmured, "Go ahead, Joan, give them doughnuts and coffee." "Sorry, sir, just trying to follow the regulations." "Many thanks Sarge, you're a good man, sorry for the misunderstanding." The coffee was great.

I dropped off my team and finally got to my quarters. I threw my clothes in the laundry bag, wrapped on a towel and went downstairs and soaked in the hot, smooth-rock stream and pool in the garden of that quaint, old, wood and bamboo hotel. It was almost dawn. There was much to do, but not now. As I sat there in the hot spring, reviewing the mission, I knew that Churchill was right: "The most exhilarating experience of the human heart is when the guys shooting at you… miss."

Western missionaries went to Korea long before the Japanese occupation in 1905. In fact some were martyred, along with Korean believers, around 1,700. During the Japanese occupation more missionaries were allowed to go to the northern part than the south. I do not know the reason, but there were many more Christians in North Korea than in the south prior to the Soviet takeover in 1945 when all religions were forbidden.

Then, many people were executed for continuing to practice their religion. In the south, however, many religions flourished. Father Rafferty, a Columbian Missionary from Ireland, arrived in that little village of On Chon Ni in 1946. He had been doing his work there for six years when we met and befriended each other. His little church was about 50 x 60 feet. The walls and roof were of wood, the floor was tatami mats. These mats were a standard measurement in Japan and Korea. Made of tightly woven straw, they measured about 3 x 6 feet. I think 6 tatami equals one tsubo (a Japanese/Korean area measurement unit). We might say how many square feet or yards is someone's home/property. The Japanese will say how many tatami or tsubo is it?

Of course, when entering the church with the tatami floor, you remove your shoes. There were no pews. We would kneel at appropriate times in the Mass and sit cross-legged or stand the rest. Father Rafferty had a parish of fifteen families or so, and a small school of about fifteen students. I am sure his garden grew well over the years but only God will know the full outcome. As it is said, the seed never sees the flower. From time to time I visited him for spiritual guidance, reconciliation, or we talked of war, weather, missionary work, politics, Ireland and more. From time to time I invited him to come to our mess hall and have dinner. Seldom did he accept, but one time he asked if he could bring the Bishop who was visiting from Seoul. Why sure. We had "a bit of the grape" before dinner and I recall introducing Andy to the Bishop as Andy Brown. He heard Andy's Russian accent and replied, "Brown? You mean Brownsky don't you?" We laughed. It was all very pleasant and we had a nice time. The next day Andy and I were chuckling about the "Brownsky" remark. "Well," he said, "You know who has the best intelligence system in the world, not Britain, the U.S., Israel, or Russia. It's the Vatican. They come by it naturally, without trying, being language literate and working a lifetime for a cause higher than self." He went on to say that the two highest avowed enemies of Soviet foreign policy were the U.S. and the Vatican, i.e., the Catholic Church, natural choices for any Communist country.

John "Mother" Murnane came across a clinic in Pusan that was run by some nuns and many helpers. There was a doctor and a few nurses among them. The lines of the refugees were very long, running the list of ailments and diseases. They needed medicines and supplies. Our own Doc Parker prevailed on his friends at the 181st Evac Hospital near Pusan to provide some of the basics. "Mother" did a lot of work for that clinic, as his time allowed. I went with him from time to time. Those good people at the clinic were at it day and night, and still the refugees came, mostly sick and very sick women and children. It was a heart-wrenching sight that created a recurring feeling of helplessness. "What's it all about, Lord?" came that question once more. The silence meant "Not yet." Big rugged Murnane had that nickname because he worried (making sure) a lot, the "kind, gentle, giant." Yes, he made a difference.

Several of us went on R&R to Tokyo: O.B., Chico, Dean Almy, and some others. What a holiday week! Not a tourist's venture, although we did learn a lot about the culture, night life, and good restaurants. I particularly remember staying in a small Japanese style, all-ground-floor hotel with gardens, stone bridges over pools of colored carp, sliding soji doors, tatami flooring, futon quilts, and polished wood and stone, nice, aesthetically in tune with the surrounding Japanese houses. It was there I first heard, in the quiet of the night, the loud *conk! conk! conk!* grouped in rhythmic 4 or 5 sets, then silence....then the "conks" again. This was the fire watchman striking two large hardwood billy clubs together as he walked his rounds. Years later, when I would be living in Japan and staying in and visiting small towns, the sound of the fire watch was very comforting. It reminded one that God's in his heaven and all's right with the world (at least in this town); go to sleep. This tradition grew out of the simple need, over the centuries, to guard against fire, a prime enemy when you cook and heat with wood and charcoal fires in towns and villages that are made of wood, straw tatami mats, soji doors, and inferior water systems. The striking of the clubs reminded people to check for fire risks, and said that the town looks ok, rest well. I also recall that in those small towns the police bicycled and walked their rounds from little sub stations. The walking fire watchers and police automatically coordinated in watching for fires and strangers in the neighborhood. The security was excellent.

Going back to Korea on the CAT plane which was carrying supplies and equipment for JACK, we met about six sergeants who were airborne rangers from the 82nd Airborne Division, and who had been handpicked for assignment to JACK. They would work basically with the paramilitary people, but sometimes train our intelligence agents regarding weapons, parachute jumping, and self-defense. I became friends with all of them, but especially Steve(?) and Tom Fosmire, who in later years would leave the army, join the Agency and rise to a high grade, for he had it all. While thinking "jump" I'll relate that Chico and I planned to do a jump on the safe, sandy banks of the Han River near Seoul. We practiced hanging in the harness, doing PLFs (post-landing falls), etc. but when the day came and we had the plane scheduled, we were ordered not to do it. The reason? If we were injured, who would replace us? Oh, isn't it nice to feel wanted and needed?

Our area around On Chon Ni had light remnants from the NKPA, which had been cut off from their support and command lines by MacArthur's superb Inchon operation. They were now trying to live in the hill country and play "hit and run" guerrilla warfare. On a few occasions we had guerrilla alerts. One time they tried to sack the ROK Field Hospital. They did burn part of it but were repelled by the ROK soldiers there. Another time, some five miles away, they sneaked up behind nine G.I.'s who were lined up and practicing on a firing range and killed them all.

One spring night there was a guerrilla alert. The moon was a blessing. The visibility was good. We went out the back gate of our compound two by two, automatic carbines in hand. Nestor and I were partners. We turned onto a small road/path which furrowed through the clustered, darkened houses. He took one side, I the other, walking slowly, looking intently, hand signals all the way. The short road we were on opened into a large grass, bush, and tree area. A two- storied building was off to the side. We spread out to cover more area, moving now in a crouched-over position. Suddenly there was a movement by a bush. We both pointed. I was a bit closer and crouch-walked toward the bush I was near. There was rustle-movement again. "Ungya!" I shouted in Korean (who goes there?) A guy put his hands up and stepped out. He kept pointing to the hotel. We could not understand him. We turned him over to the local police to sort it out. Turned out the poor guy had stepped outside the hotel to relieve himself rather than head for the faraway outhouse, and wound up answering questions from an aggressive police group. Talk about "it ain't fair."

One cloudy, black night Steve and I were going back to the JACK Headquarters from the airport over the dusty, dirt and gravel road in an open jeep. Steve was driving. I was riding shotgun. There were rice paddies all around. We were rumbling along by a small village on the right. There, in the outer beam of the head lights, we saw a Korean guy lying on the right side of the road. There was blood all over him and he was holding up his hand in a plea for help. Steve slowed down and as we came closer to him we both "actioned" the same thought at the same time: Ambush! It was too pat. The guy in the dusty road looked too alert in his pantomimed pleading. His eyes were intent, his hand was too high for such a bloodied victim, and the blood was too red. Steve gunned the engine, wheels spinning and stones flying, and I clicked off the safety, ready to fire. We roared away. No one shot at us. Later on, we figured the plan by the guerrillas was to take us alive and, of course, get the jeep. Otherwise, they could have killed us easily because we had slowed to a crawl, our jeep lights gave them an advantage, and we could not see them. I guess the "bait" was very disappointed, as he missed his chance for an acting career at the Kim Il Song Cultural Theater in Pyongyang.

I met Brian Moran, a Texas A&M grad, who was probably doing "rat line" operations for downed pilots from a crash boat and an island Headquarters on the west coast of Korea. It was customary, and mandated at JACK that all members, especially those going out on missions, live by the "need-to-know" policy and keep it compartmentalized. Anyway, we hit it off and I told him I would be going up to Cho-do (on the west coast) soon, using a 25-ton wooden Korean fishing boat. When we parted, he said he worked out of Cho-do and perhaps we would see each other up there.

About three weeks later Dosty and I went to Inchon and boarded the boat. It was a fishing boat all right, but concealed a 50-caliber machine gun and other firepower if needed. It had a huge one-cylinder Yakatama diesel engine that had to be started by heating the cylinder head with a blow torch. *Pungkata, pungkata, pungkata* (long a's) it sounded out, a noise well-known in Asia ports. We sailed for Cho-do from the 40-ft. seawall at Inchon, where we had been tied up, past Haeju city in North Korea, past Paeyangdo, another island the U.S. controlled and used for operations, and then turned north toward Cho-do. When I had left our Headquarters they had given me a duffel bag full of mail and supplies to give to Moran when I arrived at Cho-do.

Off to the west we saw on the horizon what appeared to be a Navy PT boat doing "flank" speed and heading right for us. I told the captain to hold the same course and speed, *pungkata, pungkata,* about 8 knots, and I took off my cap and stood at the bow, giving full vision to those with binoculars that there was an American on board. They came closer as we slowed down. They slowed down. Oh, lucky day, it was Brian's crash boat. They thought they might be looking at a North Korean fishing boat up in those waters and they were locked and loaded with two 50-caliber machine guns. As we slowly approached each other, I shouted that we had material for him. As our boats bumped in the open sea, with crew members holding the fender lines, I pitched the duffel bag onto the deck of the crash boat and waved goodbye. When we saw each other a month later at JACK Headquarters, he said his Korean crew could not get over how good our communications were; mail call in the open sea.

We proceeded to Cho-do and the little village there where we had a small hut with a kitchen and an on-do floor. This floor was made of clay and other material. The surface had the texture of linoleum, hard and waxy. It was about 15" deep into the ground and had 5-6 inch tunnels running through it. The tunnel started at the source of the heat which was a wood or charcoal fire in a stove or hooded container in the kitchen/ store room at the back of the house. On a cold night someone would be assigned to maintain a fire to keep the on-do floor warm. Many cold nights while in Korea I was thankful for the ingenuity of the on-do, another historical example of Necessity mothering Invention from centuries ago. From this hut we would now plan and execute an operation to infiltrate an agent onto the coast west of Chinampo in North Korea.

In the area of our hut on Cho-do island there was a communal outdoor rustic benjo (latrine). It was a deep, wide, circular hole in the ground with two long, parallel logs, about 18 inches apart set over it. When nature #2 called, aha, that was the place to go. The first time I walked out on the logs, dropped my pants, and squatted very low, so that my knees became upper arm rests, it was dawn. I was not sufficiently steeped in the culture to know if I should make eye contact and smilingly say good morning to the passersby, or just feign far-off meditation. I tried the latter while recalling the first time I saw a Japanese destroyer tied up at Yokosuka after WWII. It had two moveable platforms attached to the fantail that could be swung out so the squatting sailor could go out over the wash while the destroyer was underway, meditate, and return. A real cheap benjo, just like the one I was on. Why cheap? No reading material.

Andy had told me that whenever Dosty had to discipline a member of the group, I should not get involved but let him handle it. Dosty had been a major in the Japanese Imperial Army. Many Koreans had served in that army where it was customary for an officer to beat up an enlisted man for an infraction of the rules. The radioman, Chan, was a young man, newly trained at our radio school (Morse code, encrypting, decrypting, general maintenance and operations). In anticipation of the coming mission, and since he was just getting acquainted with the set-up on the boat, he practiced on the radio, calling the Headquarters near Pusan. It was an unauthorized transmission and could have been picked up, tying us to Cho-do and other matters. Dosty was furious. He called Chan to come in. He called Chan to attention. Chan braced. Dosty punched him in the face, knocking him down. Again. "Attention!" Brace. And Dosty knocked him down again and kicked him a few times, all the time shouting a torrent of curses about what he had done wrong. He told him to get out of his sight. Chan went to the boat. The next morning Chan came to the door and asked to see Dosty. He told him how sorry he was for having betrayed the trust that was placed in him, and asked for another chance to prove his loyalty to the cause. Dosty forgave him and walked outside with Chan, gave him some fatherly advice, and thereafter had a highly loyal, motivated crew member and radioman.

But it would be short-lived. Three or four months later Chan lost his life in a bombing attack on Cho-do. I was in Pusan at the time and Nestor contacted me from Seoul to tell me he was going to bring Chan's ashes to his home in a little village outside of Pusan. Two days later I went to Chan's home, met his family and expressed my sorrow. Shortly thereafter Nestor arrived by jeep and parked some distance from the house. From there he carried the urn, attached to wide ribbons around his shoulders and chest. Walking down the dusty village road, we, five or six of his comrades, formed a procession as the village folks looked on.

Arriving at Chan's home, Nestor slowly gave the urn to the Buddhist priest who placed it in the alcove where the other urns were displayed in accordance with tradition and fulfillment of the belief of ancestor presence in the house. The priest then performed a ceremony that included lighted candles and incense. After that he passed around a bowl of tea from which everyone present took a sip. Prayers were said, after which Nestor and I took our leave with bows and expressions of condolence to the family members and to the priest. Chan was truly a fine person, just 20, and died for a cause that was right, Freedom. May he rest in Peace.

Rewind now back to Cho-do a few months earlier. We began that mission with the agent/courier, captain, crew, Chan, Dosty, and Moose. We proceeded north in the early night along the coast *(pungkata, pungkata, pungkata)*. Some four hours later we arrived at the point, about two miles from the beach, to launch the agent in a small sampan with a crew of two. There was no moon. It was dark and misty. The west coast of Korea has the largest tide fluctuation in the world except the Bay of Fundy in Nova Scotia. That is why the Inchon Operation of 1950 was such a stunning success. General MacArthur wanted the element of surprise. He knew the NKPA would not expect an amphibious operation at Inchon because of the 30-foot tide. But more on that later.

It was an absolutely black night with no lights, radar, or navigational gear, except our compass. We launched the sampan and continued to move back and forth, north and south, at trawl speed as we waited for the crew of two to return to *Pungkata, pungkata*. We had told the agent that we would be back on the shore at a certain time and place to pick him up two months hence. If that failed, he was to attempt to filter through the battle line. I gave him a code word to use if he was able to reach and be "captured" by the American forces. I would then be notified and go to the line area and pick him up. So we trawled in that tight little area all night. We could not turn off the engine and drop the anchor because if we were challenged by a North Korean gunboat it would take too long to restart the engine, we needed instant mobility. So it was *pungkata, pungkata* for hours while peering into the moist black night and imagining many images and shapes, both friend and foe, while the boat pitched and rolled in the salty mist. Still the sampan did not return. At the first sign of dawn I ordered us back to Cho-do, lest the coastal watchers saw a fishing boat moving in a strange pattern. We hoped the reason for the sampan's unexpected absence was that it had missed the tide coming out and had been stuck on a sandbar, which was a common occurrence for such boats along that coast. Late the next day, under sail (it had a folding mast) the sampan came back to Cho-do. The agent had landed okay. Mission accomplished. The two crew men had missed the tide coming out and had to wait on a sandbar until the tide came back in.

Another time, I was doing some other work from the On Chon Ni mission. We were running out of time to do a certain planned sea launch up on the west coast in North Korea and I had to get on that boat soonest. I flew to Seoul, and from there arranged for a U.S. Army L-19, the two-seater designed for artillery spotting and observation. It could land at about 50 mph, stall at 40, and cruise at 80-90. Our "fishing" boat would sail south from Cho-do to a tiny little designated island with a tiny village and meet me there. Then we would proceed north on the sea-launch mission. The only problem was there was no landing strip, and we would have to find a place to land on that postage stamp of an island, with its bushes and rice fields.

I sat right behind the capable pilot as he maneuvered us around looking for a place to land, while that little tinker toy caught every breeze. Then we saw a trail that was used for draught animals and carts, perhaps just wide and smooth enough to take us. We would need almost stalling speed, having to watch out for ruts on the gravel and dirt surface. The pilot said okay, he would give it a go. Then we noticed there was a farmer on that pathway leading a tethered ox pulling a large cart. To give the farmer warning that we wanted to land there the pilot flew low over him, but he also was buzzing the frightened ox which bolted out into the rice fields, wagon and all, with the farmer running after it. We elevated, banked on around, came back and landed safely at almost stall speed on that very rough surface. Good job. I thanked the pilot and walked down the road with my gear, called the farmer over and apologized, and gave him some money, greenbacks, that universal goodwill medicine. He probably thought, "My, Santa looks so young." I trudged to the boat which was tied up nearby. Funny, I remember this part of the story, but not the precise mission.

On another occasion Dosty and I left Seoul by jeep for Inchon, over the Han River, through Yong Dong Po and out the road to Inchon. Our boat was tied up along the seawall and sitting on the sand which was exposed by the low tide. The crewman assigned to tend the lines there had done his job. The boat would rise and descend 30 feet every 24 hours. We climbed down a rope ladder, stored our gear, climbed up the rope ladder and proceeded to a Chinese restaurant Dosty had spotted on the way in. He wanted to talk and treat the "old man" right. The place had scars from the fighting. It was bare bones, cracked concrete floor, half a wall missing, and it was dirty, but one small area had some tatami mats and a low table. We sat there. The ratings specialists would give it zero for ambience, five stars for food, zero for presentation, and five for service. The only fresher seafood around was still in the water.

Dosty, about 45, was a good guy, cheerful, optimistic, and full of ideas to improve our intelligence mission. Sometimes he would come up with a plan, and after a lengthy discussion, Nestor or I might say, "That all sounds great, but who is going to pay for all this?" His heavily accented response always was, "Daas hokay, Hadqwuat pay" (That's okay, Headquarters will pay). Sometimes we fleshed out the idea for Headquarters's consideration, but often Dosty lost himself in his enthusiasm and we walked him down the cloud path and back to terra firma. Many years later when Mom and I lived in Japan and the Philippines, we would give a party for general representation or customer relations. She would plan it and tell me the cost, answering my "I'm not so sure" expression with: "Daas hokay, Hadqwuat pay." She enjoyed that story about ol' Dosty.

On another mission, before we sailed north from Cho-do in the late afternoon to conduct an infiltration, some 70 miles up the North Korea coast, I went to the U.S. Army major, Commander of that small island, who was also in charge of notifying the patrolling naval vessels of a friendly contact heading north and displaying the appropriate weekly recognition signals (such as three straw mats in a row drying on a line). I asked him to "clear" me to the ships for my trip. "Okay, go ahead," he said. We departed, *pungkata, pungkata,* pitch and roll, doing about 9 knots. An hour later we noticed a British cruiser out on the horizon heading toward us at a meaningful speed. I told the captain to hold his course and speed. *Pungkata, pungkata,* pitch and roll. The cruiser started to blink at us but I could not read it. Assuming we were being challenged I fired the required. Very pistol signal (flares) for that period of time (such as a red followed by a green). I told the captain to reduce his speed by half as the cruiser kept on coming toward us, and I went up to the bow and took off my cap so they could see a Caucasian on board.

I guess it was a slow day for the fleet. That British cruiser pulled right up alongside us. A 14,000-ton man-of-war and a wooden 25-ton *pungkata, pungkata,* side by side in the open sea. An officer leaned over the side with a megaphone way, way, up there. "Who are you and where are you going?" he barked. "We are cleared out of Cho-do. Major Oops was to have informed you. Call him and verify. We are going north and will return in about 12 hours," I shouted through the wind with my cupped hands. Then came the typical British understatement along with the accent: "We will contact him, but it's a bit dangerous this way you know, we were about to open fire." The Brits, I luv 'em.

We waved and resumed course and speed. The cruiser went back over the horizon. All was in good order and later the mission succeeded in the middle of the night. We judged the tide correctly. The agent infiltrated. The sampan came back and we all sailed *pungkata, pungkata,* back to Cho-do, seven North Koreans and me.

From Cho-do we stopped at Paeyang-do on the way back to Inchon. I had not had eggs for breakfast for a long time, and the "eggs-for-breakfast people" know my feelings. I asked the cook, i.e., the crewman who acted as cook, to go over to the village and find some chicken eggs. He was very happy that he was going to cook something special for me. It was early morning in that little five boat tie-up, and the next thing I knew I had a mug of tea and a bowl of garlic and hot pepper fried rice with two eggs fried hard right on top. Not so bad, except that he had fried it all in reused fish oil, I mean Ting a Ling style, change the oil every thousand fries. Well, I didn't want to embarrass the kid so I ate it all and smiled. He smiled. Ah, command is such a lonely place. The second mug of tea helped. When he had a chance to find some eggs in an island village again, I had him hard boil them in sea water. Excellent. Why are breakfast habits so hard to break?

A further gastronomic memory of that general time and place: We were *pungkata-pungkata-pungkata* coming back to a friendly island base from a mission in NK waters. I was in the wheel house. The crew got excited at seeing a school of porpoise playing off to our portside on a parallel course. It was fun to watch, as I had done so many times in the Pacific, Japanese waters, and now Korea. But this was different. They wanted to catch a porpoise and eat that traditional delicacy. Now in U.S. Navy tradition the porpoise is your friend, and will help you in the open sea in time of trouble, the myth and lore are well known. But my vibes told me not to disappoint my crew. I was in their waters, and their culture. So a cheer went up when I gave orders to slow a bit and edge toward the school. A baited line was cast out. They got a strike and when it struggled on the surface some 40-50 yards out, someone shot it and they hauled it in.

I reset the course and picked up the speed (oh, boy, from 5 knots to 9 knots) and turned to other things. In a while the crew bade me come sit on the deck and share the porpoise with them. They had cut every bit of meat from that carcass and salted most of it in empty burlap rice sacks. The porpoise is a mammal. The meat is red. The filet cuts which the cook barbecued on the hibachis (standard charcoal cooking and heating clay pots) were tasty.

Before that however, I, the big honcho and supposedly fearless leader of the ship, had to have the first portion of the delicacy of the porpoise…the brain. Now these guys probably expected this "big nose" (a common nickname by Koreans for Americans) to be squeamish in this situation, and I could read their anxiety and thoughts: "This is our delicacy, so what are you going to do, boss?" With stoic inner strength, and a smile, always a smile, I took my chopsticks and mouthed a large portion…" Mmm…mmm good!" (smile) "Ha, ha, ha, good, you like? More?" "Oh yes, (big mouthful) good (smile)!" Now everyone pitched in for the brain food, knowing the skipper liked it. Yuck! It was like a piece of beef liver with the texture of fine sand. I soon switched to the fillet, explaining I wanted to be sure all the crew had plenty of the delicacy.

All the while, as usual, the wooden boat was pitching and rocking, with the smell of the sea, the cooking, the fuel, the smoke, and *pungkata, pungkata, pungkata*…the sights and sounds of my "assigned acre," which I liked very much. Somehow, I was making a difference. God smiled.

10 THE COMPANY YEARS

Continued

ometime along the way, JACK Headquarters moved to Seoul, leaving a sub-station in the same "country-rustic" location in On chon-ni. We took over the Traymore Hotel, a western style, small, three story, brick and mortar structure. "Mother" Murnane and I shared a room on the second floor. Andy was going to leave Korea for an assignment elsewhere. Nestor would take over for him. I would continue to work with Dosty's group and Bear. Before he left, Andy, Bear, and I talked about a plan they had been hatching. It was in the "bare bones" stage. Now we would "flesh it out" a bit.

Shortly before and during WWII (more readily known in that region as the Pacific War), one Kim Mu Jong was a popular anti-Japanese fighter, a Korean patriot. He was known throughout Korea. Andy said if there had been a democratic election over all of Korea after the war, Mu Jong would have easily won. But the Soviets entered and stayed in North Korea and installed their Moscow-trained Kim Il Song, professed to have been a fighter against the Japanese. It is appropriate to note here that right after WWII the Soviet Communist takeover plan throughout Asia was ready to leave its earlier nascent setting, focusing on "their man" to emphasize to the people that he had been fighting the Japanese for them. Luis Taruc in the Philippines, Mao Tse Tung in China, Ho Chi Min in Vietnam, and Kim Il Song in North Korea are some examples of that broad picture. The U.S. wanted to see a democracy develop in South Korea, and was backing Rhee Syg Mon to lead that effort.

Mu Jong, who was not in favor of the Soviets and communism, did attempt to challenge Kim Il Song, but to no avail. Someone less well known and liked by the people might have received a typical Soviet "reward" for not singing the required song with everyone else; but they cleverly made him a General, and later relegated him to General-in-charge of artillery training, where he spent most of his time in the mountainous area of north central Korea near Kangyye, thus diminishing his political influence. His home, however, was close to the beach, in a small apple orchard just south of Chongjin according to Bear, who was related to him. That is where Mu Jong would logically go on his vacation time. The plan was for Bear, myself, and two members from Bear's group to paddle ashore in a rubber raft from a DE or submarine backup, on a dark, moonless night. Bear and I would leave the two others with the raft and SCR 300 in the securest place we could find. Then Bear and I would proceed to Mu Jong's house. I would lie down in some cover near the house while Bear proceeded to make contact. We did not know what we would find, but presumed the General would be glad to see his cousin again and would greet him accordingly.

At the appropriate time Bear would tell the general of his concern for him. He would ask him to come out with us now and he would be taken care of, and later, when unification would take place, he would have a chance to achieve his proper position among the Korean people. If all was going well, Bear would signal me to the house. I was there to show the General that Bear was in touch with the Americans. I was the "sizzle" in the sale. If he said yes, we would work our way back to the beach, go to the boat and use the SCR 300 to meet with the backup out over the horizon. If he said no, we would knock him out and give him a shot with a syringe. We would then carry him out to the rubber raft and head out to the backup. Bear was very sure that Mu Jong would want to come out. Andy asked me if I was in agreement and would do it, subject of course to final planning. Obviously there was more to go into the mix, I would see to that, but I said yes. (Yeah, I could make a difference). Imagine how we could play that defection back into North Korea and throughout the international press.

We studied and studied that area, planned and discussed. We used the three dimensional 1:250,000 inch maps and made our own for more detail. I came to believe I knew that place like my own home area. Today's brothers in such work will smile at that archaic approach, without today's sophisticated imaging, but the lack of adequate technology and the theater command structure dictated, "ya gotta go with what ya got."

We now needed up-to-date information on Kim Mu Jong and when he would take a vacation at his home near the beach. Bear went to work on that. He probably used someone he trusted in the "cover" of a smuggler to get information on Mu Jong and his intentions about a vacation. Smuggling was a good cover because it was accepted on both sides. I recall the first time I ever saw a giant Ginseng root. It had been a part of a shipment brought in from North Korea by smugglers. Once the battle line solidified, they were trading on either side, paying off on both sides, and developing more business where possible, the Asian way, war or no war.

While I worked on other activities, three or four months went by and nothing was happening, except I was still studying the maps and the plan. I had decided we would use a sampan with a folding mast rather than a rubber raft since it blended in with the usual small craft that comes and goes in that area. We also would have more space if Mu Jong had anyone there he wanted to bring with him and have the options of sailing and sculling. Also the maneuverability of a DE made it the best choice of back-up.

Then one day we got word that Kim Mu Jong had died of a heart attack. That was not at all unlikely. However, because the courier never returned, there were other obvious possibilities tied to Mu Jong's demise. We will never know. But that was a real disappointment. I really wanted to win that one.

Another plan with Bear was unusual and successful. He had a cousin, a medical doctor in the NKPA (North Korean People's Army). We learned he was in the U.S. POW camp on Koje-do, a large island, well off the southern coast of South Korea. The plan was to remove the doctor from the POW camp, take him to a deserted island nearby and train him in espionage operations for when he returned to his home area in North Korea after the war ended. The Koje-do prisoners were the ones who had elected to go back to North Korea after the war. Those who voted not to go back were at other locations. Only about 25% of the total NKPA prisoners elected to return to North Korea. The NKPR (North

Korean People's Republic) cried "foul" at the UN-monitored survey. But unless the POW was a dedicated Communist, or his family was not able to make it to the South (almost half the North Korean population had left), why would he return? The results answered that question.

As soon as I had the time I would develop that, but meantime it was winter. I was temporarily quartered in a large commandeered house on the northern side of Seoul, in the vicinity of the somewhat damaged capitol building, near the road to Wyjong-bu. A telephone message came in to our Headquarters at the Traymore from an exchange called Scotch Advance, which was a Marine battalion at the front line near Wyjong-bu. They were holding a line-crosser who had given the right code words and would I please come up and verify. I figured it was a courier we had put in up near Chinnampo from Cho-do island. John "Mother" Murnane and I drove north from Seoul on the Wyijong-bu road, that main route that the NKPA had used for their opening attack in June 1950. It was snowing hard, winter's answer to summer's discomforts. About two hours later we finally got to the Marine battalion we were looking for. It was policed by an Air Force AP unit. I don't know why. The Master Sergeant in charge asked us what we wanted and I showed him my travel orders, which asked for full cooperation to pick up a designated Korean and was signed by Lawrence Fielding Moose, Capt. Infantry. He said, "Come with me." We rode in my jeep, I drove, the sergeant next to me, and "Mother" in the back. At the gate of the compound an AP guard asked me for my ID, which I showed to him. He saluted and said to proceed. The Master Sergeant, his boss, said to him, "What's his name?" (meaning me) The guard didn't know, just going through the motions. "Be in my office at 0800," said the Master Sergeant.

We went to a holding area and found our guy, whom I recognized. Everybody was happy. I signed the papers and thanked the master Sergeant. We gave the agent some clean clothes to put on, and we headed for Seoul with the snow still falling and more to come. About halfway to Seoul, we saw lights from a stationary vehicle off the left side of the road shining out into the snow covered field. It had hit a tree. As we approached we saw an open jeep. We could see in our own lights that someone was slumped and lying down, from the passenger's side to the driver's seat. Before passing out he had pulled his field jacket up over his head because of the cold. As we drew close, I could see, through the heavy snow the collar of the jacket, lots of blood, but no head protruding. "Mother," I hollered, "where is the head?"

I stopped and then realized what I was looking at. He was unconscious. We wrapped him in some spare blankets and put him on the floor in the back of our jeep. There were two large holes in the windshield of the jeep. There was a trail of blood from the wrecked jeep to the middle of the snow-covered road. We drove to Seoul hoping the injured Marine could hang on. We asked the first MP we saw the location of the nearest field hospital. We had to drive all the way through Seoul, across the Han River to Yong Dong Po to the 81st evacuation hospital. When we entered the emergency room entrance, the nurse in charge said, "You found him up near Wyjong-bu? We have his buddy." Someone had picked up the driver, who was in worse condition, and left the other one because they did not have enough room. Both Marines had made those windshield holes with their faces and were going to need a lot of surgery. It was about 2-3 p.m. We drove to Dosty's place, where the agent would stay to get debriefed, and then headed for JACK Headquarters. "Just another day at the office, right, Mother?"

One night at the Traymore a huge explosion occurred. Mother and I jumped into our boots and pants, grabbed a carbine, and headed down the stairs, keeping low because of the smoke. We made it to the ground floor and started to elbow crawl, not knowing what we were looking for, but figuring we were under attack. Then I could see a huge hole that was blown in the thick, reinforced concrete floor of the dining room (mess hall) area. It wasn't smoke. It was steam. The boiler watchman had fallen asleep at another location. Miraculously no one was hurt, including that lucky fellow. I imagine we had cold meals for many weeks after that, but, hey, those C-Rations were just fine.

It was the usual cold winter in Seoul, which had been beaten up badly after two invasions from the north and two from the south. One Sunday I went to Mass at the Seoul Cathedral, the seat of the Bishop of Korea. The red brick cathedral was almost all intact and had received only minor damage from the fighting. No heat of course, but standing proud. I'll never forget, when we received Communion, two little street kids looked in the side door, and seeing everyone lined up to receive some "food," they came directly over to the priest, for they sure were hungry. The priest, who had helped thousands of these refugee kids, motioned to an altar boy to take them around to the rectory and get them something to eat. It was very touching and therefore memorable.

That second winter I was working out of Seoul Headquarters. I don't recall the connections, but Nestor and I were invited to a New Year's Eve party in Seoul. The hosts were a group of about eight men and women who were refugees from their home in Harbin, Manchuria. They were Russian by culture and Korean by blood.

It was an educated group. Most spoke English, and of course, Korean, Chinese, and Russian. The girls were very personable, pretty...and married. They had made up a complete Russian spread, including borsch, perogies, halumpkies, vodka, roast pork and special breads and cakes. I recall them telling us that some of their relatives had been moved by the Soviets to Azerbaijan in Transcaucasia. We snacked and sang the pedona, pedona, nosdrovia ritual for the first round of the vodka exercises. We all got a "glow" and before the meal started, shortly after midnight, we all went into the garden, sang and made noise, and looking up into the starlit night, feeling a buoyant warmth, despite the cold air, we "Happy New Year'ed" by hugging each other, and Chico and Moose, exhibiting their suave and mannerly style, fired their usually concealed guns into the air, a substitute in the absence of fireworks (which were not allowed). Back inside, the conversation about Harbin and Mukden became interesting and later the coffee, cake and brandy made the rounds into the wee hours. What a lovely group of people.

The Army fixed up the floor and walls of an old factory for a gym, hung some baskets, and when we had time, we arranged a "choose up sides" game of basketball. Those who could play, and knew how to play, were so rusty that the strategies on both sides were always "when I get the ball, I will shoot." Over some beers back at the Traymore we would give appropriate pronouncement as to who won the "gunners," "heavers," "never saw a shot I wouldn't try," and "ball hog" awards. All recipients immediately accused some other teammate as the just recipient. I'm sure that Prof would have joined in the fun.

The spring came and we could now do some more boat work, *pungkata, pungkata!* Nestor and I flew out to Sok Cho-ri on the east coast in the C-5, with Mac at the controls, to pick up our boat, another 25-ton wooden fishing boat with a radio, code pad, SCR 300 radio (walkie-talkie), a 50-caliber machine gun and some Garand rifles. We sailed north all night to get to Yo-do, an island under U.S. Marine control just outside Wonson Harbor, about 2-3 miles off the coast of North Korea. Wonson was pretty well flattened by the bombings, but the pilots and shipboard gunners had left a large, very high smoke stack to vector on. It was all highly visible in our binoculars, as were we to the North Korean coast watchers. We entered the lagoon at Yo-do about 3 p.m. and were ready to drop anchor and use the sampan to go ashore when the rhythmic whooshing of incoming shells started and would hit the land with ear-splitting explosions or a loud, crashing, "Baloop" in the water.

It was no surprise; they had seen us enter the lagoon and were ready to let it all go. I was scared. We were already in the sampan and the guy on the wiggle stick was setting new records. A few of the crew men stayed on the boat and steered it over against a protective high ground cover ridging a part of the lagoon.

As the shells were dropping all over the place, and we approached the shoreline in the sampan, I kept looking down into that clear water and then decided it was shallow enough to wade ashore (the frightened mind at work). I jumped in, boots, fatigues, field jacket, side arms, and the rest and went right under. I swam to where I could walk in, the sampan passengers arriving just ahead of me, making curious headshakes. We all ran behind some large boulders on the beach as the shells kept exploding in a scattered fashion. I sat behind the boulders shivering and shaking. It was the end of March. The water was cold. The air was cold. I was soaked and cold. The shelling lasted for a while, then stopped when two U.S. Navy destroyers were requested by the island command and came into the area to return the fire. What a sight for this "old" tin can sailor to see those two destroyers do a shore bombardment with the 5inch 38s.

We went over to our small winterized tent/office/barracks and I put on some dry clothes. Chico and I paid a courtesy call to the island commander, and later went over the mission with the boat captain and the radio operator. Our fishing boat would go up the coast at night with the agent to be infiltrated onto the mainland behind the island of Maeyang-do, under NKPA control and reportedly having a large gun emplacement. We were going to have a DE (destroyer escort) back-up out over the horizon in case we needed more meaningful fire power.

Chico had to get back to Seoul, so we boarded the boat and headed back to Sok Cho-ri. It was night and I was sleeping fine, becoming accustomed to the pitching, rolling, and diesel and fish smell of our "flagship" *(pungkata, pungkata)*. Suddenly, I had a nightmare. It was the shelling again, only worse. I jumped from there, my mind scrambling for a real thought, scared. I woke up Nestor, who was in a bunk nearby, and told him I didn't want to go back up there to Yo-do. He said, "Moose, you have to go back. Too much is depending on this." I was fully awake now and said something like yeah, yeah and went back to a half sleep, trying hard to sink into a better comfort zone. We arrived at Sok Cho-ri early morning. We said our good lucks and God blesses. He walked to the short landing strip and the waiting plane. We pulled over to the fuel facility to load diesel. I asked the Navy "motor macs" at the floating dock area to have a look at our "one lunger." Now those guys knew PT boats, crash boats, DEs and others. They smilingly looked over ol' *"pungkata,"* watched as our motor mac got it started with the blowtorch. They looked closer, thoroughly, could hardly keep from laughing, revved it up a few times, and said, "It looks okay, do you sail in this often?" I said, "All the time," and they got that "who is this guy" look about them. They gave us a pack of ground coffee as we said our thanks, seven North Koreans and me.

We went back to Yo-do and arrived during the night. In the afternoon I went to see the Colonel who had his quarters/command post at a high point on the island. He was happy to see me. He liked to talk with this "outsider." He could express himself freely and not worry.

He pulled out the map of the island and briefed me on the defense. There were trip flares along the beach at many places, machine guns' field of fire, mortars to catch them at the waterline He said the NKPA shelled the island almost every afternoon when the angle of the sun was just right to make it difficult to see the gun flashes. I didn't tell him of the watery experience of my baptism of artillery fire. He said they were lousy shots or they would have blown away his command post a long time ago.

The firing started later on when he was talking about how the war was, and was not, going. We had maps of the mainland before us and he gave his views on the strategy that should be employed to win it all. We were sitting in a large winterized tent. The shells were not very close, but with random fire they could get lucky. "Do you want to go to the shelter?" he asked. "Nah," sez I, "I'm okay" (big breath). So he smiled and proceeded. One swooshing "freight train" hit close enough that some very light gravel hit up on top of the tent, but he just kept talking and pointing to the map. Someone must have called for the destroyers because the shelling stopped. We finished up our conversation, both agreeing there was no substitute for victory and cursing the policies that were working against freedom for the North Korean people and a unified Korea.

He wished me well and the next afternoon I, and my guys, with the agent, headed north, *pungkata-pungkata*. We would rendezvous with the DE just over the horizon at the same latitude as Maeyang-do. We arrived there at dusk, and there it was, waiting in a moderate sea. What a nice sight. I only needed the DE to help us out if we ran into trouble. We had radio contact with them via our SCR 300 backpack.

I was in the wheelhouse with the captain going over the charts again when a crew member asked permission to test our 50-caliber machine gun. "Yes, of course." I heard the short heavy burst of the gun as I kept looking at the chart of the Maeyang-do area. I thought, "Good, the gun works fine." We were about ready to move toward our target area on the beach, waiting for complete darkness. A crew man came up from below and said, "Sa, we 'av hut mon." (Sir, we have a hurt man.) He led me below to a bunk where a crew member named Kim was lying and moaning, unconscious, with bloody gauze wrapped around his head and over his eyes. I lifted the bandage. The left eye was all torn and bloody. It was a mess. He had fed the ammunition belt as they test fired the gun and a piece of a faulty cartridge casing blew into his eye. He was in very bad shape and would not last the mission unless he had medical treatment beyond our first aid kit. What to do? Go for the mission and lose Kim? Go back to Yo-do, and lose the mission, and perhaps Kim?

I took the SCR and told the DE that I was coming aboard with a badly wounded man, and we would go through with the mission. I gave the SCR to the radioman, who spoke the best English. I told our captain that I would get Kim some medical help and God willing we would complete the mission; that I would be in touch on the SCR300 circuit and help them in on the SG radar. I had noticed the DE had SG and SP radar that I knew from seven years ago. We pulled alongside in the open sea. The DE medics lowered the wire basket stretcher down to us. Our little 25-ton wood chip was rocking and rolling and bouncing up against the 1700 ton DE. We tied Kim in, and our captain told him what was happening, if he heard, and they hoisted him up. I climbed up the Jacobs ladder they had dropped for me. I briefed the DE captain on the situation. It was dark now and our North Korean fishing boat headed for the beach area facing Maeyang-do at a slow trawl. The DE had a doctor on board! Great luck! In COM DES RON 12 we had one doctor for four destroyers.

They got Kim hydrated and sedated. The Doc said he did not usually give morphine for a head injury but this was necessary. Meanwhile I went into the radar shack with the skipper's approval, said hello to all, and asked for the SCR300 mouthpiece. I took a stool next to the Plan Position Indicator (PPI). From there I could tell if anything was approaching and from where. I also started to vector them into the chosen shore area. Often what would happen in these boat operations, a local fishing boat would be moving around in the dark, and, realizing another boat was close by, would shout a "Hello; are you catching anything?" "No; how about you?" "We were trawling a little farther out, but we are still looking." "Good luck." Common fishing talk around the world. To shorten the story, they got in okay, infiltrated the agent, and came back out. I told them to go back to Pusan and wait for instructions as the DE headed east and away from the area. The captain and the doctor had arranged that we would sail all night to go aboard an aircraft carrier which was conducting battle operations in the Sea of Japan. That was the nearest medical facility that could treat Kim. I was exhausted. I talked some encouragement as best I could to my wounded shipmate. His eyes and head were bandaged. He was barely conscious. I "crashed" in a bunk for a while, clothes, boots, side arms and all.

Just before daybreak I had some food and coffee. Oh, that Navy coffee, what an engine starter. Do they grow their own? I went out onto the deck and there on the dawning horizon was the carrier which Kim and I would board in the open sea. "What carrier is that, Chief?" "It's the Boxer, sir," he replied, "flagship of the task force." My thoughts jumped back seven years to our task force group with the Boxer. I felt some pleasant vibes that told me it was going to be all right. Kim was still alive. Now we had a better chance.

We would go aboard onto the hangar deck at the fantail (rear). Both ships were doing about 10 knots. We pulled up into position, keeping a safe distance, so that our port amidships was lined up with the large opening that we would be pulled into on the starboard fantail. The thick hawser line which would hold the pulleys and the harnesses was rigged and ready. The medics brought Kim out in that special wire basket stretcher used for such transfers. His head was bandaged, he could not see, and was groggy. In my limited way I told him I was with him. It was okay. "We are going on a big ship with many doctors and I will stay with you." But I doubt he understood much. He could not see, was in pain, and was heavily sedated for that and what was coming.

The medics tagged him with notes on treatment and strapped him into the stretcher hanging from the hawser, and then the rhythmic pull, pull, up, down, rolling waves, rolling DE; a wave almost hit him. They were pulling him uphill with a pull, pull. The main deck of the DE was about 14 feet above the water line and the hangar deck of the carrier was about 50 or 60 feet above the water line. Up, down, bouncing around, without his sight, could be a fright. Finally he was on board and they were taking him to the sick bay for treatment and x-rays. Now it was my turn. I sat in the harness hanging from the hawser line. Pull, pull, up, down, rolling waves, rolling DE. I looked up and along the edge of the flight deck, and other viewing spaces, there must have been 1,000 or more sailors watching. We were way above the bomb line in northern waters. They were all thinking, "Who is this guy?" It was show time, baby.

I was wearing Marine fatigues, jump boots, packing a Colt .45 and Colt Cobra, had not bathed for a long time, had a 5-day beard, and smelled like a swamp critter. I wore no uniform markings except a little brass U.S. pin on the collar and cap. A Commander met me as I swung aboard and slipped out of the harness. He said, "Admiral Suzak would like to see you on the bridge. Please follow me, and let me have your guns, sir." We started the long trek up to the bridge. I tried to engage him in conversation about the Panther jets on the hangar deck, but he would only say, "Follow me, please." The whole task force had slowed down temporarily for me. The Commander opened the hatch to the bridge. I "hunch-stepped" through it.

Admiral Suzak was there, and the skipper of the Boxer was Capt. Kelley. In Suzak's watchful presence Kelley said, "Who are you and what is your purpose for coming aboard my ship?" I said, "Sir, I have a badly wounded man who needs treatment and then a transfer, somehow, to an Army hospital." I gave him my name and unit to contact in Seoul to verify who I was. "And sir," I said, smiling, "I could use a hot shower." He replied, "We will let you know when we get a response, and Commander, get him a hot shower and some clean clothes, and stay with him." I shaved and showered, oh, the unheralded blessings of life. The shipboard Marines donated a clean set of fatigues. We went to see Kim. His head was heavily bandaged. The doctor said the eye was totally destroyed. He was on medication to prevent infection and pain. The shrapnel was near the brain and had to come out. He had eaten some food and was a bit better. I let him know I was there with him and went through my same limited comments about not to worry and it's going to be okay, though I couldn't fully believe that.

A quick response from our Seoul Headquarters to the Boxer said, we concur that is Howard Newhard. We do not know the Korean, but if Newhard vouches for him it is all right. Captain Kelley told me that when I was called back to the bridge.

The stern-faced task force commander was close by and watching. I turned to him a bit, while talking to Capt. Kelley and said, "Along with our regular intelligence procedures we come across OB (order of battle) information that we disseminate laterally to the fleet." I also mentioned that I had been a radar man on the Vesole DD878 when COM DES RON 12 escorted the Boxer from Norfolk to the Third Fleet in the Pacific in 1945. The admiral's serious "game face" softened to a kind, fatherly mode. He looked straight at me and said, "Thank you, son, good luck." We shook hands. I left the bridge. I was nine feet tall. The Commander walked me by the panther jets and answered my questions, gave me back my guns, and we had coffee in the ward room.

Late that afternoon Kim and I were again rigged for a ride on a hawser line, this time to an ammunitions ship. At chow time I was able to confirm the rumor that we heard when I was in the fleet: ammo ships get the best chow to discourage crew members from asking for transfers from that hazardous duty. We sailed through the night, and the next morning, in South Korea waters, we transferred to a Korean frigate bound for Pusan. When we docked, I cranked up our sub-station at On Chon-ni on the old combat phone system, going through an operator, imagine that.

Our own Doc Parker made arrangements at the 181st evacuation hospital in Pusan. He pulled some strings and obtained Kim's admittance. We waited and he showed up with an ambulance at dockside and guided Kim through the procedures all the way. I hugged Kim and said so long and rode to the On Chon Ni mission house with Doc Parker. I probably took a long soak in the hot springs. The next day I flew to Seoul. I had to see Bear about our plan for the POW operation and tell Nestor about Moose's nautical adventures.

First Nestor and I agreed that we should round up some friends and take a week of R&R, schedules permitting. About five of us coordinated the chosen week and took a CAT flight to Japan. We stayed in Tokyo and studied the nocturnal cultural life. We took language lessons, while sampling the finer Japanese beverages in the night clubs. The teachers were gorgeous. When we returned to Korea it felt like we had been away a few weeks.

Bear and I flew to Pusan and I left him in town while I looked for Larry McDonnell, "MaGoo" to close friends. He had agreed to help me sail a 21 ft. plywood craft with a 25hp outboard engine from Pusan harbor to Kojedo. This was an American made runabout and easily blended into the Kojedo docking facility which had many recreational boats for use in the area.

As mentioned earlier, the plan was to meet with Bear's cousin, a doctor and POW, and, if he was willing, take him off the island of Kojedo, to a small deserted island for seven days' training and planning for long term intelligence activity upon his return to North Korea after the war. Why not longer training? The answer will be in the telling of the tale. MaGoo was a Lt. in the Navy Reserve, he had been in underwater demolitions in WWII. I would not expect a fine ocean swimmer to come out of Kansas, but that was Larry McDonnell, from Abilene, Kansas. His father, "Six" McDonnell, had been a good semi-pro ball player in that region. At Abilene High School he had played the outfield along with a guy named Dwight D. Eisenhower. Larry was thoughtful, humorous, intelligent, and a good athlete.

We both agreed, "Let's get to it." We packed some sandwiches and water, took a couple of hydrographic charts, and in the morning, headed across that South Korea sea for Capri (our informal code name for that deserted island) to drop Bear off and then go on to Kojedo. It looked simple enough. As I recall, we figured five hours or so without pushing it. Capri was easy. But there are so many islands in that area. As we sailed our plotted southern course, we found it difficult to determine major island references, looking from the map to the course ahead. Different sizes, different heights, distance perception, and sea haze were all in the mix of uncertainty. Then it really got bad. The engine balked, and then died. The good news? The sea was calm. MaGoo talked to the engine while taking out the plugs and cleaning them, kicked it, talked some more, and it started to run on one spark plug. That was slow boatin'. A long time passed. We were out of sandwiches and water. It was hazy and night was coming on us. We were lost.

As it became dark, lights from the various and plentiful islands were visible.

We could not determine how far away any of them were, and decided to aim for the largest group of lights. We would ask them if we could stay there that night and ask them for directions to Koje-do in the morning. We were going slower and slower. We had not planned to be on the open sea all day. We were sunburned and in need of water. We finally arrived at the cluster of lights with a change of luck. It was a small U.S. army outpost. I forget what they were all about, but they had some boats and "motor macs." They might have been connected to the Koje-do command. We told them our problem. They were happy to have some visitors in that lonely spot, and we were in time for a late supper and some cold beer, which never tasted better.

The next morning they fixed our engine and gave us specific directions to Koje-do. I guess we had about 15 miles to go. The sea was still calm, and along the way, right off of a small island, we came upon five or six women diving for shell fish, conch, and sponges. An interesting culture was there at the time. The men would stay in the village and take care of the kids. The women would get into small boats, tended by a man, and go out and dive, using face masks. We were close to them. We slowed down to watch. "Choge isumnika?" I shouted (Do you have clams?) "Isumnida!" (have) came the answer. A couple of the gals swam near our boat, dove, and came up with some clams in their cloth tote bags. They dumped six or seven softball-sized ones into our boat. We offered some money and gestured we would give it to the guy in the boat, but they would not take it. Who doesn't want some extra money honestly earned? This was their expression of thanks to Americans who made it possible for them not to have to live under the Japanese or the communists, but as free Koreans. Those gals could stay in that water and dive for hours, while the guy tended the boat, sorting the catches of the day. Some "clever" remarks about the importance of women in the workplace come to mind, but I'm not going there, no way, not with you daughters listening to this tale. The clams? I cut them open with my knife and they were delicious, similar in taste to the chowder clams of New Jersey and Long Island. How could I have forgotten the horse radish?

We arrived at the Koje-do prisoners' camp and tied up away from the open dock area and general view, but near enough to the U.S. Army Headquarters building. MaGoo stayed with the boat. I went to see the Officer in Charge of G-2 (Intelligence). He was a Major. I showed him my travel orders from way up the line of theater command (no Lawrence Fielding Moose, this time), which read to "please provide him with any and all possible assistance." I asked him for a private place to talk. He was glad to see me. He was steaming. He needed a sympathetic ear for the venting to come. "Do you know what this is?" he asked, showing me a North Korean flag, about 9"x13" made of cloth. "Sure, it's a North Korean flag." "Yeah, but what's it made of?" and before I could guess, he said, "G.I. boxer shorts. These prisoners never wore underwear in their lives, and the UN inspectors come around and say we must give them underwear. They use it to make flags to keep up their morale." He went on to say, "We would not allow them to wear their hats with the red star, their national Communist symbol. Under the Geneva Convention prisoners become neutral and are no longer militarized, but the UN voted to allow them to do just that." Many in the UN worked for the Communist interests.

Unfortunately, the war was a UN operation under international law, although the U.S. carried about 90% of the burden in casualties and financial expenses. We were a willing party to UN "suggestions," so caught up in the law that we forgot about planning to win, which some of our U.N. "friends" did not want us to do. That is what got us to the absurdity of a peace table farce and allowed the North Korea Communists to continue to enslave their people and retain power, corrupt and cruel.

The Major went on to tell me that the UN periodically sent inspection teams such as UNCACK, United Nations Civil Assistance Commission, Korea, to see that the NKPA prisoners held in South Korea were cared for humanely. U.N. prisoners held in North Korea prison camps were not allowed to be visited by the U.N. officials.

One time they came up with the idea to keep the little dears busy. Let them work with their hands and make things. They brought in some 55-gallon steel drums (empty gasoline drums) and gave the workshops some hammers and chisels and other implements so they could make ash trays, lamps, and the like. Before long they made knives and spears to enforce the organization they had already established to carry on their disciplines inside the camp. They held "kangaroo courts" and even executed prisoners who did not stay in line. The Major went on to say, "That is the situation. They control their own captivity inside the fences. We know they have the means of transmitting information from one compound to another. Some time back, you will recall, the situation was so bad that one of our generals went there to talk to the NKPAs in charge of their own, to get matters back to a more peaceful setting. He walked in, unarmed, and they captured him. They made many impossible demands. The army called in several companies of paratroopers and in full battle gear they entered the camp and rescued the general. The international press had a field day. Here were the big paratroopers attacking the poor POWs. It was not true, of course, they just put on the pressure with their presence to release the general. But the press played it otherwise for weeks. Do you remember?" "I sure do, Major," I replied.

The watchful eyes of the NKPA group leaders controlling the prisoners was going to make my job difficult. I told him my mission on a limited, need-to-know basis. I gave him the name of the NKPA doctor I wanted to take off the island for a week. He worked in a clinic in one of the compounds with American medics and doctors. If we were going to take him off the island surreptitiously, we would need a good cover story for the time of absence to avoid suspicion by his "comrades." We talked to the American doctor in charge. I gave him a limited briefing, emphasizing absolute secrecy, and asked him to bring out our subject under the pretext of consultation in seeing a sick American, who possibly had a rare disease found only in that area of Asia. I met the doctor, Bear's cousin, in a small room, alone. I gave him Bear's name and talked of our friendship. He spoke good English. I outlined the plan. We would transport him by boat to a small island to be with Bear for a week. I emphasized that we wanted to free his homeland from the Communist devil. He was a Christian. He agreed. I also emphasized that Bear was waiting to meet with him. I called in the chief doctor and the G-2 Major and we, mostly they, set up a plan to make our North Korean friend "sick," (fever, chills, and weakness). He would be removed from his quarters and taken to the main clinic and "isolated." They would write it up as a possibly contagious disease. They gave him a shot and in the morning he would have the mild symptoms mentioned (he could fake the rest). The clinic staff would come looking for him, take him out to go to isolation, the Doc in charge watching carefully, but on the way I would take over, give him some clothes to cover his POW outfit, and walk him down a secluded path to our little boat, and Larry MaGoo.

It worked as planned. The Doc got aboard and went into the little cabin and I sat in the back with MaGoo who started the engine and slowly headed out of the area, two Americans on the usual boat outing. Half an hour later we set course for that deserted island, Capri. It was fairly small and well-vegetated. There was a well-built concrete and steel two-storied gun emplacement there. It would serve as the training and living quarters. The gun had been dismantled and taken away after the Pacific War. Well, Bear and his cousin had a nice reunion. Now the former Kempe Tai sergeant would teach the Doctor about espionage, communications and security, and go over a long-term plan for his intelligence activity after he returned to North Korea.

I sailed back to Capri by myself when the seven days were up. I picked up the Doc and took him back in the way we came out. En route to Koje-do we had some time together. He was pleasant and solid, the manners of a gentleman. Suprisingly, he had been a motorcycle enthusiast before being drafted. He knew about the Harley Davidson bike. We spoke of many things: life, family, politics, American jazz, the war and our ultimate victory with a unified, democratic Korea. The chief doctor took over when we arrived and "released" him from isolation. He was pronounced well enough to resume his duties and join his NKPA comrades. But I was long gone before all that. Many years later, long after I left the Company, I visited MaGoo in Maryland. He told me that at one point on his career path he had served as the Chief of the Korea Desk, and that the Doc had been productive a long time. Then one day it ceased. Nothing more was heard from him. It could have been a natural death. His communication link might have been severed or compromised. There were many possibilities; we just didn't know.

I had to go to Yo-do to check on some matters and left Sok Cho-ri by boat (what else?) *pungkata, pungkata, pungkata,* the night ferry right up the North Korea coast. We arrived in the morning and tied up at a dock in the lagoon. I looked up to where we had our Headquarters winterized tent, and there, running down the sandy hill to greet me was Kim, he was so happy to see me. He would not let me carry my duffel bag. His glass eye was a perfect match. I, too, was happy, and glad to see him well again. He kept bowing and thanking me to a point where I was uncomfortable, but I didn't show it. I had not yet lived in Asia long enough to know the ways, and develop my "transfer button" in unfamiliar situations; but I lived there long enough to know the basic rule that says do not cause embarrassment. I waited and stayed caught up in his enthusiasm and gratitude until he was satisfied with his full expression of thanks. Then, feeling a growing joy, I came to realize I had made a difference, and as the discomfort left me, I bowed to him and shook his hand, not only for friendship, but for helping me to learn something about myself.

I went to see the commander of the island and then I walked around and scanned the nearby North Korea coast. A group of young Marines were on duty in a large open slit trench. We talked about common matters, the war, the shelling, island defense, waiting to go home on a 6-month rotation. They always spoke to me using "sir." Finally I said, "Please don't call me sir; I'm a civilian." "A civilian? What are you doing here? Why don't you go home?" "I will when the war is over." I went on, "Why are you here?" "Well, we're here to fight the gooks." They were thinking, "That's what we're supposed to do, Semper fi." They had little knowledge of what it was all about or why they were there. From the time the Korea war started and General MacArthur called into immediate action the lightly trained barracks troops of the Occupation days, who had become a bit soft, living the good life that was readily available, I can assure you most of them didn't know why they were there. Even the rank-and-file troops sent from the States didn't know why they were there. Many of them were draftees and had not been in service very long. They should have been instructed about the evils of Communism, a short history of Korea, and the subjugation of Korea in recent history.

The Pusan Perimeter had developed because we were out-manned and out-gunned in the initial phase of the war. But the thought prevails that almost all of our troops did not know what it was all about. Those were the circumstances when General Walker issued his famous "Stand and Die" order in those dark Pusan Perimeter days.

Certainly those who carried the heaviest of the load early in the war, and those brave heroes who did not return, should have been told what it was all about, and why they were there. One aspect of the answer had to do with Congressional interference. In 1950, or 51, Senator Fulbright was the head of the Senate Armed Services Committee. The Joint Chiefs of Staff recognized the problem: Troop attitude, motivation, and morale is affected by lack of knowledge about the overall mission, i.e., why am I here? So the Chiefs planned to have the troops lectured on the politics of the world, Communism, democracy, Stalin, Kim Il Song, etc. Fulbright heard about it and wrote a searing letter to them saying he would never allow military leaders to teach political matters to the troops. It was dangerous, he claimed. Well, many melodies make up the full orchestration, and there is myth and reality, images and true pictures, but in the final analysis, if you are sending troops into combat and they do not know what they are there for, and risking their lives for, then you do not deserve to be the Commander in Chief, or the head of the Armed Services Committee. How many of the 120,000 casualties and 50,000 KIAs could have told us why they were there? How many in those groupings had motivational problems because they did not know why?

Times have now changed regarding this matter because we have a professional all-Volunteer Armed Force (VAF), but if we have to go back to a military draft, that experience should not be repeated. In fact it will be highly necessary to teach the "whys and wherefores," given the low level of government, civics, and American history knowledge the average high school senior possesses. Why is that?

I recall some fun times at the little bar in the Traymore when some of my buddies happened to be there at the same time. Dean might break out his guitar and give us his 5-chord repertoire of western songs, cowboy, that is. The two of us composed and sang "Cobalt Blues" (never published, heh, heh). One tune that made the rounds, sung in country-western style was "Itazuke Tower." I still remember the words: *"Oh Itazuke tower, this is nine seven niner, and I'm about to freeze. My canopy's blown off and the engine keeps missing; Landing instructions, please. Oh, nine seven niner this is Itazuke Tower. Sorry for you old friend, but the General's coming in with a plane load of Brass. You'll have to go around again."*

We kept working on our operations. The war was going to wind down and it was going to end without a unified Korea. The geopolitics of the time in that Northwest Pacific area cried out for a unified Korea. It still does. A unified Korea would been self-reliant with hydro-electric power, timber, and some minor mineral resources in the north, heavy agriculture in the south, and good fishing all around the peninsula. That Naktong Valley was the "rice bowl" of the country. Another reason for the importance of unification at that time in history was to provide a substantial buffer zone against Communist China and the Soviet Union. Our foreign policy in the Cold War vs. the Soviet Union was containment/encirclement. Russia was not going to go to war, or chance a nuclear war over little North Korea. They were too busy in those days solidifying and communizing their hold on Eastern European countries which the U.S. allowed them to continue to occupy after WWII. They were an economically weak country in those days and had very little military power in the Maritime Province.

Communist China had used her best and only mobile troops to fight in Korea. She didn't have anything left to put into the Korea War. We had control of the sea and the air and we could have gone back to the Yalu and secured the country. Why didn't we? Did our enemies in the UN have something to do with it? Did the media influence public opinion? Did the UN really help us in our cause?

Another reason to have a unified Korea was that Japan, for the first time a democratic country, was starting to rebuild its industrial strength and a nearby democratic neighbor with raw materials and a future growth potential would make a good "win-win" situation, and provide a solid containment buffer, fitting nicely into our foreign policy, or what was supposed to be our foreign policy.

Well, the average person was misinformed and did not know what it was all about concerning that "forgotten war." The left (communist-influenced) element of the media, had done its job well, postulating that the war was three years old, and, well, let's settle for the old line of demarcation, we have lost so many now, etc., etc. The déjà vu chimes ring loudly, as one follows our current history, while our casualties and KIAs cry/cried for justice and victory.

Most people were now convinced to "call it quits." "Bring the boys home" was the popular cry. Eisenhower, our hero, he of the "unconditional surrender" philosophy and the "no substitute for victory" West Point mold, ran for the Presidency on the "Bring the boys home" platform, to fit the mood of the time which the powerful media had developed, and, of course, obtain the Vote. He even went to Korea in October 1952, just before the U.S. elections, to see President Rhee Sygh Mon and visit the troops, his first step in the "giving up" process.

I was in my jeep driving the road along the Han River in Yong Dong Po the night Eisenhower arrived. His small motorcade passed by on its way to Seoul from the old Chinampo Airport. None of us were happy. I didn't know anyone American, or Korean, who didn't want unification. Rhee, of course, wanted unification and hoped to be president of all of Korea. He was always arranging for demonstrations to be held to support reunification. "Pukchin, pukchin!" (go north, go north) chanted the demonstrators in powerful, rhythmic unison, while jogging through the tightly packed streets of Seoul. These massive demonstrations were impressive. They went on day after day. Almost half of the people had left North Korea when the battle lines were broken and shifting up and down the peninsula. They, and the South Koreans, hated the Communists. They wanted unification and freedom,

Now I am not suggesting that Rhee Sygh Mon was our man in the long term. He was the only horse in the race at that time because he kept it that way. He professed to be a long time fighter against the occupying Japanese (1905–1945), providing "cheerleader" support for many years from his comfortable "digs" at Princeton University where he had earned his doctorate, absorbing our culture and becoming friendly with FDR and others whose support he cherished. But he ruled with an iron hand disguised in a friendly glove. Because of this, he was not as popular as the questionable number of ballots reported; nor was his Austrian wife, who looked so out of place on special occasions, wearing the formal high-waist, long-skirt, flowing-sleeves dress of the Korean culture.

Mike, a radio instructor who the Company trained abroad and sometimes a translator/interpreter for me, a possible team member in the planned Kim Mu Jong action, had a brother who ran for office as a Congressman from the Pusan area. He was in a political party that opposed Rhee. He took a flight to Seoul one day, was picked up on an "attempted assassination" charge and put in jail, where he was regularly beaten. Mike went to see him and was devastated. He asked for my help to somehow save his brother. I was sad and empty because there was no way I could help him without compromising myself, my missions, and JACK. We were good friends. His brother died in jail from the beatings; such is the dictator's way.

A popular candidate in a fair election would have replaced Rhee in setting up a democracy in all of Korea. It was in our power to win the war and help implement the peace (see Appendix B: Korea Lesson. In War, If You Don't Win, You Lose). But it was the politics at home, not national security, nor the geopolitics of the N.W. Pacific, that determined that hurtful decision. We are still paying the price for the way Korea was handled, and you ain't seen nuthin' yet. The Communist brothers help each other openly at times, covertly at others, but their bond of the perceived common good is always there, and our strategies should be developed accordingly.

Korea was the first war in which we compromised our principles. It was a just war, fought for a noble cause. Some of the UN and most of the media manipulated the minds of our populace to the point where no one got angry or outraged with "wimpy Washington" settling for a draw. It was a very bad mistake. We who were there knew it. A few Chicom divisions in north central Korea would fake a frontal assault to the south again, as if to start a major campaign. The whole intention was to get the bells and whistles going off all the way back to Washington to get assurance we were really sincere about quitting and sitting at the peace table. They did that two or three times. They played us like a violin with the help of much of the media, some of the UN, and other friends. Now, fifty-four years later we are still dancing to the changing tunes that North Korea chooses to play in the political/war-plan arena, while we ask their Communist ally, China, to help us negotiate with them. Many feel it wasn't even a draw. They won, and are winning. Why?

11 | AFTER KOREA

What's Next?

In July, 1953, the firing ceased and peace negotiations started. The Korean people would not be re-united as the northern part remained dominated by the communist regime of Kim Il Song. The Central Intelligence Agency was a young, inexperienced, developing organization before and during the Korean War. Our mission there was, naturally, under much pressure for immediate results. Our case officers had to learn their area and language knowledge on the job, a poor approach at best. But there was no other way, and the determination and spirit of those participating was exemplary. I did not think about it then, but years later, I have always been proud to have been a part of that group.

Andy came over from Japan on a survey. We talked. He congratulated me for my work. "Ol' piss and vinegar" would have been proud. (I had never seen him again, nor knew his name.) We went to see Dosty, and then Bear. It was a sad time, but buoyed up a bit by the determined character of all concerned. Bear, who was about 50, told Andy that when he first met me (at 24), he was not enthusiastic that we would work well together, but as time went on he realized that he had never seen anyone work with such determination and effort, and he became pleased with our teamwork and friendship. That meant more to me than any "atta boy" the Company might have provided. I worked my heart out in Korea. Generally, but with exception, it was 24/7 with breaks to sleep, eat, and listen to radio Moscow and USAF radio around 9 p.m.. At one stretch, working out of On chon-ni, I was feeling very tired, which culminated in falling asleep with my head on the breakfast table in the mess hall. They put me to bed. After the examination Doc Parker said, "You're lucky, you're the type who doesn't get a nervous breakdown, but just runs out of gas." After 3 days sleeping on my cot, all was well.

Andy and I talked of the whole Korea situation, and the future of the Cold War. I recall his comment that, in addition to the educational arena the Soviets had long since had agents which influenced much of the information/media and entertainment spectrums of the U.S.A.. The name of the game is psychological warfare (psy war), designed to influence the way the populace thinks and feels about a variety of chosen subjects. Through this, the Soviets cleverly worked on the irrefutable themes, that this is a free country, the people have the right to know, and "sunshine" must encompass all government activities. This influenced the laws to be friendly to openness, which is good; but even in very sensitive matters, which is not good. Therefore, working from that base of complete openness, Congress, the media, and others will peel back the "secrets onion" layer by layer. That was 1953. Andy knew, and we have seen it happen over the years. The Soviet Union is now gone but Communists and other obvious enemies prevail and know the "psy war" game.

I would soon leave for D.C., and looked forward to vacation and then language training and area studies for the Northeast Asia region. We had stopped on a small knoll overlooking the Han River; it was a pleasant summer day. I was troubled because I had never told my Mom or Dad about what I did or what I was doing. Andy showed surprise, saying, "Moose, when you get home tell them once, in a couple of sentences, but tell them." We drove back to Seoul, said our goodbyes, and agreed we would touch base somewhere down the road.

U.S.A....SOME READJUSTING

Soon after, I checked out of the Mission Headquarters, flew to Japan on CAT, changed into strange-feeling civilian garb, and flew first class, so much more appreciated now after 22 months in a war zone, to D.C. I spent some time at the Korea Desk being debriefed, writing reports, taking the end-of-tour polygraph, adjusting to the routines, and finding a place to live. It was evident that it would be necessary to lose some of the acquired rough edges, if possible.

I had one month's leave, and was homeward bound, in this comfortable Penn RR coach (oh, everything was cozy in the land of milk and honey). I had taken this ride a few times while at Georgetown, but now there was a difference, that had to do with my re-adjustment to this society of my birth. At home, Nana asked me to shop for some groceries. The multiple choices for bread and other goods against the background of the vivid memories related to my time in Korea were astounding. I found myself covering my resentment of how good it all was. Remaining polite, I didn't like these loving people trying to please me with special foods, clothing, presents, and general comforts. I eventually worked through the whys and wherefores of it all by myself. It was not the kind of thing that was talked about, and counseling then was an extreme, not general, consideration.

Tied into my overall mindset at that time was some dilution of my spiritual sense. During my stay at home that month, Nana noticed some changes and commented about faith and hope and God's overall goodness. Thinking of the conditions in Korea, I recall replying, "Well, he hasn't done a very good job." (Oh, bite my tongue, I hurt her.) There was more than "rough edges" to consider.

While I was away, the New Jersey Highway Dept. decided to build the Garden State Parkway. They needed a thin strip of the Water Company property, a proper use of the Right of Eminent Domain which is so abused and discriminatory to the landowner today, so they moved the house down Morris Ave. to an area across from the Suburban Golf Club entrance.

We had some nice parties and dinners and times to just hang out with family, relatives and friends. I picked up lost time with Digi and Bob Teuscher; Joe and Julie had moved on to Chicago. I bought a new car and Nana and Pop-pop and I broke it in on a drive to Florida, We got a lot out of the trip. I was 26 now and we three adults got to know each other better.

We almost had a big disruption of plans. It was late evening and I was driving through the Okefenokee Swamp in Ga., going a good clip, along a desolate stretch when a big buck deer jumped out of the brush into my light beams. He was on the right side of the road, made a quick motion to cross, then "shake and bake" stutter steps, and jumped back off the road. WHEW, we never forgot it.

We went to St. Augustine, Vero Beach, across to Clearwater, then up through the Carolinas and home. It was October 1953, and I have fond memories of that trip. We had nice ocean front accommodations in Vero and sat on the beach, walked, talked, and Dad and I threw a ball back and forth (like from the time I was 5). We looked out at sea and saw all the shrimp boats moving around, and some coming in, so, FLASH, "I will go down the road to a restaurant and get us some fried shrimp to go, and we will eat it right here on the beach." Whistles and applause followed, and I proceeded as planned. "Three large orders of fried shrimp with slaw and fries," sez I. "You got it!" and she started to take shrimp out of the freezer. "But don't you have them fresh; I see all the boats out there." "Oh no, we get all of our shrimp frozen, and those boats out there sail straight to the freezer and are under contract." It was great eating anyway, but it shows how the increasing demand forged a system of distribution, even then.

Dad and I eagerly took to the surf. Not as good as Long Beach Island in season on the Jersey coast, but it was great. We even had a lot of porpoise milling around out there. Mom, a non-swimmer, just took it all in and was very happy. The kid was back.

The good and lasting memories of the trip were not places and things, but just being together and enjoying that companionship. None of us forgot it.

Upon returning to D.C., I looked up OB and Brian and moved in with them out in Glass Manor. Some time after, OB met a lovely girl and married. He left the Agency and pursued a successful career with Mutual of New York (MONY). Two other guys returned from Korea and we all shared the apartment in Glass Manor for a while.

I was reporting to the Korea Desk and doing various Headquarters tasks as assigned.. The Chief of the desk called me in one day and said, "They have a case officer project for you in Japan." "What's the cover?" I asked. "You will work out of the Embassy." "But I want to speak Japanese before I go there, what about language training?" "That's okay; they will put you in touch with an English speaking PA (Principal Agent)." I thought it over for a day and then turned it down. Reason: No language preparation. Working with an English-speaking PA, and not knowing the language, is like walking with a crutch when you really need full mobility. I moved to the Japan Desk and continued with perfunctory tasks. They sent me to language training for a few hours a week, given by an old American whose reference book was written in Romaji (phonic transliteration to English letters). About five years later, having left the Agency, I studied basic Japanese at the Maryland U extension program in Misawa Air Base, Japan. We learned Hiragana from the beginning, so I could phonetically write, in Japanese, everything I could say. A Japanese teacher conducted the class.

I moved into a large apartment on Connecticut Ave. with Magoo, Art Rosen,

Brian, and Bob Coughlin, all former JACK devotees. We had a party every Saturday night that usually lasted more than a while. The Salty Dog was a popular drink for some of us. The girls were pretty and the music cool. Most times we would end the evening watching MaGoo (off with the shoes) do interpretive dancing to Aaron Copeland's inspiring Appalachian Suite, and cheering him on in our state of imbibement.

I saw Ed George in one of the hallways at Headquarters. An excited exchange ensued. "Hey I got married while you were away!" "To Chickie?" "No, to her mom, Libby." Well, that was great news. They were both super people with great human qualities, and they were a fine match for each other. We had some nice times there in DC and from time to time I dated Chickie who was pretty, fun, and had the personality of an aspiring actress.

While I was waiting for something to "happen" in my career, they sent me for a potpourri of ops training at "the farm" in Virginia. It was nice to see other friends from Korea days, Tom and Steve, who were there at the "farm" with some other former airborne rangers to demonstrate their expertise, along with demolitions etc. It was a hodgepodge of some 22 people at different career stages and job descriptions. I learned some new things and refreshed on others. Having been trained by Andy and worked with Bear and Dosty on the job, I was a bit advanced for that program but I realized it should be on my 201 file.

Most mornings at the "farm," I ran with Tom and Steve and a couple of other former Rangers. They ran most of the time with their fists closed and arms extended straight up. "Hey guys, why are we running this way?" "Because it's harder." "Oh…"

One night Tom and I were having some drinks by ourselves, talking Korea, friends, future, having a pleasant time, when two guys sat down nearby and we all had more drinks and talked. Seems these guys had been with the OSS and started to tell us that the newer officers, like Tom and I, didn't really have it, and couldn't handle themselves in a real fight. Tom responded with some expletives. They both stood up and went for Tom, and I jumped at one of them and bashed him against the wall. He just sat there on the floor, playing "tweety bird," while Tom was out in the nearby garden doing a body slam on the other guy. Mutual apologies took place and we all got friendly again and had another round, the end of a nice day at school. (For the gals not catching on to this, it's a guy thing.)

Back in DC Headquarters after the course, I saw Col. Ben Vandervort walking in a hallway. It was a pleasant meeting. "What are you doing?" and I explained my situation and mild frustration. He liked me because I always volunteered to get a job done back in the early days of JACK when there were only about twenty in the whole mission. He told me about a special staff that he was in. It was an inner group and, while he couldn't spell it out for me, he said I would like it, that it was important. I agreed. I would probably be working for him and that would be great.

A week or so later a man came to my office and said that he was in the group that Ben was in and could we go and have coffee. We started for the cafeteria, me jabbering all the way, thinking oh boy, here comes some real good news. He was very nice, was high up in that unit, and was a good friend of Ben's. He explained that Ben was very enthusiastic and in his drive and energy sometimes thinks too far ahead of himself. The short shot was that they weren't really looking to add personnel, maybe later. Subsequently, Ben looked me up and said he was sorry how it turned out. Me too, but it was nice to know he gave me a good evaluation as a professional and recommended me.

In the summer of '55, Andy came to the DC Headquarters. He looked me up and we had a nice "catch up" time at lunch. We agreed to do some fishing on Saturday up the Potomac River near the Falls. It was a great day with good weather, lively rapids, and we caught and roasted some fish. He was in his element. He told me if he could do anything he wanted, just considering himself, he would be a forest ranger and live in the woods. Then he told me he had to leave the Agency because he had no way to prove his background story and someday it might well happen that a congressional spotlight could shine on him as had happened to a Soviet defector the Agency had hired. What to do? He was going to look for a business position using his education and talents. Well, I saw that good friend shortly thereafter and then we lost touch, only to pick up some years later.

LAURIE...A ROMANTIC INTERLUDE

About this time I ran into Nestor who had come back from a short assignment. "Moose," he said, "I want you to meet a girl who was in our support activities on the last assignment. There will be a party tonight and you should meet her." Laurie was a tall, shapely, blue-eyed, copper-red-haired knockout. We "clicked" and fell into a natural fun time routine of parties, outings, dinners, walks in Rock Creek Park, movies, and shows; it was a good script. She worked for the Agency and she and her roommate had been roommates at Northwestern.

We fell in love and that created a problem having to do with religion. One evening she asked me why I seemed sad. "Because some day soon I will ask you to marry me and I'm not sure of your answer." Though she herself was not actively religious, her mom was, to the exclusion of all others, especially mine. Ecumenism was yet to become a known word. Sometime later her dad stopped in D.C. on a business trip and the three of us sat in a lounge and talked over drinks. The conversation flowed nicely. It seemed he liked me. Laurie was happy, but her mom, who never met me, was against it. We kept dating until 1957.

Nothing was happening for me on the Far East desk. The language training had all but ceased. Personnel Planning got involved and asked me about transferring to the Near East and Africa Division. I had shared a home in Arlington with a few I.O.s for a short while. One of them was Byron Engle who later became the first Director of USAID. He advised me to study Africa for its role in the future, so I was assigned to the office of the Chief, Near East and Africa.

While I was there, I had a minor part in a very productive activity in New York City. We had set up a deep cover operation there to recruit foreign students. I would pick up a recruited student in NYC, take him to a safe house in D.C., work on his motivation, emphasize the need to defeat Communism, build freedom and democracy, and coordinate for some special training. Later contacts would be in New York or DC with more of the same and the appropriate geographic Desk would pick up on the student before he returned to his homeland. I understand this produced many healthy, sprouting, seeds later on.

I hope the Agency had a similar operation in all major cities (many schools). Now, it is my understanding that Congress passed a law making it illegal to recruit foreign students. One wonders. The Soviets were here recruiting. The ChiComs still recruit here. Some members of Osama Bin Laden's family were at Harvard with an office to provide student loans. That smells like recruiting. They all left immediately after 9/11 on Saudi Airways. You could look it up. I also recall that Congress stopped the Agency from using USAID and Peace Corps, two good sources of information abroad. One wonders.

I was seeing Laurie often and neither of us dated anyone else. I had a little outboard that I kept up by the Georgetown rowing docks near Key Bridge. We occasionally went down the Potomac off of Haines Point or near Mt. Vernon for a day's outing. Sometimes we would picnic at Rock Creek Park. We had a good softball team with Magoo, Almy, Jim Delaney, Johnny Coyle and others. We played in a league at Haines Point. Laurie often went there with me.

Around this time, 1955, Laurie left the agency for a non-government job. She was not sure that we had a future together because of her mom and her own views of not wanting to be in an organized religion. Still we kept seeing each other. I recall that we attended a lovely Easter sunrise service at Arlington Cemetery.

I was working as a staff of one for the Assistant Desk Chief, Near East and Africa. He was very studious, tweedy, pipe-smoking, masters degree holder, and was cozy in his headquarters assignment. I myself seemed a long way from a foreign assignment, my favorite activity, so I decided to leave the Agency and get into the commercial world. I wrote a letter of resignation pointing out that language and area studies were lacking, as was security, that money was wasted, and "paper mills" flourished because we were always fast with the buck, looking for the easy way. Lastly, they did not handle their personnel very well, me for example.

Many people were surprised, officials and friends. The agency told me it would require three exit interviews. My Division Chief, Ben Smith, who had worked for OSS, was very professional, a friendly and good leader. He asked me to stay on, but I told him I had waited long enough. I next saw Richard Helms who was Deputy Chief of Plans then. He had read my resignation and said he agreed with my observations; and that if I would stay, I would see those changes come about and would have a good career. I thanked him for his time. The last interview was a gal from Personnel Planning who asked me to stay and offered me the next level to do so. That was a GS–12, equal to a Major. At 29 that was not bad, but I told her I had not been talking about a pay grade, and we said our goodbyes. I probably had a final polygraph, I don't remember. One thing I did know, I did not have a job to go to.

I guess I really wanted out, driven by my disappointment. Truth to tell, aided by the clarity of time's focus, I wanted language training in D.C. because Laurie was there, and that attraction clouded my thinking. What I should have done to properly follow a career path in that love-of-my life job, was to take the Japan assignment and do the language and area studies there on my own, but then would I have met Mom and had you, my lovely daughters? Ah, sweet mysteries of life!

The *New York Times* classifieds showed that Prentice Hall Publishing, College Text Division, was looking for salesmen to call on professors at various campuses. Their main office was in Englewood Cliffs, New Jersey, but they still retained some presence in the old book publishing area on 7th Ave. That is where I went for a battery of psychological tests. It took two days to complete the process. Prentice Hall was looking for people who could travel and work on their own and sell texts to the colleges in their given area. I was hired, and met Carl who was the V.P. of Sales. Carl was a big, straight shooter, honest and direct. He had played guard on the famous Iowa football team with the great Nile Kinnick. He insisted that all applicants for sales have athletics in their background. I was given a lot of rules and procedures to read and a list of all the college texts, with authors and titles. There were 300 of them and I was told I must have them memorized a week hence when I was to report to a motel in Englewood Cliffs for a one month training program with some fifteen others.

Laurie and I made flash cards and we both drilled and drilled; by the deadline I had the 300 titles and authors memorized. They wanted certain people who had attitudes and personalities that would lend toward their goals. It was all very interesting. Here was a sales situation where the buyer knew more about the product than the seller. How was that handled? I would call on the chairman of the biology dept and one or two of its members, and present the newest book we had. That would be *The Biotic World and Man* (Bio 101). Before doing the presentation, I would find out, early in our conversation, what he liked in a 101 text, and how he would write one. Then I would pick out those parts of the text that lined up with his thinking. "Well, Dr. Polywag, if I could show you a text that provided the osmosis process early, and the ecosystem toward the end, would that be of interest to you?" We were trained to avoid questions that would get a "no" answer. Often those in the same field know each other as friends or by reputation. We had 300 authors and titles in our heads so we could look smart and get friendly by saying, "Well, professor, do you think Dr. Knowall had that in mind when he wrote *The Civilized Ape?*"

I was very interested in the academics of the job. Ask a college professor a question in his field and you are right back in the classroom, and he is doing what he likes, teaching, making a point. After training, they gave me the Maryland territory and I took residence in Beltsville where I had a large room with a private entrance in a large home. I was centrally located and near enough to Laurie. I called on professors at Maryland U., Towson State Teachers, Peabody Conservatory, Johns Hopkins, Villanova, Mount St. Mary's in western Maryland and others. There were some state teachers' colleges over on the eastern shore and I liked to visit there, not only to present my books, but it had its own homey social style, and of course I cannot forget the great crab chowder, fried clams, and other Chesapeake Bay sea foods which that area kept a secret from the outside world for so long.

I took over the Maryland territory from Jack Finneran who was a graduate of William and Mary. He had met his wife Myrna while working abroad. She was employed at a U.S. Embassy. They had decided to open a miniature golf course by Maryland U. They rented a house and grounds for the course from an old lady who owned the seven acres which would contain the golf course. There were three houses there: one was the old lady's residence and the other two she rented. Jack was an avid golfer. They designed and built the course, and were hands-on, meet-the-community owners who set up tournaments with prizes. Their friendly great Dane added to the scene, and they became a great success. It had been a gamble. They put up everything they had and called it Monte Golf. I stopped by to see them periodically, Jack giving some observations and ideas about my job and the Maryland territory. We became good friends. Jack, an unsung hero, had seen the heavy side of war as a gunner on a B-17 over Germany. He lost many friends, and half the squadron at one time, often coming back to base heavily shot up. Honor, duty, country.

Ordinarily you would think that the head of a department would want other opinions before choosing a text book. I was a little surprised to find that sometimes the department head would choose alone. For example, we had a book, Government of the People by Hofstadter, Aaron, and Miller, historian, economist and sociologist. Hofstadter, a well known professor at Columbia U, came over to Englewood Cliffs to address us at a periodic gathering of field salesmen. It was a great book. We were all pumped to get back to home base and present it. When I did so at one of my larger schools, I ran into a stone wall. The 101 U.S. History book they were using was noticeably thin and authored by the department head. With a large number of students, who all must take U.S. History, it makes a nice "bonus" along with tenure, sabbaticals and other perks. Knowing the mission was to teach students to their highest attainable levels, I really "burned" over such chicanery, a choker of progress, crying out for reform.

Going out to Western Maryland in those days was a trip to the frontier. The only " hotel" in the town near Mount St. Mary's was an old, square concrete building, perhaps two stories, with very high ceilings, and a few bare light bulbs. No rugs. Hey, don't complain, it's a long thankful way from the sleeping bag in the field, or a bunk in a *"pungkata-pungkata"* fishing boat, and that countryside was beautiful, and the small St. Mary's college was a pleasure to visit.

Carl had asked me to visit Gettysburg College in PA while in the area, so I did. It was a Saturday morning. One appointment I remember was the biology prof. He was late. He and the class had been out in the field for a day or two and he had many jars of creepy, crawly things, including snakes. He was so happy. I became very attentive as he described various projects. I began to ask questions as he explained. We had lunch. He talked. I got the short syllabus. By the time I started to present The Biotic World and Man, tying in some of the things he had told me, time was short and he had to move on. I could only give him a copy of the book and ask him to review it so we could cover it on my next visit. That is not how I was trained.

As I called on the professors, I came to realize that I liked finding out about the academic subject and its inherent teaching challenges more than I did the sale and its closing. I was not sales-minded enough in those circumstances. That's not to say I was not making the sales, it just didn't fill me up, but this problem would soon be solved. I attended a periodic meeting and had been thinking that my pay scale level was far below my effort, customer relations, and results. I grumbled to some of my ex-training friends, who concurred. A few weeks later Carl called me into Englewood Cliffs and asked me why I had spoken to them instead of him. He said I had demoralized them. He was right; I should have taken it up with him. He was "steaming" and told me to write out my resignation showing I was leaving for personal reasons.

I went back to Beltsville and began writing my resume. I told Laurie I really wasn't getting anywhere with this job. I paid more attention to the academics than I did the sales, so I was thinking of getting another job. Laurie: "So you were fired." Me: "Yes, now let's write my resume."

Marriage? Quiet as a cemetery at midnight. The little guy in me said, "What do you expect, Moose, you don't even have a job." I went to Nana and Pop-pop's in New Jersey and made a list of 200 or so companies, most of them headquartered in that general area, and sent my résumé to their presidents. Meanwhile, Ben McAlpine, a Korea mission colleague, invited me to visit him at his Wall Street office. He was a stock broker. I went there and he told me to come with him, learn the business, and I would be set, but that daily commute to Wall Street, and the "money culture" there, was not my bag.

I acquired appointments and received job offers with Lurline, Armstrong Rubber, Remington Arms, American Express, Standard Brands, Texaco, Firestone, Aramco and several others. At each interview I inquired about going abroad to Asia. They all had interesting jobs for me, but only Aramco and American Express had positions to fill abroad. Lurline had a position in D.C. to work with an exadmiral, keeping in touch with the National Labor relations Board (NLRB) and the Maritime Board. Remington Arms in Hartford, Ct was to assist the International VP with correspondence and promotions to customers abroad. Texaco was the highest paying, as an economic analyst, in New York, writing reports and related matters for the management. The Arabian American Oil Co. was a 3 years assignment in Saudi Arabia, living in a large complex with other Americans, and with high restrictions on your activities due to Muslim laws and culture. The living conditions were comfortable, lots of activities in the compound, but the only plus was that you could bank your tax free salary and they would fly you out to the Mediterranean Sea free once a year for a scenery change. This was a "no brainer" for me. Some 3-4 years later I was managing an American Express bank at Misawa Air Base in Japan and a guy who had retired after twenty years with Aramco in Saudi Arabia came in to transfer some funds. He was visiting his son. He kept talking about the money he had saved, not about the twenty years in Saudi Arabia.

THE AMERICAN EXPRESS CAREER

American Express (Amexco) was my choice. They ran military banking facilities (MBFs) in Europe and Asia, under U.S. Treasury license to provide home town banking on the various bases, including car and housing loans insurance, and travel services at some locations. They offered me a short trainee time in northern Japan and then a management position from there. We talked in July, 1957. I took some basic training, received my shots, got the passport and visa, and briefings from Dick Taylor, VP Personnel and a couple of international banking officers. I commuted from Union, New Jersey to 65 Broadway NYC. Amexco had just entered the credit card business by purchasing CIT with 300,000 members. Diners Club was the only other player in the game at that time. In training with the Travelers Cheque Division, I met Bob Bishop, who was going to have a good position in this new credit card subsidiary, and he kept asking me to join him. He had that vision. I did not. My vision was focused on the northwest Pacific. I don't know why, but it just came naturally Another ifa, woulda, coulda. A very good man, Bob entered eternal life about 4-5 years after that.

During this time I had been going back and forth to D.C. to see Laurie who could not solve the problem (one way or the other). I told her I was going to Japan, and if she wanted to marry before that, or in Japan after, that was her decision. I was tired of drinking the weak tea of that conversation. By now I really wasn't sure what I would do if she would show up in Japan, an outside chance. By November, I was ready to leave. I called Laurie and she came to New York. We had a lovely evening, dinner, wine, some walking, but it was the same tea, probably for the best. I took her to the airport for the flight back. We said goodbye at the departure counter and held a long kiss amid the gawking travelers, for she was very attractive. That was the last time I saw her. Many years later a mutual friend told me she married a famous TV anchor and had five children. That was nice to hear. I had prayed for her well-being.

JAPAN

Back in New Jersey there was a round of parties and a couple days later I took off on a 3 year assignment. The flight was from New York to Tokyo, probably on a DC8 prop, with a stop at Shimya, Alaska. I was met at Haneda Airport by an Amexco meeter/greeter, and went to the Imperial Hotel, where I would meet Karl Kircher, G/M for Travel and Tourism, and Ted Jennings G/M for Commercial Banking. We would become lasting friends. They briefed me on Amexco's activities in Japan, including the Military Banking. The District Manager of Military Banking was at Misawa Air Base and reported directly to New York, as did Karl and Ted. Next day I flew from Tokyo to Misawa Air Base, home of the 39th Air Div in Aomori-ken, in Northern Honshu, on a Nippon Airways DC-3, the commercial configuration of the ol' gooney bird, C-47. Ray Hoffman, the D/M for us there, met me at the flight line and showed me to my quarters, which were field grade officer accommodations. Jack Van Wagoner, the assistant manager, showed me around. Friends to this day, he lives in Lakewood, New Jersey.

Misawa was a huge air base with the Pacific Ocean a couple of miles to the East and a large lake to the Northwest. It was part of the containment policy we had for dealing with Communist Russia, China, and North Korea. Aomori-ken had rolling hills, small mountains, hot springs, wooded areas, farming and fishing, and a shoreline on the Tsugaru Straits facing Hokkaido. The cumulative snowfall for a winter was about 17 feet, November to April. That little farm town had markets, shops, restaurants, a movie house, bars, a few hotels and one paved road. The train station nearby was Furumaki. The town's economy was mostly dependent on the base, the Japanese who worked on the Base and lived in town, and those Americans who went in to town from the base and spent money. My training at the bank was all "hands-on." I worked at every position we had. No one in cash and accounting left for the day until we balanced our books. All posting and recording was done by hand, a bit archaic, even then, but accurate, functional, and economic.

HOKKAIDO

By late December I transferred to Chitose Air Base, Hokkaido. It was part of the 39th Air Div complex. We had F-86 pilots there who were training the Japan Self Defense Forces (JASDAF) pilots The Amexco manager there was Bud Towson, also a friend to this day, who was scheduled for a transfer to Germany. We had a small bank there in the Headquarters building, 7 employees, all efficient and reliable, and, while I had the title Manager, they helped to polish my training.

We had an office party that Christmas, a farewell to Bud and welcome to me. One guest was Hiakawa-san, Manager of the local branch of the Bank of Hokkaido, where we bought Yen with U.S. Treasury Checks to use for our foreign exchange service at the bank. He had been a catcher in his amateur playing days, and I, a pitcher, the initial ingredients of a good relationship. I befriended the staff, and we talked of their friends, families, and backgrounds between speeches, impromptu singing, acting (the birth of karaoke probably took place that night), and Tanko-bushi, the coal miners dance and song, somewhat like a slow conga line dance. After six years in Japan, I still know the tune and some steps; but I need a bit of saké to twinkle the toes.

Hokkaido was a charming place, 20% of the land area of Japan and about 5% of the population. For years the government tried to get more people to go there to live, but most of them do not like the snowy, cold, winter. The Japanese are basically a warm climate group, having moved from the southern seas over the eons to settle when they ran out of mild weather. The aborigines they encountered were taller, lighter of skin and eye, and have a facial structure that suggests their origin to be in the northern Asia mainland. Apparently they did not easily intermingle and marry. The only Ainus (aborigines) I saw in my six years in Japan were in Hokkaido and Okinawa, the very north and south of the archipelago.

In Hokkaido the Ainus had the ceremonial sacrifice of the cub bear. The Ainus, similar to our Native Americans, had lived in nature, took only what thy needed from nature, and found their religion in nature. The bear was at the center of this nature worship, and in the ceremony they would shoot arrows into the bear cub in the belief that it would release the soul of the precious cub to God for the benefit of all who had this faith. In the later years of my stay, the government was trying to effect a change in the procedure, whereby it would be symbolic gesture rather than killing the poor little fella. That would be the family of the big brown bear that is common in our Northwest, Canada, Alaska, and over into Hokkaido, Kamchatka, and the northern Asian mainland. They are very big, powerful, and lightning fast in the first 100 yards, and just fast after that.

12 | AMERICAN EXPRESS
First 3 years ... Japan

Author in Asamushi, 1959

HOKKAIDO

When spring came, I bought a 50cc Tohatsu motorcycle and would go, dictionary in pocket, through the fields and hills to a town I had chosen from the map.
This was done without research, something like "pin the tail on the donkey."
Those bike rides were exhilarating and, surprise, no watery, humid, rice fields, but
forests, rolling farm land with red barns, dairy cattle, sheep, horses, apple trees,
corn, asparagus, and other vegetables, a true touch of the farm country in the
northeastern U.S.A. I learned that before and after the Pacific War the University
of Hokkaido and, I think, Massachusetts, had exchange programs for students and
professors in the agricultural and livestock fields. The influence was dramatic. As
I rode the rolling farm and woodlands, were it not for the signs and occasional
bill boards in Kanji, it was easy to feel some familiarity with the New England
scene. They even made cheese there. It was Admiral Perry and his task group that
visited that isolated archipelago of the Sun God about 1840, a milestone in the
slow opening up to the "gaijin" (foreigners.) Here I was just four generations and
one big war later, traveling around and making friends in that lovely Land of the
Rising Sun. Nice place. Nice people.

Arriving at a pinpointed town, usually on the coast, I would check into a
hotel, and walk around, the only gaijin in sight, jubiki (dictionary) at the ready.
Oh, the sights and sounds of those small coastal towns: bicycles and mopeds
aplenty, mostly small wooden structures, narrow sidewalks with little shops with
soji (wood and paper) doors, and the call of "Irashaimasu!"(welcome) when you
opened one to the aroma of steamed rice, miso soup, cooking and grilling of sea
foods and meats, various noodle dishes (soup or fried) and of course the sushi and
sashimi (raw seafood). My favorite was squid, fresh off the boat, cut into thin
strips, like thick noodles, and eaten with chopped green onions, soy sauce and
wasabi, that green mustard, so famous for attacking the sinus if used in excess. A
cold Sapporo beer would enhance the pleasant thought of the next course.

Of course each town had its own personality, "beat," and physical characteristics. There was a small one that I found on the east (Pacific) coast using my
"donkey tail" method. Upon "putt-putting" in, on my "powerful" 50cc bike, I
discovered the heart of its economy was the big King Crab of the northern
Pacific. All up and down the beach were 6-9 feet mounds of crab shells, the waste
of the canning process. Those hills attracted hundreds of plump, happy, seagulls,
crying out in a concert of appreciation. That sight, the sweet/sour, acrid odor, and
the clouds of flies kept my hands in drive position as I continued south along the
Pacific to another quaint fishing village, but with a clean beach. Somehow, the
"irashaimasu" there had a better ring.

On these trips away from the air base and English-speaking Japanese, my jubiki fell into the make-do communication mix of hand gestures, facial expression,
hop, skip, and jump English, and some Japanese words I had learned, all in the fun
of socio-cultural exploration.

A Japanese friend, with whom I hunted pheasant and duck, had a farmer friend who was having some trouble with a bear breaking into his storehouse, probably looking for food prior to hibernation. Around sundown he visited the farm, just to look around. He walked up and over a rise, carrying a Savage 308 rifle, and on the way down the slope he heard a loud, rough, snort, and there, standing up on its hind legs, was a big brown bear sniffing the air and facing his direction. It was 50-60 yards away and he knew that when the bear came down, the charge was on, and all you would have is a frontal head shot. He was scared, shaky scared, and as he raised his rifle he was getting "jelly knees." He fired a lung shot and the bear went down, another shot and it was over. He vowed never again, for a lot of reasons, but mainly because that beautiful animal is such a prominent part of nature in those mountain woodlands. Perhaps leaving plenty of food out as the hibernation time came, say, all of November, would be one answer.

Another Japanese friend was a distributor for Nikka Whiskey Co. They had a distillery in Hokkaido and made a good blend whiskey. He invited me to attend a big bash at an auditorium in Sapporo, the capitol of Hokkaido. It was a charming city with a beautiful architectural blend of Japanese and Western designs. On the main avenue was a small Christian church with a tower clock. It was all wood and clapboard, again right out of early New England.

Nikka was having a promotional party to get publicity to kick off that well-known whiskey in newly designed bottles to pump up the sales. I was the only gaijin there. I had a nice time, conversed with some of the English-speaking Nikka officials, and watched the way it was all done. There were about six gorgeous models to whom my friend introduced me who did not speak English, and after I got past "Haji me mashte…I kagadeska?" (Pleased to meet you…how are you?) it was all a wash-out, and all the back and forth smiles were not going to get it done in this boy meets girl world. But it was nice, and the whiskey was smooth.

One day, looking to break the routine at Chitose base, I headed for Sapporo after we closed the bank. I got into the car and started the 50 minute trip. It was winter. I was crossing a river bridge at about 40 mph, realized I was on ice and should be going slower, so I hit the brakes, and then I went into a skid, hanging on to the wheel, knuckles white, eyes bulging, as I did a 180 degree spin in the middle of the bridge. Luckily there was no traffic at that instant. Then I slowly drove the snow and ice road to Sapporo over that rolling single lane road, a bit shaken from my stupidity, looking forward to a large pre-dinner cocktail in the Grand Hotel dining room, complete with fireplace, deer trophies, leather, polished wood, and brass, in an alpine atmosphere. Lamb, beef, venison, or salmon was always a good choice. Long winters? Who cares?

Bud left for the U.S. around February and I became the manager of that little "home town bank away from home." Shortly thereafter, the Command at Chitose Air base asked me to consider a much-needed bimonthly mobile banking service at Wakkanai, the northernmost tip of Hokkaido, an overnight train ride from Sapporo. The Air Force operated a loran station and a listening post, similar to the ASA (Army Security Agency) at Chitose. I took a trip up there to meet the Command and make decisions on feasibility, especially the security of my staff members who would undertake such a long, valuables-toting journey. Deep snow and wind was common for that area, as I looked out over the cold sea to the Kurile Islands of the USSR. I wrote it up for all concerned. We would take a car to the Sapporo rail station with a large metal footlocker of cash, travelers' cheques, and bank papers and forms. Two male tellers would board the sleeper train and chain the footlocker under the bunk bed, to be met at Wakkanai by the Air Police jeep and go onto the base for business, returning the same way at the end of the day. New York Headquarters approved, as did the military command, and we started the program about 2-3 weeks later. I was never fully satisfied from a security viewpoint, but weighed that against the service those military people needed at Wakkanai.

In the beautiful summer, a Japanese friend told me about an uncle who was the caretaker of a large pristine estate set in a forest, with a crater lake anchoring the scene. It was a preserve held under the Emperor's seal and privilege. He never used it and few people were allowed to go there. We got permission to go there and fish for a day on that sparkling, clear lake with the birds calling to each other, probably about us, from deep within the forest. My, how the slightest sound traveled in that stillness. The caretaker said the lake was loaded with Masu. Imagine a cross between a salmon and a rainbow trout. That's Masu. We fished very deep for it, as suggested, but caught nothing after 5-6 hours. No matter. It was a memorable experience, that pristine setting existing in its ancient charm.

One day in winter I was in Sapporo walking along and as I passed by two women bundled in fur coats and hats. I realized they were speaking Russian. Curious as I passed, I looked back to give a courtesy nod and to see their faces, expecting light eyes and hair. Surprise! Two middle aged Japanese women acknowledged my nod and continued talking in Russian. I found this was not uncommon in that area, since migrations over the years entailed Russians and Japanese living in Kamchatka, Sahkalin and the Kuriles, which Japan had taken after the 1905 war with Russia, and Russia took back after WWII. One of our MBF employees was born in the Kuriles, lived on a farm, and migrated (escaped) to Japan after 1945.

Sapporo was the home of the winter Olympics many years later, and the first place I vacationed with Mom after we were married and living in Misawa. We have Ainu wood carvings of bears which prompt fond memories of that trip. In the fall of 1958 Dick Stewart came up from Tokyo and Meryl Hoffman joined us from Misawa to do some deer hunting for a couple of days in Hydaka, in the southern area of Hokkaido's mainland. We had three Japanese locals to guide us in those woods. We took turns at driving some deer from over the next ridge to the general vicinity of the standers. We all had some shots, but no rewards. It was a fun outing nevertheless.

A nice place to go, especially in winter, was a hot springs lodge. One place was a resort with many hot spring pools and a large swimming pool. It was fun to swim in that hot/warm water which emitted steam, while the snow was drifted high around the grounds. There was no heat in the bedrooms, but after swimming/soaking in that hot water sleeping on a futon covered with a quilt guaranteed refreshing sleep. Some time after I met Aiko, in 1958, I occasionally had "pie-in-the-sky" thoughts about us owning a small hotel in the Jozanke Hot Springs area. Ah, Shangri-la revisited.

The plan was for me to manage the Chitose MBF for a year. Then Meryl Hoffman would take over at Chitose, and I would be the assistant District Manager at Misawa, reporting to the D/M, Jack Van Waggoner. I rented a nice Japanese style house in a six tree apple orchard, while retaining my quarters on the base.

After I had been in Japan about three months, I received a letter from Laurie telling me that she could not bring herself to make the trip. I was more relieved than disappointed because I had come to realize it would not be a good match. Since there was nothing left to say, I did not answer. Two months after that, I received a letter from her roommate saying that Laurie was unhappy and would like to hear from me. I was busy with work and other things and did not bother. "Other things" mostly had to do with Aiko, a tall, lovely girl, from Asashikawa City on Hokkaido. She played the koto, a pleasing, melodious, ancient, string instrument. She had left home at age 21 because she had been looking at a future molded in the past. She wanted to know more and see more than staying at home, for the times they had been a-changing in post-war Japan.

AIKO…THE NAME MEANS LOVE

I walked into a local tavern one night and there she was, tending bar, in her bright, charming manner. I took a stool at the end of the bar. No table for this young fella tonight. Her English, though limited, was sufficient to roll an understandable basic dialogue, broken up by waiting on customers. I showed off my limited Japanese, which at the time consisted of my often used words and phrases, the equivalent English competence level of the beginners' "See Jane Run" and "Jump Johnny Jump." Pretty suave thought I, with the jubiki as back-up.

At another time I stopped in and we enjoyed our conversation-solving. She was pretty and very charming. After another visit, I walked her home to the small place where she was staying. That happened a few more times and then I asked her for a movie date for the next Sunday. The plan was to meet in front of the theatre. I waited and waited and then figured something had happened. As I started to walk home and was a couple of blocks from the movie house, Aiko appeared. She was dressed in a beautiful kimono (her Dad was in the kimono

Aiko at beach near Misawa, 1959

business). This was, obviously, a special time for her. We were happy, saw a double feature, and then went to a nice cozy restaurant. Afterward I showed her my house among the apple trees. The kitchen and breakfast nook over-looking the garden and trees were Western. The rest of the house was Japanese with sliding doors, tatami floors, and a big tiled ofuro (sunken bath). We drank tea. Talked some more. Laughed a lot, and enjoyed our own futon fantasy ("Oh, boy, Moose, this can get complicated," said my little inside guy, "and it's just starting." "Shut up," said Howie, like he was in control.)

It was not long before Aiko moved in with me. I still retained my quarters on the base. (Little guy: "I told you this would get complicated, and it's just starting." Howie: "Shut up. Go away.")

Springtime is such a joy in areas with long snowy winters. The changes which nature creates awakens all the senses, a tonic of its own, refreshingly recalling to me that line from *A Day in June* by James Russell Lowell: "Every clod feels a stir of might, an instinct within it that reaches and towers, and groping blindly above it for light climbs to a soul in earth and flowers."

In June, the Obon festival is celebrated in honor of one's ancestors. Aiko and I attended one on the outskirts of Chitose, in an open field. A 20 foot wooden tower was constructed with a topping platform large enough to hold a few drummers and two huge special wooden kettle drums. This was to provide the rhythm for dancing the traditional Bon Odori. It was summer, so I wore a yuka-ta (summer kimono) and gettas (raised wooden klogs), all chosen by Aiko. As the night approached, the people gathered and had some hot tea, saké, or beer from the nearby stalls. Those marvelous deep drum beats were building up and soon became hypnotic, as a circle of dancers gradually formed, growing larger as more people arrived. It was an easy, line-style dance to learn and with the singing and clapping that went on, along with the thunderous drums, I was soon on cruise control, fueled by that excellent saké. What a lovely time and tribute to one's ancestors. It was all love and friendship and a pleasant, warm, feeling that such an environment can create. We danced well into the night with its country fresh air and late spring aroma. On the last night of the two or three day festival those with a true feel for the festival's meaning would place special lighted candles in little boat-shaped floats and take them to the nearest waterway that would carry them with the currents to a place unknown. It was inspiring to see perhaps a thousand candles lighting up the darkness and water as they drifted away.

In early summer, Aiko's father came from Asashigawa, looking for her, and the trail led to that little house in the apple trees. There was a knock on the door and Aiko went to answer it and then stepped outside. After a while, in my curiosity, I opened the door to find the reason for her absence. Aiko was sitting on a step, looking forlorn, and the man standing on the ground had a placid expression. "This my father," she said. "He say to come home; I want stay here, nothing for me there." With Aiko interpreting as best she could, he asked me about me, where from and where going? I invited him to come in for tea. His gentle refusal indicated he was in anguish and wanted to leave, so I answered all of his questions and he asked me to please take care of his daughter, whom he loved very much. I responded in the affirmative without much feeling, a bit shaken by his demeanor and sad expression, realizing this was very serious. ("I told you, Moose, this would be complicated and..." "Oh please, I'm in charge here, right?" "Are you? It's not right and you know it.")

Life went on. My district manager thought I was doing a fine job. My friends, American and Japanese, had some good times arranging outings and parties, or just plain get-togethers. Aiko and I went off on our own some weekends, usually visiting hot spring towns in the mountains or going to Sapporo. Toward the end of the year my "on-base" friends planned a New Year's Eve party at the Officer's Club. Almost all had a Japanese girlfriend. Now it was an unwritten rule at the time that members of the Officers Club did not bring their Japanese dates into the club, so we asked the Base Commander for a review so we could participate in the base's party. He said sure, that's the best way, share the fun. Ah, for sure, the times, they were a-changin'.

Chitose was a small base and there were not more than forty couples there at the Officer's Club party, including our group and some couples from the ASA (Army Security Agency). There was a band and a singer. Incidentally, Miyoshi Umeke of Flower Drum Song fame got her start singing at a military base in Hokkaido, the temporary home of the 1st Cavalry Division at one phase of the Korean War. The music was great. I recall one of the flight instructors grabbed a hula hoop and put on a show with the improvisation of the band, and Capt. Vic Saldania with his Philippine heritage also brought out encouraging shouts and applause with his dancing (it's in the blood). Everyone mixed just fine, even the base commander's wife. All the girls were lovely and the wine superb. Some ASA people asked some of us, including Aiko and me, to go over to their quarters for a mini-party afterwards, which we did. The ASA group was intelligent, knowledgeable, cosmopolitan, and of course multi-lingual. One lady played a fine piano and we all sang. An older woman, a Russian specialist, made it a point to talk with Aiko and me, wishing us well, and saying she was so impressed with Aiko's beauty and charm. (Little guy: "You're really into it now, aren't you Moose? I told you this was wrong and...." "Will you please shut up?")

One wintry evening I was walking along a street in Chitose and stopped in a small noodle shop. Upon opening the sliding door, I was met with the nice warm aromas from the kitchen, and a voice, "Newhard-san." It was Hyakawa-san from the Bank of Hokkaido sitting on a low stool at the counter. "Ona skimashtaka? Nodo kawa kimaska?" (Are you hungry? thirsty?) he asked, and we started chatting, eating, and sipping saké. Two hours or so later, having resolved some very intricate matters regarding the Japanese economy, the cold war, and baseball strategies for winners only, he suggested that we go to his house so I could meet his wife and three daughters. I begged off. It was late. He insisted. So we walked the snow covered streets and when we reached his house he banged on the front door and shouted, "Everybody up, we have a guest." We ate some good local cheese, drank beer, and chatted away, as the ladies waited on us, such was the way of the day (which was slowly a-changin'). The surprise was when he sat down at the piano and played a whole medley of Stephen Foster songs. I knew some of them from way back in grammar school and needed no encouragement whatever to sing the ones I knew. It was a real fun time.

Meryl Hoffman came up from Misawa for orientation to the Chitose operation. He was going to take over from me and I was going to Misawa as assistant D/M. He was serious about his work and did well. He also liked to go hunting for pheasant and duck, which we did often, in both Chitose and Misawa, I even have an old newspaper clipping and picture from a village newspaper in the hills of Aomori-ken showing Hoss and I with our "bag" of pheasant (the two "gaijin" hunters must have been news in that little town that day.) He always had a funny story, or was doing something different. Once he bought a little pocket monkey at a pet shop. "Hoss," Meryl's nickname, would go into a neighborhood bistro, sit down, order a beer, take the monkey out of his pocket and put it on the bar, and watch the fun of the monkey's antics. It would draw an interested group. The owner was delighted, and Hoss made a lot of friends.

I told Aiko that I would proceed to Misawa, get established at the MBF, and find a house, and she planned to come down in about six weeks. "Look at yourself," said the little guy inside, "You are living with this beautiful woman and you don't go to church anymore, you are palsy with the devil because you are living in sin, and you are ignoring it all and just going along in 'la-la' land, ssooo...hhmmm?"(No back-talk this time). I prepared to leave Chitose, going around and saying goodbyes, and signing responsibilities over to Hoss.

The new job was bigger and with more action. Jack and I again shared a field grade BOQ (Base Officers Quarters). We were friends and he was my boss, and the two never blended or interfered with our mission concerning correct banking and accounting procedure and service to the customers. We had a good relationship. An avid golfer, he would often play 36 holes over a weekend, sometimes 54. He encouraged me to play. I knew the game a bit from my caddying days in my teens, but never played. "But you are an athlete, and will have much fun, once you learn," Jack assured me. Still no interest.

I received a letter from my Korea days buddy Tom Doolittle, who was going to be assigned to the American Embassy in Manila. He and Becky and the kids would be going on the U.S. President Lines from San Francisco with a two day stop in Yokohama, so how about getting together there? Sure. So, when the time came I took the overnight sleeper from Misawa and booked into the Silk Hotel which was on the waterfront in Yokohama, near the President Lines docking area. I went to the dock when the ship was arriving and being slowly positioned for tying up. As I stood there looking up at the various decks of passengers, trying to locate the Doolittles, a loud voice called out, "Hey, Georgetown," and I gazed along a high railing and stopped at a waving arm. It was my old dormmate from "Yah-yah Father, you can't ccaaatch mmeee!" taking a cruise with the family. And there along another railing were the Doolittles. We all met when they came down to the dock. It was a nice way to travel with the family in those days. In Tom's case he was going on authorized PCS (Permanent Change of Station), and would not be charged for the time en route. Now that's a "bennie." We had dinner at the hotel that night and caught up on a lot of news, and the next day just "hung out" and browsed around. They invited me to visit them in Manila when I was on my way back from my home leave, a year or so hence, and we marked it down. That evening I took the overnight train back to Misawa.

Late one day Jack and I were standing at the Service Counter in the MBF, talking and watching the activity in the lobby and at the tellers' windows. A master sergeant came in and asked us about a car loan. "Sure, no problem, just fill out a form and if you qualify we can have it for you late tomorrow." "Great," he said, "I'm the "top kick" for the Base Provost Marshal," and smiling: "Anybody gives you any trouble around here, I'll lock 'em up." As we kidded around, I knew I had seen him before. "Sarge," I said, "I know you from somewhere. I'm from New Jersey, went to school in D.C., spent some time in Maryland, was in Korea and..." He said, "Korea might fit." So we sifted through that, and sure enough he was the Master Sergeant at Wyjong-bu who helped me pick up the line-crossing courier in the middle of winter. For the rest of the time he was at Misawa, he always said, "Anyone gives you a problem, I'll lock him up." It's nice to see a guy who loves his job.

As mentioned, this was the Headquarters of the 39th Air Division, the north-

Author and friend, manager of offices, in Misawa, 1962

ernmost large unit in the Western Pacific in that Cold War, with its shifting and maneuvering and planning. Misawa was, of course, just "across the table" in the electronic sight of a Soviet missile crew. Very serious, but amusing at the same time, was to answer the common question: "What do we do in the case of a missile attack?" (atomic, that is.) We had no air raid shelters. One idea that circulated was that everyone should seek shelter in the larger tunnels housing the steam lines that went all over the base from the central steam generating unit. But if a steam line was hit, it would be "lobster-likeness" for those nearby, nah, no good! How about everybody get as far away from the base as you can? Yeah, but how much of a head start would there be? Nah!......I know, how about everybody stand up straight, feet wide apart, bend forward, way over, hands grasping your ankles, look up, now kiss your ass goodbye. It was American humor at work again in trying times, a true weapon in the morale arsenal.

Seriously, the alerts were frequent, and the Air Force professionals were dedicated, intelligent, and knew their jobs. They stood the Watch, always on guard. They continually practiced. I recall Col. Davenport who had command of a tactical fighter squadron. As a Lt. he had flown a bomber in the famous Doolittle raid over Tokyo in 1942. One evening he and others, including Texas Tom and me, were sitting around in a large group, sipping some brew, and making the usual noise in the men's bar in the Officer's Club, when Davenport banged his drinking mug on a table, jumped up and loudly said, "Okay! My squadron has an 0600 takeoff tomorrow and I am going to bed. Let's be ready, gentlemen." He was a warrior leading warriors, and I did notice a decrease in attendance to the bull session after that. He was about 40 then and flying a fighter jet. One night, sitting around, he talked about the fighter plane weapons contest they had that day. Davenport had come in second of all the pilots and said, "I don't know how that could have happened. Some shave-tail beat me out." There were many of his character and persona in the Air Force, heroes all.

I had some nice friends at Misawa. "Texas Tom" Martin was the G/M for the Post Exchange (PX) operation in Northern Japan. The PX is the department store of the military personnel, one of the non-appropriated fund activities which was allowed to make a small, limited profit, which was then used to support various activities such as hobby shops, libraries, athletic equipment, and other community activities. Our MBF had all of the non-appropriated fund accounts, the PX being the largest.

Tom was talkative, funny, played guitar and knew many popular tunes. He played in a small group of Japanese musicians that he organized, The Fuji Mountain Boys. They would sometimes go around to the restaurants and bars in Misawa town and play their country western and hillbilly songs. He and I enjoyed our friendship which involved many days of duck and pheasant hunting.

Helen and Tom Ige were from Hawaii and he was the Deputy at the exchange. His parents had migrated from Okinawa to Hawaii. He had spent three years of his youth in an internment camp along with the many others of Japanese descent who were rounded up during the Pacific War. While he understood the reason for that drastic security measure, the innocence of those he knew, and himself, stood in the way of a full acceptance to what had been done to him and his family members. Friends that we were, we seldom talked about that. I could see and feel why it was done, and also why it was highly objectionable to those who lost their freedom.

In late winter I read an ad in the Stars and Stripes newspaper that the motor pool at Tachikawa Air Base, in the Tokyo area, was selling some vehicles "as is." Being in the market for a 4-wheel drive jeep, I called that motor pool and got the reply, "Come on down," so I arranged for a few days off, and took the overnight train from Furumaki station and showed up at Tachikawa the next day ready for a wintry drive north. It was snowing hard. The motor pool had a couple of jeeps for sale, that old WWII and Korea vintage. I told the sergeant in charge of my intention to buy a jeep "as is" and drive it to Misawa air base, and he said he could not recommend any of his "as is" jeeps for what I had in mind, but if I was going ahead anyway, the one "startable" jeep (I needed someone to hold the palm of their hand over the carburetor) might get me back to Misawa. So with a big bottle of water, map, jubiki, some gas cans, and a guideline briefing from the senior Japanese employee at the motor pool, I headed north in the general direction of Sendai on the Pacific coast, about a day's drive south from Misawa. There were no modern highways. Some secondary roads were dirt and gravel. It was most interesting and challenging; stopping to ask questions, getting someone to hold their palm over the carburetor, or work the starter as I coaxed the carburetor, finding lodging and food from time to time. The locals in those small towns surely thought I was crazy driving from Tachikawa to Misawa in the falling snow with a faulty vehicle, but a little adventure is a spice of life. Besides, my Japanese improved rapidly as the need urged me on. A mechanic helped me out with the carburetor in Sendai and after that it was cool (heh heh). At Misawa

I had a wooden top put on and so I had a vehicle for hunting, field trips, and general driving.

Shortly after, Aiko arrived from Hokkaido. We chose a small house on the outskirts of town. She had brought her koto and played it often. I had been enrolled in the basic Japanese course at the Maryland U extension program on the base and Aiko congratulated me on my proficiency, probably more for encouragement than a true measure of progress, but I knew I was on a roll. One long weekend we decided to drive along a coastal road going south toward Sendai, swim and relax at a small beach resort, and return the same way. About two hours out of Misawa, driving on the left side of course, along a dirt and gravel road, about 60 feet above the sea, a truck coming the other way forced me to the left. I hit the brakes, skidded, and ended up tottering on the edge, two wheels off the edge, and two wheels on the ground. As the jeep rocked, I pushed Aiko, shouting, "Jump, jump," out the right side door and followed her on to the road. We lay there holding each other and counting our blessings. Three truckers from the swerving truck had stopped and were running toward us. When they found we were okay, they backed up the truck, rigged some rope on the jeep, and pulled all of it back on to the road. They had swerved to dodge a large hole in the road and were most apologetic. We traveled on and found a nice hotel along my favorite beach in that general area. The waves were super and we returned to Misawa late the following day.

Jack and I had the MBF in good running order. The staff was well-trained and instructed as to company procedures and policies, the Command was pleased with our services, and we had good audit reports. I was due three months' home leave in November and was asked to return to Japan as District Manager, MBFs, to which I agreed. Jack was scheduled to work at the Amexco bank in New Delhi, India. Our career paths were forming and looking good.

At the end of summer "Texas Tom" Martin suggested we have a baseball game, American Express MBF vs. the PX Services, and play for bragging rights around the base with the loser paying for the ensuing picnic to be prepared by the PX snack bar. I talked it over with our staff and everyone was excited about beating the PX team. They had many more employees than we did so the prospect of fielding a better team was in their favor, but we had a secret weapon, a gaijin "ringer" who was going to pitch for the MBF. All of these pencil-pushing desk and chair jockeys shifted gears and started to work out and practice. Game day gave us nice weather and many employees and families attended. There was much give and take, razzing on both sides, in the field and in the stands, not quite like our Georgetown team, but you get the idea. Working with my tailing fast (well almost) ball, Circle Change-Up, and Uncle Charley, I did okay. Not well enough for some scout to come out of the stands to ask me how I was feeling, am I working out all the time? and would I be interested to hook up with a Tokyo Giants farm team, but okay. Except not okay enough. We lost by about 3 to 5 because of critical errors, and I saw my last chance at a comeback fade into the halls of history. But it was a great time on a summer Sunday afternoon and goodwill and friendship abounded as all went on to picnic at the expense of American Express. It was "Hadquat Pay," as my Korean friend Dosty would say.

As the early autumn began painting its annual colorful woodland fantasy, my calendar more prominently showed I had 3 months of leave starting in November. That little man inside was pressing hard for a decision about Aiko. "You can't go on like this," he said "It's wrong. Either marry her or break it off (as difficult as that might be in our mutual attraction). You have been living in sin and not practicing your faith in exchange for the pleasure and comfort of playing 'love nest'." I really struggled a great deal, and did not recognize some of the weaknesses in our relationship at the time. Although we shared a strong physical attraction and natural compatibility, I kept getting warnings, "Don't do it." We had cultural and educational differences, and a need for better communication to support our deeper thoughts. Also, the little guy was winning and his name was conscience, and a good conscience is to the soul what health is to the body, and I should marry her, but I was afraid, timid, whatever, to take on the challenges of our differences. I did not consider all the possibilities, like seeing if she would accept my religion. There were some Canadian missionaries living near Misawa who could have given her instruction, if she chose. There was an English course taught at the Maryland U extension on the base for those who wanted it, and there were Japanese classes there for me to continue to take.

Overall, I felt it was not meant to be and made the decision to part. However, I have always felt sadness and guilt concerning Aiko, who loved me so much. It was a very painful parting and goodbye for both of us.

Sometime in November, I made the rounds of friends and the Command liaison folks with a "so long, I'll be back" and picked up my flight to Tokyo. I had heard that Connie Hines was living in Malibu and had become very successful acting in a TV series called Mr. Ed, The Talking Horse. I contacted her and arranged to stop by on my way through California. Having lived and worked around those air bases with the adjacent small towns for three years, produced some contrasting discomfort as I sat there in that luxurious setting in my old, tacky, tweedy, sports jacket, sipping a cold drink and looking out over the Pacific. There was that pretty shortstop I knew back in the plain folks setting, now a star and well known actress. Connie was as attractive as ever and living the life one would expect of a successful actress. She invited me to go to the set that day and see how the TV film was made, but I said my plane schedule was tight and we continued talking of common interests and "the old days."

A LONG HOME LEAVE

I went home to Union thinking: three months' vacation? What will I do after three weeks? It was winter. Everyone was working. Of course, I caught up on the time with the family, and Digi, and Bob Teuscher and Mary. I recall attending the

Water Co. Christmas party that Pop-pop organized each year at the storage and equipment center for repairmen, outside crews, trucker drivers, i.e. non-office personnel. They loved "Newt." He ran their summer picnic, not to mention Christmas party, and was one of them, even if he did wear a tie and jacket now; he was always "in the field."

I recall I spent many morning hours over that vacation working out in the Elizabeth YMCA with my gym rat instincts still flourishing. I started by buying an old car, several levels above the Ed McGrath hot shot special from the Georgetown days, and drove around to see friends and relatives. Of course there were some parties and a lot of time was used up loafing and reading. It was winter. Something was going through my mind. I was missing Aiko. I was 33 years old and I had no one to share my experiences and travels. I felt that in the natural order of things I needed the other half of the circle to create that synergy of the whole, God's plan, as otherwise described in Genesis. Perhaps seeing the nice families of Marion and Bob, Rich and Joyce, Digi, Bob, and others had a subliminal influence. But regardless of my course in the future, my heart, soul, and the little guy told me I had to reconcile my life and its meaning with God, which I did through a kind and understanding priest at the local St. Michael's Church.

I stayed with Mom and Dad and Gram Newhard. It was such a pleasure. It was home. I would like my next assignment, but this was home. Nana and Pop-pop were planning to build a retirement home to the south in that pine country in Howell, New Jersey, five years hence.

Uncle Jim, Nana's brother, was living somewhere in a New Jersey shore community. He invited me down so we could play catch up and talk and share a bit of the grog. He was a Merchant Marine Officer in WWII and stayed in a while after the war. I recall looking for his ship when I was in Tokyo Bay, aboard the Vesole, DD 878, but had just missed him. He was torpedoed once, near Cuba by a German submarine and avoided talking about it. A man of principle and straight talk, his idea of a good vacation was to get in the car and drive north into Canada until he ran out of people. Then he would find some connecting lakes, rent an open boat, hook up his outboard, get a map and provisions and load in the tackle, bait, and a .22 rifle for plinking small game. He sometimes took an Indian guide. Two weeks in that pristine setting refreshes the body and soul.

I arrived early evening. Aunt Clare and my cousins were out. Jim put a bottle of Canadian Club on the table and also poured some cold beer. Snacks abounded, and we launched into a non-stop conversation that didn't end until the level of the bottle indicated we might want to think about a possible tomorrow. We talked a bit more. We had a lot in common. It was a great time. One for the road. A goodbye hug. It was snowing. "Do you want to stay over?" asked Jim. "No thanks, I'm fine," not knowing I was lying. I started the engine. It was snowing. I arrived at the Garden State Parkway. It was really snowing, and I was drunk. With a mantra-like chant I sounded off, "The more you drink, the slower you drive." I got into the right hand lane and aimed that car to stay in the middle of it, but it was snowing hard and the visibility was dropping like a hawk on a prairie dog, as was the temperature. "The more you drink, the slower you drive, drive straight, go slow; don't fall asleep." Not many cars or trucks were on the road that night and I pressed on. Finally, with the big flakes falling on the windshield creating that hypnotic spell, the snow being high and my concentration low, I edged into the right side emergency lane, and over a little more. I parked, shut off the engine, and gave in to that over-powering temptation and demand from Sleep. It seemed like a week later, there was a loud pounding on the window and a flashlight beam in my face. "Are you okay in there?" hollered the State trooper. "Yeah," I shouted back while wind and snow danced the Swirl. "Well, you can't stay here; it's dangerous, get back on the road and keep going." He waited until I was underway. "Now follow the lane," my little guy ordered. "What lane?" "Why, the dim red lights in front of you," and repeat again, "The more I drink, the slower I drive." I mustered up all the determination I could, fought off the insistent call to sleep, and finally, slowly, made it home with a reinforced admiration of state troopers and the job they do protecting people from their own careless inadvertence.

There were many good times with friends and relatives. Pop-pop and I liked to have some good nibbles, usually cherry stone clams, a wedge of cheese, or some ham chunks, to go with a beer or two when watching a TV sporting event. Early one evening there was a good event coming up, so I said to Pop-pop, "I'll go to Elizabeth and get some clams at ol' Joe's," the family's favorite fish store for over twenty years. He replied, "It's late; if Joe's is not open, I would not buy from anyone else." Well, Joe's was closed and I went to a neighboring shop and bought the clams. They tasted great, as usual, with the hot sauce and lemon juice. Dad munched some cheese instead, loyal to Joe's place all the way, and we had a nice father-son game-watching session.

When the time came to go back to Japan, I drove that old car cross country (Rt. 66) to San Francisco. It was winter, so I took that southern route through the desert and Arizona. During my vacation, a recurring thought reflected a growing feeling. I was 33 years old and did not have anyone to share all this traveling, going places and doing things, with. Some people can be very happy without the other half of the circle to complete the whole. In fact, they do not see their life as shown in that graphic, but rather are complete unto themselves. But I saw myself in such a graphic, as I moved another measure into my future, and away from those recent years, where I had fallen away from practicing my faith, during the consecutive Laurie and Aiko affairs. That had given me a feeling of spiritual restlessness (the little guy's action), but with the love we had shared, I was not that lonely. Now it appeared to be the other way around, as I was naturally seeking both. Ah, analysis in retrospect is so much easier and more accurate than in real time.

I cashed in my NYC/SFO ticket, sold the car, and stayed a few days at the Drake Hotel, where those young, "salty" sailors stayed on their way home many years before. I had booked my return trip from SFO to HNL and then MNL and TKY in following up on Tom and Becky's invitation to visit them in Manila for a week or so. I boarded my flight in first class, started talking with my seat partner, and heard a familiar Russian-accented voice jovially responding to the flight attendant's greeting as he came aboard. Our happy reactions from such a coincidence prompted my seat partner to suggest a seat swap, and Andy and I had the San Francisco/Honolulu leg to play "catch-up" before we split at HNL. He was returning to Japan, and had been working with TRW Company setting up various businesses for them in Japan, Fuji Valve Co., and parts for Boeing. He was obviously pleased with his situation and I was happy for him. I told him about my work with Amexco and we agreed to stay in touch and get together along the way. Perhaps I would go to Tokyo and visit or, recalling that we had hunted along the Naktong River in Korea, he might come up north during hunting season. We parted in Honolulu, looking forward to our next meeting, as good friends do.

ZENI…AND THE BAND PLAYED ON

Tom was living like a "big mahoff" with the clubs, good restaurants, maid service, golf courses, and PX privileges. Among the first things I learned was that the language of the courts and education was English, having been instituted after the U.S. established the Philippines as a Territory soon after the Spanish-American War. We did some sight-seeing which included Corregidor, that famous shrine of American Valor, even in defeat and surrender, at the mouth of Manila Bay and the foot of the Bataan Peninsula. It was eerie. It was pretty much as the battles of 1942 (the Japanese occupation) and 1944 (American retaking) left it: the destroyed barracks, the Malinta Tunnel, that last headquarters of hospital and refuge, burrowed into the rock with many connecting rooms and tunnels from where General Wainwright walked out to surrender to the Japanese Army.

As a few of us stood deep in the dark, almost black, deathly silent recesses of what had been the underground hospital, the tour guide said softly, "Now stare into the darkness, or close your eyes, and listen to the moaning and groaning of the wounded and dying." I did just that and heard in soft sounds just what she said. I never forget them. Honor, Duty, Country. I also recall seeing the strange sight of a couple of batteries of mortars, posted on high ground, behind a stone wall, facing the sea. They were permanent emplacements, huge cast-iron barrels with bulbous bottoms that recoiled into gigantic springs set in a bedding deep in the ground. I believe the design went back to the 19th century.

Tom and Becky thought it would be a good idea to go to the Sky Light Room for an evening out. That was a night club on top of the Jai Alai stadium, good food, band, and Jai Alai action right out the curtain and into a box seat. Tom had asked Jun Navarro, a senior pilot at Philippine Airlines, and his wife May to join us and see if they could get me a date from among the flight attendants they knew. They called their friend Zeni Buhain, but she said, "Oh, I just got in from a long flight schedule and I am tired." "We're not asking you to marry him," said Jun, "just go over with us, have dinner, listen to some music, and we will take you home." "Well, okay."

So Tom and Becky and I arrived, had a drink, and began to enjoy the atmosphere. I was well into my second martini when they came in, but wow! Zeni was gorgeous, with beautiful dark almond shaped eyes, a lovely smile, and a happy personality; and, I soon learned, a storyteller par excellence. We had dinner, danced, tried the jai alai a bit, and it was an exceptionally pleasant time. Zeni and May had been classmates at the University of Santo Thomas where Zeni degreed in Journalism in the College of Arts and Letters, which meant a heavy touch of philosophy in that Dominican school. Crash! Bang! Well I was thunderstruck by it all, and before the evening ended, I asked her for a date, to which she agreed.

A couple of evenings later I went to her home, met her mom and dad, and we went out to dinner with her brother Efren and his wife. The Philippines had been a part of the Spanish Empire for 400 years, and much of its traditions, religion, and culture had a lasting effect on Philippine society, and even had an effect on lil' ol' me. Zeni's mom and dad were born during the Spanish rule and one of the social norms was that nice young ladies do not go out on dates without a chaperone or two.

It was all very pleasant with beautiful Zeni entertaining us with tales of flying, childhood, and Santo Thomas University. Efren had been three years with the guerrilla forces in the mountain areas south of Manila, along with his older brothers Moy and Vic. Amado, the youngest brother, was too young, and stayed at home during the Japanese occupation. He later distinguished himself by serving as a 2nd Lt. with the Philippine Expeditionary Forces in the Korean War. Efren and his wife, also a Zeni, were with the Philippine National Bank. In later years he would become EVP, Chief of Security, and Head Cashier for the whole system of 300 branches. I guess I told some St. Benedict, Georgetown, and Amexco stories, among other things. We all connected so comfortably. This thunderstruck roamer was already thinking of the ultimate possibility.

We had our last date before the night I would fly to Tokyo and then take the overnight train to Misawa. Zeni enjoyed dancing and also the bongo drum rhythms. So we went to a little place in Quezon City that she knew (and they knew her). I forget our escorts but recall the bongo music was great. Zeni came by dancing naturally, and this clod obviously forgot all the teaching of Mrs. Watson. Perhaps another Cuba Libra (rum and Coke) would help. For sure I was on Stardust Boulevard, and before we said goodbye and parted, we exchanged telephone numbers and addresses.

Waking up at the Doolittle's next morning, I felt a bit warm and weak. I said thanks and goodbye took my flight to Tokyo, and checked in at the Imperial Hotel. The next morning I called the house doctor who said I had the flu and to see a doctor when I arrived at Misawa, which I did after the overnight train trip. By then I had the yellow tinges of hepatitis on the skin and in the eyes, and absolutely no appetite. I spent six weeks in the base hospital, four on intravenous feeding. They told me that the incubation period for that germ was 2-3 weeks which coincided with the cherry stone clams I had bought in Elizabeth. It was a bit ironic, considering all the diseased places and bad food and water situations I had experienced in prior years, that I had to go to my clean home area to get hepatitis. I can still hear Pop-pop: "I told you to buy only at Joe's." Yeah, yeah.

One evening after the second week I had a visitor. It was charming Aiko, in a lovely kimono and with a present, bedroom slippers. We talked a bit, but not much. I was thankful but embarrassed about the situation as she showed a loving face in the quietness of it all. The frequent and awkward silences were prevalent and finally she said she had to go and kissed me and left. There was a Master Sergeant in the bed nearby who said, "Sir, I'm the last one to interfere in the personal matter of a stranger, but if someone loved me liked that, I would be sure to love her back." I thanked him, for he was right. Had I not met Zeni, I think, looking back, I would have made it all happen with Aiko. I never saw her again. I prayed for her. Years later I heard that she married a man who owned a resort hotel in the Japan Alps.

I was there a total of six weeks. I had no appetite the first four and was intravenously fed. Oh, what fun. The nurses would come by looking for new veins every other day. One was learning and one was teaching. "There's a good one. Pop it up a little more. That's it. Good. Didn't hurt a bit, did it Howard? Howard, stop faking, I know you didn't pass out." One time the very new Lt. was trying to find the vein among the collapsed ones and was wiggling the needle around inside. "Komata ne, can we get a little help here?" I asked. "What's that mean?" she inquired. I translated: "I'm in a bad way," and happily a nurse-Major and voice of experience came on to the scene and I was saved.

Jack, of course, was waiting for me to get well so he could turn over the district management to me and take some home leave before his assignment to India. He would visit often and jokingly comment, "C'mon, you're not sick. You like the nurses here and the food, and the soft bed. I need you. Hoss will come down from Chitose to be your assistant and I will send the new guy to Chitose." And so it was. I recovered my strength, exercised, and have never had any recurrence, or questionable blood test.

.

13 | COURTSHIP
International, that is

I had been away from the MBF job over 4 months, and went back to work re-connecting with the staff, seeing friends, and calling on the Base military officials, taking over as District Manager, and setting the business plan for the year ahead. I kept my residence on the base, from where I wrote some long letters with a humorous twist to Zeni on my old reliable Olympic script typewriter, stories about my trip to the Philippines, the hospital stay and Japan. Jack was about to depart and we had a party for him, that good friend.

I later found a small Japanese house in Misawa machi (town, village) among a loose cluster of six others owned by an elderly Japanese widow, Mrs. Ito, whose beautiful Siamese cat was a big part of her life. I spent much of my non-office time at the base gym (still a touch of the gym rat), the officer's club or my little Japanese house with no Western furnishings, but having the tatami floors, futon quilts (no bed), sliding soji doors, and sunken ofuro, keeping me in my Japanese mode, and, therefore, finding my best self in that bi-cultural situation. Other non-working hours might find some friends and me enjoying a local bistro.

Mrs. Ito was a kind and good person, a rarity in my experience regarding landlords. One time she was telling me about the centuries-old history of that area, mentioning a road and small fortress used by highway robbers who had controlled that area, near a large crater lake, Towada. It had a history of tribal warfare in which the fortress was a prominent centerpiece with the Samurai of the Bushido code, good guys winning out over the bandits. I was interested, and we drove out there in my jeep on the dirt road, through the mountain forest and finally to the ancient "fortress," more of a 200-year-old dilapidated walled-in stone house than a fort. The breath-taking overview of Towada remains with me today. That lake, with its high algae content had continual color changes from varying reflections by moving cloud formations. It was so quiet. No cars or people. Just the sound of the wind and birds and animals among the rustling trees. A fine setting for a possible film coming soon near you, The Towada Samurai.

That year, as the Obon festival came along, Mrs. Ita's big cat died. She was heart broken. It was very touching to see her put the cat's body in a box and then on a wooden float with some lighted candles and float it out on the current in the darkness with the hundreds of other candle-lit floats, toward a nearby lake, and so including her cat in that historic pageant.

A few weeks after, I wrote to Zeni; she replied saying that she and her flight attendant friends enjoyed the "laugh-gem" stories I had sent. Such a compliment from a qualified journalist, whom I liked very much, made my heart sing. Our writings progressed to a regular beat.

Our MBF provided loans for off-base housing and to purchase automobiles, along with insurance coverage. To improve this service I contacted the American Foreign Insurance Association (AFIA), in Tokyo to provide a local adjustor, which they did. A young man came up from Tokyo Fujikawa-san, with his mom, sister, and sister's little girl. His dad, deceased, had been a general in the Japanese Army and had a string of embassy assignments as military attaché to many European countries before WWII. They needed a place to rent in our little town and I introduced them to Mrs. Ito, who did have a house available, almost next to mine. They were nice neighbors, and he did well with his assignment.

In one of her letters, Zeni mentioned that she had a Tokyo stop a couple of weeks hence. I called Manila, no easy feat in those days, to get the details. We arranged to meet and have dinner. It worked out fine. We had dinner in the Prunier at the Imperial Hotel and afterwards walked around talking and enjoying the sights. Later, we chanced by a German bar (Ratskeller), with an attractive ornamental front and a cozy environment, so we went in talking some more. She had to get back to her hotel shortly and be ready for an early flight next morning, but we stayed on a while enjoying the moment. On the way out, we were both commenting on the nice design and style of the displayed beer mugs, particularly the 16 oz. ones of blue glass, shaped like a boot, with the Ratskeller coat of arms on it. I bought a box of them for her, my first present (the big banker from the north).

I saw Zeni to her hotel, as we commented on enjoying each others' writing. I said I would call once in a while and that I was thinking of coming to the Philippines for a week or so around Christmas to see the Doolittles and perhaps we could have some dates, to which she agreed. We said a warm goodbye and I walked back to the Imperial feeling the world was totally attuned and in "synch."

Early the next day I called Andy's office, apologizing for not letting him know I was coming to town, but how about lunch? Yes, the morning schedule was easy to move around, come on over, and he gave me the address. His office was about 30x40 ft. (very large in space-scarce Tokyo) and designed with an artful Eurasian blend. I walked in and said, "Wow, you've come a long way from On Chon-ni." He laughed, and never forgot that remark, mentioning it many years later in San Francisco. He was the TRW (a large engineering company) representative for Japan. TRW had several partnerships: Fuji Valve, a company making parts for Boeing, and some others. In his usual genial manner, he told the story of when he first arrived there, and addressed a gathering of some twenty important business and government people as to what TRW could and would be doing. He wanted to be known and do more business by explaining how TRW could be helpful in their search for a good investment or in the purchase of TRW products. He purposely started his talk in English, and could see many leaning forward, straining to understand, and then he said, (in Japanese) "I think it would be better if I used your language," and he proceeded to do so. They were so pleased that he spoke so well that they relaxed and enjoyed the talk to the extent that he was immersed in requests for appointments, more info, and business offers in the coming days. I was not surprised; Andy had it all. We went off to lunch. I told him about Zeni. He was happy to hear that I was thinking of settling down at last and wished me well, agreeing to keep in touch.

The next day I went over to the Amexco office which was nearby and went to lunch with Dick Stewart and Karl Kircher, filling the air with my news about this fabulous girl I had met. That evening "Night Train Howie" jumped aboard with renewed vigor and ready for the Future's tricks and surprises. Ah, nothing could faze me, I was focused. God smiled.

It was early summer and the MBF audit had a good rating, which pleased me, the Amexco New York Headquarters, the 39th Air Division Command, and the U.S. Treasury Dept. overseers. About that time Tom Martin talked me into playing some golf. Well sure, after all, I had played Wack Wack in Manila (shooting about 115 and using the baseball grip of the stubborn and uninformed). Well, I'm a natural athlete, right? So just keep playing and you will do fine. We played a foursome; but before teeing off, I hit a bucket of balls and listened to some advice about grip and stance. Gosh it felt awkward…overlap grip, left arm straight, draw back slowly, head down, 3/4 time like the Skaters' Waltz, and follow through. I knew I had improved from the last time because I said fewer "good mornings" to those we let play through, but I still wasn't all that keen about that being a good way to get my exercise. I preferred walking those dirt and gravel country roads. However, I wanted some improvement so I could play a little better when I got to Manila, and perhaps play with Zeni's oldest brother, Moy.

I began thinking "Zeni" often, and called her with the bright idea of flying to Manila for a week in September. She said she could probably arrange her flight schedule to be in town part of that time. Her letter some ten days later said all was well and Moy wanted to meet me and play some golf. Yes!

The summer moved fast and we were always busy at the bank. On weekends I often went to a nice beach with a good surf, about 90 minutes south along that Pacific coast. Near Misawa we had a couple of company picnics with invited guests. By the time mid-Sept arrived, my NWA ticket had been confirmed and off I went on All Nippon Airways, connecting at the old Haneda airport with NWA. Five hours later I was talking with Tom Doolittle as he drove me to his place in San Lorenzo Village, Makati. I told him about Zeni, and, realizing I came down in Sept and would repeat in December he said, "Moose, you have a great life, no large responsibilities, other than your work, lots of freedom, you call all the shots, why do you want to get serious with this international romance?" He was right in his mind, but wrong in mine, and I didn't choose to explain the feeling about needing a beloved other half of the circle to create a synergistic being in a holy union with God. We went on to chat about our mutual Agency friends and who was assigned where, no sensitive ingredients, ever. Tom and Becky, as usual, were hospitable and we enjoyed some trips to the Sea Front Club and pool while I was there; and little Tom Jr. had a good time swimming with his uncle Moose, as the tyke called me.

I called Zeni and arranged to pick her up the next evening. She said some friends were having a small get-together, so I drove over Hwy. 54 to her home in Quezon City. I met her sister Luz, a nurse, who lived there, and said hi to her parents, chatting and watching some boxing, a favorite of her Dad's, while I waited for Zeni. Then retired, her father was from Cavite province, son of a fishing family that had a fleet of boats. He had made up his mind very early that he would go to college in Manila and not pursue that family business. After college, he joined the postal service and for many years worked in the northern part of Luzon helping to improve the system and put in telegraph lines. There he met and married Isabel de Jesus, who was from Tarlac in Nueva Ecija province, of a hacienda family. Zeni was born in Cabanatuan, Nueva Ecija province; the family moved to Manila with children Rocing, Moy, Vic, Luz, Efren, and Amado when she was one year old. Vicente Buhain, Zeni's dad, went on to become the Post Master of International Mail.

We went off to the party which was at the home of Gen. Castaneda, retired Chief of Staff, and was given by some of his children (our age group). Seems that Moy, a young lieutenant, fought in Bataan and was in the infamous Death March. He suffered from malaria and malnutrition and escaped at night during the march, crawling off of the roadside and into the brush, was sheltered by the locals there, and finally got to the Manila Bay shore line and was taken in a banca (outrigger) across the bay to the coast near Manila. It took him a month to get to Cavite and his relatives, being sheltered and cared for by local folks along the way. Thereafter, he went off to a mountain location where he found Castaneda, who was running guerrilla operations, and Moy became his aide. After the war Moy was his aide when Gen. Casteneda became Chief of Staff. Hence the families were very close.

They all were such warm and friendly people that I went away feeling I had known them a long while. It was a super evening and, of course, I was near Zeni all the time. She told me that if it was ok Moy was inviting me for golf the day after tomorrow. Later, I drove Zeni home sans escort, and with a kiss at the door, which surely emphasized that progress was in order. Then I went on to Doolittle's.

Zeni did not play golf, so at the appointed time and country club I showed up and met Moy in the lobby. He had invited an American friend to play with us. Lou Gleeck was the Consul General at the U.S. Embassy, an experienced diplomat, fluent in Tagalog, the largest native dialect in this country of some 58 dialects in this most interesting 1,500 mile long archipelago of 7,000 islands. An historian on the Philippines, he specialized in the American era, and was the custodian of its largest pictorial aggregate, housed in the library at the U.S. Embassy. I imagine they both played around 85-90 golf, with me still trying to break 100, but all that was just a good excuse for our conversationally stimulating walk through those lovely grounds. The Colonel's educational and civilian background was in journalism and after the war he attended the U.S. Army School of Psychological Warfare in Carlisle Pa, and the U.S. Army Transportation School. The elicitation skills of both of these gentlemen were silently applauded by this trained and experienced former I.O. They wanted to know a lot about me, and with good reason. Who was this 34-year-old guy who was writing, calling, and traveling from northern Japan to see Moy's youngest sister? Where was he from?

Married before? Have children? and so on. I enjoyed it all, telling of Nana and Pop-pop, St. Benedict's, U.S. Navy, Georgetown, sports, Korea, and American Express at appropriate times in our four hours or so together. I liked them from the start.

At another time Zeni and I went to a movie with Efren and his wife. Zeni was scheduled for a flight the next afternoon and I would not be seeing her anymore this trip, so we agreed to meet for lunch at the airport restaurant before she had to report. When I walked in she was in uniform and seated at a nice sized table. The waiter was putting a serving platter full of Chinese noodles, veggies, chicken and mushrooms in the center of the table. "Who else is joining us?" I asked. "Oh, that's for me, do you want some?" We laughed. She did some modeling and had an hour-glass figure. I had a portion and she finished the platter. Yeah, go figure the figure. She talked about studying journalism and writing prose and poetry along the way, did some interning, and was offered a position as assistant editor in a small women's magazine, a job she really wanted. But her brothers Moy and Vic counseled their old father against her moving around in the world of journalism, with which they were familiar and considered it not fit for a respectable young woman like their sister. Such were the times. So her dad said no. She was very disappointed. "What did I go to school for?" she asked him...silence, case closed.

She talked of applying for a flight attendant position and he said no to that also, away from home too often. Such was the culture of yesteryear which would have to make its changes for tomorrow in the repetitive cycle of history. Her sister Luz had been allowed to be a flight attendant with Philippine Airlines sometime after the war. In those days you had to be a nurse before you could apply (a fact not well known due to the efforts of the marketing dept). Anyway, she had a winning point and so applied to Trans World Airlines, the famous Howard Hughes operation. She flew the Manila, Sri Lanka, Bombay, or Delhi route and later was selected to represent her region in TWA's Miss Jet International Contest in Paris. The jets were just coming into the market. She placed second, won a trip to Egypt, met many celebrities, and had a happy, memorable experience as the newspapers picked it up from Paris to Manila. Later they asked her to go to Paris and base from there, but of course that was not agreeable to her father and mother. The old school and ways were still pre-dominant, so she stayed based in Manila and flew the Asia routes.

Later on, Philippine Airlines planned to go international and Zeni took a job with them. One of the qualifications was to be adept at rescue procedures in the water and they trained by going off-shore and practiced using life rafts. She enjoyed learning those procedures and started to fly domestically with PAL hoping to fly international. Meanwhile, World Airways, a charter company during the Vietnam War was flying military personnel across the Pacific to Wake Island, Manila and Saigon. Zeni applied and was made Chief Purser, hard work and good pay. We met in that period of time. She had been doing some modeling,

Zeni in Paris, in TWA uniform

and occasionally wrote a feature article. Her real love was journalism and that's what she wanted to do, but, that story has been told.

The time ran out, lunch was finished. We said our parting words and from the observation deck I saw her plane take off. With a mild emptiness, or "stuck in neutral," I cabbed it to Tom's place, where that evening we had a nice family dinner and a few bon voyage toasts to uncle Moose.

Back in Misawa all was well, with Hoss running the show in my absence. Hunting season was about to open in October in that northern clime and during several evenings over a mug or two in the "O" Club, Texas Tom, Hoss, and I planned some trips into some good duck and pheasant areas. The day before the season opened we rode in Hoss's jeep out to a desolate place on the beach to practice shooting birds, using a hand-held contraption to throw out clay discs as in skeet shooting. We were experienced shooters and soon established the rhythm of it all. We were ready for our predawn trip tomorrow. It was late afternoon as we rode a dirt and gravel road on the way back to the base. As we passed along a high, sloping, brush-filled embankment lining a small lake, I said, "Stop, Hoss, let's walk up and have a look at the lake," and I jumped out holding my shotgun which I had been cradling against the bumpy ride, still loaded with the light # 8 or 9 shot with the safety on. I hurried up the long slope ahead of the others, reached the top, and there in the water were about 20 ducks starting a noisy take-off from my intrusion. Instinctively, Bam! Bam! Bam! and about seven dropped, as they were well clustered. Hoss and Tom came running up, shouting, "What the hell are you doing? We start TOMORROW." Response: "I don't know why. I just lost it." Tom replied, "We can have big problems with the local authorities and our own Misawa Airbase officials." Then he broke into a smile, seeing the humor of it all coming from a mix of stupidity and hunter's instinct, as he surely anticipated telling the story to as many friends as would listen while sitting around the "O" Club bar, the home of humor and wisdom.

So we waded out into that cold shallow water, retrieved the seven, and hid them in a tote bag in the jeep. They were placed in Tom's home freezer for a few days (well into the season), then thawed out, and taken to a local butcher for gutting and cleaning. Obviously 3 good criminal minds were at work. I was an average bird shooter who got lucky with a modified choke and # 8 or 9 bird shot, usually too light for ducks. Texas Tom probably still tells that one, wherever he is, or he has set it to some folksy guitar lyrics.

Before the snows came in late November, we spent much of our spare time in the field, or studying and discussing potentially good game areas. A Japanese friend knew a good duck lake and drove us there in his jeep. He knew a farmer who owned land right on that shallow lake with intermittent areas of rushes and cattail reeds. The farmer had a dog he called "Em," a mongrel about the size of a beagle. We put the decoys, gear, and ourselves, along with Em and the farmer, into his long cigar-shaped poling boat and headed for the opposite shore, pushed by his slow rhythmic poling. It was early dawn with a heavy mist in the area, poor visibility until it lifted. We were poling through some rushes and the farmer stopped. We sat still, the universal "sshush" finger/lip signal in play, as the farmer watched the highly alert Em, standing still with head up, then dove and splash! into the rushes and disappeared. We sat there for a while in the silent mist. Then some thrashing around in there, and suddenly in a small opening there was Em with a duck by the throat coming to the boat, as the poling farmer shortened the distance. What a duck dog! When we later reached the other shore, we set out decoys, the mist lifted, and the ducks started to fly. Bam! Bam! Bam! Em was right there retrieving each one that hit the water. Here's to Em in salute of that happy rumor that all dogs go to heaven.

Our correspondence kept humming along and Zeni and I enjoyed it. I also called a few times. I made plans to visit Tom and Becky for a week or so over Christmas and Zeni was going to take off most of that time. The more I thought about her and my planned trip in December, the more I saw this as a focal point. I sat down and talked with Texas Tom Martin, the G/M of the Exchange, my buddy, about getting in touch with his diamond suppliers and arranging a good deal on an engagement and wedding ring. I wanted that with me when I made my trip. I mean, if I did decide to ask her to marry me and she said yes, it would be a bit like, duh, what do I do now? But with the presentation of the ring right there on the spot? aha, what a smooth, suave, suitor of the fair maiden! Well Texas Tom was beside himself, couldn't wait to spread the word, and I had to give him some friendly advice. "Look, this might not go through. She might have a 'sometimes' boy friend and they have rekindled the flame, or I might not want to go through with the asking, for whatever reason, and I'll expect a refund. Regardless, I don't want you talking about this until there is something positive to say. Otherwise, I will have a couple of guys from Shinjuku (the Tokyo area where Mafia types were easy to find) come up here to arrange for your candlelight representation in the next Obon festival, wakari maska? (understand?)"

Laughingly, "Wakari mashta (understood); good luck, I'll get you a good deal. Say, if this goes through and you marry in 5-6 months where will you live? In that little one room tatami-floor castle of yours?" "Thanks Tom, hadn't even thought of it, but I will work it out," said the game-plan strategist, obviously not at his best.

Hunting season was over all too soon, but we had frozen duck and pheasant in the PX freezer all winter, awaiting creative preparations by Tom, or Tom and Helen Ige, or other volunteer hosts. The snows came and would continue through March. I recall looking across the airfield on many winter days and seeing only the tail of an aircraft whooshing along above that high snow line, which had been piled up along side the runways by the huge snow blowers. Our guys were always ready. Alerts were frequent. We had the Amexco Christmas party, including spouses, around the 18th, complete with music, dancing, speeches, and a touch of karaoke by those with more chutzpa than talent. I think I sang Sakura, Sakura, the cherry blossom song, thus proving that point. It was a nice, warm and friendly time. I left for Manila a day or two after with a few presents and that little ring box tucked away in my pocket.

I called Zeni from Doolittle's house and she told me about the Misa de Gallo (Mass of the Rooster) tradition. Five days before Christmas, very early in the morning, the Church there has a 5 a.m. Mass (about the time the cock crows) to say hey, wake up and relive the first advent season awaiting the promised Savior. The tradition was to attend the Mass 5 days in a row. She added, "Do you want to go one time? How about tomorrow? Hot chocolate and pan de sal afterward?" So we went to that early morning Mass with some of her friends, a chilly winter morning of 67 degrees, cold for this country, and everyone wore a jacket, while I, fresh out of the snow country, was just fine in a shirt. The Mass itself was the Advent Mass for that date which was read and said throughout the world; a lovely tradition anticipating Christmas Day.

The next day we had dinner and Zeni invited me to go to the Christmas Midnight Mass, which we attended along with Efren, his wife and Luz. I had been attending Mass on Sundays since my Reconciliation while on home leave, and was slowly returning to my spiritual training and ethics.

It was in a large cathedral-like church with such an overflow of attendees that they put some loudspeakers up over the doors facing the crowd in the street. We had to stand but had a clear view of the altar and the several co-celebrants. The centuries-old Christmas music was played and sung. To be involved in all that color, sound, pageantry, and familiar-from-boyhood Liturgy, Creed, and Eucharistic prayers, with this woman whom I loved, touched me deeply, and as I walked with her to the altar rail to receive the Body of Christ it all came to a meaningful focus. Faith soared, and inside, along with that little guy, I had a "clock-cleaning," joyful cry.

The Mass finished in the early morning and we went somewhere, I do not remember, for a light meal of delicacies. I told Zeni that going to Mass with her was very meaningful for me and I appreciated the invitation and she said she was glad I was there. We planned to go to a movie that evening after a snack at Ma Mon Luk, a famous noodle house chain.

I went back to Doolittle's to sleep and share some of the Christmas Day with them. Afterward, I borrowed Tom's VW again and had another tight-fisted (10 and 2 o'clock position) adventure along Hwy. 54 cluttered with taxis, cars, people, jeepneys, pedicabs, and dogs, nicely blended into the chaotic overture of The Unsolvable Traffic Problem.

It was a beautiful December day in the tropics. I arrived at the Buhains', had a pleasant chat with Mama and Papa (Zeni's parents), and we went out without any travel companions. "Where are we going?" Zeni asked. "Oh, toward Los Baños, through Laguna; Tom suggested that for a nice drive in the country." "Yes," she said, "nice plan, and Laguna has some good country restaurants." We rolled along and shared a happy feeling. I was in love with her and she, I knew, had a strong feeling for me. I had my first out-of-Manila look at the Philippine countryside and I liked it very much: the small towns with open markets, a variety of wood, bamboo, stone dwellings, the nipa huts, and very friendly people. "Hi Joe" was still a kid's greeting for an American, extended from the war days, when it got its start from the standardized phrase "G.I. Joe," meaning the common soldier, or "grunt" as in the jargon of WWII. That all started from the Army's formal classification of G.I. meaning General Issue, as when we "grunts" got our clothing allotment in boot camp.

We went to Los Baños, drove around the Agricultural School, the surrounding countryside with its tropical foliage and streams, talking and having fun with it all. On the way back I said I wanted to stop the car for a while, and wound up choosing a large patch with grassy coverage, well off the road, which the grazing goats and carabao (water buffalo) kept low. A stream meandered nearby and some carabao were soaking in it. I said, "What a great spot!" and Zeni had a "what-are-we-doing-here?" face. But I was thinking about the end result, not the implementation. A blanket was produced from the car and Zeni kept that questioning expression. I, near my beloved, talked about my good job in Japan, future travels, and finally brought it to us and my feeling for her. I asked her to marry me. She must have had an inkling or two, but she showed downright surprise. "Oh my, I can't speak." "Just say yes." "I can't right now, I have to wait and think." Unknown to me at the time, the reality was that in keeping with the tradition of the day, as practiced and moved along by the older generation, her mom and dad had to have a say in the matter. I said, "I really want to marry you. Here, I want you to wear this ring while you are thinking it over." She was very surprised and obviously happy. "Oh, I can't do that." "Well just keep it until you say yes." (the "presumed close" by this crafty rascal.) So I talked some more, about what a nice future she and I and our children would have. She took the ring box and said, "When you get back to Japan, please write to my father for his permission, and I will marry you when he approves." Oh boy! was that going to be some letter! Exaggerate, but do not fabricate. "I'm gooder 'n good" in Snuffy Smith language.

Over the years we laughed at the time, place, and substance of the whole situation. I can hear Mom, "And he chooses this place, out in the country, near a creek where the carabao soak and wade and the goats are grazing. Whatever happened to a little glass of wine reflecting the candle light, while the violin music soothes the mind, body and soul?" So here was this dude, whose Agency efficiency reports said he can plan well and implement, botching the biggest operation of his life because of poor prior intelligence and bad choice of location and timing. But Love did have its day and the rest didn't matter.

The lunch and ride back was a cloud nine adventure. Zeni would be on duty for the next few days and I was leaving during that time, so I said I would be calling and writing to Papa. I had dinner at her home, talked with Luz and Papa and Mama, and watched some TV for a while. She walked me to the door. We kissed, and again. I left, thinking about that letter all the time. I told the Doolittles the whole story the next day. "I knew it!" said Becky. "Now your troubles are just starting," said Tom, the advisor on worldly matters.

Back in the snow country, I pounded out the "request for permission" letter with all of the reasons to support an affirmative response. Some serious praying prevailed at that time and off went the letter in the post-haste class. Two weeks went by without a return. I called Zeni and she explained, "Well you know he is old and he wants to talk it over with Moy." "Well, where is Moy?" "Oh, he is at the SEATO (South East Asia Treaty Organization) Conference with the Speaker and will return next week." Time went on as Zeni and I corresponded some more and, finally, I received a letter from Papa Buhain granting approval and giving us his blessing and love (see Appendix C: Papa Buhain's Letter of Approval). My friends and I closed the "O" club that night, having sampled a bit of the bar stock and handling all the known problems and eschatological considerations with imagined class and profundity. I sent another letter to Zeni, and after sleeping, I called her, full of love and excitement, to discuss the how, when, and where plans for the wedding. She had moved ahead on that: It would be June 16, at The Immaculate Conception Church in Quezon City. She also said I had to be there at least ten days before to follow the law regarding blood tests and administrative paperwork. Father Cogan, a Columbian missionary priest and friend of the family, would provide the pre-marriage counseling and conduct the ceremony. She also enlightened me as to another Philippine custom: the bridegroom pays for the wedding expenses. "No problem, what's mine is yours," said he, of the "pay a little more and go first class" perception, who was only now getting serious about personal savings. I sent most of what I had, except for taking care of the immediate future, including the two-week honeymoon, which Karl Kircher was going to arrange to include the Imperial Hotel in Tokyo, and Fujiya and Karakuen Hotels on the Isu Peninsula. My first investment should have been in the Nippon Telephone and Telegraph Co., because our writings almost ceased in favor of the telephone. There were no telephone cards and cell phones then; it was all station to station (when you connected). "I hope we are married before we go broke," I

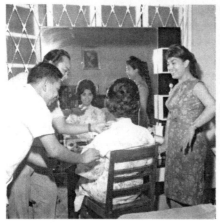

Beauticians at Zeni's home, helping the bride get ready.

quipped. "Going broke?" she answered. "Even before we have children? Oh, what am I getting into?" I had that lovely laughing face in my mind.

We talked and talked many times a week along with intermittent letters. The announcement had been published. She was now wearing the ring and she was busy planning the whole affair. Because of the heat in June (and not wanting to have our wedding night in Manila, easy pickin's for prankster friends), the wedding would be at 7a.m. followed by a wedding breakfast at the Club Filipino, after which we would go to Zeni's home; she would change from her gown, the limo would be loaded with my two suitcases and her many. Hey, she was packing for good, a PCS (Permanent Change of Station). But seriously, looking back, this was an awesome change for her. Zeni had lived in Manila from age 1, the youngest in a large family. She was there during the war, ages 8-12, when the atrocities involving relatives came close to home, and in the final horrendous fight for the city. Now she was 29 and would be leaving friends and family to go off with her husband to live in a foreign country for the first time. She had visited Japan before, as a guest of Dr. and Mrs. Arakawa, a personal friend of her uncle (Tito) Pepe, going back to the pre-war days. This helped to temper her attitude of distrust toward the society that had caused so much pain and hardship in the Philippines, 1941–1945.

I asked her to leave her flying job to make it easier to work on the wedding plans, and of course because of my concern about the risks involved. She said she was planning to do that and with "notice time" she would be flying just another month. About ten days later I picked up a copy of the daily Stars and Stripes and there on the front page was the story that a World Airways military charter flight, headed for Manila and Saigon, had taken off from Wake Island and disappeared somewhere between Wake Island and Manila. Oh, my God, Zeni often did a turn-

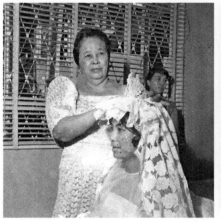

Left: Lola helps Zeni put on veil for wedding. Right: Zeni leaving Buhain house for the church.

around at Wake. How many WA charters could there be? I was frantic. I called Manila. Luz said Zeni was away on a flight schedule and would be back in a couple of days. I was more frantic and could not get any more information. When Zeni returned, she told me the story. There were two turn-around crews at Wake. They had a nice social the night before that flight, which was assigned to the other crew, took off. They waved goodbye as they boarded. Many of them were friends of Zeni. She was very sad as she spoke and I talked of my love and concern, and relief that it was not her flight. She replied with a simple "It wasn't my time," a phrase she would use at other times as we traveled our path together.

STEP ONE...THE MOST IMPORTANT

In the spring Zeni took a cruise ship to Hong Kong with her Uncle and Aunt Pepe and Conching Roy for a shopping trip with her future in mind. Among her purchases was my wedding ring, custom designed, by her, etched, wide band, with an inscription inside.

I wrote at length to Nana and Pop-pop about Zeni and me, asking who might be coming to the wedding, knowing it was not likely that anyone from my family would make the 16,000 mile round trip . The same was true for good friends, so I asked Tom Doolittle, a good friend since my Korea days, to be best man. Tom, a non-churchgoer and perennial critic of the Vatican and Church who had advised me not to do it, accepted without hesitation (maybe there was some hope for him after all). Zeni, Becky and others had to laugh when the pictures were passed around to see Tom and I standing there at the altar waiting while (out of picture) Zeni was walking up the aisle with Papa and Tom looked downright

Left: Luz Buhain, maid-of-honor. Right: Lolo walking Zeni down the aisle

nervous and tense. All the while a well known classical soprano sang the Ave Maria. The church was beautifully decorated, including a bouquet at every pew. A goodly crowd was gathered for the ceremony, steeped in rich tradition of not only the Church, but Philippine custom.

I was enlightened as we progressed through it all, to the Consecration and Reception of the Eucharist…I was elated; my Faith again soared. Faith, the yeast in the dough of immutable Truth, as I felt the "full circle" of our oneness come to life. "Hey, it's not about you anymore," said the little guy inside; I could not have said it better myself.

After the final blessing ending the Mass, we walked the aisle, hand in hand, smiling, nodding, and grateful for the comments, kind looks, and gestures of all, wishing us well. Here I was immersed in a different culture, without any family

Left: signing of the wedding contract. The bell, candle, cord and contract are Spanish Catholic wedding traditions. Right: the newlywed Newhards laugh as well-wishers throw rice.

Left: Zeni and Howard exit the church. Right: the newlyweds pose between a jeepney and car.

or friends from the U.S. except Doolittle, and yet I felt very comfortable and "at home," such was Zeni's love for me, my acceptance by her family, and the kind and hospitable nature of the people. Those quotation marks would disappear in a few years.

Outside the church the rice was thrown and we all went to the Club Pilipino for the wedding breakfast. Fr. Cogan and all eight sponsors were at our table. There was the champagne toast and later the cake cutting, a couple of short speeches, and then the release of the doves. Someone pulled the long silk ribbon to open the door of the cage hanging up on the ceiling and one of the two doves flew out. The people laughed. The other bird stayed in the cage. The people laughed some more. Auntie Conching told me that the tradition said if the two do not leave at the same time it means the woman will

Releasing the doves

Left: Zeni and Howard say goodbye to guests. Right: tossing the bouquet

rule the family, meaningful in that macho depicted society. I laughed too but, hey, whether it's the Philippines or the U.S.A., "If Momma ain't happy, ain't nobody happy."

All too soon it was over, some of us looking at our watches, knowing it would be a "squeaker" to make that flight to Tokyo. After many goodbyes, we went in the car to Mom's home where she changed, the baggage was loaded, and we sat in the car waiting to pull out, waving to Mama, Papa and Luz. Standing in the doorway, Mama called to Zeni in Tagalog, "Are you sure you don't want to take a maid?" Zeni laughed, and when she translated for me she added that Mama was concerned for me. Way to go Mama!

Moy made an early start to the airport and asked the security people to hold

The wedding party. Left to right: flowergirls, Luz, Lola, Zeni, Howard,
Lolo, Tom Doolittle and son (the ringbearer).

Zeni and Howard at the airport

the plane for us, if necessary. He could do things like that. He knew all the military and security people well and was the aide de camp for the Speaker of the House of Representatives who was with the controlling Liberal Party at that time, along with President Macapagal; and so it happened. We were late and they held an international flight ten minutes for us. We arrived at the airport. A few pictures were snapped, the bags were toted out to the waiting plane, and we walked the tarmac to the stairs at the First Class entrance and went up and into the cabin. Zeni with her corsage and both of us with our wedding rings gave the waiting passengers a clue of the situation as we sat down and hugged and kissed. The passengers clapped, showing a kind spirit, prompted by the thoughts of "now we can go," and "who are these guys?"

Left: a quick group photo at the airport. Right: the newlyweds hold hands on the tarmac as they walk to the detained plane.

After the take-off and the climb to cruise level, we had some wine and hors d'oeuvres, but Zeni begged off the meal to lie down—and in those times some of the best meals in the world were served at 30,000 feet in first class. She was just too tired. She and a few friends had stayed up after midnight talking, singing, strumming guitars and giving her a nice send-off. So there was my bride with two pillows off to the side, covered by a blanket in a deep slumber all the way to Tokyo, while I enjoyed the scrumptious meal. Upon arrival a meeter/greeter arranged our car transfer to the Imperial, which provided us a lovely suite with flowers and a bowl of fruit and a welcome message from the G/M, a nice touch by Karl Kircher in arranging our trip.

Our wedding night was the night of nights. We were up late, very late. I recall joking about what happened to the chaperones. We sipped the wine and talked of our future together as if we knew all about it. God smiled. We surely rested well and in the morning we decided to have our breakfast in the main dining room and arranged for the hotel to store most of our luggage until we returned about ten days hence. Later in the day we took the train to the town of the Fujiya Hotel on the Isu Peninsula. Nestled in the hills and the surrounding hot springs, the hotel was a mecca for rest and relaxation. Some buildings on that estate were in the Japanese style and others were European with a Swiss flair. It

Zeni on the grounds of the Fujiya Hotel.

was a perfect place to honeymoon. The natural beauty of it all, hills, woodland, gardens, stone bridges over pools filled with carp, and marvelous June weather, make it memorable to this writing. After five or six days there, we took a train to the town of the Karakouen Hotel in the same general area. That was a western style hotel set in the hills and surrounded by a golf course. Aboard the train we had gone into the club car, ordered a drink, were talking, and there a few tables away was Don Newcombe, the future Hall of Famer who was in Japan either playing baseball or negotiating to play there. I went over to say hello. He was from Newark, so we had some talking subjects. I sure wasn't going to tell HIM about my circle change and Uncle Charlie. He was a nice fella with a style to match. I recall hearing an interview in the U.S. with the great Roy Campanella, who was "Newk's" catcher, commenting about his fastball. He said, "Ol' Newk, he can really hum that pea." How true.

We walked those beautiful grounds and took in the view from a couple of look-out towers. The next day we played nine holes of golf, Zeni's first attempt. I wasn't much better, but we had fun, and the girl caddies were highly amused. We were really enjoying being together. The next day was a Saturday and our telephone rang. Who would know we are here? Must be a wrong connection. Not so, it was our tour arranger, Karl Kircher. "How are you guys doing? Everything ok? Want to play some golf?" "Are you nuts, I'm on my honeymoon." "Yeah, but I'm in the lobby and I brought my clubs." I had to laugh and Zeni thought it was funny too, and when she met Karl she said, "You guys play and I will walk with you, maybe I'll learn something." "You won't learn from him, just watch my form and swing," said the caddie from Union. We had a grand round, not of golf, but conversation. Karl's girlfriend Kay, later his wife, was Japanese and a flight attendant with BOAC (British Airways), currently on a flight. We had a lot to talk about and we did. After the round, Karl left to go off to another course, and we agreed to have dinner back in Tokyo, my kind of tour arranger. Our lovely time at the Karakouen ended too soon and we headed back to The Imperial, met up with Kircher and Dick Stewart the next day, and they were charmed by Mom's personality and beauty. We toured the city a bit and the next day we flew to Misawa Air Base.

I had given "Hoss" our ETA, so when the DC-3 taxied to the commercial parking area on that large air base, there was Hoss, Texas Tom, Helen and Tom Ige, and a few other friends. It was just a fantastic "homecoming" for me. Right there, on the apron, next to the parked plane, they broke out the champagne, cut up a cake, and Texas Tom took his guitar out of the car and serenaded the group, a real fun time. Did the Air Police mind? Nah, we were all part of the family. From there Mom and I went into Misawa machi to move into our first home. Mrs. Ito came out of her nearby house to greet us, and the mother and sister of Fujikawa-san, the AFIA rep, also gave a neighborly welcome to Mom. We went over to our little Japanese house (not yet a home) and went in. I had prefaced the door-entering ceremony with "Of, course we are going to look for something more suitable," (since the entire house was about 700 sq. ft. of tatami mat flooring on which we would be sitting, sleeping, and eating.) "Well, I always wanted to be a girl scout," said the new bride with a smile. Actually, I had notified New York Headquarters of my situation and had asked for the funds to build a house and was awaiting a reply.

It was about this time that Mom divulged that your Lola, a great cook, had given her little opportunity or encouragement to acquire such skills. However, she said with a smile, that she could make jelly rolls (oh, for joy!) The love-struck bridegroom replied, "That's ok, we are members of the Officers Club, so until you learn, we can eat out." She liked that idea and we not only frequented the "O" Club but some little restaurants around town. One small sushi and noodle shop in particular was homey and cozy and served a soup of freshly made ramen noodles with spring onions and thin slices of pork loin. We always remembered that place.

When she finally figured she really could make it happen, Mom decided to practice making spaghetti. She did fine in our tiny kitchen, and a week or so later we asked about six friends to come for dinner. We all sat at the low table on the tatami floor, in the usual Japanese style, and ate the spaghetti and meatballs, bread, and salad. Cheese and fruit followed, along with some port wine. The comments of the parting guests acclaimed the evening a success; I am sure the martinis and wine had some small part. All were happy, especially Mom, who was so pleased to give a successful dinner party for six or seven in a tiny Japanese house way up there in northern Japan (see Appendix D: Mom's letter to Nana and Pop-pop, 1962).

Later that summer, Mom accompanied me on a business trip to check on the Chitose MBF office in Hokkaido. We took the train to Aomori City and crossed the Tsugaru Straits on a two hour ferry ride to Hakodate, where I recalled and told her the story of when I visited there from my ship, the DD878, 17 years before. Then we boarded the train to Chitose where I introduced Mom to the MBF staff and conducted the necessary business. The next day we proceeded to the Grand Hotel in Sapporo where we did some sight seeing and shopping. Zeni was as surprised as I had been at the change in climate, landscape, and lifestyle. We bought two beautiful Ainu wood carvings of bears, one a head, the other the full body. As we wandered through the various stores and open markets, it was interesting that when I would start to talk to a sales girl in Japanese she would invariably reply looking directly at Mom and not me. We could not figure that one out. Perhaps it was more natural and comfortable for the salesgirl to talk to the Asian face rather that of the gaijin.

While we were away, New York Headquarters had approved the expense to build our house. Mrs. Ito had picked a perfect place to set the house, western style but with an ofuro, among a stand of pine trees. I gave her half of the approved funds and with the plan she proceeded to organize the builders and establish a starting date. Just a few days later I received a telephone call from Dick Taylor, VP

Personnel saying that I should plan to report to Okinawa within the week to take over the 6 MBF's there as District Manager. Okinawa was the largest island in the Ryukyu archipelago that stretches some 600 miles from Kyushu, Japan to Taiwan.

I cancelled the housing plans, Hoss took over my job and, after four or so days getting ready to leave, saying goodbyes, we took the overnight train to Tokyo. Several people came to the Furumaki station to see us off, and, of course, all stood and waved as the train was pulling out. But Fujikawa-san's sister, our neighbor, walked along with the train, broke into a run as it gained speed, waving and crying, to the end of the platform. She and Zeni had developed a friendship. They had often talked, and played with the sister's child. She had asked Zeni for advice from time to time on personal matters, and here was her best friend leaving for good. It just added to that touch of sadness that was already there, a scene so well known throughout the world, but, of course, we had each other and we did look forward to the new challenges.

In Tokyo we saw Dr. and Mrs. Arakawa. He was a most interesting, highly intellectual, and well-connected gentleman; a walking history book on Japanese and Asian history in the 20th Century. We would meet several times later on. Then we had a lunch with Dick Stewart and Karl Kircher and on our last evening in Tokyo we had dinner with Andy. He and Zeni, two great storytellers, really hit it off and Andy was happy to see that his friend Moose had married such a charming and personable lady.

Mom and I arrived in Okinawa in early September, 1962. I would be the District Manager for the six MBF's on Okinawa, reporting to Ted Jennings, who had transferred down from Tokyo to be GM Okinawa, over the MBF's and our commercial bank at Naha, the capitol city, reporting to New York. Sam Halsted, an old timer with Amexco, was the Manager for the commercial bank which included arrangements with the local sogo (savings) banks, construction loans for military and non-military projects, and a field warehousing activity. Ted and Shirley Jennings were two of the finest people I have met along the way and they made us feel right at home immediately. Ted was the kind of boss who let you run with the ball and call the plays, except for an occasional "where are we and what are we going to do?" check.

The company had just built four ground level apartments with a common parking area for four of the six MBF managers. These accommodations were new, furnished and typhoon-proof. The Okinawa area was called "Typhoon Alley," which came as no surprise to me, recalling that night of the "close call" on the USS Vesole, except now we had a safe haven apartment and would actually have typhoon parties whenever mother nature did her noisy dance.

The MBF's were scattered all over the island and provided banking services, plus auto insurance and travel services, to the Army, Navy, Air Force and Marine Corps installations. Later, I opened a new bank to serve the 3rd Marine Division at Camp Hansen. The Director of the 9th Logistic Command was my main military business contact on the island. Col. Ashenfelder was a solid, intelligent, professional soldier and finance officer. We worked well together. The U.S. had not yet given Okinawa back to Japan from the days of Occupation and the entire Ryukyu archipelago was on U.S. currency (greenbacks), no military script or Japanese yen. As agreed, it was in the best interests of both countries that the U.S. maintain that military fortress, which was an anchor in the containment strategy against the Soviet Union and Communist China during the Cold War, and included protection for Japan under that umbrella. The Japanese civilian population there was administered by The United States Civil Administration, Ryukyus (USCAR). There were about 40-45,000 assigned military plus support elements spread over that 60 x 15 mile piece of very important real estate in that part of the Pacific (and that aspect, in time, has not changed, except in added importance.) The Cold War was in full "face-off" mode. The Berlin Airlift and Korea War were in the history books and the Vietnam War was in its nascent stage. The First Special Forces on Okinawa were already taking short tours of duty there to help against the communist Viet Cong, led by Ho Chi Min.

I replaced Dick Arsenault who went on a banking assignment to NYC, then on to India, and later to Taiwan. Ted and Shirley Jennings gave a cocktail party for Dick and Zeni and I at the Sukiran Officers Club, attended by some 300 ranking well wishers, mostly from the military and USCAR. Ah, Zeni was super-charming; she was going to like it here. We left Okinawa some 19 months later and I was replaced by Bud Towson (from my Chitose days). We hosted 400 guests in a similar "goodbye-welcome" party, an indication of how our military was building there at the time.

Our time there was very full with business, personal, family, and outside friendships. The Army Headquarters was the location of our main bank, my office, and central accounting for the district. The flow of the U.S. dollar currency on the island was that military and Ryukyuan personnel expenditures in the off-base economy would work through the savings banks, controlled by the Bank of Ryukyus, BOR (Central Bank, 51% owned by USCAR), and accumulate there. I (Amexco) had a U.S. Treasury account and I would write a check favoring BOR for, say, two million, the day before the troops' payday, which our cashier would hand carry to the BOR along with a few of his staff and an MP escort. The check would then be cashed by placing appropriate amounts in mail sacks and deliver them to our outside underground vault at Sukiran. From there we would provide the MBF's with cash for payday check cashing. I never liked that whole routine for security reasons. The underground vault room was guarded by two Okinawan civilian guards. We went to the BOR in Naha with two small trucks and military guards to pick up the many mail bags full of bundled cash. I wanted to change the system and have BOR deliver the cash to our Sukiran vault in exchange for the check.

One day I told Col. Ashenfelder of my concerns and that BOR refused to deliver the cash to my vault. It was a security problem. We agreed that I would write a U.S. Treasury check payable to his command in exchange for some of his reserve cash right there on the Sukiran base. It worked fine. I notified the BOR that this was my future plan. Two weeks later I received a "rocket" of a telex from New York Headquarters that they had been notified by the U.S. Treasury Dept. about this change. BOR had protested and the Treasury was mad at Amexco, New York, and New York Headquarters was mad at me. So we went back to the old system. Some years after I had left Okinawa, someone told me they had word from Okinawa that one payday morning some 18 mail bags arrived in Sukiran under guard and went to the big vault for counting and distribution. They were two bags short, some half million dollars. The police and CID had no clues. Two years later, a former employee was living in Tokyo, having too much to drink in a Shinjuku bar and playing "big spender." Someone tipped off the police and they traced it to a matter of unexplained wealth. They contacted the guy and he confessed and "ratted" on his buddy. It seems he was assigned to the cash transfer detail at BOR, was walking an alley, a mail bag on each shoulder, and threw the bags over a fence into a vacant lot where his accomplice waited, then turned and walked back in empty-handed as if he was returning from the truck. A nice amateur heist. I guess a company traveling auditor told me the story in my early days in the Philippines. It did not occur to me to telex NYHeadquarters with a "nah nee nah nee nah nah!"

Okinawa was the last big battle of the Pacific War (if you are Japanese), a.k.a. World War II (if you are American). It had an armada assemblage bigger than D-Day. Kamikazes were all over the sky and, on the island very dirty, tough fighting took place with day by day face-offs. They used many fortified caves to a strategic advantage, and toward the end, many Japanese soldiers and civilians committed suicide by jumping off the cliffs in the southern region rather than surrender. Before the war, Okinawa was the poorest province in Japan, with low-grade sugar, pineapple and rice growing out of its inferior soil. Then, with the U.S. presence having been there about 18 years, priming the economic pump in a variety of ways, the economy became stronger. This has made substantial contributions to the overall Japanese economy. The number of Okinawa employees who were on the payrolls at all the bases and sub bases, and USCAR, was enormous. In fact many Ryukyuans became millionaires. A common occurrence was that a family that experienced some benefit from the post-war land reform, though perhaps somewhat poor, would work out a rental arrangement with a U.S. military unit that wanted to use some or all of the property to help meet its mission goal. If, for example, the Air Force wanted to extend a runway over your property, voilá! instant millionaire! I would see several of them, 1962-64, at Awase Meadows Golf Course, learning the game and forgetting about those inferior pineapples.

One man who worked very hard for his wealthy status was Charlie Chang, a postwar Chinese immigrant to Okinawa who started by working in a bakery that made bread and rolls for the U.S. military contracts for mess halls, clubs, and the PX grocery stores. Eventually he owned the company and was the chief "honcho" supplying baked goods on the island. Incidentally, a "honcho" in the old Japanese army was a squad leader. American G.I.'s in the early part of the Occupation were taught to ask "Who's the honcho here?" Anyway, Charlie (shall I say living the Okinawa dream?) was a very nice, charitable, family man, who opened a restaurant, jewelry store, and later built a small mall right on the main road.

Mom and I made many close friends in the community. Willie Yu, a Chinese-Filipino, was a contractor who built a variety of buildings, runways and roadways for the military and was a long-standing customer of the Amexco commercial bank there. Mark Carr, from California, was the Bank of America rep, and his wife Annie had been born in France, where they met after the war. She taught French to the First Special Forces, which of course was applicable in Vietnam. Other great friends included Louie and Delly Uy, a Chinese Filipino, representing The American Foreign Insurance Association (AFIA), along with Ted and Susan Harriman, Ray McGill and his Chinese wife Vi, representing Mutual of Omaha, Col. Ed Garner, USAF and Kathy. Ed had a fine career that included several attaché positions at embassies in Europe. Many years later, when on "home leave" from the Philippines, Mom and I visited these good friends at their retirement home in Ft. Lauderdale. Mike Ladau, from the Philippines, worked for USCAR, and Lucy his wife, managed the insurance sales at our MBF in Sukiran. Unice Mohhadeen and his wife were from India, charming people. He ran Charlie's jewelry store. Back then he often spoke of his fail-safe retirement program. In that era there were only about 10-14 companies in the Wall Street Dow Jones averaging, and so he would place the same amount each month in a different Dow Jones stock, betting on the strength of the over-all economy for the long run, in his own Dow mutual fund (not known at the time). I am sure Unice retired with a great portfolio.

I recall that Willie Yu had a nice home on a main road. He entertained a great deal. When you walked in the front door, you walked into a large well furnished living room with a bar running across the entire rear, lined with a dozen very comfortable stools. On occasion, 5 or 6 of us would stop by Willie's after work to have a "sun downer." But invariably it was a very slow sunset and our wives were tired of keeping dinner warm, so, being friends, they decided that they too would meet at Willie's. And so a weekly Willie's meeting developed and we would all go off to dinner from there. A word about Mom's drinking; she could buy a bottle of wine for a special occasion and a year later she would have gone right through it, a real tippler. We had a truly international community of friends, very good friends. They made our Okinawa stay a lasting memory.

Shortly after our arrival on-island, we bought a new green Volkswagen Beetle and I started to give Mom driving lessons. She knew absolutely nothing about driving so to be safe I drove us to an old abandoned Japanese air strip on a plateau about ten miles away. It was a great way to start (stick shift and all) because she could drive all over that runway, making the early mistakes without the tension of traffic. In time I took her out on the roads where the maximum speed limit was 35 mph and then found a professional instructor. She had her license and the Beetle. Oh, my, was she happy, and I was so happy for her.

As in Misawa, we had military privileges and could use the PX, commissaries and "O' clubs and the Harbor View, the Dept. of Defense civilian club in Naha. These clubs were visited by name entertainers who were touring the Asia circuit. I recall that Mom, I, and some friends had ringside seats for dinner, dancing, and to see the world renowned Katarina Valente (she sang in four languages) and her ensemble. These clubs were non-appropriated fund activities and could not make more than 5% profit, so inexpensive dinners and entertainment were common-place. But, hey, those military personnel deserved all their benefits and I was happy to be of service while having those privileges.

Time moved along very rapidly for both of us. We were very happily in love and had active schedules whether together or apart. About February Mom gave me the great news that I was going to be a father, and, of course, the good news went out to New Jersey and Manila. We flew to the Philippines for a brief hello. As the birth day came closer, our lady friends would stop by more often to be of help to Mom. On the 12th of Sept Maria Luz arrived.

She was born at the U.S. Army Hospital in Sukiran. The night before, Mom was lying in bed in the pre-delivery room and I was sitting in a chair holding her hand as the night wore on, both of us sleeping and dozing. Then another labor pain and she would cry out and we would both be awake awhile, mumble-talking, half asleep, and repeating the cycle over, and over, oh, so tired. In the middle of the night the nurses changed shifts, and a very pleasant Lt. Nurse came in, making her rounds, lifted the sheet, smoothed her hand over Zeni's large stom-ach and proclaimed, "My word, that baby's going to be big enough to go to work right away." We all laughed and that really broke the painful monotony of it all for Mom. Shortly thereafter she gave birth to our first daughter, made in Japan. All those fine women friends, to whom we are always grateful, worked out sched-ules to be at our apartment to cook breakfasts, make dinners, help Zeni with Maria, and give advice, as they were all mothers, such good friends. When Mariellos, as she was called in the early years, reached the "roll over" stage we would put a quilt on the living room carpet and play with her. We noticed that Schnappsie, our daschund, was jealous, so we had to find him a home which Mike and Lucy Ludao readily provided, what are friends for?

One day in November I was going to the office very early in the morning, and decided to stop for the Amexco's mail at the big APO there in Sukiran. I walked into that usually busy place and nothing was going on. All the soldiers, most of whom knew me, were sitting around in a corner of the big receiving room, listening to a radio. "Hi guys, can I get my mail?" was returned by blank faces. "What's wrong?" I called out. Their looks of deep anguish accompanied their reply, "President Kennedy has been shot." Whacko! It hit me too. I was numb. The nation loved him and the First Lady, Jackie. It was the American Camelot at its height, and the mourning and long term press coverage would reflect how the nation felt about their President and Commander-In-Chief and the whole personae that projected out from his family.

The Cold War was heating up. Who do I think did it? Facts:

1. The Soviet Union, a communist police state, always taught their controlled population, cradle to grave, that the U.S. was the hated enemy.

2. Kennedy tried to destroy Communist Cuba with that poorly planned Bay of Pigs fiasco, which prompted the Soviet Union to plan and implement a response.

3. Kennedy was an avid anti-communist, which contributed to his popularity, and his campaign speeches, and others that followed in that Cold War rhetoric arena.

4. He had a showdown with Premier Kruschev and refused to allow the Soviets to build missile bases in Cuba, after they had already started, and sent their ships, loaded with missiles, to Cuba, only to be forced to turn back by the U.S. Navy ships involved. It was a nuclear standoff according to many, although I do not think, for a variety of reasons, the Soviets were going to go to war over Cuba. Basically, Cuba was not as important in the Polit-Bureau's foreign policy guidelines as a closer-to-home Soviet "buffer" state.

5. Kruschev went to the United Nations and gave his "We will bury you" speech and pounded the table with his shoe, heard and shown around the world. He wasn't talking about Ireland or Denmark, as he practiced that "scare tactic."

6. Lee Harvey Oswald was a Marine Corporal or Sergeant billeted in Japan. His specialty was radar. His unit had worked on tracking our special U-2 spy plane out of Japan and over the Soviet Union to add a variety of electronic intelligence data to our growing files. The U2 was the state of the art design of its day. Soviet intelligence had eyes and ears for such young men in technical fields who were billeted in Japan, where they had easy access through motivated bar girls and their controls (see index), to elicit information and try to recruit to their cause. The Soviets were good at that. Oswald had a record through most of his Marine Corps days of speaking out on his belief that Communism was the answer to the world's problems. He even studied Russian. It is unlikely the communist principal agents and their operators in the area would have missed him.

7. Oswald was a qualified Marine marksman, ie, 2-300 yards in a mild breeze with a high powered rifle was not difficult for him.

8. He left the Marine Corps in September 1959.

9. Soon after, he applied for, and was granted, a visa to go to the Soviet Union and live. It was a defection.

10. The Soviet Union granted tourist visas prior to and during the cold war for reasons of their choosing, not the whim of the traveler. Soviet visas had the implication of invitation, not what the visitor wanted but what the

Soviet Union wanted. No one was given a Soviet visa without careful scrutiny, and with the interest of the SU in mind. They were wary of visitors and spent much time and effort to watch and follow visitors even those with diplomatic privileges, whom they suspected to be intelligence agents anyway.

An example of the whys and wherefores of the Soviet Union issuing visas was Bill Clinton in his student days in London It was public knowledge that he had refused/ avoided the military draft in the U.S. and had been leading public demonstrations, in London, against the U.S.A. for carrying on the war in Vietnam against the Communist Viet Cong. The USSR backed the Viet Cong, and noticing Clinton's actions (they knew he was a protégé of Senator Fulbright of Arkansas, who had been the Chairman of the Armed Services Committee), invited him to come to the USSR to "tour" the country. They of course had an interest in recruiting students, and it must have scared the socks off of my fellow alumnus when he realized this was no longer just about a student protest. They would want to see how angry he really was and if they had a friend worth cultivating, for that is the way the game was played, and still is, by those who sit at the table of chance called espionage.

11. Oswald went on to live in Russia a year or more and married a Soviet citizen. The Soviets would have never approved that, and they controlled everything, unless they wanted it that way.

12. He and his wife were allowed to leave the Soviet Union. Just to change location? They didn't like it there anymore?

13. They applied for and were granted a U.S. visa for her and a re-entry permit for him. I'm confused. Was he now a Soviet citizen? Did he lose his U.S. citizenship after taking permanent residence in the SU?

14. Anyway, it appears likely they were under the control of the KGB for use in the U.S. in the future. Oswald was a pro-Soviet, anti-American, now a Russian-speaking pawn, and the wife, whether agreeable or not, had relatives in the Soviet Union. That situation customarily controlled and forced co-operation with KGB intentions.

15. Oswald was in the area of the Kennedy shooting and was arrested there, in a movie house. It was near his place of work and distant from his house. His own gun was found, with his finger prints on it, at that book storage company where he worked. He had set up some available card board boxes for partial cover and rifle support at a location overlooking the planed motorcade route on which President Kennedy was shot.

16. Oswald was seen on the 2nd floor of that book depository building by a state trooper right after the shooting, but he did not question him because a passing employee said he (Oswald) worked there.

17. Oswald was shot and killed while in Dallas police custody by a man who ran a strip joint in Baltimore. He died of cancer while incarcerated and

awaiting trial for shooting Oswald. It was truly a bizarre and "crazy," almost fictional, ending that continues to diminish in understanding.

Those are the facts and thought processes from which I concluded that the Soviet Union assassinated John Kennedy. Legal proof? No. But perhaps I have more intuitive dots to connect from my experiences and past environments than others who have tried to influence us to conclude everything from, the butler did it, the Mafia did it, or the CIA did it, for heaven's sake, spare me such drivel. However, I can somewhat see the reasoning that he acted on his own, but my vibes tell me it was the KGB, who, in their usually clever fashion had said something to the effect of "Oh, we looked at him for possible use but we concluded he was a bit screwy and couldn't be trusted." Hey, they were missing their own criteria, which is, can he do the job? Another clever comment of the former KGB after the Soviet Union was no more, was that they thought Oswald might be a CIA plant when he was in Russia and did not go near him. Well, they had full control, and if they truly had an unknown to be resolved, certainly they would have given him a polygraph test or two, and another interview or two using something like sodium pentothal truth serum. If it worked out he was a CIA agent he would have assumed room temperature. No, he went to the U.S. with his wife.

We were truly overjoyed with Mariellos. She was very bright, cheerful, and responsive. Among the great and meaningful experiences that life affords us are those fascinating moments when you look into the eyes of that beloved baby, arm around the mom, and let the whole meaning of it all overwhelm you, and feel God's presence. There was a lot of excitement around our families in the U.S. and Philippines. The doctor told us we must wait two months before Mariellos could go and meet her relatives in the Philippines, about a two hour flight.

Thanks to our wonderful friends I was a well-cared for "bachelor" during the month they were away. After work I spent a lot of time at Willie Yu's or another friend's house and invariably the evening would end with some putting competition on the rug and the usual give-and-take "ribbing:" "Why do you keep letting me win? I really don't want your money," or "Is that the same crooked putter you used in that horrible round on Saturday?" I discovered how well the wives cooked. We surely had a memorable group of friends.

Ted and Shirley Jennings would soon leave for NYC, where Ted would be promoted to V.P. in charge of the New York Agency, the company's multi-currency clearing house and transfer station. True friends, they send a Christmas card to this day. That responsibility for Okinawa was taken over by Dick Stewart and run from Tokyo. He was another fine guy to work for, a good banker with a great personality. He was an excellent representative for Amexco in Asia. Early on, he came down from Tokyo to look over the activities of Sam Halsted and me. One Sunday I rented a boat and several of us went out to snorkel. Okinawa had very clear sub-tropical water and the healthy coral reefs supported a myriad of beautiful fish and plants. We were in the water most of the day and then headed back to shower and change and meet at our apartment for dinner and drinks. Mom, ever the gracious host, said a picnic fare would fit into the day's activities, so she went ahead and prepared hot dogs, hamburgers, chips, pickles, potato salad. Oh, those drinks and nibbles were great after a long time in the water. Mom finished making the potato salad but of course it was very warm.

So she suggested another round of drinks, an easy sell with that group, which included me, to have the time to "fix" the potato salad, meaning she put it in the freezer to chill it, then joined the party which was in full sail. Several stories later she recalled the potato salad and rushed to the kitchen to find it frozen in its large ball-shaped mold. Cleverly, and at the suggestion of another round (we all had a "glow") she put it in the oven on low, hoping to thaw it. Well, it worked, almost. We sat around the table full of compliments for all the food (we were so hungry), and there in the middle was potato salad, in a big bowl and shaped like a large ball. There was an ice cream scoop next to it. The more hungry (which we were) and clever (which some were) scraped the outer, thawed potato salad off of the ice ball inside, claimed it to be delicious, and took turns with an original comment about such a situation, insuring a lasting memory of Mom's picnic cook-in. It all added to the fun of the day.

While Dick was visiting he wanted to discuss an idea for the Amexco commercial bank lending with 6-7 Okinawans who owned sogo savings banks on the island. Sam Halsted arranged the invitations and dinner at his house. Dick figured dinner first and then, over brandy, the idea would be presented and discussed. Unknown to us, the tradition and culture of Okinawa did not allow for that approach to the matter. The idea should have been discussed during the early round of drinks and over dinner, because when the white rice was served at the end of the meal, there was no more drinking and adjournment was in order. There was Dick standing at the door with a bottle of brandy in hand, trying to encourage "one for the road" and stay a while, as the guests were departing. We were learning. On another occasion, he made the rounds and called on them at their offices. It worked much better.

Sometime in 1963, the U.S. and China signed the "one China" policy agreement. The U.S. then closed its embassy in Taiwan in favor of a "trade representatives' office." There were two U.S. military bases there which were going to be closed and so we had to close our MBF's that were there. So Dick came down to Okinawa and asked me to join him on his trip to Taiwan to help close the MBF's. It all went smoothly. We set close-down dates with the military commands and advised New York. It was interesting. The trade representative office still did diplomatic and consular work as well as shipping and trade matters, but as long as it was not called an embassy and no one had the title of ambassador, the Communist China Government did not complain.

The night before we took our flight to Naha, we ate in a superb restaurant, Chinese of course. Dick wanted to give Mom a treat and he arranged with the owner to prepare two very large wrapped bags of freshly boiled lobster to be picked up by us on our way to the airport in the morning. At Naha we each took one package and threw our top coats over them and carried our suitcase in the other hand. The customs clerk did not ask us to open our bags, but waved us through. Oh, what a feast we had that night with happy Mom adding some Chinese dishes, thus showing off her ever-improving culinary skills. That first home dinner in Misawa seemed so far away.

About March '64, Dick Stewart and Trev Benney, President of world-wide Amexco banking, visited Okinawa. Bud Towson would be coming to replace me, my second 3-year assignment was up, and I would be moving on. Trev said, "I have been hearing about you, tell me what you would like to do next in the company." I said I would like to stay in the banking division and take some international banking training in New York and then move on to another foreign assignment. So in June, Mom and I, with Mariellos all of nine months, said a tearful good bye to good friends, many of whom we would see again, and our unforgettable Okinawa tour of duty, and flew to NYC.

NEW YORK

En Route to the Philippines

Bonvoyage party, Okinawa, May 1964

We left Okinawa for New York, via Manila, where we stayed a couple of weeks. I recall happy Mariellos, nine months old, in her playpen under a ceiling fan, for it was the hot time before the rainy season. Her Lola (grandmother) watched her constantly, so pleased we could stay there a while. I don't recall what we did, undoubtedly we went to visit relatives and friends and show off Mariellos. Then we flew on to New York and Nana and Pop-pop met us at JFK, tears in their eyes as we walked into the waiting area. It had been a long time. We were all like that except for little Mariellos ("who are these people?") Zeni was her charming self, having looked forward to meeting them. "Oh, Howie, Zeni's so pretty," Nana whispered to me.

We had reservations in a NYC hotel so I could get to the Amexco Headquarters for a couple days and then take some leave. We then stayed with Mom and Dad in Union, and soon found a new garden apartment in Fords, near Perth Amboy. The commute to NYC meant taking a bus at 7 a.m. to the NYC bus terminal, then the 8th Ave. subway to the lower west side of Manhattan, and walk to 65 Broadway. It was 90 minutes each way, except in bad weather. The apartment was nice and we figured 14 to 18 months and then an overseas assignment.

The training program was only partially what I expected. I had been managing "home town" type banks overseas at the MBFs for six years and had many successful internal and external audits. The trainees, about 10 of them, were a mix of new employees with backgrounds in shipping, insurance, etc. and the training was tailored for the entire group, whereas all I really needed was the training in international bank lending such as spreading balance sheets, loan appraisals, letters of credit, and loan processing. I also took evening classes at the New York Institute of Credit for a year, which was quite helpful. The program was all "on the job" which meant more time than I needed to effect the training.

After a year I was anxious and asked for an overseas assignment. I liked the company very much for many reasons, not the least of which was the integrity and caliber of the people who made it all happen. Trev spoke of sending me to the Philippines to try to get a banking license while working in the Travel Division which had a Manila office (travel, foreign exchange, travelers cheques and credit cards), if John Stewart, the head of the Travel Division, approved. John had been an FBI agent and joined Amexco to manage the security division world-wide. That was his job when the famous De Angelus field warehousing case exploded in the headlines. He helped save the company from serious losses.

John Stewart and I "hit it off" and talked about the Philippines and an assignment. The manager there was going to Madrid about six months hence, so it was all shaping up for the Philippines, and of course, my Zeni and I were delighted, as was her family. All this planning took place in the summer of 1965. The banking division was shifting its assistant manager in Tokyo to another location and would need an assistant manager until March 1966. That would be me.

Our time together in the U.S. was full, interesting, and memorable. Mom and Dad visited our apartment often, sometimes to be all together, occasionally, to let us have a "date" out by ourselves. Early in our stay, Mom became pregnant and she was into her fifth month when I came home from work one Wednesday evening and she was changing Mariellos in the bedroom. As I came in, she said "Oh, I don't feel so good." "What's wrong?" "I don't know," and I was watching her go into some kind of shock. She lay down on the bed, next to Mariellos, as I threw a blanket over her saying, "I'll get the doctor." I headed out the door. As I flew down the stairs, I thought it was lucky that our obstetrician's office was in the basement of our building. Oh, no! The sign on his door read " Closed Wednesdays." Panicked, I knocked anyway. He jumped up from his backlog of paperwork and opened the locked door and read my distress. "Doc, come quick, it's Zeni, she's having trouble," as we vaulted the stairs and I excitedly jabbered about her situation. He took one look at her moaning on the bed with an arm over Mariellos and grabbed the phone, calling Perth Amboy General. "Emergency call. Send an ambulance right away and get a room ready for Zenaida Newhard." He said, "I'm going down to the hospital to be sure they are ready for testing her; there are a few possibilities but let's wait and see."

The ambulance came. I picked up Mariellos, a bit in shock myself. They carried Mom out as she rose up from the stretcher, in pain and vomiting. Walking to the ambulance with Mariellos in my arms, I hardly noticed the rain as I started to follow Mom into the ambulance. The EMS leader said, "Sir, we will take good care of her. Why don't you call someone to mind the baby and then come to the hospital?" I called Nana and Pop-pop and when they arrived, I hurried to the hospital. The doctor told me she had blood poisoning caused by a miscarriage about ten days ago that did not abort. I was really troubled when he said he was waiting for the chief obstetrician for consultation as to the proper antidote. I went in to see her. She was swollen, her face like a pumpkin, her eyes, those beautiful eyes, just thin slits. She was groggy from medication. I told her that she would be home real soon, that Mariellos was fine, and that I would be right here with her.

They gave her the antidote and I stayed the night, praying and trying to bribe God ("If you let me keep her, I promise…and….I promise…"). By late morning she was coming out of the woods as the doctor wore his "good news" face. "She can go home tomorrow." I wanted to sing something loud and heavy, but considered a possible relapse; so I tenderly kissed her, held her hand, and cried. "I guess it wasn't my time," she smiled.

Back at home a few days later, I got the real "skinny" on the how and why. It seems that the guys who carried in some new pieces of furniture put it all in the places Mom wanted it, but with a mind-change in interior design, she later did some rearranging on her own, rather than wait for me, pushing the sofa, pulling on a table; and that caused the miscarriage. It was your brother, to be named Andrew after the grandfather I never knew.

That was not the only time we needed Perth Amboy General. My hibernating back injury woke up and I was in continual traction for three weeks, well medicated for the pain. They poured me the old plaster of Paris cast, waist and hips, and after a week or so with my 50"+ new pants size, I went back to my 90 minute commute. About three weeks later, following the therapy drill, I was back to normal.

We stayed close with family and friends: cook-outs at Nana and Pop-pop's, Aunt Marion and Uncle Bob's, Uncle Richie and Aunt Joyce's, the annual two week summer rental at Long Beach Island, other trips to the beach, crabbing in Barnegat Bay, Broadway shows, and going with Nana and Pop-pop to orchards and farms in South Jersey to pick/buy produce. It was especially pleasing to be with the growing families of Rich and Joyce, and Marion and Bob. We all had fun with our picnics, cookouts, trips to the beaches, garden parties and the like.

Maria, ca. 1967

Mom became friendly with many neighborhood wives in that lovely garden apartment complex, since the wives were at home all day with their children and the husbands were out working.. One memorable time was when we gave a party for several couples and as we stood near the door greeting our guests, there was Mariellos, two years old, nicely dressed, and copying our mannerisms and words, "Hi, nice to see you, please come in," along with a hand shake, way up there.

I recall that some of the guys in that commercial bank management class decided to have a Christmas party for our group of many nationalities at someone's NYC apartment. It was a happy time and we all got to know each other better; partly because we had that additional time in a social setting, but more important to talk with the co-worker and wife at the same time. It truly improved our friendship and allowed each other to understand the whole person, for surely a person married in God's grace is only a half of the whole. As the organizers got a little "glow," they decided there would be a secret vote among the men, the next day at work, to decide whose wife was the prettiest. That morning at a little "koffee klatch" one of them opened the envelope and announced the winner was...Zeni!... hardly a surprise to me as I tried to act in disbelief (clever rascal).

So it was set, and in early October in anticipation of leaving in November, we moved out of the garden apartment in Fords and moved in with Nana and Pop-pop in Union (my teenage dwelling). One day the phone rang. A man said, "Is this Howard Newhard?" The sound was as if the voice was talking in a breezy tunnel. "Yes." "Do you remember what you were doing in 1951-2-3?" (Korea). "Yes." "Would you like to consider doing that again?" (He forgot to say, "Do you really want to make a difference?") I was curious, and a "quick-think" told me he was talking about Vietnam, which was starting a build-up in military strength. I said, "Yes. I'll consider it, what's the action from here? I am leaving for Manila in a month or so." "We will send you a paper and then follow up on that." "OK," and the line closed. Today it is easy to second-guess myself and say why would you do that? But then, I did not know about all the self-defeating issues and circumstances that were allowed to interfere with the mission in Nam. I felt I might be answering the call again, but if I did, I would resume that career, ask for an appropriate pay grade and stay with it on into the rocking chair years: honor, duty, country. I envisioned Zeni and Mariellos living in Manila while I was in Vietnam, just a couple hours away. Of course, I did not tell Zeni about this at the time, since it was only in the tentative stage.

I assumed they would check me out from the time I left the Agency, about ten years before, but what I received was the standard, very thick, Government Employee Application forms starting from DOB. I just didn't have time for that and was somewhat surprised. In thinking it through I envisioned that they were probably following all likely leads to fill those planned positions and it was a matter of placing both former and new potential I.O.s into a common clearing pool.

Some years later I told Mom what had happened and she completely agreed that if I had wanted to answer the call, she understood. Her background and experience about war and subjugated people conditioned her thinking. Gosh, how I loved her.

15 | FIRST STOP, TOKYO, THEN
My Philippine Home

Gathering in Tokyo. 1st row center: Jack Scotland; 2nd row center: Zeni; top row center: Bill White

Nana and Pop-pop drove us to the JFK airport. It was a tearful good-bye. We had all become family-fun close, as the relationship garden had been seeded and watered along the way by all concerned, starting with Mom's letter to Nana and Pop-pop dated July 15, 1962 (see Appendix D). However, our low mood lifted as the flight proceeded and, much later, after a good dinner and a fitful sleep, we arrived in Tokyo refreshed. The "meet and greet" worked fine and we checked into the Imperial Hotel where we would stay for the next three months. Jack Scotland and Karl Kircher came over to welcome us. In a day or two I went to the American Express offices (Travel and Banking) which were near the Dai-ichi Building in the Hibiya district to fill in as assistant manager banking, reporting to Jack. I had first met him when he visited Okinawa. He was then in charge of corporate internal audits and headquartered in London. Then he transferred to the banking division and was assigned to Tokyo. Jack Scotland, from Ireland, was thoughtful, intelligent, fun-loving and sociable. We became friends and are to this day, although we lost contact some time back.

It was nice to be back in Japan. Jack introduced me to the bank staff and all went smoothly. After three weeks or so, the excellent accommodations at the Imperial aside, Mom was understandably a bit bored with the daily routine of being transient and looking after Mariellos all day and night. She suggested that she go to Manila with Mariellos, prep for our arrival and come back in 4-5 weeks. Mama Buhain (Papa had suffered a stroke and had entered Eternal Life in 1963, about the time of Maria's birth) and the rest of the family were delighted to have them. I personally didn't care for that arrangement with the lonely nights and not having my family. I had many late dinners with friends like Kircher, White, and Scotland. By then Kircher was the V.P. of credit cards for the Asia area based in Tokyo and Bill White, a fine British fellow, ex-RAF bloke, was the Manager of Travel Tokyo.

The various suits of cards; political, social, psychological, and military were being played in the Cold War game, and Japan was full of Communist sympathizers and activists. When the Japanese constitution was formed, the use of labor unions was wisely given a legal base, to assure better employment standards. One target the Communists had was American companies, and they tried to take control and make crippling demands. The creation of, or penetration of, labor unions for control was a tactic from the very early days of the international Communist movement.

The Amexco Bank in Tokyo had a labor union; the Travel Office (another subsidiary company) did not. One day a non-union employee gave Jack Scotland an original memo that was written by the union leader at the bank which defamed American Express, called for higher wages and better benefits, employee involvement in management decisions, and spouted the Communist line. Somehow the leaders knew that Jack possessed the memo (he had already made copies for safe keeping) and at closing time Jack and I were sitting in his office talking of the problems which the union would now be presenting. Three or four of the leaders pushed in and with threatening voices and fiery eyes demanded the paper. They were afraid we would go to the authorities and make a case against them. They were ready to fight. Jack was a big guy who could handle himself, and I was ready to go for two of them real quick if he made the move. But he out-shouted them and then reduced the noise of it all to a loud conversation, then a civilized discussion, and then a logical talk; whereupon he gave them back their memo with an appropriate admonishment, which they completely ignored. The next day our Japanese lawyer concurred that it was properly handled and filed a complaint using the retained copy.

I recalled from my CIA training and studies that right after WWII our expert thinkers and planners were very concerned that Japan would go Communist, based on:

1. Many ex-Japanese prisoners, military and civilian, in China, Manchuria and North Korea had been given Communist indoctrination programs prior to being freed to return to Japan.
2. Once the Emperor allowed for peaceful surrender, it was logical for many people to look for a better system of government.
3. The political and social psyche of the Japanese became based on adopting something considered better than the one they had lost with. For years they had copied the better-manufactured items. Whether connected or not, these things happened. The Soviets wanted to go into Japan and help disarm the Japanese, concurrently, as they had aggressively done in North Korea, but the U.S. would not agree with their wishes.

General MacArthur and his staff were aware of the Soviets' ultimate intent and he pushed his authorities to set up a new government and complete the new constitution which included democracy, land reform, and women's suffrage, an amazing accomplishment considering they had been in their age-old feudal system only five years before that was achieved.

After 3–4 weeks, I flew to Manila to pick up Mom and Mariellos, meet with my in-laws, and return. On the flight back, they were in the two seats in front of me and my seat partner was Raymond Burr, that famous actor of the Mr. District Attorney TV series. He had been in Vietnam thanking and visiting with the troops. His right hand was all swollen and blue from shaking so many hands. He was a very impressive, intelligent, and humble person. He and Mariellos hit it off particularly well and she sat next to him for much of the flight. I think he needed the playful ways of a happy child after being in a war zone a couple of weeks, great therapy.

Sunny days! Life at the Imperial was never better. One evening we were having our dinner in the main dining room. Some folks were on the dance floor and Mariellos, about three, wanted to try the dancing, so I shuffled around with her and she was laughing and talking aloud with a joy that a three-year-old can infuse into a small crowd. On his way out, Pat O'Brien, a top line Hollywood actor for many years, passed our table and commented how enjoyable it was to watch such a happy child, and Zeni, my theater and film buff, joined Mariellos in the child-of-happiness genre.

One Saturday morning we walked to nearby Hibiya Park to enjoy the beauty of it all on that brisk and sunny day. Mom and Mariellos were feeding the pigeons and I was sitting on a bench watching across a wide walk way. A young fellow came along and asked me in English if I was American, and then asked if it would be okay if he practiced his English with me. Of course. Shortly after, he asked me if I was a Christian, and when I said yes, he wanted to discuss The Sermon On The Mount, that beautiful exhortation and guideline extolled by Jesus. I sensed his surprise when it became obvious he had much more to discuss and a broader view of the matter than I did. I was a bit embarrassed, this "I" who had taken religion courses from the Benedictine and Jesuit fathers. That was an awareness whisper to me that I knew little about the Bible. Looking back, my religious studies had revolved around the Seven Sacraments, Papal encyclicals and the theological writings of some of the Church Doctors such as St. Thomas Aquinas and St. Augustine. The celebration of the Mass has always included liturgy from the Bible but it seems that studying the Bible was not emphasized to the laity until the Vatican II Council in 1962.

Our Tokyo assignment was about finished. Jack had the bank running well, with a good loan portfolio, and the permanent assistant manager would soon arrive; so we said our goodbyes and arrived in Manila in March of 1966. Going to the Philippines to live was an important aspect of my life. Not only were the people generally warm and friendly but it was pleasant to see my sisters- and brothers-in-law, mother-in-law and Mom's aunts, uncles, nieces and nephews, and make new friends. I was readily accepted and it was a comfortable feeling.

GETTING SETTLED

The American Express Office was in the PhilAm Life Building on United Nations Ave., conducting a broad business in Travel, Travelers Cheques, Credit Cards, and Foreign Exchange. The operation was modest in size, the staff was experienced, and we had "two old-timers" who had worked for Amexco in the pre-WWII days when the company was basically a shipping operation, its international forté then, historically extended from the U.S. domestic shipping of the old stagecoach and pony-express days a century before. Later, as we all became friends, they told me of one American manager in those "shipping" days who spent most of his time at his reserved table in a cantina a few doors from the waterfront office, reviewing mail and shipping papers, having lunch, talking business with steamship and shipping company execs, and returning to the office to check the books, sign papers, and balance the cash at the end of the day. In those days, the 1930s, almost all communication, unless very important, was by surface mail, and New York Headquarters mail came in about twice a month.

They enthusiastically recalled seeing the first trans-Pacific commercial flight by Pan American Airways splash-land in Manila Bay in 1934 and dock at Sangley Point Naval Station, in Cavite Province; but air mail would not become common for a while. Thirty-plus years later I had telex, daily mail, and seldom-used telephones to support and strengthen my activities, and, of course, today's overseas managers and the Headquarters have many communications choices; but when I now think of that manager in the waterfront cantina, in that pre-WWII tropical setting and way of life, my vibes have a nice ring.

Bill Reardon, the manager, was most helpful in explaining the business to me and introducing me to people in the PTA (Philippine Travel Association). I recall Cecilia Laurel, the very capable president and many other active members. Later, Joe Aspiras, The Minister of Tourism, would have the lead in the PTA. One year

Howard and Zeni pose with Maria on her 3rd birthday, in Manila.

I joined his contingent on a trip to Seoul Korea to attend the Pacific Area Travel Association conference. I had not been back to Korea since I left in 1953. In those days there was one bridge over the Han River from Yong Dong Po into Seoul. It had been destroyed and rebuilt several times as the battle lines moved up and down the peninsula. Going in from the airport (about 1975), I asked the driver how many bridges crossed the Han. He said fourteen!

Shortly after I arrived in Manila, Vic Chua joined us. He was returning home after earning his MBA at New York University and working for American Express in New York. We became good friends and later he went on to Singapore to run the company's banking activity there.

STARTING TO BUILD THE BUSINESS

Once I had a feel for the operation and took over from Bill, I wanted to expand the business which had been ambling along on loyal corporate and individual accounts. So in 1967, I opened an office in Makati to meet the needs of that growing city in the greater Manila area.

In my early days in the Philippines I realized that the base of our Travel business should be large international organizations that we could bill in U.S. dollars, avoiding foreign exchange fluctuations; and I began a personal program to talk with and offer Travel, Credit Card, Travelers Cheque, and Foreign Exchange services that fit the target. I even tried the U.S. Embassy, which was our largest one in the world at that time, through Lou Gleeck, who was Consul General; but the regulations concerning establishing a commercial business on Embassy property prohibited such activity.

Nevertheless, as time went on, I offered various organizations a deal they couldn't refuse, whereby I established their own in-house travel office, using my Amexco employees, communications, and services, saving them time and money in arranging their travel affairs. Over a year or two, I signed up The Asia Development Bank, World Health Regional Headquarters, United States Agricultural and Industrial Development (USAID), International Rice Research Institute, U.S. Peace Corps, and UNDP (United Nations Development Projects), and of course made many friends in those organizations. Over time, I also expanded the business by fusing the Travel, Card, and Travelers Cheque activities, which were under my general management, into a cross-selling pattern. They reported on a separate line back to New York, but that marketing plan, while not a show stopper, made progress. At a managers' meeting around 1970, Frank Erickson asked me to say something about my operation and why it was successful, (while some were not). The idea moved up the corporate ladder and eventually helped give birth to American Express Travel Related Services, Inc.

In March 1967, while living in Bel Air Village, Makati we were blessed with our second child, Maria Anna, now known as Mari, Mariana, or "Muning." We

Maria cuddling new sister, Mariana

were all thrilled and thankful for that little charmer. Maria (Mariellos) was on cloud Happiness now that her sister had arrived. Later on we had some concern over some allergies that troubled Mariana and changed to soy milk until she got "on track" about a year later.

Mariellos was three–and–a–half and just thrilled and talkative about her baby sister. My mind sees her holding, cuddling, and playing with Mariana in those early years. As was customary, Mom and Mariana stayed in the hospital about 4–5 days and the large room was full of flowers and well-wishers, all expressing their joy of the newborn cutie. And a joy she was. We were a happy family.

Recalling that interim, the four of us flew to the NYC/New Jersey area on vacation and stayed with Nana and Pop-pop at their retirement home in Howell,

Mariana (left) and Maria (right), ages 3 and 7

New Jersey. Mom and I took turns walking the floor many nights holding the precious Mariana in our arms while she cried her frustration at the world, and we prayed for her comfort. Perhaps all that had a purpose. Today, that beautiful woman, Mari, remains youthful and has a sideline proficiency in her knowledge of nutrition and exercise.

It was during that trip that Mom and I took you, Mari, to see Gram Newhard, who was staying in a nursing home in Bricktown, New Jersey. She was about 92 then and totally blind. She sat propped up in bed with plenty of pillows, quite strong for her age, and talkative, upbeat as usual. I said, "Gram, this is our daughter Mariana," and I held you close to her so she could "see" you with her hands, and she gently caressed your nose, checks, ears, eyes, and lips, she softly said, "Oh, Howie, she's an angel." Mom and I were deeply touched. Gram always had that cheerful attitude of playing in the game of Life, though her pilgrimage had been difficult.

THE CURSILLO STORY

From the time of our arrival in the Philippines I got to know and became friends with Mom's brother and sister-like friends in the Castaneda family. The Cursillo movement was sweeping the greater Luzon area at that time and some of the group invited me to enter the program by way of a three-day retreat in a country setting well outside of Manila. I did, and found it to be so spiritually uplifting that it was truly a milestone mark of spiritual progress in my life's journey. There were about twenty men in that Cursillo group and after the last session, wives and families were invited into the auditorium area for the closing exercise, which consisted of speeches by the priests and lay organizers and each participant was called upon to talk about his feelings and reaction to it all. We were all brothers and sisters in Christ, and the Grace and Love that flowed around that place from everyone's heartfelt rendering of their state of mind was a joy to behold and remember. Mom was inspired and signed up for the next session for women. Our ride home that evening, with the clear country sky and full moon, just added to my indescribable happiness.

About a week or so later Mom and I were in bed. It was about 5 a.m. and we were awakened by the sound of guitars and a small group singing a beautiful song from the Cursillo: "How beautiful the morning, with the star dust and the dew, And God's early morning blessing, With pleasure we sing to you. On the day that you were born, All the flowers came to bloom, And at the baptismal fount, All the angels sang their songs. The dawn, it now is breaking, the rays of the sun shine through, and with God's early morning blessing, we give our love to you;" more inspiration from my sponsors and friends.

At the end of the song they were all standing around our bed holding guitars and lighted candles, smiling and laughing from the joy of it all. We all went downstairs to the dining room where the maids had prepared breakfast, chattering happily that they had a big part in the "surprise awakening." Of course, Mom had worked out the coordination of it all and shared fully in my happiness, and a couple of weeks later she entered the Program. A few weeks after that Moy did likewise. We were all so very close.

PLARIDEL BULACAN...THE FARM EXPERIENCE

About 1967, Moy told me he would be retiring from the Army and wanted to go into a business in partnership with me. "Hey, Moy, I already have a very important job." "No, I don't mean to leave American Express. I will run the business and you will be an invested partner." "Well okay," I said, "But what will you do?" After many considerations, and finally a talk with Jun Rivera, it seemed that a pig and chicken farm out in Bulacan Province, Plaridel barrio, was a good choice. I knew Jun. He had married into the Castaneda family. A graduate of the Philippine Air force Academy, he had been the Federal Air Administration Director at age 30 under President Magsaysay. He had some property in Plaridel and would provide about 3 hectares of his 16 or so for the farm, plus an area for a feed mill.

The plan was to build fattening pens for 270 hogs and raise broilers in eight weeks in screened sections built a few feet above the ground. 1,000 chicks were purchased every week and 1,000 sold. There was always one section left empty during the week for cleaning. The property had a small house which Moy planned to use during the week, and return home to Makati on weekends. Jun built a new house for himself there. Plaridel was his home town, but he lived mostly in Makati.

Lou Gleeck retired from the State Dept. after a long career and he took a position with USAID. His knowledge of the Philippines and fluency in Tagalog made him an asset to any employer in the region. He had a natural interest to helping the farming people and told me several times about sorghum. It seems that sorghum uses the same soil mechanics as corn and, generally speaking, is an equally nutritious animal feed. Now for the pluses. Sorghum stalks contain sugar and can also be used for feed, or they can be processed to extract the sugar. Sorghum yields about 15–20% more grain per hectare, and if I recall correctly would produce an additional crop per season in our conditions there. I talked to Moy with the idea that we could help the low-income people in the barrio by getting them to break with tradition and plant some of their land with sorghum (a gigantic task to plant a portion of the rice field to a new crop until the proof was in).

The "what's in it for me?" We would start the farmer on sorghum, provide the seed and instructions and he would turn it in to the feed mill for finished piglet feed, at which time he would be given a few free piglets to raise. As he grew the sorghum and exchanged it for complete feed and raised piglets, a whole new vista would develop. A few opted in and benefited from the plan, but the lesson we learned was that out there in the farmland in Luzon, asking the farmer to break with tradition about what to grow is an overwhelming task. The answer probably is not only in the entrenched customs, but its cause, that is, lack of education and understanding. The more educated are likely to create and evaluate new methods, and understand "what's in it for me."

Jun, Moy, and I agreed, and we started the partnership and signed the papers. Moy was the G/M and he hired workers, built the feed mill, and hired a consultant, my friend Sol Blum, who had a doctorate in animal nutrition from Iowa U, married a Filipina, and had recently retired from USAID. In a very short time the operation was up and running, feed mill, housing for 8,000 broilers, a water supply and drainage system, and housing for 270 fatteners. Moy bought 1,000 baby chicks every Friday and sold 1,000 broilers the same day. The workers had a bunk house that Moy built for them and they could grow their own vegetables for food, and sale in the local market in addition to their salaries.

I was out at the farm most Saturdays and Sundays and we had many fine barbeque picnics there with our families and guests. Sometimes we would just "hang out" and enjoy the day. I recall the time Moy and I were watching a worker plowing a piece of ground behind a carabao with the common single plane flat plow. One hand and arm controls the plow, the other controls the reins. At my casual comment about that action looking easy enough, Moy responded with, "Oh, sure, easy, suppose you could do that?" "Of course, how tough could it be?" So Moy told the guy to let me have the reins and the plow so they could all watch a "pro" take over. Well, that big smelly water buffalo wasn't too happy with the new "driver," and I quickly realized that keeping the flat-planed plow on an even keel, with one hand so it did not cut in too deep, or ride too thin near the top, was a true responsive gift acquired only through practice. Moy and our workers had a long-lasting, big laugh, and a story to tell in the days to come about the American trying to learn in a half an hour what it took them years to perfect. Besides, the carabao didn't even like me (which added to the humor of it all) and tried to run away from me, more hearty laughs in that friendly happy setting. Really, I could have gone "on the road" with this one and sold tickets.

When the farm and feed mill were ready for opening in that little provincial town, Jun got the mayor of Plaridel to organize a celebration in and around the feed mill area for our visitors. I had arranged for the representatives from UNDP and USAID to attend, as they were interested in such projects. On the Sunday of the grand opening, into the barrio drives the Administrator of the UNDP, UN flag flying, and the Philippine Chief of USAID, with the U.S. flag flying. The local town band was playing loud if not clear, and the open area around and inside the feed mill was set up with tables, chairs, food, cold drinks, and a sound system. The town's folks were delighted at the unexpected fiesta, with music, lechon (roast piglet) and all that rippled out from the mill area. It was a real bash with a barrio flair, and many nice things were said about hard work and having a vision to make a difference.

Lou, Sol, Moy, Jun, and I were especially pleased, and Jun, who would be running for governor of Bulacan Province, got an extra PR "bump." He was in the Liberal party and would run against President Marcos' candidate in the Nacionalista Party.

The farm activity started up. Sol advised Moy on the feed mill activity and feed formulation at the different stages of animal growth. We put in an underground storage tank at the mill for sugar molasses (sugar land started just to the north). Sol would say, "Be sure that hog feed has those black gum drops on the last month" (for fattening). I recall a book that was the bible of its day on raising broilers, written by a Dr. Schnabel at Indiana or Illinois U. I read it all and understood about half, but hey, those farm weekends were fun as I understood most of what was going on.

The barrio folks were friendly and supportive, pleased to see that our little group was interested to help them. One day I was in the open market and noticed a little girl who was blind in one eye. Moy and I found a doctor in Manila who agreed to see her on a pro bono basis. We brought her and her mom to Manila and the doctor operated on her eye, restoring her sight.

We kept some firearms at the farm for security reasons. A few Communist insurgents were purported to be over in the nearby San Rafael area, but we never experienced any trouble. Jun usually had some personal hand guns at his house there, and I had a small German magnum. On a few occasions some of us had a shooting contest right off of his back porch, firing at tin cans. Oh, the "ribbing" and joshing that went on, in accompaniment to the many misses. "Maggie's drawers, again?" "What did you do in the war, Daddy?" All "macho" stuff that the ladies and children enjoyed watching from a distance.

COCK FIGHTS...A PIECE OF THE CULTURE

Jun was a fighting cock aficionado and on some Sunday afternoons we would go to one in that area. A rustic, dirt floor, corrugated metal roof, wooden, weather-worn building with a bleacher seats grandstand, held about 300 shouting, screaming, betting, tuba (fermented coconut milk) and beer-drinking men, staring down into the fighting arena. Each match would be all over in a couple of minutes or so, and the din in that smoke-filled arena was deafening, but not uncomfortable, as I was caught up in the excitement of it all. A common expression of a fan who lost his bet was to holler, "Ay naku (translation: for gosh sakes/doggone it), Kentucky fry," meaning, his losing bird should be cooked. The most intriguing action aside from the fighting itself was the betting system. The "bookies," working for the house, were scattered throughout the crowd, drifting through their sections of the noisy audience before each match, as the "build-up" to battle progressed. He would see a bettor's hand go up 10-15 feet away. In the pandemonium they would shout back and forth about making the bet and also use hand signals, the more reliable way. The bettor would show a couple sets of fingers, the number of the bird and the amount, and then the bookie would confirm by a fingers sign, including the odds, thus confirming the deal in the pandemonium of it all. The bookie took the bettor's money in making 20-30 bets around his area. After a match, he would go up and down the packed bleacher seats to each bettor (how could he remember them all?), and pay off where necessary, including the appropriate odds. Amazing! and not a math major in the bunch.

One time Jun invited me to an "invitation only" cock fight, staged in some "inner sanctum" of the Araneta Coliseum (where the great Mohammed Ali/Joe Frazier "Thrilla in Manila" heavyweight championship fight took place). "Jun, I don't have that kind of money to bet, and I wouldn't anyway." "No problem, you don't have to bet, you're with me." We went, and he introduced me to some of his friends there. What a change at the cock fighting scene. There were soft comfortable seats, waiters serving drinks, air conditioning, and very expensive fighting cocks, about 60 spectators; it was "a classy joint." But that place in the barrio was my kind of Philippines, the common tao, hard-working country folks, having a good time at the cock fights.

Jun and I would sometimes fly in his Beechcraft to Subic Bay NAS, the Bulacan or Zambales Provincial airports (turf runways), and elsewhere. One time we went up to Zambales and the town and birthplace of former President Magsaysay, then deceased, whose brother greeted us and kindly signed and gave me a biography of the President who was so instrumental in defeating the Hukbalahaps (communist insurgents) in the mid-1950's. As mentioned elsewhere, the Soviets had a policy in the 1940's to win the hearts and minds of the people in various countries that were or had been under Japanese rule by propagandizing that their man was a Japanese fighter. In this case it was Luis Taruc, and Hukbalahap means something like fighters against Japanese. Zambales Province with the beautiful beaches and sea, mountains, farm lands, and big yellow mangoes, was a lovely place.

I flew in a small plane many times, usually a 4-seater Mooney with retractable landing gear that I rented for business travel to the Clark and Subic military bases. The pilots, whom I came to know, would give me some "stick time" and teach me some of the very basics of flying. One time, two of us took off for Subic, using the domestic portion of Manila International Airport. As we lifted off and retracted the landing gear, the pilot and I noticed the light for the landing gear did not indicate it was locked in. He flew past the tower and asked the controller to look and see if his landing gear was up and in. The controller responded, "Are you declaring an emergency at this field?" "Well no, just tell us how it looks when we do a fly-by." The Tower said they could not see anything unusual, and so we had no real answer. It was early morning and we had full gas tanks. The pilot took a heading for Subic out over Manila Bay and did a little maneuver, a mild dive and pull-up to see if the gear would drop down, no, it seemed normal. I said to him,

"Look, if you are not real sure, we could get a wheel collapse on the Subic run-way, and with all this gas it would not be pretty, I would just as soon you tell the Subic tower you are going to slow it down, keep the nose up and touch us down in the Subic Bay, and please hurry with the crash boat." But he said he thought (thought?) it would be okay. I was on high anxiety, white knuckles showing, as we banked left around the Santa Rosa communication tower in those surrounding hills, lined up with the runway as we dropped down over that final ridge, and he put it down as smooth as silk. I went on to conduct my business and we flew back with the same problem of the landing gear's light. Again he asked the Manila tower to look at it, and again all seemed well and we landed at the domestic port. The pilot said he was going to take it straight into the maintenance shop. About 3-4 weeks later I was told by one of the other pilots that the plane crashed because of a landing gear problem. The pilot was killed. "What's it all about, Lord?" I guess Mom said, "It was his time."

NANA AND POP-POP...TRIP OF A LIFETIME

In the "winter" of 1968-69 when the temperatures might range from 67 to 80 (situated about 14 degrees above the equator), we surprised Nana and Pop-pop with first class around-the-world tickets on Pan Am #1. Retired then, they had the time of their lives on a 3-month trip. They stayed with us about two months and were met and accommodated by our Amexco friends in Tokyo, Hong Kong and New Delhi, and of course the usual "meet and assist" in other places, like Paris and London. Their enjoyment from being with us, and especially the grandchildren, was contagious, making their visit "gooder 'n good" (that Snuffy Smith expression again).

Clara, your Uncle Bob's mom, made that trip with Nana and Pop-pop, trav-eling together on a three-month trip. Were Sol, the dad of Bob, alive, he would have been there too, such was the goodwill and love of all concerned.

At that time we were living at Bel Air Village in Makati. Karl Kircher, visit-ing on business from his Hong Kong Headquarters, where he was VP of Credit Card Asia then, came over for dinner and he and Dad had a nice time later in the evening standing around our small bar out in the lanai telling their stories, includ-ing their German backgrounds. At my office the next day Karl commented "Hey, your Dad speaks pretty good German (another first in my knowledge bin)."

Mom and I planned to take them to the mountain provinces, joined by Moy and Luz, nine in all, including the yaya (nanny). After about five hours of driv-ing, our two-car caravan arrived at Baguio, 5,000 feet elevation, with its pine forests, morning mists, and fresh mountain air. Those old mountain roads were an interesting adventure. We started off at the Baguio Country Club with its log cabin architecture and unique 5,000 yard golf course. The "greens" were packed and rolled sand. There were sharp changes in elevation with several demanding blind shots to the green. One hole, "Cardiac Hill," was about 250 yards of straight, well-maintained fairway (the last of the good news). The green was "blind" with an elevation angle of about 35 degrees from tee to green. There were two shelves on the side of that slope at about 120 and 170 yards from the tee. Off to the right side were steps cut into the soil with wood slat supports. Adjacent to the stairs was a rope-and-pulley contraption from tee to near the green. Push the button, the motor starts, grab hold of the rope, and you are pulled along as you walk up the stairs, and get off at the appropriate level. When you finally putt out, you pull the hammer chord of a large heavy bell that echoes through the hills telling the next group, waiting blindly, that all is clear.

Moy and I played the course while Mom, Dad, Zeni, Luz, Mariellos, Mariana, and yaya went over to the pony rides and walked through the town's open market, which displayed the various wood carving, weaving, and other skills of the local folks. Moy had a retired Army friend, Col Khawid, who lived with his wife in Bontoc. They had converted a large house into a "bed and breakfast" accommodation (small village, mountain air, clean and comfy, might read the travel guide). We arrived there on the old gravel road, large pine trees all around. After we checked into our rooms and the dogs stopped barking, we settled down in the large living room, fitting to the location in design and ornamentation. Dad, always the congenial companion, noticed that sundown was upon us and smilingly suggested we all "get a glow" as he produced a bottle of "happy tonic." The Khawids joined us. Interesting and funny stories filled the air, Zeni and Dad leading the way, but Maria and Mariana also had their say, as they sipped their icy sugar molasses with kalamansi juice drinks. Of course, there was no menu and toward dinner time Mrs. Khawid asked, "Would you like pork, chicken or fish?" We all chose unanimously to make it easy on the cook, pork would be fine. The conversation continued; then later it stopped temporarily when the squealing of a pig was heard from way off in the distance. Ah, the supermarket of nature: fresh provisions, take only what you need. The dinner was superb with cooked rice, vegetables and fresh tropical fruit to go with the roast pork.

The next morning we were on the road to Baguio, pointing out all the different birds and animals of the woodland and occasionally seeing a real native Igorot walking the road. Moy said, "Mom, it wasn't too many years ago that the natives up in this region were head hunters, and believe me, when they see that beautiful head of white hair that you have, some will get nervous." Nana's expression showed the anxiety which that rascal Moy expected, as she peered out intently as we drove past the objects and people of interest along that forest road. I commented that she should not worry because there had been no problems of that kind since last Tuesday. She "got it" and laughed, saying she was going to start wearing a veil.

Going on to Baguio, often called the summer capital, we also visited the vacation home of the U.S. Ambassador. It was probably built in the early 1920's when summer in Manila made one dream of the cool pine forests at 5,000 feet. It had been turned into a landmark. It had its own minor history, but assumed prominence because it was where the post-war trials of some of the Japanese generals took place. The last of the Philippine fighting in WWII took place in the mountain provinces and General Homma and others were captured and their trials took place on that property.

Over at Camp John Hay, an Air Force communication station, we walked around, did some bowling and played mini-golf. In the course of that activity we chatted with an American lady and her companions. She was the wife of General Abrams, the Theater Commander in Vietnam. She invited Mom, Nana, Clara, Luz and you children to a ladies' tea that she was giving the next day. They all had a lovely time. Moy and I played golf. The next day we all motored back to Manila. Our family visited Baguio many times over the years staying at the Country Club, a friend's home, Camp John Hay, or in later years, the then new Hilton Hotel. We always returned with that invigorated spirit which good vacation generates.

THE BULACAN AGGIES...AND OTHERS

We stopped at the farm as we passed through Bulacan Province heading south to Manila. Pop-pop the perennial vegetable gardener had brought tomato seeds with him to plant on the farm, maria globes and beefsteaks, as I recall. On his first visit to the farm he made many rows in the soft rich soil, placed the seeds (no starting cups) right into the ground, watered them, and inspected them on each return trip. Soon they were high enough to tie to stakes, and they were healthy, while the prevailing thought of experts was that using seeds from one soil culture to another does not work well. One day Dad was working in his little plot, watering the plants with a garden hose right along side of the garden of the workers. I hollered over, "Hey Dad, spray some on those other plants." "Nah, they can take care of their own." I laughed. In his mind, he was in competition with our guys to see who would have the best tomatoes. Well, he won before he left, and we dried the seeds of some of those large beefsteak tomatoes, and later in the year the workers used some of the seeds. They started off very well, but halfway through the growth period a destructive wilt grew on them.

One Saturday I drove from Makati to The Agricultural College of The University of the Philippines in Los Baños. I found a vegetable expert, a Ph.D. from Indiana U. We talked about sorghum and other matters I was interested in. When I mentioned the imported tomato seeds and the ensuing wilted tomatoes, he said it was a common occurrence for the imported and next generation of seeds to grow into wilted plants. It was something about weak resistance to various microbes in the soil, but no one had yet pinned it down (I'm sure they have by now). But that big tomato was so good and in such demand, especially by restaurants, that an American agriculturalist, whom I visited in Antipolo, was using a hydroponics system to avoid the wilt. With standard cement hollow building blocks, he built long troughs about 40 inches high, 50 inches wide, and 30 feet long. He boiled, and then dried, saw dust, and placed it in the troughs, adding selected nutrients. He started the seeds in small cups filled with the saw dust and later transferred the seedlings to the troughs, and presto! The problem of import-ed seeds creating wilted plants was solved for the high-priced market places, while the search for the bad guy soil microbes went on.

Nana and Pop-pop did and saw many things while they were there. One day we took them to Pangasinan Falls, a long drive north from Manila, and two by two we got into dugout canoes with two paddlers each and went up the river to the falls. It was all woodsy, jungle-like, a few monkeys chattering, with two sets of rapids that we walked past to lighten the dug outs while the boatmen muscled them through. At the falls, we broke out the snacks, some of us swam in the river, or sat around talking, enjoying the beauty of it all, with the high falls, light mist, and sunlight shafts through the foliage.

Another time Mom took Nana and Pop-pop to Zamboanga, in the southern region. She had some good friends there and in addition to sightseeing around town they went out to a nearby island to the Menses Plantation, known for its advanced agricultural methods. Before leaving Zamboanga, Pop-pop, being so impressed at the size and delicious taste of the lobsters there, had a chef cook up enough to fill two very large insulated boxes, and they brought them home on the plane, then into the house, onto the dinner table with chilled white wine and a rousing toast to Zamboanga!

One night we visited a casino on Roxas Blvd. along the Bay (probably still Dewey Blvd. at that time) and Pop-pop was having a nice time at the dice table. It seems he knew all about the game and would just bet the safer side bets. (My total lack of knowledge about it all is obvious as I try to explain.) He never took the dice but just bet that side bet area. He knew his math and could figure the odds. He was a steady small winner and finally the manager came over and cour-teously said he was glad Pop-pop was there and enjoying himself and he would like to buy our party dinner, and "if you will all just come this way, Pablo here will take care of you." (i.e., please don't play here anymore) It was a nice dinner and we liked the price.

Then there were the many parties. My extended family surely made Nana and Pop-Pop feel at home, the well-known Philippine hospitality at its finest. Tito Pepe (Senator Roy) and Tita Conching hosted them more than once, as did Moy, Efren, Luz and others. Zeni and I gave them a Bon Voyage dinner at the Casino Español with about 35 guests, where they again met my old buddy Ed George who had recently arrived to work at the U.S. Embassy.

From Manila, their tickets read Saigon, New Delhi, Paris, London, and home. Zeni, Moy, and I took them to the airport. Moy apparently arranged with Security that the three of us would escort Mom and Dad across the tarmac and up the first class steps and into the plane, which we did. Then we said goodbye, after we escorted them to their seats, just like a "head of state." Not bad for a couple who started off raising their family in a tenement house. Oh, how I love them.

Pop-pop loved to tell the story that Tito Pepe gave him a present when he left the Philippines. It was a beautiful walking cane inlaid with mother of pearl with the well known artistic skills of the Philippine wood carvers. When they arrived at JFK International, a customs officer with an experienced eye for expensive items noticed that Pop-pop had not declared the cane. "Nice cane," he commented. "Yes," said Pop-pop, "It was given to me by Senator Roy when I was in the Philippines." "How much did it cost?" "Ah, gee," replied Pop-pop, "If Senator Javits gave you a present, would you ask him how much it cost?" to which the official replied with a smile and his clearance stamp.

AMEXCO...CONTINUING BUILDING THE BUSINESS

I had always liked and enjoyed working for Amexco, especially with this assignment in the Philippines. It was "a natural" from the time John Stewart decided to appoint me there. John was a respected and productive leader as Vice President for the global travel division. As mentioned elsewhere, he had been an FBI agent and was the VP Security when he joined Amexco. The De Angelus case came along during that time and his action prevented severe losses. The Board of Directors then appointed John to run the travel division as a rewarding promotion, a wise choice. The De Angelus case had to do with a lending activity called "field warehousing." De Angelus, trying to corner the market of vegetable oil, would import the oil by tankers, store it in a tank farm (like diesel or gasoline) and would then put up the filled tank(s) as collateral for a loan to purchase more oil. The lender would then take physical control of the vegetable oil used as collateral, a "field warehousing" action similar to a lender taking control of a silo of corn out in the field.

Using many financial institutions, De Angelus spiraled the procedure upward. Then, needing even more money to achieve his goal, his operatives filled many of the oil storage tanks with water, leaving enough oil on the top to stick to the long dip sticks which the lenders' inspectors would periodically use to validate the collateral. I do not know the details of the story and how it broke when the scheme was uncovered. I was not in the U.S. then. De Angelus went to jail for many years.

As mentioned, in those early years, from 1966-75, I improved the Amexco Philippine business from 3 profit units to about 18, which gave it a good base for the future. As any business person knows, such a job requires a "long hours, hands-on" approach. I opened offices in Makati, Guam, Angeles City (next to Clark Air Base in Pampanga), on Subic Bay Navy Base, a representative office in Saipan funneling to Guam, Cebu in the central Philippines, and in-house offices in World Health Regional Headquarters, United States Agricultural and Industrial Development, Peace Corps (with some 200 volunteers), Asia Development Bank, and The International Rice Research Institute in Los Baños.

From time to time I had a representative in Zamboanga. In 1978, I received a new assignment as Director, Industry Relations, Asia/Pacific. When leaving the G/M position, American Express International honored me with a dinner and silver tray reading, "To Mr. Howard Newhard, one who is loved, respected and held in the highest esteem by people in the Travel Industry and particularly the Amexco staff in the Philippines, in profound appreciation. January 20, 1979."

CHALLENGING DAYS...MANILA OFFICE BLOWN UP

Amexco had its office on the ground floor of the PhilAm Life Building, which had a nice cafeteria, also on the ground floor, where I would occasionally stop for coffee and conversation after attending early morning Mass at the Ateneo University nearby. The cafeteria workers were employed by PhilAm Life, which decided to "pay them off" and contract with a food company to run the cafeteria. Those employees objected and then demonstrated every day, but to no avail. So they went out and got the backing of the Communist Kabatan Makabayan, a hard-core group that thrived on such matters. They picketed the PhilAm Life building, happy to take action against the leading domestic insurance company and its capitalistic philosophy. I arrived there for work and Mac, my driver, let me out in the street near the main entrance, where the red banners were flying amid the dense, shouting crowd that " pumped up the volume" on seeing the tall American wanting to cross the picket line. Some of my staff met me at that point, not being able to cross through the line either. In high decibel tones the leaders and I had a short conversation. "Look, I don't have a place in this argument. I pay rent to PhilAm Life to use that office space and I have a legal right to do so. Don't make any more trouble; you have already injured one of my employees (one of the travel consultants was kicked in the ribs by a roughneck goon sitting in a jeep as she tried to pass through the picket line)." They all jeered me with curses and shouts of "Yankee Go Home!"

I went next door to the Third Precinct, which was between the PhilAm Life Building and the World Health Regional Headquarters on United Nations Ave., and told the Capt. I needed help. He sent four or five patrolmen to open a hole in the line and we all went right in. The whole staff came to work that day. I was proud of them. That was the same staff that was unionized when I arrived there but a year or so later decided to dissolve the union as we all found common ground to work on in advancing the business and employee concerns.

At the end of the work day, I was leaving the building around 5:30, out the front entrance and on to the esplanade, between the building and the sidewalk on which the heavy picket line was well-replenished with its red banners and loud activists. I had arranged with Mac to pick me up across the street at the Hilton Hotel. A couple of friends, who were PhilAm Life executives, were watching from the front door when the pickets started to curse me in Tagalog with their "bull horns." "Do you know what they are saying?" asked Ramon, obviously upset. "No, I don't." "It's awful stuff," he said, "I want to sue them. You should sue them. We are your witnesses." "That's okay, Ramon, let's take it a day at a time." My path was already set for me in a psychological automation as I walked the short promenade to the sidewalk where it was all fire and brimstone. "Hey, Yankee, how many did you kill in Vietnam today?" screamed a fiery-eyed woman holding a banner. I could not hold back, like the little guy inside had told me to do. "If they were anything like you, I hope we got 'em all," I shouted as I pushed across the sidewalk and out into the street and over to the Hilton, as the shouts, screaming, and bull horns filled the air, stopping the traffic.

That whole scene was repeated for a week or so, and then PhilAm Life raised the "pay off" level and completed the contract for outside food services. The bargaining went on. A few evenings later, I was at home in Urdaneta Village and a telephone caller said, "Is this Mr. Howard Newhard?" "Yes it is. Who's calling?" "Well, Mr. Newhard, you will be a dead man within twenty-four hours." *(Click)*. Needless to say, it was a near-sleepless night. I kept checking around the house, somehow sensing I had a couple of days before they/he made their move. If he had indicated Mom and you children were in danger (a bit contrary to Philippine thinking unless he was into terrorist tactics, not common then), we all would have been out of there on the next plane.

The next day I telexed New York Headquarters the reason I was hiring an armed guard at the house, which was of course approved. I then went to see "Johnny" Juan Ponce Enrile, Minister of Defense for a license to carry, which he immediately approved and I bought a nice-packing German magnum. Two evenings later I received another "dead man" call at home. I remained a light sleeper. Mom and you "guys" slept just fine as I had not yet told her about it. When the third threatening call came in a few evenings, later I said, "Look, you know where I live. Why don't you come over and we'll see what happens." *(Click)*.

There was much turmoil there in those Cold War days. In another instance, after having lunch at the Army/Navy club, I drove myself out onto Roxas Blvd, right among that red banner crowd who were picketing the U.S. Embassy (and fire-bombed it a few days later) along with like-minded foreign "guests." I had slowed to a crawl, windows down, nice weather, when a stocky, well-built, Caucasian guy came along giving out pamphlets. "Hey, where are you from?" I asked. "Canada," he replied. "Here, this tells all the bad things the Americans are doing in Vietnam and why the Viet Cong will win." I took the pamphlets, gave a quick look as he moved away, held them out the window, and tore them up and dropped it all in the street. "Aw buddy, you don't want to do that," he said, coming toward me, obviously intent on "punching my lights out," which I am sure he could have done, judging from his build and line of work. I packed that magnum almost everywhere I went for a few years, and I had it then, and made up my mind that if he tried to get into the car or pull me out of it, I would shoot him. But the traffic opened, and I moved along, past the intermittent, temporarily inactive, policemen.

Those were trying days with bomb threats at the International School from time to time, you guys coming home and telling us about the bomb drills, bombs by insurgents, but also aerial bombs if the Cold War heated up. Recalling those conditions, I was home early one evening and received a call from an Amexco colleague. "Howard, your Manila office has just been blown up." After dinner at Alba's, which was across the street from the side entrance to the PhilAm Life Bldg., he was walking toward his car when back down the road a loud explosion shook the area. The bomb took out most of our Amexco office and part of the Far East Bank and Trust Co across the hall in the PhilAm Life Building. Whether or not the timing device did not work properly or it was purposely set for around 7 p.m., off-business hours, we will never know. When I got there the police had secured the area. The damage was heavy; we had to close that main ground floor office and support our retail operations from our Makati office. There were piles and piles of thick broken plate glass all over the area during the clean-up and repair that followed, while we did our best to keep the overall business as normal as possible for our clients. Our Philippine staff was superb.

From about 1970 to 1979 we lived in Urdaneta Village in Makati, No. 7 Farol St. It had a large dining and living room with a bar, accommodating for large but friendly parties, a nice lanai, and a lawn and garden beyond. I remember doing exercises in the garden four or five mornings a week, then going around to Mariellos' and Mariana's bedroom, rapping on the window and making noises like a big ogre. They would pull back the curtains, see the ogre, and amid screams of delight and fun, jump back into bed, covers over head, while the ogre did his howling dance. Then it was "everybody up" (Michele too when she was old enough) and we marched around the garden and lanai with high-lift legs and arms swinging to the tune of a John Philip Sousa march. They laughed as Dad took exaggerated steps like a drum major at the Michigan football game. Then they would do their things like see Mommy, bedroom play, breakfast, whatever, and I would run through the Makati business district, or into the Ft. Bonifacio grounds, a mile or so away.

Our family was expanding. As with "Muning," Michele was also born at the Manila Doctor's Hospital, a half a block from my office. After a long wait in the early morning, the nurse was taking me to see Mom and in some narrow passage another nurse was carrying a newly born who had a smear of blood and whitish powder. My escort said, "Here's your little girl," and reading my face (as I thought, she looks funny, that can't be my kid, it's not even tagged), so she continued, "Oh, we have to clean her up, she's a healthy and beautiful baby." So she was, and she became a beautiful woman. Mom laughed at the story. Both Mom and baby were fine and we were on top of the world with our growing family, many friends, and nice lifestyle. It was 1970, December 28, Innocent's Day in the Church Calendar. Michele later gave Mariana her other nickname…somehow at the age of two "Mariana" was hard to pronounce and evolved into "Munining"

Baby Michele at swimming pool, ca. 1972   *Baby Christina, November 22, 1974*

or "Muning" for short. The whole family thought it was cute and the name stuck.

On November 20, 1974, Christina was also born in Manila Doctor's Hospital. Funny, we never asked them for a volume discount. I had to be at my office that day rather than be in the waiting room as before, but was in continual touch with the head nurse, and in the afternoon I got the call: "Sheez heerre!" Whatever was so important on the business scene that I could not wait in the hospital disappeared like poof! I ran across the street and down the block and there was my cute little daughter all nice and bright and pretty and quite comfortable there in the nursery with all of her new room mates. Mom, smiling and well, already had some visitors The very large room was full of flowers. Life was good and we gave our thanks then, and again about a week later, as we celebrated the American Thanksgiving Day at the Mother Earth Chinese restaurant which was shaped like a large Chinese junk.

Mom's idea was to have a Hawaiian-style luau in our garden for Christina's Baptism and my birthday. That Urdaneta house was designed to entertain. From the front door one looked across the large living room, with the square bar and stools off to the side, out into the lanai with the green grass and flowery garden beyond. The low tables and cushions around the main garden lawn seated about sixty guests while near the high stone wall in the rear the Alba restaurant caterers rotated the dressed calf over the coals, set up the buffet tables, and Senor Alba made his famous paella. Christina was awakened and shown to the crowd among appropriate cheers, blessings and congratulations. Zeni had placed many fish nets with the shells of various crustaceans on many of the walls and screens. The lighting was superb. The music was pleasant, and the hula dancers, from a local dance school, exemplified that musical and rhythmic part of the Filipino heart. Mom, a natural dancer herself, was a marvelous hostess and storyteller…and the band played on….

Author strikes a pose next to a floating picnic table on a family outing at the beach, January 1969.

FISHING...THE CAVITE WAY

As mentioned, the Buhain lineage has its roots in Cavite, that coastal province with Sangley Point at the mouth of Manila Bay. Moy arranged for us go see a relative who owned some fishing boats and then go out on one all night. They would be fishing a few miles to the west of Corregidor Island. These were large boats with an outrigger design, a somewhat misleading description because outrigger usually connotes a Hawaiian paddle boat race, or the banca boat in the Philippines handled by two or three paddlers. These fishing boats could berth 6-8 crewmen and go out three or four days. There were two outriggers on each side to compensate for the roll of the large hull in a rough sea. Moy wanted me to see how they fished.

   We headed out toward the selected fishing area right after sundown in a warm, moist, tropical, starry night with no moon. The engine had a strong smooth purr (no *pungkata-pungkata* here), as we moved in that gentle sea, cutting a wake that sparkled from the phosphorous, splashing through the small dark waves while some flying fish played and went *splat!* here and there. The crew was upbeat and talkative as we arrived in the selected area, and I guess we all had our afternoon nap for the sleepless night to come. The fishing system was to drop anchor, and then put a large fishing net deep under the boat. The nets were lowered way down, almost to the bottom, and a small hooded floodlight on each side of the boat was turned on to attract the fish. We would wait until the captain thought it was time to haul up the nets, sort the fish into ice-chilled compartments, and do it over again, and again.

While the crew waited for the captain's command to haul in the nets, they would go out on the outriggers' supports and fish for squid with a hand line. That was part of their remuneration. I needed no encouragement to get out there on the supports and try my hand at catching squid. We used no bait. A little piece of white tape wrapped around the top of the hook did the job of attracting squid. Of course I was a bit awkward squatting down on the supports and manipulating my two lines, making my mistakes, but learning. Moy and the captain and crew were good- naturedly amused by it all, sort of like my "quick learn" when I tried to plow using a carabao.

The routine went on through the night and we headed to home port and the fish wholesalers while it was still dark, to arrive at daybreak to beat, or at least compete, with the other boats coming in. It was interesting to watch the fish traders work, bargain, settle deals, make future deals, and keep steady suppliers happy; probably the same basics applied at seaports around the world. Anyway it was a great time. I slept most of that day at a relative's home and then drove to Manila with my well-earned squid packed in ice.

THE CORRUPTING POWER OF POWER

In the early days of the Marcos presidency, 1966-67, the general conditions and economy improved. He and his wife Imelda made a striking couple and they were popular. Philippine-U.S. relations were on a high. Shortly after his election, Marcos addressed a joint session of the U.S. Congress for about forty minutes. It was carried by several TV networks. He was warmly greeted and his fine oratorical skills were on display as he spoke of our countries' friendship, the sacrifices that both countries made in WWII, MacArthur's return to the Philippines, our partnership in the Cold War, the Philippine participation in the Korea War, and I especially retain that part wherein he spoke of Lt. Marcos fighting in Bataan and the time he was holding and comforting the dying American soldier, whose blood was seeping into the Philippine soil. He had our Congressmen mesmerized and they went nuts.

Much later on in his presidency there was popular talk and media coverage of the many medals he had won for his wartime activity. Moy, who did fight in Bataan, and escaped from the death march, was a journalist by education. In the immediate post-war era, he was given the assignment to research and write the wartime history of the Philippine army. Querying Moy in regard to Marcos' purported military accolades, Moy told me, "I never heard of him."

A reversal of that early favorable trend was predictable as we noted the changes taking place concerning "how business was done." For example, the government was setting up "co-ops," or "associations," owned 51% by the "government" and 49% by private investors (favored and privileged). We had the rice, tobacco, coffee, corn, sugar, coconut, mining, lumber, etc. "co-ops." It was widely understood that Marcos had large, cover-up holdings in those and other organizations, eventually including banks, and the Manila Electric Company (MARALCO) formerly owned by the Laurel family of Batangas Province. All this is a book in itself but this was the evolving power situation in those years which would create the crippling graft and corruption. Marcos increased his power by declaring martial law in 1972. He claimed it was necessary because the Communist activists had become too strong.

Jun ran for governor of Bulacan Province on the Liberal Party ticket, loyal to that party since the days when he was FAA Director under President Magsaysay, the same party wherein Marcos had been Senate President but jumped to the Nacionalista Party when President Macapagal reversed his agreement with Marcos to only run for one term (Oh, how they do love that job). Jun campaigned hard, going all over the province, but the Marcos folks could really "spread the bread" and Jun lost. Intermittently, he flew Sergio Osmeña, Jr. around the country in a Lodestar (overhead wing, twin engines, seating about fifteen) on his presidential campaign against Marcos in that summer and fall of 1969. It would be a very close contest indeed, one that would go to the Supreme Court for an unresolved final decision (while Marcos took office for a second term).

One day while taking off from the provincial airfield outside Cebu (Osmeña's home territory), Jun felt a yawing motion in the plane as he approached take-off speed; the rudder would not respond. He immediately cut the power, hit the brakes, skidded off the end of the runway into a corn field, causing some contusions and other minor injuries among the ten or so passengers. The investigators determined that the cable line to the rudder had been cut clean, a prelude of the "grungy" tactics to come.

THE FADING FARM

About 1970, just when the farm operation was ready for phase two, pig production, and pushing the plan of sorghum swapping by the barrio farmer for finished pig feed to start his own pig feeding activity for more income, I visited the farm one Saturday and nothing seemed to be going on. I asked Moy what was happening. He did not have a straight answer, saying that Letty, his wife, was unhappy that he was at the farm during the weekdays, and he would have to try to find someone to replace himself (meaning, he was stepping out of the picture). Wow, what a shock. I mean, we had always discussed things and kept each other informed. Letty had agreed to the farm plan two years before. It took about 3-4 months after he hired an experienced farm manager to discover that the new guy had the right amount of experience to know how to steal from us, making deals with our suppliers and buyers. We tried another manager and that did not work either; our workers were leaving us.

The short read is that the farm had no management and we sold off the live-stock, and the grass grew, and the winds blew, as the tropical vines nestled their way over the pig pens and feed mill. I was in a quandary. There was more to it than Letty's purported decision, and I was very disappointed. I had been asked to go in on a one-third partnership of the profits, invested an amount as required, and then he surprisingly bailed out without a valid reason. I asked for my money back. I surely needed it. Nothing happened and, in terms of the farm, time stood still, but all else was rapidly moving on.

AMEXCO CONFERENCES…HIGHLIGHTS THROUGH THE YEARS

Back in 1968 Frank Erickson and John Stewart decided we should have an annual Asia managers meeting at some place in the world, and that continued on after they both moved into retirement. What a marvelous idea! Not only did it help achieve the intended goals in the overall business, but the camaraderie among the multi-national managers added to the pleasant experience of being a part of the American Express family. The established pattern was two full days of company business and two full days of recreation at a nearby resort location. One such meeting was in NYC at the inaugural luncheon ceremonies for the new and very impressive American Express World Headquarters, before mov-ing on to Boston for the meeting itself. Howard Clark, that fine gentleman and superb CEO, addressed the group with, "I am pleased to invite you here to this exceedingly expensive lunch," also a nice sense of humor. Over the years I recall we had managers meetings in Hawaii (twice), Hong Kong, Taiwan, Berlin, Beirut, Bangkok, Tahiti, Singapore, Auckland, Las Vegas, Mexico City, Tokyo, Sydney, and Manila.

The side trip from Las Vegas was to the El Travar Hotel on the rim of the Grand Canyon. Frank Erickson arranged for all volunteers who wanted to fly in a small prop plane into the canyon to sign up and be ready. With our fleet of 3 four-seaters we took off. I was next to our pilot. As we approached the rim, descended well into the canyon, and saw little planes going in all different verti-cal and horizontal directions, I asked our pilot how many hours he had accred-ited in doing this. "Oh, about thirty," was the reply, which I was sorry I heard, but helped me recall this story.

Another time we went to Beirut, Lebanon, the Paris of the East. On "free-time" some of us drove north past miles and miles of beautifully cultivated vine-yards to that ancient Roman outpost city of Balbaak where the tile designs in the public baths and court yards were still bright with color, and the camels still smelled. As of this writing it is the headquarters of the Hezbollah. I wonder what the history that little town will have recorded by the middle of this century.

While visiting Lebanon, the Ministry of Tourism hosted us at two events. One evening we boarded buses and went along a mountain road to a huge cavern complete with stalactites and stalagmites that the Ministry was going to make into a beautiful underground concert hall, about 20% finished. The basic lighting gave emphasis to the natural contours. The idea was to have the audience sit comfortably and enjoy the music in this beautiful and unusual natural environment.

The other tourist attraction was the largest casino I had ever seen up to that time, about 1977. Run by the government, it was two-storied. The ground floor was the sprawling casino. The second story was a sloped dinner theater for about 1,000. There were no tables or chairs. It was designed like the seats similar to the large first class airline seats of that time, with folding serving trays. There was ample room between the rows for the waiters. Common now throughout the world, that was the first of its kind I had seen.

While thinking "meetings abroad," around 1980, I was invited by the India Hotel Association to attend its annual meeting in Calcutta. Mom went with me, and we met many Indian hoteliers in that productive and friendly environment. From there we went to Delhi, Srinagar, and the Jaipur area, where we visited a pinkish red-brick town; streets, esplanades, amphitheater, buildings, all brick. It dates back to 1200 A.D. Long since abandoned, it is maintained by the Indian government in its promotion of tourism and history. Today, in that region, when the hot summer breezes drift in from the desert, people turn on their fans or A/Cs. In 1200 A.D. the architects had designed vents to carry cooler air from outside openings three stories high, into special lounge rooms just below ground level. On the outside of the buildings were stairways leading up to a level above the openings facing the desert. The coolies would carry bags of water up the stairs and pour it into troughs which were designed to spill off making water screens which cooled the desert breeze as it passed through and down into the chamber below. A/C in 1200 A.D.!

MARTIAL LAW...THE FOX GUARDS THE HENHOUSE

One night the car of Juan Ponce Enrile, Minister of Defense, who lived in Urdaneta Village, was shot up near the main gate. He was not in it. No one was hurt. The headlines next day proclaimed that Communist activists were becoming bolder. A month or so later a hand-grenade went off on the front lawn of Senator Roy's home on Broadway in Quezon City. Eyewitnesses saw a truck pass by and something was thrown over the wall. The newspapers blamed the communist insurgents. The general reporting about the insurgents went on, some factual, like demonstrations at Malacañang Palace, the presidential residence, and some unsubstantiated.

I was at an American Express Asia Travel manager's meeting on a small resort island near Auckland, New Zealand in 1972. We were having breakfast when Frank Erickson, the VP for Asia Travel, came in and told me that he had just heard that Marcos had declared martial law in the Philippines. I ran to a telephone and could not get through to Zeni on two tries. I told Frank I would try once more, but failing that I would book the earliest flight out to connect to Manila. Finally I got through. Mom said not to worry. The schools and all business offices were open and all was peaceful for the most part. But the Communist activists were running for cover and some had been jailed, and there were some troops in the streets, giving the populace a feeling of safety. So I stayed at the meeting and about three days later we all went on to Auckland and shortly thereafter I returned to Manila.

Within the week we attended a family party at the Roy's. Tito Pepe (Senator Roy) was laughing when I asked him about the grenade exploding on his front lawn. Suspecting it was a staged job, I said, "Gosh, it would be easy to throw a grenade through the window. I wonder why it was thrown onto the lawn." He turned to me and quietly said, "That was the Marcos people." Tito Pepe was a very popular senator. Obviously the Marcos clandestine group chose his place, just as they had chosen to shoot up the Defense Minister's car, to get the publicity to blame the communist sympathizers through the media. It was all in a developed design for more power (martial law) and especially necessary to quell the possibility of a Supreme Court decision to award the 1969 election to Sergio Osmeña. This had been pending since the votes were counted. It was that close and fraud had been charged. Now there would be no Supreme Court decision.

Jun had been on a trip to the U.S. and when he returned he was arrested and charged with conspiring to assassinate President Marcos. I knew Jun pretty well. He would not do something like that. It was payback for running against a Marcos man in Bulacan and strongly supporting Osmeña, piloting the campaign plane, and being anti-Marcos in a clear and outspoken manner.

Around 1974 our nephew, René Buhain, Moy's son, who was a top executive at Ayala Corp. urged us to buy a lot in Alabang and build our home there. That area was formerly a mango plantation of about 1,000 acres. Long since dormant, the Madrigal family had sold to the Ayala Corporation, the developer of Makati and Alabang. We committed to do just that and chose an elevated lot in the rolling hill countryside that was totally vacant at that time, except for the country club, 50 meter pool, golf course, and polo fields, which were already built to help project a "futurama" and spice that's nice for the coming sales. Way off in the distance we could see the South China Sea. We agreed that Mom would design and build the home of her dreams (within our budget). I did not have an interest along those lines. As long as we had a home, the house could be most any configuration and style. She did a marvelous job and we were the third house built in Alabang, which, I understand, is now a city. Back to the Alabang days later.

Since Jun's property in Plaridel had increased in value from the fixed assets of the farm operation, and Moy had decided not to manage, and since I needed funds (my Amexco benefits were good but my salary was modest), I told Moy I would like to have my investment back. Both he and Jun could easily afford the small amount involved. He did not like my request and his demeanor showed it.

From his view I had taken a business risk and that was that (still no plausible reason as to why he dropped out). He went to talk to Jun's wife about the matter, and although resenting my request, they agreed to pay me back my investment. First we would have to dissolve the partnership and the necessary papers were drawn up for me to take to Jun for his signature.

I asked Minister Juan Ponce Enrile for permission to go to the Intelligence Security Dept. where he was being held to obtain his signature. I went there and the major in charge looked at the approval paper and said, "Newhard, I remember that name, you were taking target practice out there in Bulacan. I was going to bring you in." The hair on the back of my head felt like flies were crawling around there and I said, "Well, I'm here now, what did you want to talk about?" With hard eyes and a bigot's mind he responded, "Well, you people feel that we all look and think alike, so what's the sense in talking to you?" "Sir, I can assure you that I can distinguish my many friends and family members from each other." I don't think he got it. He asked why I wanted to see Jun and I told him about the farm and showed him the partnership dissolution papers for Jun to sign. He brought Jun out and we three sat at a table with the Major holding a newspaper in front of his face as if reading (oh, that clever rascal). Jun and I said hello, how are you, etc. He had lost a lot of weight. We did not have much to say with the paper reader sitting there, but Jun's unsmiling straight face I took as his attempt to convey he was being mistreated. At a later time, after they moved him to Ft. Bonifacio, I heard that one tactic to keep him unsettled was to take him out of his cell in the middle of the night, put a bag over his head, walk him around the large grassy open spaces there, and occasionally snap the bolt of a rifle into place, as if putting a round in the chamber for his execution. I explained the negative situation at the farm and the need to dissolve the partnership. He signed in the right place, we shook hands, and held an eye-lock of friendship and understanding.

I brought the paper back to Moy and he made arrangements for us all to meet, i.e., a few of the Castenedas who were helping to handle Jun's affairs, Moy, and myself. Moy and they were highly resentful of my actions. Zeni was absolved of any of their hard feelings and she quietly felt I had done the right thing (in our interest). Well, I met with them. The air was icy and brittle. I thought, aren't these my good friends whom I have loved from my earliest days in the Philippines? The fellow Cursillistas who came into the bedroom with candlelight and song, "How beautiful the morning...?" It was not an easy time for me. Many years later I figured Moy left the farm management because he did not want some Marcos goon squad after him. After all, he was in the Liberal Party camp all those years as aide de camp to House Speaker Villareal. He was a staunch Liberal, and upon retiring, joined up with Jun, a vocal Liberal, who also was anti-Marcos. They paid me the money I requested, but to this day I do not know the reason for his action, only guesses.

Ambassador Bill Sullivan was an excellent diplomat and representative of our country. He was our Ambassador to the Philippines a few years prior to his assignment to Iran where he was Ambassador when the Shah was overthrown by the followers of the Ayatollah Khomeini. Our acquaintance grew out of our similar habit of often using our lunchtime to swim laps at the Army Navy Club. So we often had some good conversations on a variety of subjects while taking a break along the shallow end of the pool. About 1979, our new CEO Jim Robinson was visiting the Philippines and I made an appointment for us to visit Ambassador Sullivan. We walked into his office and Sullivan, ever the wit, said to me "Hi, I didn't recognize you with your clothes on," and we laughed, as I quickly explained to Jim in order to lower his raised eyebrow. We went on to discuss the general economic conditions in the Philippines and surrounding region.

Speaking of good representatives of our country, our dedicated Ambassadors and State Department and other Government personnel serving abroad do an adequate job at representing U.S. interests, views, and making friends; but I must comment on that part of history wherein those Americans who lived abroad and represented an American company naturally represented the company and America well. They got to know the culture, integrated easily, sometimes intermarried, and were well accepted as they spoke of various social, political, and economic problems involving the U.S. and the host country or region. Our country was better understood and accepted in more countries in those days thanks to those American expatriates. But sometime back, always looking to improve profits, American companies with overseas activities realized they could hire foreign English-speaking, U.S. or home country college graduates to work in their homeland at much less cost, and of course they had the benefit of having an executive who thoroughly knew the culture and language. It made good business sense. Of course, this change in American business representation abroad had a negative effect on what formerly was unofficially keeping the wires humming with the whys and wherefores of U.S. policies. For example, the U.S. Chamber of Commerce of the Philippines in Manila had a membership of about 110. These were well-known companies with one to three American executives representing them and working with and socializing among Philippine business and government officials all the time. Lies and twisted stories about America and/or its "policies" found almost no place to grow in such an environment. That was the best representation America ever had around the world. It's mostly gone now and the results are obvious.

As the Vietnam war was quickly closing down, Bill Sullivan called me one day. He asked me if I would set up a travel processing unit in the ballroom of the U.S. Embassy to sell air tickets and related services in exchange for U.S. travel vouchers to that flood of non-military personnel that would be processing through the Embassy on their way home. "I'll be right over," I replied. The emergency was obvious and the need was now. We set up about six desks in the ball room and I put some of my best people on the job. In the next month or so transactions through that travel funnel were voluminous. I went there one day to check on the operation and as I was coming out and starting down the stairs off to my left, there were Tom Fosmire and Jim Delaney, old friends from the "Moose" days. "Stumpy!" I shouted (I had hung that on Tom when we first met because of his "pulling guard" or "linebacker" build.) They stopped and looked up and I ran down and hugged them, knowing their pain, and happy to see them. They were really hurting and I tried to cheer them up. I invited them to lunch at the Casino Espanol. In time, with the help of the Paella, Sopa de Mariscos, and a San Miguel beer, we were able to move off of their immediate concern and talk about fun things, as friends can do. Of course, the cloud remained. Afterward we said our goodbyes, friends to this day, but having had no contact due to life's circumstances.

Also, around 1972 one of my good friends from my CIA days (we go back 57 years, and I recently visited him again at his home in the hills in West Virginia) was assigned with his family to Manila. We all had a happy reunion. After a while, he got the idea of using me as a principal agent and, along with Moy, we could work with him on various assigned projects. I contacted Moy. Would he do it? Yes. Would I do it? Yes. And all were happy. Shortly thereafter though, I realized that my cover was fragile as some people suspected me of such a connection because of my friendships at the Embassy and that I put the Agency on my resumes when I sought other employment in 1956-57 (allowable procedure). I had told several people, including Mom and some of her family, that I had worked for the Agency. In addition, after approving the plan, the D.C. Headquarters contacted my CEO in New York City seeking his approval. That fine gentleman and ex-Navy officer was delighted to approve. However, I felt an exposure that would have probably earned me an early "retirement," considering the Marcos regime's modus operandi (MO) when aware of such matters. We were all disappointed, especially me, who always retained his love for the Agency and its purpose and mission.

16 MY PHILIPPINE HOME

Part II

*The Newhard family, ca 1976. From left to right: Michele, Maria,
Zeni, Christina, Howard, Mariana*

MORE AGGIE FUN...TRYING TO MAKE A DIFFERENCE

About 1976 Lou Gleeck told me about a plan to try to introduce sorghum to the corn farmers in a particular region in Zambales Province. He planned to establish a corporation with a mission to grow and expand sorghum production in that area. USAID had approved the project and would provide "seed" money (no pun intended) to develop a cooperative for the benefit of all who joined. We had to wait about a year or so for the Army to drive the New People's Army (NPA), the military branch of the communist insurgency organization, out of that area. In picking his team, Lou asked me if I would sit on the board for economic/financial advice and general "buttinski" work, no pay, same as Lou, but some interesting weekends in the field and occasional meetings in Manila. Lou then hired a CEO, Augusto, and we set the plans to move ahead. Gus brought in three others for the top positions and went into that area in Zambales to talk with the locals about joining the cooperative, planning crop rotation, etc. They hired mechanics and other staff, built a motor pool, barracks for workers, offices, purchased some tractors and laid the physical ground work.

Early one Saturday morning Lou and I headed for Zambales in a very practical vehicle, the old universal, open, 4-wheel drive, jeep. On the way to the little Headquarters deep in the rolling farmland, he wanted to check out some other area. The growth became heavier as the road disappeared and we drove in a dry river bed. Then we heard a child crying loudly and looking up into the growth on the embankment we saw a child of say eight with her daddy who was dressed in the usual loin cloth and carrying his bolo (machete). We waved and stopped. I went up the embankment and gave the little girl a treat from our knapsack. She had never seen or heard an engine before and was afraid. These folks lived deep in the hills there. They are the Negritos, the aborigines of the Philippines. During the Pacific War they were fiercely loyal to the Philippine/American cause against the Japanese, aiding our guerrilla operations. In fact, after the war General MacArthur personally decorated one of their chiefs. They were friendly to Americans and even named some of their children after prominent Americans. One of our trained tractor drivers was named Roosevelt. Naturally, they remained hostile toward Japanese. Hardly a generation had passed since the deplorable actions of the Japanese army in the Negritos' territory.

After probing around in the dry river beds and heavily wooded region, we broke out onto the open rolling hills and farm land again and arrived at the Headquarters, near nothing, in the middle of nowhere, but there was a lot of arable land there and our co-op had contracted to help farm some 200 hectares of land (about 420 acres) with sorghum, a good start. We met with the workers, about eight, and Gus and his staff of two or three and they talked about the plans for the future. There was an information program for the farmers to explain the advantages of sorghum and reasons to join the co-op. Meanwhile Lou and Gus had plans to ask various corporations and banks for financial donations to move the program along to a "take-off" point. I probably asked the American Express Foundation to donate. Lou and I stayed overnight after a nice BBQ chicken, corn, rice, and mango dinner. It had been a long day and I slept very well on an old army surplus cot.

The operation grew and more farmers joined the co-op. Gus was a real dynamo and his enthusiasm was contagious to all the employees. The few roads in the area connected to an old, unused, docking facility on the nearby inlet. Some Japanese business men, who specialized in the importation of grain, apparently heard about Gus and his fledging group and looked him up in Manila. They talked about a possible venture in which they might invest. One weekend, Lou, Gus and I, along with two Japanese gentlemen, "jeeped it" up to Zambales from Manila. They liked the program, noted the potential of using the wharves for shipping, and in general we all had a productive day. Lou, Gus and I envisioned the possibility of the co-op farmers being able to improve their local economy. As the afternoon moved toward evening, our two guests became a little nervous when we suggested that we have a cold beer and dinner, sleep in the barracks overnight, and drive to Manila early in the morning. They made it clear they must return to Manila that afternoon. Actually they were afraid of the Negritos and would not stay. Rumor had it that a year before a Japanese business rep did not return from a trip into that region, corporate loyalty at its finest.

We all went back to Manila, and Gus would be following up on their proposal. I was away for a while on Amexco business and lost the trend of the sorghum project, being only casually involved anyway. I believe Gus made a trip to Japan concerning the matter, and Lou had moved on to other endeavors, but one day he called me for lunch. He told me that Gus had died in a strange way. They found him on the grounds of a large hotel in Manila and the report said he had fallen from a high level (presumably out of a window). Some weeks later his brother told Lou and me that he had no broken bones. The riddle was never solved. There was a lot of speculation, useless as to facts. So the sorghum plans crumbled. The Japanese did not re-enter the picture; donations dwindled. I was an outsider, but that disappointment marked the second time I saw a good farm project, designed to help the common tao and his community, dissolve to nothing.

A FRIENDSHIP FOR ALL SEASONS

Mom's uncle, "Tio Paquito," Francisco Nicholas, was a lumberman and coconut plantation owner from the Naga area. He owned a furniture store chain around Manila. We became friends. A hard worker and early riser, I recall he often played an early round of golf at dawn on a short course by the Intramuros before going to breakfast and work. Occasionally, I joined him in that invigorating way to start the day. One night Mom and I went to his home for dinner, and one of his guests was his Naga home town friend, Monsignor Florencio Yllana, who was the

Cardinal's official designee to conduct the Church/State Liaison Office. During the war they had both conspired to help the local guerrillas who were hiding from the Japanese soldiers. In the post-war period they took the lead role in building the cathedral there, a beautiful structure with that old European flair that I would visit some years later when my (by then) very good friend, invited me to attend the celebration of the 50th anniversary of his ordination. Another time the whole family flew there for a week at the Yllana ancestral home with several trips to the beach house, about ten miles away.

Tita and Tito Nicholas were marvelous hosts and a nice evening ensued as Msgr. and Tio Paquito told many stories of their long friendship. Msgr. had his office in the Intramuros, and on some occasions after I finished work I would stop by and have a "sundowner" with him and other friends who might stop by for a chat, sampling from the fine liquor cabinet that was kept stocked by well-wishers and visitors.

HOLY YEAR…AN "ATTA BOY" FROM THE POPE

1975 was Holy Year (every 25 years) and many people around the world would be traveling to the Vatican and St. Peter's Basilica for the various scheduled events or just to make the visit, attend High Mass, and visit noteworthy places fit for the occasion. Since martial law had been declared in 1972, those people wishing to travel abroad had to acquire permission through the established channels. On behalf of the Cardinal, Msgr., as Church and State Liaison, got permission from President Marcos and the Security Dept. to have 2,500 pilgrims apply for exit permits. Msgr. and I talked about setting up a basic tour with some side trip options. I flew to London, to confer with Amexco's Europe Tour section that had the experts who knew how to package tours to specification. The best in a complicated business, they came up with a variety of options and prices after they made all of their local European contacts. Back in Manila some more discussion went on and final choices were made; then London printed and sent the Holy Year Brochures to me in Manila.

The Holy Year Pilgrims departed in groups of 30-35 with one or two priests in each group during the late spring and summer. In October the last tour was scheduled and Msgr. and I and his brother Fred, also a Msgr., along with two other priests, escorted some forty people on our Holy Year Pilgrimage. We were all good friends of Msgr. Yllana, who had chosen this last grouping. We flew to Rome, went through the Holy Year Door in St. Peter's Basilica (opened every Holy Year), went to Mass in the Basilica, attended the Wednesday afternoon talk and blessing by the Holy Father from his apartment balcony, visited the Sistine Chapel and other famous places, immersed in the art and beauty of it all.

When we entered the huge square in front of the Basilica to attend Mass, it was all highly organized, and each group from all over the world had to stay together to reach the seating assigned to them. The Swiss guards had strict rules and security was firm. I, of course was with the Philippine group with my start-ing-to-gray blond hair, blue eyes, and 6'3" frame. While our group, tightly packed in that immense crowd, was moving to its seating destination, we entered anoth-er check point. A guard saw me, totally out of place in his mind. He held up his hand commanding, "No, no, go back." Our whole group responded, "No, no, he is with us." The over-worked guard rolled his eyes skyward and held his hands up in a pleading gesture before waving us through. There were about a half million in the square that day. We all proceeded with our participation in the Mass, that continuation of the Last Supper.

From Rome we took the train to beautiful Lucerne, Switzerland, for local sightseeing, then to Paris and its main tourist attractions including the Notre Dame Cathedral. Then we boarded a train to Lourdes (Our Lady of Lourdes) in southern France. The exhibits of so many cures of the faithful, characterized by the crutches and canes they left hanging there at the cave of the apparition of the Blessed Mother, was truly impressive for me. Msgr., who had visited there before, kept encouraging me to be dunked in the stream of healing waters. Healing through faith is known from the Bible and various examples around the world up to the current time, but I wasn't sure about that water bit. Anyway I didn't need healing (at that time). "Yeah, yeah, but it's part of the visit," he said. So we went into that area for dunking, stripped down to our shorts, walked down the steps into that frigid mountain spring water where a guy was waiting, waist deep, to dunk you completely underwater (and make sure you didn't drown or have a heart attack). Msgr. had told me that there would be no towels provided. You just put your clothes back on and in no time, poof! all is dried. Well, that's exactly what happened, a minor miracle, within say, forty minutes; there was no sense of wetness. I recall that we went to Mass there at the large church and the beauti-ful evening candlelight procession of thousands of pilgrims was most fitting to the purpose of the occasion.

From Lourdes we took a bus through the Pyrenees Mountains into Spain and its northernmost rail head. We had a long wait at the station, so we sat around and snacked and entertained ourselves with sing-alongs, and some of us went solo with hardly any encouragement at all. It was a fun group. Mom did not join us on this trip. You children would be running the show by the time we returned, but the year before I arranged a long trip for her and Mariellos (then 11), includ-ing Hong Kong, Delhi, and Paris.

Madrid was sightseeing, good dinners, bull-fighting for those so inclined, and a flamenco dance exhibition. From there we flew to Lisbon, Portugal, for a bus ride to Fatima. We would be there for the annual celebration of Our Lady of Fatima on October 16. We arrived a couple of days before and checked into our comfortable accommodations. Portugal at that time had a strong Communist influence in the north, but was one government, not broken up. Mid-October was very chilly at night and we were most impressed to see the poor farmers and peasants coming in with their families in donkey carts, many walking, to spread blankets and sleep on the cold ground awaiting the Mass and other celebrations in honor of the Blessed Mother. I recall Msgr. Fred saying to me: "Howard, we are looking at Faith in action." That night there was a candlelight procession, breathtaking by its massive number, moving through the night in prayer.

The following day, in the beautiful fall sunshine, the Mass was conducted by close to 100 concelebrating priests at the upper level of the stairs on the esplanade in front of the entrance to the Basilica, and the sight that holds my mind was to see those priests come down the stairs and spread out into the crowd of a half million or so to distribute Communion.

I left the group the next day, parting at Lisbon Airport. They were going on to a side trip, which I had arranged. I went back to the Philippines via New York/New Jersey to see Nana and Pop-pop et al. It had been a trip to remember.

Of course The Holy Year had continual publicity in the Philippines. In early 1976 some of the newspapers covered the story with a picture wherein a Dominican priest at the University of Santo Tomas, on behalf of the Pope and Papal Nuncio, presented me with a plaque of appreciation and blessing for the Amexco Filipino employees and me for our efforts to the Holy Year Pilgrimage.

MARION AND BOB, A WELCOME VISIT

Sometime about now, Aunt Marion and Uncle Bob decided it was time for them to come and see us. Of course, we all were delighted to see them. All you children were still home, at about ages 13, 9, 5 and 1. I recall Mom took the lead in showing them around, arranging some parties, shopping, meeting the Buhain family, and the like. We lived in Urdaneta Village, Makati then, and they journeyed from that base to points of interest like Baguio and the Banaue rice terraces. It was a pleasant stay for all. I am a little light on the details of this. I probably had a loaded business plate and could not give it the time it deserved, but one memory comes out of the fog. Aunt Marion laughingly told me, after returning from an afternoon of shopping with Mom, "My goodness, it was so much fun. I didn't know you are supposed to haggle over price. It's expected of you. I enjoyed watching Zeni bargain with a store owner, tell a funny story, get them laughing, go around behind the counters, look at merchandise, and come away with a good deal."

Writing this now my heart sings as I recall the sights, sounds, aromas, and action in the open air markets around the country. Whether in a barrio or the big city the bargaining action goes on. Mom would usually have her "suki" (a personal vendor of veggies, fruit, nuts, or flowers). Then after the friendly banter and "wiggle-waggle" about the price, the deal was closed, and usually, a good "suki" wanting you to come back, would provide the "dagdag," a little add-on, like the old "baker's dozen." Just thinking as I write: The "dagdag" strategy in this home-grown selling practice goes back into ancient times around the world. Today, the eager student in Marketing 101 is happy to pay his tuition in learning for the first time that fantastic marketing concept, under whatever name it is addressed.

RUNNING......A PERSONAL BEST

As mentioned, working out has always been a natural part of my life. When we lived in Urdaneta Village I expanded my daily routine from exercising around the house to jogs around the block, to covering many blocks. After we moved to the new Alabang development, I slowly, not planning or thinking about it, increased my distance in that rolling hill countryside. In Manila, I would occasionally run at lunchtime from the Army/Navy club on Roxas Blvd. along Manila Bay toward Parañaque and back.

I started to read about running. Of the many books, I recall one by Coach Bowerman of Oregon U. who paid a lot of attention to the style and biomechanics of long distance running. He taught his students to use a heel-to-toe roll technique which I found useful, along with his teaching on body position, arm movement and the rest. Then there was the great New Zealand coach of that world class miler Tom Landry. He had them running the hills, beaches, and sand dunes, and eating a prescribed diet in the pre-race preparation days, but the one that provided me with the most information and motivation was written by a marathoner cardiologist from New Jersey. He wrote a best seller or two for the layman to understand the physiology, aerobics and general benefits from running. He had a sense of aestheticism in his writing and lectures that made him the running guru of his day, as he emphasized running for a personal best: whether you win or not. He opined that the true value and joy of it all is an internal, spiritual happening.

Oh, that feeling of the runner's "high" and the fun of running five miles out in the open rolling hills at the break of dawn is an outstanding memory. In 1980-81, as Director of Industry Relations, Asia Pacific, I traveled about 25% of the time. My routine was to leave my hotel at dawn and run 3-4 miles before starting my business day.

A few memories: A bright dawn was breaking as I ran an almost desolate highway in Katmandu, Nepal, with the goats and sheep grazing in the fields nearby, the lush valleys in the far distance below me and the snow-capped Himalaya Mountains above me, as the scattered locals walking the road watched this strange foreigner in shorts (it was summer) and t-shirt, running (for heaven's sake). Another time I was running, in the early dawn, on the outskirts of New Delhi, India, when I discerned in that vague hazy light a group of some 50-60 monkeys scattered across the road and on into the fields and brush on both sides. I thought they would just run away as I came closer (you know, like squirrels), but they stayed where they were. I shouted and clapped my hands, hoping they would leave and I could run on, but at about 50 yards the thought hit me that I was doing a very stupid thing, which could have disastrous consequences for this guy in the shorts and t-shirt, who might be found without ID after he had assumed the temperature of the day. I kept on running, but in the opposite direction and back to my hotel for a shower and breakfast and some "monkey talk" with whoever would listen.

Another time in Bombay, India, I went out from the Taj Mahal Hotel, running in the pre dawn light, and turned a corner into a very narrow street when out of a shanty a huge (like an English Bull Mastiff) mongrel of a dog came right for me with all the fury and sounds of death in the jungle. He hit the end of the huge chain and flipped over as I ran away a bit faster than I had been moving. Really, I was scared and ran back to the hotel, showered and had breakfast, and probably three cups of strong coffee to soothe my old jitters about big dogs that don't like me. But after the monkeys and the dog scenarios, I was more careful about choosing my early morning running routes in strange areas.

When I was at home, I naturally took to running more distance, about 25 miles a week. Alabang was all open country then, a runner's dream land. I loved it and would hit that "high" and go into cruise control, enjoying the whole world, praise the Lord! I decided to run a marathon. Which one? I decided on the Marine Corps Marathon in Washington D.C. in July. I was accustomed to my tropical environment, so the heat of a D.C. July was not going to bother me. I signed up, paid my fee, received the confirmation and running number and was ready. I notified Mom and Dad and others in the U.S. I wrote to Larry "MaGoo" who lived in Arlington, Dean Almy, and Doolittle in Manassas. "C'mon, watch ol' Moose try to finish a marathon in July, which of course must be followed by a hydration procedure of Moose's choosing." I was 52 and finishing a marathon was still in the dream stage. MaGoo, a fine tennis player, had national ranking in the senior division for his class.

I went into serious training and kept to the 25 miles a week including about seven on Sunday. I moved up to 30 and 35 a week. The books that I read advised not to run the whole 26 miles in preparation for the marathon, because at my age and level of conditioning a professional trainer would consider me "injured" upon completing 26 miles, and prescribe rest and therapeutic workouts accordingly. Rather, I should go up to 15-17 miles, a couple of weeks apart. One Sunday I was up to 10 and planning to do 14 or so around Alabang streets and the grass of the side-by-side polo fields nearby. I left the road and ran onto the perimeter of the polo fields, made one loop around and then hit a low spot on the turf with my right foot and youch! I had a sharp pain in and back of the right hip. I hobbled to the grandstand fence, held on, stood my left leg turning and twisting the right foot trying to get a reading, hoping something would "pop back in." I could walk, but it hurt.

The doctor measured the length of my legs, took x-rays, and I told him about the old back injury. They discovered a slight curvature in the spine, but no definitive answers were forthcoming. I started an extensive therapy program but could not proceed above a brisk walk pace. Even to this day I can hear my old Korea buddies, to whom I wrote about canceling my run. "Sure, yeah, Moose is going to run the marathon in DC, like when the Cubs win the World Series."

Although it's only walking, and some swimming, I still work out. The human body is designed whereby the legs are 50% of its length. Fortunately, that means we are programmed to walk and run, for if Man were a short-legged little rascal he would have been unable to make the "flight or fight" choices in time of real emergencies. I believe it is important to walk and/or run to maintain good health. Simply put, when the legs go, you go. When I visit NYC I notice there is a lot of walking going on, 4 or 5 blocks that way, then 6 blocks this way, and walk up and down the subway stairs, etc. Almost everyone is walking. Whereas those who live in a suburban or semi-rural setting walk to the car in the driveway, and walk from the car in the parking lot to the supermarket or the office. The plump, chubby, or obese are more numerous in the latter group.

GOLF, ANYONE?

As mentioned, even though I caddied often, ages 13-17, and knew something of the game I did not play it, being in favor of the more "action" sports. Jack Van Wagonner's urgings at Misawa, Japan were not successful, and I did not become a regular participant until I joined the Awase Meadows Club in Okinawa and took lessons and started to understand the finer points of the hand and feet positions, swing, lie, and sand traps, then the light went on in that dark place: "Ah, so this is what it's all about." All those years in Okinawa and the Philippines, I played at nice clubs and caddies were a part of the scene, golf carts were not used, and the general trappings were those of the current day pros, oh, what a lovely game. I had many friends with whom I played in both countries. Louie Uie, Ray McGill, Mike Ladau, Willie Yu, Grau Roses, Lew Gleeck, Moy, Jun Riviera, Ed Uhde, come to mind right now.

From time to time I, with the help of Ed Uhde, would hold a little golf tournament on a Saturday morning for about 12 golfers from the World Health Organization Regional Headquarters. After we totaled up the score, I would give some golf balls or other prizes to the top three players, with high praise for perhaps breaking 88, to the laughter of all. Dr. Han's wife operated an excellent Korean restaurant and he usually invited all of us to lunch. Bulgogi, rice, kimchi, and a cold San Miguel, along with prevailing friendship, ensured that the lunch would be long and pleasant.

APRIL 1976... OH, THOSE NECESSARY GOODBYES...

I went to NYC on business, and having heard Pop-pop was sick and in the hospital, I stayed a couple of days with Nana. Then Nana, Marion, Bob, and I drove over to the hospital to see him. Afterward, I would proceed to the airport to return to

Manila, stopping by San Francisco to see Andy whom I heard was suffering from ALS. Upon arriving at the hospital Marion said to Nana, "Why don't we let Howie see Dad by himself, then we can see him, and Howie can catch his plane." He was in an ICU. He was not on a respirator but coughing some and spitting up. He had mild emphysema, but the real problem, unknown to me then, was that he had cancer of the liver. To me he looked a bit sick, but I assumed he would recover and be home soon, knowing his toughness and resiliency. He was happy to see me. I brought him up to date on his four granddaughters (including Christina, whom he had not yet seen) and Zeni, and the Philippines (he never forgot how much he enjoyed his trip there), and said we would be coming over for vacation around the first of July and would see him then when he was home. We would be there, at his house, for the 4th of July, which would be the 200th anniversary of our nation's birthday, The Declaration of Independence, and we recalled the "4ths" when I was a kid and we would go to the doubleheaders at Yankee Stadium. We talked some more and it slowly dawned on me that this might be the last time I would see him ("why don't we let Howie see Dad by himself?"). I told him that I loved him and thanked him for all he had done for me, held his hand, and kissed him. He was probably crying inside, as I was, but did not want to show it and said, "Hey, you better get going so you don't miss your plane. I'll see you in July." As I walked out, purposefully erect, as he always instructed me those many years ago, I looked over and said goodbye and thank you to the attendant nurse who had been watching through the tears she was wiping away. That was the last time I saw Pop-pop before he entered Eternal Life. We missed him by two days when we arrived that July 1. He had long since left the hospital and was cared for by Nana and Marion and Bob at their place, with frequent visits by Rich and Joyce, and the visiting nurse. I broke down many times trying to do the eulogy and was a bit embarrassed. Uncle Larry said, "That was okay, that's good, it was from the heart."

Leaving Dad's bedside that day in April, I proceeded to San Francisco, en route to Manila. My dear friend Andy was suffering from ALS, the Lou Gehrig disease. Somehow we had been in touch and he asked me to stop by and see him. When I arrived at his garden apartment, he was in leg braces but moving around as best he could with the aid of crutches. Here was another tough fighter. Andy and Dad would have really "hit it off." Olga, knowing my liking for perogies, halumpkis and other Slavic dishes, prepared a nice lunch for us and we were joined by a relative of Andy's whom I had previously met. We had a fun time talking of the days in Korea and all the personalities we knew and remembered, and the bishop's remark, "You mean Brownsky don't you?" We never forgot that, and our activity in Korea. He also enjoyed repeating my comment when I saw his TRW office in Tokyo, "Wow, you've come a long way from On Chon ni."

After lunch, to my surprise, Andy said he wanted to take his two hunting dogs out to the park so they could get some exercise. I knew of his love of animals but he was in leg braces and using crutches. He drove us to the park with the happy dogs who obviously knew the drill. It was a pleasure to see him work the dogs on long leashes and respond to his commands, crutches and braces or not. Back at the apartment we continued to talk and reminisce until it was time for me to leave and go to the airport. We hugged and quietly fought the tears through meaningful words of friendship. We knew this was goodbye. He waved to me from the door as his relative drove me away to the airport. I cried, knowing I would not see him again, missing a great friend and one of the best persons I ever knew. I reminisced later, while in flight, recalling my return from Korea to the D.C. Headquarters and the Desk Chief saying, "They want you in Japan." It must have been Andy's request. Who else in Japan knew me that well and what I could, and would, do? But he never said, and I never asked.

GOLF....SERIOUSLY THOUGH

With Howard Clark, our American Express CEO, being on the board of the International Golf Association, it was natural that we sponsored Pro-Am tournaments in some parts of the world. We started to do that in Asia and I was chosen to arrange the sponsorships and give out the prizes at many places on the Asia Circuit such as Hong Kong, Taipei, Kaohsiung, Manila, Singapore, Djakarta, Colombo, and Bangkok, which I did several times over the years. It helped public and customer relations and it was fun.

Our local offices would arrange the pairings, the golf club chosen would run the tournament, and I, representing American Express, would provide the trophies afterward, silver engraved trays to the first five amateurs and Travelers Cheques to their professional partners, all based on "best team" scores. Snacks and other refreshments went along with the award ceremonies, and we always saw the ensuing evening before breaking up and departing, leaving pleasant recollections for many.

Sometime around 1976 Howard Clark was the President of the IGA. He contacted me to say that the IGA board would like to have the next IGA world championship in the Philippines. He asked me to see if President Marcos would agree and suggested a date in December. I was reminded that IGA would be inviting the two players whom the South Africa Golf Federation would choose to represent S.A. Since the Philippines had voted against the Apartheid Policy of South Africa in the United Nations General Assembly, it might be a consideration for the president in making his decision. So I contacted him through our mutual friend Tabby Tabanyiag, a member of the Philippine golf association (RPGA). Pres. Marcos, an avid golfer himself, in fact he had just come off the 18th green at Wack Wack Golf Club, when we approached him about the matter. He said he would be very pleased to host such a well-known tournament. Concerning the South African apartheid matter, he said that any problem this decision might create, he would take care of. And so it was. I was in charge of the welcoming committee for those players coming in from all over the world.

When Gary Player and Hugh Baiocchi, the South African players, arrived at the airport, Security met them with a limo at plane-side and took them, baggage and clubs, straight to their hotel, without the customary airport publicity or document recording and clearance.

No one I ever knew or met wanted the apartheid policy to exist, including the SA players. I recall that if Mom and I had ever showed up in SA we would have been arrested. In fact the American Express manager at Johannesburg and I had some nice conversations at our international meetings and he said, "Why don't you and your wife come and visit for a week? Johannesburg is a beautiful city." I explained why I had to decline. That brought a high level of venting from that former British Army officer as he railed against such an inhuman system.

Fred Corcoran was the Executive Director of the IGA and visited the Philippines to help set up the tournament. I showed him around, arranged press meetings and coverage, photos, and meetings with the top sports reporters and others. Fred was a New Yorker's New Yorker, who was born to be deeply involved in sports. "If a guy don't like sports we're not gonna have much to say," was his remark, as we moved along to a nice friendship. A guiding developer of the Professional Golf Association in its early days, he is one of the two or three members of the golf hall of fame who was not a player. That golf guru was a walking rules book and fountain of information, a friend and manager of many well-known golfers and other famous athletes, such as Walter Hagen, Arnold Palmer, Stan Musial, and Ted Williams. I recall he mentioned his close relationship with the great Hagen. Back in the 1930's, he was telling Hagen of his frustrations regarding an upcoming tournament and Hagen, a carefree, fun-loving personality, advised him, "Fred, don't hurry, and don't worry, and don't forget to smell the flowers as you go by." Fred talked sports all the time, was a great storyteller, most interesting and informative. He had dinner at our home a few times and also joined us for Mass on Sundays. He liked Mom and you children very much. President Marcos, who was the honorary chairman of the tournament, had a special trophy designed and struck, The Corcoran Memorial Trophy. I saw Fred at his IGA office a year or so later when I was visiting NYC. We had an enjoyable lunch. He was talking sports and telling stories and making plans. My kind of guy.

As a very minor worker bee among the many, I think the World Cup Tournament was pleasing to all and "mission accomplished," but unfortunately I spent the actual tournament days in the hospital with my neck in traction because of a "flare-up" from an old injury. Howard Clark visited me there with a bottle of wine, a smile, and a thank-you; also my kind of guy.

GROWING SPIRITUALLY—"BUT I HAVE CHOSEN YOU"

The essence of my spiritual life was touched and nurtured along during my years in the Philippines. The Cursillo initiation, an increase in weekday Mass attendance, the Baptisms and First Communions of you, my daughters, and our family going to the Sunday Masses, all come to mind. While we lived in Makati, we went to different churches at different times. I recall the lovely Spanish-style church in Forbes Park, and St. Joseph the Worker, pastored by Msgr. Mempin, and the St. John Bosco church and school. When we moved to the "wilds" of Alabang around 1977 there was no nearby church. The old St. Susana chapel that was in the then defunct Madrigal Plantation had long sat in disrepair.

While driving through the open country side of Alabang, I saw a bearded man in a simple gray robe and sandals. That's how I came to know Fr. Tardite. I later learned he had been sent to the Philippines, along with some other priests, to help establish a seminary in our general region, and that he had previously worked as a missionary in South America. He spoke Italian, English, Spanish, and Tagalog. He certainly helped the "nuturing" of which I speak.

My first impression of him on that dusty, road-side meeting, seeing the beard, well-worn simple robe, sandals, and his moderate stature was that here is a bit of a country bumpkin, and a kind, caring, saintly servant of God. Well, I did it again. Remember the fabulously wealthy Chinese businessman with the rubber sandals, shorts, and t-shirt who looked like he could not even afford to buy a sweepstakes ticket? Yes, one day, early on, Fr. Tardite and I were discussing something in the philosophical/theological realm and I, not aware of being way out of my league, came to realize, as the declining action of my mouth became directly proportional to the opening of my ears, this guy was a mental giant. I would later learn (not from that humble soul) that he had several high level degrees, including one from the Gregorian University in Rome. He was a member of the Somascan Order, named after the town of Somasca, near Naples, Italy, where its nascent workings had started around 1500 A.D. to answer the needs of the many poor, sick, and homeless, struggling in the great famines and plagues of that time. It was led by a young priest named Jerome Emiliani, whose main effort was directed to the care, education, and raising of orphans. Well, from little acorns big oak trees do grow (the gardener's name was Trinity). Going through the struggles and calamities that the next 4 centuries would bring, the Somascan Order, lived its coat of arms (Christ carrying the Cross) and motto ("My burden is light") and the disciples of Jerome have followed the mission and built vocational schools, seminaries, and colleges in Europe, South and Central America, Mexico, and the Philippines. Jerome entered the Church's hall of fame as Saint Jerome around 1750 and was proclaimed "Father of Orphans and Universal Patron of Needy Youth" by Pope Pius XI in 1928.

We, sparsely-scattered residents of Alabang, and our live-in servants, had no local church to attend, so Fr. Tardite held Sunday Mass for us at our little community center, which was a painted concrete slab of some 60x40 feet with a roof for shielding from sun and rain, screen walls to allow for the prevalent breezes, a couple of ping pong tables and some card tables and chairs, and the green grass grew all around, all around. About that time Fr. Tardite told me, "I want you to go to a Eucharistic Minister seminar for three evenings in Manila, get the certification, and then come and see me. Then you can visit the homebound sick and also serve Communion at Mass." He did not ask. It was a case of "just do it." I am most grateful for those happenings. The biblical quote, "You have not chosen me but I have chosen you" comes to mind.

Shortly thereafter I also did the prescribed Biblical readings as Lector in the Sunday Mass. One year we had a Christmas midnight Mass in the cool outside setting of that little center and I similarly participated. In that quaint and practical place of worship about 1982 Christina, age 7, had prepared for her First Communion and one Sunday we all went to Mass at the center, Christina very pretty in her special white dress and veil. During his homily Fr. Tardite commented on choosing a good name for one's child, and not going with the trend to choose unusual and strange-sounding made up names and nicknames. In that marvelous Italian-accented English he said, "Look at this lovely child. Her name is Maria Christina. Such a beautiful name. I hear so many people naming or nicknaming their children with all kinds of crazy sounds like Baboo, or Icky, or Picky, something I would call my dog, but not a child of God." (I think his unintended humorous delivery helped me to remember that comment.) A year or so later, knowing that Christina was an outstanding reader, I told Fr. Tardite about her and suggested that he have her do a reading at a Sunday Mass to encourage the other youngsters. He wasn't sure, and one day he took her off to the side, talked with her, she did a sample read, and he decided to do it. She read fine and everyone was happy, for many reasons.

While thinking about Christina this way I am reminded of the time when she was about three (story from Mom). Little Christina was standing outside the den room one day, looking very different and thoughtful. Mom asked, "What happened, honey?" "God spoke to me," was her reply. "Oh? What did he say" "He said, 'Crissie, I love you,' but I could hardly hear him and said, 'Can you talk louder?' Then he said, 'CRISSIE, I LOVE YOU,' real loud and it hurt my ears!" (as she put her little hands over her ears). Mom tearfully stood there in bewildered belief. How could an innocent three-year-old not tell the truth?

About 1981 the Somascans opened the seminary and a year later two or three of them were assigned to the new church of St. Jerome Emiliani and St. Susana that was built by the local Archbishop's Council at the site of the replaced Madrigal Chapel (St. Susana). Alabang was growing. Fr. Cesar was the Pastor of that church that covered a very wide area, starting off with 1,800 registered families. I would do some liturgical readings at the Sunday Mass and serve as a Eucharistic Minister. I vividly remember the day Cardinal Jaime Sin established the church and installed Fr. Cesar. About six of us laity met him and escorted him into the over-crowded church where he conducted the Inaugural Mass. I had the honor and humble privilege to be the Lector that day. I knew I was making a difference in God's service for my brothers and sisters and myself.

Fr. Cesar was blessed with all the qualities to shepherd that growing flock in those early stages. Guide groups were formed for such matters as Liturgy, Christian Education, Bible Studies, Cursillo, Charismatic Renewal, Marriage Encounter, Retreats, Charity Assistance, and many others, as well as the proper care and administration of the Church's core activities, the seven sacraments of Baptism, Eucharist, Confirmation, Reconciliation, Marriage, and Blessing of the Sick; the 7th, Holy Orders, the ordination of priests and deacons is done by the bishop.

One of those clear flashbacks: Fr. Cesar was giving the homily, after his Gospel reading one Sunday. He started off by saying, "If the doctor told me, 'Father, I have some bad news, we give you only five months to live,' I would say, 'Alleluia!'" Wow, there were some slack jaws and serious eyes in the audience, as we digested the words of that saintly man. No, it wasn't because of his somewhat crowded schedule and overworked situation (which I jokingly opined to him afterward).It was more to the core of one's faith, practice, or lack thereof, and preparation to enter Eternal Life. Perhaps I was getting closer to the answer of my "what's it all about Lord?" That active community, centered in and around that large Spanish Mission style church, scores big in my Philippine memories.

During those Philippine years, my work did not allow as much time with you, my children, as I wanted, not an unusual feeling for a loving father. There have been many times when I wished I could have been a better father. Looking back on large-family growth and development, and training of one's children, seems sort of like slowly riding a horse over an open plain with no reins.You can talk to it, use your legs, pull the mane, pat the neck, slap the behind, but you don't have full control. Now my aged wisdom tells me my smiling God planned it that way to assure sufficient growth, ability, and knowledge. It started of course with the marriage and work in Northern Japan, Okinawa and NYC, with most of the story having been created in the Philippines and finalized later in the U.S.

As stated in the Introduction:"They have contributed much, much more to my life's journey than what can be written." What this means is from the time our family started with my marriage to Mom, my life, time, and attention was re-centered to your welfare. Even today, I care, and stay in touch, and sometimes worry about your normal life problems, not necessarily appreciated, but a fact in my character's make-up.

So many happy memories come to me, my lovely daughters, from those days as you grew through your childhood and youth. Our traditional evening meals together helped our sharing and growing as a family I recall the parties we gave for family birthdays, Christmas, and any cause we could find; family "get-togethers" at Uncle Moy's, Efren's, and Auntie Luz's; the various times we went to Auntie Conching and Tito Pepe's and also the big New Year's "bash" they always had, complete with the Chinese laureate and fireworks; Mom taking you to her long-time friend who made your dresses, our many visits to the Makati Theater and the Philippine Cultural Center Theater, our trips to Cavite, Baguio, the Zambales beaches, the trip to Naga with Msgr.Yllana, our vacation trips to the

Maria's high school graduation, 1981   Acting headshot of Mari, 1991

U.S., the many trips to the farm in Bulacan, the visits over to Laguna to the hot springs and "Uncle" Tony Laforteza's vacation house there, our continual visits to the local clubs for some weekend or evening fun (Army Navy, Elks, Metropolitan, Casino Español, Alabang Country Club), your many school activities, rides out of town on a Sunday like Los Baños or Tagaytay and I am sure we can all add something to the list. But while holding these thoughts my "happy vibes" oscillate and recall even more.

Maria reached an age when, in her mind, her childhood name, Mariellos (Maria Luz) needed changing (sort of like me wanting to change from "Junior"). After we, the family, saw the first of many viewings of "The Sound of Music" with the main character Maria doing all that beautiful singing, Mariellos was no more, it was Maria, right to this day. With her abiding love for music, the choice was hardly hers to make. It was just going to happen. Of course there were her choir performances in high school that we enjoyed, and later at the Fine Arts Theater of the International School, I mostly remember her terrific performance in "Fiddler on the Roof" and that touching "going-away-for-good" song she sang to her "family."

Mariana followed her big sister around in the very early years, in predictable sibling manner, but later (also predictable) moved into her own styles and interests in studies, choir, dance and theater. Muning, all of your awards at graduation I have mentioned elsewhere, but the performance at The Fine Arts Theater that impressed me the most was your portrayal of Antigone in that Greek drama of the same name. Your strong projection and the long extended lines of the Greek drama style were done with a flair that held the audience. I asked myself. "Is that my Mariana?" "How did she get here so fast?" I whispered to a happy-tears

Mom. The answer of course was hard work, all those practices and late practices in both theater and dancing. Also, to my regret, I had not been watching all that closely. But you exemplified the work code of my coach Joe Kasberger: "You play the way you practice." Now that belongs on a plaque because it holds true for all activity: a student, trumpeter, violinist, truck driver, painter, surgeon, dancer, mechanic, ball player, CEO, a father, or a mom, "You play the way you practice."

Michele, a tall, slender beauty today, was built like a bowling ball when she was 3 or 4. Very athletic, she would go hand-over-hand while hanging from the horizontal ladder in the playground, bump into and knock down some kid who was playing too rough, and was the chief "keeper" (so she thought) of our large rabbit "Thumper" and the quail hutch, which she sometimes got stuck in and had to be pulled out of. It was at Baguio, ages 3-5, riding those mountain ponies with her sisters, going around the track with the handler, insisting the handler let her

Top: Maria, Mariana and Michele riding ponies in Baguio, ca. 1975.
Bottom: Michele riding Raven, 2007.

The four Newhard daughters in descending order of height:
Maria, Mari, Michele and Christina, 1977

"ride" by herself that she started her lifelong love of riding. Michele, I recall that day when you were registered in a jumping tournament at Clark Air Base; you were 11 or 12 and rode Celeste. It had rained the night before, but the judges determined the conditions were okay to proceed. Only one horse and rider had made the round without a knockdown and it was your turn; you were ready. You did all the jumps with a nice style, but after clearing the next to last hurdle a left diagonal was needed for the final run and jump. Upon landing and veering left Celeste's hind quarter gave way on a moist spot, tumbling her and you to the ground with your left leg under Celeste. I came running out of the stands as Celeste, unhurt, was standing there while you, still holding the reins, were trying to get up to remount. "Stay down," I shouted repeatedly, as the standby medics got to the scene. Your left leg was broken above the left ankle and they took you to the Clark Air Base hospital for treatment, where they made a soft cast, wrote a report for whichever doctor in Manila would handle the recovery.

The trip going home that night was an adventure in itself. I drove and Michele sat with her legs extended across the back seat, a bit sedated but not without some pain. It was dark, no lights anywhere, as we drove south at a careful speed, aware that lawlessness was not uncommon in that area under those conditions. The "rest stop" for me was any bush along the road. The "rest stop" for Michele was a little two-stall building so marked (seen in the head lights, which I turned off as I drove up next to it so as not to attract any unwanted visitors). I picked Michele up and carried her into the stall, back out, and on our way, watching all around for those "visitors." Finally we reached some lighted area, then the outskirts of Manila, a memorable day for sure. Michele did not win that day, but a personal best was in the making and she was learning a lot.

Christina was watched, played with, and cuddled by her sisters, but as she grew away from babyhood the age differences showed and she competed for attention in the family. Naturally smart, this honed her skills at talking, thinking and getting along. Her strong suites were literature and art. Christina, I remember you often coming to the table with a book to read while everyone else was chatting, usually about mundane things that did not need your attention. Years later, Christina would graduate high school with a 4.35 GPA and a college scholarship. Gifted and insightful, this pretty gal works in the literature and art fields, and for vacations and pleasure writes on her blog about backpacking in Bolivia, kayaking among the whales off of Vancouver Island, or swimming with the whale sharks in the central Philippines.

I can't leave these thoughts of family-building days without a word about Beau. Michele was always bringing home neighborhood cats and dogs or strays. She had begged for a dog for years and Zeni was not too keen on the idea. But when we moved to Alabang and got settled, around 1978, we bought a Dalmatian pup and called him Beau. He grew fast. We all took turns taking him out for walks on a leash, over to the polo fields nearby (and seldom used). Beau of course loved to run and as he grew bigger he would run all over those polo fields chasing us and we, him. As our group of four children and myself (Zeni wasn't into this particular activity) would run away from him, he of course would catch up, single out the smallest, Christina, and playfully knock her down in the grass. Christina would cry, get up, and chase Beau with the rest of us, and the cycle

Christina kayaking with the orcas in the waters off of Vancouver Island, Canada, 2004

would continue, with all of us calling to Beau and each other and running all over the place in that open grassy plain in that lovely countryside. What fun!

The seasonal changes in the Philippines are wet and dry, rather than the hot and cold variations of the temperate zones. I recall April and May as the hottest and driest months, and then it moves into the rainy season, which sometimes was a real problem. During one rainy season there were three typhoons in tandem, to the east of the country, traveling north. They slowed down and then stopped for 3 days as their low pressure systems pulled in the monsoon conditions from the Asia mainland. There was a torrential downpour for three straight days, and disastrous floods for an extended period.. Now some people, trying to find a way to pick up their spirits at such a time might philosophically postulate, "Well, you can't know pleasure, if you don't know pain." I say, "Try me."

BEGINNING OF THE END...IN THE PHILIPPINES

Around 1980, I was told I would be "promoted" to a new position of Director, Industry Relations, Asia Pacific, reporting to Karl Kircher in Hong Kong who also had a similar title. Since I would be going from an on-line to a staff-type function, and since Karl had been previously on-line all those years building the Card business in Asia, a sense of uncertainty prevailed. The position would require me to travel often, calling on top line executives of national flag carriers, hotel chains, and the tourism ministries with the mission to develop business with and through those enterprises and where possible interface card and travel activity, or card and banking activity for the mutual benefit of Amexco and the hotel chain or airline involved. It would be a two-man show, just Karl and myself.

First I had to find and hire my replacement as General Manager Philippines. I had been auditing the M.B.A. program evenings at the Ateneo University. I asked the Dean if he knew a former graduate who could handle the position. His candidate had a good résumé and personality, but the pressure of the job, and his only average acumen, attitude, and ability, caused me to look for and find Tom Meneses to replace me. He had good business sense and could do the job, having had his own business in transportation. As soon as I had him in tune with our goals, mission, regulations, budget preparation, and major customers, I started the new job, coordinating with Karl. In hiring Tom I used my AAA method for employee selection that I developed in building the Philippine operation. Quite simply, rather than put all the value on the résumé and a personality-affected interview, I placed much emphasis on Acumen, Attitude, and Ability. i.e., don't tell me the grades until we know the applicant can do the job. President Lincoln made Grant the Chief of Staff over many senior generals. Grant's résumé was not impressive aside from being a West Pointe graduate. He had left the army, failed twice in business, and was called back to duty because of the war, but now he was winning his assigned battles in the field at that dark and critical time of the Civil

War: Lincoln chose him based on acumen, attitude, and ability.

With a growing uneasiness, I sensed that New York Headquarters was going to "pasture" me with this new position, as they had Karl. We were similar in that we both had unusually long, continual careers in Asia, and had produced. All the senior officials in my line of report had retired, and the recent ones did not know me, nor I them. George Waters had been a colonel in the Air Force, a colleague of Defense Secretary McNamara when they were at Ford Motor Co., and the guiding light of the American Express Card Division for about 25 years, from its inception. He was a traveling consultant for the Company when he stopped by Manila to see me and play some golf together. We had a pleasant round at Wack Wack along with our conversation about Asia, the Company's growth, and management concepts. He left the same day. Apparently he had been asked to "size me up," and it came back to me through Karl Kircher, who was his good friend, that his report to New York was that I was being "under-utilized."

I traveled the various countries working on the missions assigned and about 1982 Karl had a heart attack and died. Kay, his wife, took the body to Wiesbaden for burial in his hometown. Soon after, I was notified that my position would be eliminated and I would work for the area Card VP (Headquarters Hong Kong) and cover the Philippines, Guam and Korea, and I proceeded to cover those assignments. Sometime thereafter I wrote a memo explaining to one and all why the Philippines and Guam should be under the area Card VP Headquarters at Singapore, and Korea under Hong Kong. Before any action was taken, the Chinese VP at Hong Kong said he wanted to discuss my fitness evaluation. I had only worked for him a short while and I had never sat down for an evaluation in all those years. Naturally I was evaluated along the way as I received more responsibilities, but no one ever sat down with me, that I can remember, and said you're doing this well, and here's where you need improvement. Perhaps Frank Erickson did it once. The V.P. from Hong Kong flew into Manila. We went to an airport restaurant to go over his evaluation of me, and he went back to Hong Kong immediately thereafter. He was very nervous, and started off by telling me he had never seen anyone as socially unacceptable and biased as me. (He only knew me through our business contacts.) He then went on to show me that he had given me low and very low scores throughout the evaluation. He asked me to sign the paper to show that I had seen it. Maybe he was irked by my memo, or he had some kind of prejudicial quirk about me, which gave basis to his possible role of a "hatchetman" for someone who did not want me to stay in the Philippines. I never did know.

My memo was approved and I started to report to the VP in Singapore who was a top of the line executive with a West Point, Army Ranger, and M.B.A. background. At a budget conference he held with his managers in Singapore shortly thereafter he gave me the top rating for my budget plan. About March of 1983, I was notified that the Company would be letting me go and when would I decide to leave?

I wrote a lengthy memo to the CEO Jim Robinson asking for reconsideration based on my record of results in Asia and pointing out that in four more years I would be 60 years old and have 30 years seniority, the basis for a full pension. (Otherwise, I was looking at a 40% reduction.) His reply made it conclusive that I would be leaving the company that I was proud to represent and liked so much. American Express was a fine company, noted for a good employee relations record. In fact it was the first company in the U.S. to start a retirement fund for its employees. I still had the status of a permanent resident in the Philippines and an attorney friend told me I was entitled to a payment from the company of one month salary for each year worked in the Philippines. That was 17 months' salary. But since it was not offered, I felt if I pressed for it I could be assigned to a job in the U.S. and then released from there, when what I really wanted was to remain in the Philippines; so I did not pursue the matter. My final official discussion concerning my severance from Amexco, and there had been a few with my then in line boss, took place in Hong Kong with some Human Resources VP who was visiting from New York Headquarters. In going over my departure and the papers we were signing, she said that I might want to tell a prospective employer that Amexco was reorganizing in Asia and there did not happen to be a place for me. She meant well and thought she was helping me.

So about October 1983, they gave me a "retirement" dinner, flew in a couple of former colleagues with whom I had worked in my MBF days to say some nice things, as did some others, and presented me with a large shiny wood plaque, with an embedded metallic replica of an American Express Gold Card. The inscription read:

HOWARD NEWHARD
AMERICAN EXPRESS INTERNATIONAL, INC.
1957-1983

With Sincere Gratitude and Appreciation
For Your Dedication, Loyalty, and Commitment
And Special Thanks For the Contribution
You Have Made To Our Business in the Philippines

I had been asked to invite whomever I wanted to the dinner from among my many friends, but I chose not to do so. Not even Zeni attended. I was heartbroken, frustrated, and bewildered. I was well-known there and didn't know what to say to people. I surely was not retiring, and I now had to think about continuing to earn the income to pay the bills, I.S. tuition, mortgage, and send you, my bright and deserving daughters to good colleges.

Mom and I had agreed we would stay in the Philippines and I would try to build a business. That was home for all of us, and to uproot ourselves and restart our lives, as a family, in another culture would be difficult indeed (which would become the case.)

Naturally the business I knew the best and planned to pursue was the travel service. The plan was to open an office with my name on it in Makati and advertise accordingly, do some strong networking with the various airlines and hotel chains, let all my friends in various commercial and governmental organizations know I was ready to handle their travel arrangements, network among friends, build a good staff using my AAA procedure, and go from there. I went to see Joe Aspiras, Minister of Tourism, to obtain my travel office license. "Sure," he said, "Fill out this form and we will process it, and you should have it in a week or so." I followed up twice in person. The second time he seemed agitated and called over to one of his staff members inquiring as to why my license had not been processed for his signature. The guy came over to Joe's desk and half-whispered as he leaned toward him, "Sir, the Meralco group does not want it approved." That was sort of a code name for "Marcos Inc." Right after the declaration of martial law his group took over The Manila Electric Rail & Lighting Company (MERALCO), which had been owned by the Laurel family of Batangas Province.

I was shocked. I needed that license. My plan for our future depended on that license. The bearer of the bad news left and I said, "Joe, you are my friend and I have always recognized your good work in the industry. You know I have a legal right to obtain that license since I meet all the necessary qualifications." His expression verified his agreement and regret that he could not do what was right. "I am sorry, Howard." I walked out mentally staggering under the weight of my new problem. I quickly found out that the reason the Marcos group would not allow the approval was they were going into the travel business by becoming the franchisee of the American Express travel operation in the Philippines, using a newly organized bank, under the Marcos umbrella, to do so. I knew I was legally right but if I pushed too hard some bad things might happen, very bad things. So I had a legal right to the severance pay and the license as allowed by Philippine law and came up with neither.

Mom and I talked some more. What to do? We agreed it would be best for the children if we did not go to the U.S. until the summer of 1985, after their graduation from The International High School, Middle School, and Grammar School for Mariana, Michele, and Christina respectively. (Maria at this time was already attending college in the U.S.) Meanwhile, I would obtain a tour sales license and sell tours of the Philippines abroad and some tour packages of other countries. If I was successful, we would remain in the Philippines and our home in Alabang. So I opened as a one-man show. It became obvious that I could not add anything of value to Philippine Airlines tour programs, and other airlines had little interest because the Philippines was not exactly a hot destination in those days. I went to Taiwan and through my old friend General Charlie Chang (retired), was able to meet with the President of China Airlines and others and with the help of a professional tour consultant I traveled around Taiwan and packaged some programs, made the brochures using China Airlines and my name, and introduced it to the travel market in the Philippines. I even took a group of American Express travel people (former employees) on one of the tours I had packaged in Taiwan.

I worked very hard trying to make a go of that tour activity, but by the late summer of 1984 it was obvious I was not going to develop an adequate income, and our resources were rapidly depleting. This was the beginning of a long process of change for all of us. I would go to the U.S. and look for a job while Mom and you three daughters would remain until you graduated in May 1985.

Mom was depressed and apprehensive for our future. Over the years she had exhibited changes having to do with her special attention to food, a slow steady increase in weight, and a growing need for anger control. She seemed to have her ups and downs as with a mild form of manic depression or a bipolar condition. Again, I am thinking with the wisdom and hindsight of age. At those times such clarity was not forthcoming.

The plan was I would go to the U.S. in November 1984 and look for a job, while Zeni and the girls stayed in the Philippines so they could complete their year at I.S. (International School). Zeni would do all the preparation for shipping our furniture and selling the house, taxes, foreign exchange etc. So we followed the plan, and I said an anxious and sad goodbye to Zeni, children, relatives and friends over many days. It was November 1984. Maria was at Manhattanville College in New York, and Muning, Michele, and Christina would stay home with Mom, whose anxieties, coupled with her physical condition, did not make it any easier for them in that final year at I.S. Not that it was all bad, but it sure wasn't getting any better.

17 | THE U.S.A.
A Slow Homecoming

Author and grandson, Danny, 1994

Going back to my country of birth, which I have always loved with a patriot's zeal, was a most difficult, "stretched-out" milestone. I was weighted down with the cumulative baggage of an understandably unhappy wife, uprooting Christina and Michele from their home culture before college age, my self-grief fostered by my involuntary retirement, and the unsuccessful attempt during that ensuing year to revive the "retirement." The unrecoverable financial losses, resulting from our decision to have Zeni and our graduating I.S. children remain in the Philippines (which was really our home) for those two years after the "retirement," handicapped our family in our efforts to improve and reach short and long-range goals. It was apparent that we would now be going into debt while I looked for a job and we supported our daughters in their college pursuits.

Aside from the interim 16-month assignment at New York Headquarters in the '60s and home leave vacations, I had been away in Asia for a full generation (1957–1984) and the changes that had taken place in the U.S., and in me, were enormous. I remember wondering, as a foreign visitor might, while walking the streets, or riding a bus full of strangers, "What do all these people do? Where are they going in such a hurry? How do they live their lives?" It was just natural that I left a piece of myself in the Philippines and Asia after all those years, and brought a piece of Asia with me to fill the void.

Obviously, getting to be "at home" here again was going to take some time. My last boss, the VP in Singapore, said a New York Headquarters type told him, "We left him out there too long." I was not sure what that meant, and the historical lens has not helped except in its declined level of importance.

I am eternally grateful to Marion and Bob for having me stay with them and use their home in Union, near Livingston School, from which to conduct my job search. Ah, the old neighborhood. Most mornings, quite early, I would walk past the old school, with all its memories for me, to the new church nearby to attend Mass. Therein lay my strength and my life and my ability to challenge my challenges. Through many obvious and imperceptible changes, I had given God center stage in my life.

My mind now drifted back across the many years and the countless times I had been to Mass in all the various locations, always "at home," and following all the rituals, prayers and readings of that given day, regardless of location or language, whether Indonesia, Japan, Lebanon, China, Korea, Philippines, India, wherever, I was "at home," understanding and participating in the same Mass as celebrated for that day throughout the world, seeing more clearly the total Church as the sacrament of universal salvation.

I had been away so long, and with the shock and hurt of the more recent events, my perception was distorted. That image of the curled leaf in the shifting breeze out there on the lake seemed to reappear. I was nearly 59 and was somewhat ashamed to try to seek help from disconnected yesteryear friendships. Over 200 resumes, each with five solid letters of recommendation, were mailed to the presidents of companies, and to government organizations. There was no reply from most. Many responded that it was a great resume, but they had nothing for me. A few of the government addressees said the same, but advised I was going about it the wrong way and should review the government employment notices and respond accordingly, which I did. There was always a call to make, a follow-up letter to write, the want ads to review, interviews, and other related action. Of course PC's were not yet in the standard loop.

I was sometimes turned down for being over-qualified for a particular job as the interviewer figured I would not be happy. Most often, I think, I was not called back because of age. And so it went, on, and on. All that winter and on into the spring I searched. I had to find a job and then a house for the arrival of Mom, Mariana, Michele, and Christina in the summer. This separation was difficult for all of us and left its mark.

JOB SEARCH...58 AND OUT OF TOUCH

I explored many different job opportunities. I checked for a franchise with Carvel and Dunkin' Donuts. The long "hands on" hours (easy for a younger man), and the start-up costs, negated that comeback road. I interviewed for a job in the State Department, a GS-10 in Tokyo, working in the travel section at the Embassy. I also interviewed in NYC for a GS 10 agent job with the Drug Enforcement Agency. A guy in Augusta, Georgia owned a company in Hong Kong that had a patent on a special material that was used in their production of sport sneakers. He needed a manager. I interviewed in Augusta. He liked me and showed me around Augusta National Golf Course. Then he asked me to wait and went out and talked with his son, about 26, who had just returned from the HK operation. The kid "nixed" the arrangement his father was making with me (I assume he wanted to be the manager). That would have been nice. Mom would have liked it and the I.S. schooling would have continued in HK for Michele and Christina. Some "head-hunter" group in New York said they would get me two good interviews (not jobs), for $5,000. At a small town, near the Jersey Shore, I interviewed to manage a Kentucky Fry franchise and the owner could not reconcile my résumé with my being there. He was thinking, who is this guy talking about poultry raising in the Philippines, and his management acumen, applying to manage this small shop? It seems strange. Such was my situation.

Another time I went to interview at the Junction Music Promoters in Orlando: Big Music Business. They were nice. Their offices were in beautifully furnished and modernized railroad Pullman cars from another era. Seeing my age and whiting hair, they honestly said they made a mistake, and good luck! Then there was the housing and condo real estate mogul in a well known town near Orlando. He was planning to add a commercial real estate company and wanted to train me for the team he was building. I liked the idea and would have followed up except that the town was full of drug dealers at that time, preying on the teenagers. Late in the search I answered an ad from a Met Life broker around Saddle Brook, New Jersey. He and the company would teach me that broad range of business over a two-year period, paying a base salary, and then I would "graduate" into the good stuff. I was not sure. I had been walking with an uncertainty for a long time (a subtle depression?) We agreed I would think it over, and he gave me many manuals and programs to read, plus the schedule of commissions, to help my thinking.

I was bitter against Amexco and did not contact the New York Headquarters for anything. Some years later I was in New York to visit the headquarters regarding some administrative matter. They needed my signature on something. A clerk asked, "Why didn't you come in and use the out-placement service?" My unforgiving stance had precluded such action. I thought, why should someone hire me after Amexco said goodbye while "playing odd man out" in the alleged reorganization?

From time to time during that winter I drove over to see Maria at Manhattanville College, finishing her senior year, in Purchase, New York That helped my mental frame, as did driving down to Howell, New Jersey to stay with Nana, dear Mom, that quite solid rock, and also being with Marion and Bob. I decided to go to Manila and be with Mom and you daughters awhile, even though I did not have any good news about a job and our future location. Nevertheless it did us all a lot of good. I believe that was the time I saw Mariana's performance in "Antigone." I went back to New Jersey somewhat refreshed and ready to live that Churchillian code that we were adopting: we will never, never, never, ever, ever, give up.

FINALLY...THE SLOW CHANGE STARTS

Later on, Digi and I were talking on the phone. I explained my situation and he told me about his friend Paul who was formerly Exec. Director of the New Jersey Builders Assoc and later Miami Builders Assoc. Paul had the California territory for the Whitestone Corp., selling savings and retirement plans with an insurance policy and annuity rider to employees of small and medium sized companies for as little as $1.00 a day. In his own inimitable way Digi, my teammate, classmate and friend through life, sold me on this being my answer for the future. I called Paul in San Diego and he laid it out. He was a licensed insurance broker and was doing well with the savings/retirement plan, which contained term life insurance, an annuity, and a savings account, which in those days paid about 12%. Projected and compounded out to 20-25 years at $10-12 a week, payroll deducted, made a lot of sense for the average wage earner. Even the smallest contribution of $1 a day had meaning for the lower end of the wage scale participants. I liked the program from the beginning as I could see myself traveling around an assigned territory, calling on the owners of companies, and providing them with something they needed for good employee relations. They did the payroll deductions; a contribution was optional. Most important, while I would be explaining the program to all levels of employees, I would mostly be helping those on the middle and lower rungs of the ladder with this program designed for them, and which many needed for their families. I would be making a difference.

Paul told me to give him some time to call Stanley Channick, the owner of Whitestone Corp in Philadelphia, and one of the finest gentlemen I ever met. Well, Digi had given Paul a background briefing on me and Paul passed it on to Stanley who asked me to come over to Philadelphia and talk a few days hence. When I arrived at the big gray stone downtown building, I climbed the stairs and walked the corridor of the first floor. There, on the side wall up over Whitestone's door, was a big banner with leaf designs in the margins that read "Whitestone Corporation Welcomes Howard Newhard." We talked a long time and went to lunch. He asked, "Where would you like to work? I can give you Illinois," and named a few other states. I responded that I felt the need for some precise product knowledge and sales training before I could move out, obtain my license, and be productive. He agreed, "You could go out to California and work for Paul or you could go down to Florida and work for Rush Mizell. Both of them are excellent producers and run good operations, know the business, and could give you top level training." "Which one would you choose, Stanley?" I inquired. "Rush Mizell. He is in Miami Lakes, has agents in Tampa and Jacksonville, and needs someone for S.W. Florida."

Rush, and Patty his wife, both top line sales people, met me at the Miami airport, and we drove to a motel in Naples. We talked, went to dinner, and later in the evening we agreed on a plan to train me, after which I would sell in the S.W Florida territory. For the next week I went through all the phases of training with them. I practiced with them, and on my own, went on sales calls with them, and put a canned sales presentation on my tape recorder so I could go to sleep with the plug in my ear. Finally at the end of the week I did one sales call on my own under Rush's observation, and "closed" a small air conditioning company owner, setting a time to see his employees. It was July. You girls would be arriving from Manila. Mom was going to come as soon as she could sell the house in that collapsing economy. The schools in Florida start around August 15, so I signed a one year lease on a furnished house in Ft. Myers, a bit old, but adequate for the basics.

The Mizells returned to Miami Lakes and I joined the Naples Builders Association and the 5 County Builders Association in Ft. Myers. Later on I added the Charlotte County Builders Association and met with those executive boards. I started to make some calls on company owners in the area, but shortly thereafter returned to Union to await the arrival of you girls. I bought a used mini station wagon (overlooking that it did not have A/C), choosing to pay it off on time, Cousin Frank signed the note for me because I had no credit record in the U.S.

In the spring of 1985, Maria graduated from Manhattanville College *Magna Cum Laude,* Mariana graduated High School at the I.S. (International School) with awards of First Place in Acting and Poetry and second place for Dance, and was planning to study Acting at Sarah Lawrence College in Bronxville, New York. Michele was a good student when she graduated from the I.S. Middle School, and was developing her artistic talent, but her main thrust was with the horses in dressage and jumping, at which she excelled. Christina graduated I.S. elementary school with straight "A"s. Wow! How I have loved you guys over the years, not for grades and performance (though that sure fires up the parental engine), but for who and what you are, in my inner sense, where that comforting glow is helped by your everyday actions of compassion, justice, kindness, and love.

Muning, Michele, and Christina arrived and we all stayed at Nana and Poppop's. Muning would go on to Marion and Bob's who would take her to Sarah Lawrence College for registration starting in September. We, Florida bound pilgrims, with an uncertain but hopeful future, loaded up that little vehicle and took that long miserable ride south, packed in around luggage and other materials, plus Marion's contributions to our household needs, in July yet, and with no A/C. Christina and Michele were thinking that this living in the States was not the way they had heard it, but we finally made it to Ft. Myers. The change was penetrating. Yes, it was still the tropics, but the similarity to the lifestyle we had known, ended there.

Rush "mother-henned" me a bit. Naturally he wanted me to make a successful transition and be productive. He called me daily, "How did it go?" and we would discuss the business of the day. When he came over from Miami to make some sales calls with me, and oh, he was one of the best I ever saw, a real "Zig" Ziegler from the old school of sales know-how, he would always take us out to a good restaurant for dinner and a pleasant time. "What'll you have, girls?" he would ask, before ordering martinis for both of us. "I'll have a Perrier with a twist of lime," responded Michele, as the typical dad pondered her early sophistication. "Coke for me," was Christina's choice (that's better). Michele and Christina started calling him Uncle Rush.

Rush had been a poor Texas farm boy who was a good athlete and played on some of the great SMU football teams in the late '40s with Kyle Rote, the All American and New York Giant great. At lunch one day he said, "You know, I made Leon Hart (that great tackle from Notre Dame and the Chicago Bears) an All- American." "How did you do that, Rush?" "Well, he played against me." Rush was in the airborne in WWII, and, as with Eddie George, I said, "Wow, that's patriotism," and as with Ed he said, "Hell no, I jumped for the bonus money!" Humorous, but not all true.

Stanley was right; Rush was very helpful in getting my training to a level where I was really involved and could handle the general situations and problematical matters of the sales to the owners and the presentations to the employees, usually at a job site around 6:30-7 a.m. Really needing the money, there was no better feeling than to be driving to my office after a presentation, with a batch of signed applications in the car, especially if it was a Monday, and there was the whole week ahead to develop some more "apps" for dispatch on Friday.

Michele and Christina enrolled in school. Michele, trying to adjust, was not a happy camper. Christina started 6th grade right where she left off at the International School. Zeni arrived in October and that made our family matters better. I was very happy that she was there. She was happy too, although disappointed about the house in which we were to live for the next nine months. We all tried to move on.

As mentioned, Maria graduated from Manhattanville College in May '85, and Fordham U. offered her a five-year fellowship to do her doctorate in clinical psychology. She turned it down. "What?" I exclaimed, "Why did you do that?" "Well, Dad, I really want to get out and work in the trenches before I go back to the nice orderly classroom." And so she did. Using her B.A. in psychology she worked as a mental health aide and then as a child abuse caseworker, and later took her Masters at Fordham, specializing in social work. She and Michael, a close friend from high school, stayed in touch over the college years. Michael, having graduated from Berklee School of Music in Boston, was teaching music in the White Plains area. A natural and expected progression ensued, and at their wedding, in a lovely old stately church in Manhattan, I gave Maria to Michael in Holy Matrimony in August 1986. The families were there; many I.S. friends were there, Beth, Maria's roommate at Manhattanville, who visited us one Christmastime in the Philippines, was also there and played the guitar and sang. Blind from birth, she has two degrees and is an accomplished musician. Beth is family. It was a marvelous wedding and ended up, as expected, with all of the I.S. classmates and theater mates singing away, accompanied by Mike at the piano.

GETTING SETTLED

Mom had looked and looked for a house that fit our budget and found a nice corner house to our liking. Shortly thereafter our furniture shipment came in from the Philippines. All those familiar items, a complete house of furniture from our home in Alabang, were very good for all of our vibes. Later on Zeni and I both made adjustments for the better. She made friends with a young couple in our neighborhood who had children and she spent some time there taking care of the kids, teaching them to read etc, we all became good friends. Also we had joined the Ft. Myers Recreation Center. Zeni liked to swim and for a period of time we swam laps there.

Our church, St. Cecilia's, and the adjacent Bishop Verot High School are administered by the Oblates of St. Francis De Sales. The church mission, in part, reads: "We give honor and glory to God through worship, prayer, social justice, education, service, and example." My association there has been a "long happening" in my life. I started, and continue, after twenty-two years, to attend Mass early in the morning several times a week. In such a situation, faces become familiar and everyone says good morning. One morning, after Mass, a familiar face said to me, "Would you like to go over to Publix coffee shop for some prayer and discussion of today's liturgy?" So Jim Fabick, along with Lou Marrone, and I sat down and talked Jesus. There were others who had been joining Jim and Lou. Henry LaRose, Dan Stramara, and Gerry Manning come to mind, and a bit later we called ourselves The Brothers in Christ, keeping it light in structure and rules. Jim, the founder, made the simple mission statement for the members: "To help raise the spirituality of my brothers and myself to the highest level possible." Later, we held our small after-Mass meetings in the church all-activity center, which we still do, starting each "koffee klatch" by praying the beautiful and all-encompassing Prayer of Thanksgiving by St. Thomas Aquinas. Our garden of friendship grew in size and strength. Not friends in the "let's go bowling and have a couple of beers" sense, although that is good and worthwhile, and we might do that also, but friends where our love blends in God's love through our Faith, and we live the Church's and The Brothers in Christ's missions, as we do our various independent ministries and other voluntary works, interfacing with each other with a joy found only in such situations, having relationships tied to a higher calling in Jesus.

Our friendships jelled. In those days I might stop by Jim's condo and watch a golf match on TV or sit around the pool. Much older than I, the stories of his youth, and adventures, like paddling a canoe down the Mississippi from St. Louis to New Orleans, were right out of Mark Twain. A graduate of St. Louis University, he was an ex-Air Force officer, an avid reader and liked to delve into philosophy and theology. One day we had breakfast at a little bagel shop. I got his attention with a quickly homegrown quote of my own. "Jim," I said, "Faith is the yeast in the dough of immutable truth, that's Tolstoy." His eyes lit up, "Wow, that's great, let's have a close look; what's he saying?" As I started to respond with my eyes lowered and a weak smile on my face, he said in a slight tone of condescension, "Oh, that's you." So there I was up there in the ratified air of Tolstoy, only to drop onto that wire-back chair in a common deli in Ft. Myers, Florida. A few days later I took that "close look," and have come to like and understand it. I have used it many times over the years. I recognize that Faith is a gift from God, and the metaphorical "yeast" is that ingredient which enhances the taste and texture of the bread (Truth), thereby making it popular, sought-after, and enjoyable. By extension then, I see a progression in Faith, Truth, and Freedom, or, another way, no Faith, no Truth; no Truth, no Freedom. Out of that casual, half-thought remark to have fun with Jim, I have been blessed with a better understanding of Faith, a greater faith in Faith.

My "homecoming" neared completion as time moved on. Going to Mass often and meeting afterwards with my brothers for scripture reading and thoughtful discussions were, and are, important elements in my life. With all this, a certain forgiveness, giving way to unimportance, developed as time passed, and the resentment for the way I was treated slowly dissolved. Forgiveness is tied into Love. For me to love God and not forgive another of God's creation raises a fallacy, and there's really a joy and freedom in releasing the baggage you have been carrying. Anyway, while one is peeved and laboriously dragging that "anger anchor" around, the objects of that umbrage are oblivious to it all, as they enjoy a golden sunset, the concert music, that walk on the beach, or the blossoms of spring. The "are-you-sure?" test was passed when I amusedly, and without animosity, mailed in my Amexco credit card, as requested, for failure to meet the requirements. Years later, in 1997, I looked back on this time in a letter to my in-laws in the Philippines (Appendix E: Advent Letter to Buhain Family in the Philippines, 1997).

Understandably, at fourteen Michele had the most difficulty adjusting to the new environment and culture, with the focused Christina, ten, seeming to be bothered the least. It was agreed that Michele would go to live with Maria and Michael in Yonkers, New York, and attend high school there. I have always been extremely thankful to them, married a short time, for what they did to help in those difficult times. Another "help" developed as Michele became friendly with a classmate, Eila, who has come to be friends with all of my daughters over the years. She is family. Her mom and dad are exemplary citizens and parents, the kind of people you would like to have for neighbors. Though we have seen each other just a few times over the years, I did attend the Seder Passover festivities at their home in Yonkers a few years ago, coupled with Christina's invitation.

Michele returned to Ft. Myers, having graduated from an arts-focused "magnet" program, diploma in hand, and proceeded to obtain a hair stylist license. She later moved into a fashionable salon, and took the basics to pursue a fine arts major. She stayed with us for a while and then found an apartment. She entered an art contest at Edison College and received awards for a painting and a marble sculpture. It was a nice evening at the Barbara B. Mann Theater. The exhibit was held in the grandiose marble and chandeliered lobby, complete with hors-d'oeuvres, wine, and live chamber music. Yes, Virginia, Ft. Myers was no longer just shrimp, squid, pelicans, and lizards (Guess who wore a casual shirt? hhmmm?)

Around 1987 my friend Rush had a heart attack and entered Eternal Life. I attended the funeral service for him in Macon, Georgia, Patty's home area. She continued running the business from their Miami Lakes office. Not too long after that Stanley, that humble, efficient, gentleman, who had built Whitestone, and a successful mutual fund company, invited all the agents to Ashville, North Carolina for a few days of business talk and sightseeing, which Zeni and I enjoyed very much. At the awards dinner for the past year's performances Stanley awarded me the trophy for the most policies sold with the comment, "Not bad for a rookie." I was 61.

While any improvement that was evolving in my spiritual life was of course a blessing, it was painfully obvious that our old lifestyle was gone forever, and the new one would be likely to settle in the middle income category, and, as I put on some more years, to the lower one. That's where the real adjustment challenge was; acceptance, from what was to what is, and will be.

Around '89, Stanley called a meeting of his agents to introduce us to some officials of Preferred Financial Corporation of Englewood, Colorado, owners of the Colorado Bankers Life Insurance Company (CBL). PFC was going to buy the Whitestone Corporation and we were going to proceed with our program of savings and retirement with an annuity rider using CBL. It was an improvement in my income because now I was an insurance broker reporting to PFC, thereby providing me with a higher commission. Shortly thereafter they brought in about twenty reps from around the country and I went out to Englewood, Colorado for that orientation, meeting several officials including the CEO and digesting their philosophy and general practice of business. Those folks were of the highest caliber and, in time, I felt proud and at home to be representing PFC.

It was a class act. After 2 full days of business discussions, the Marketing VPs gave a Colorado Rockies cap and bottle of wine to all who had followed the instructions that we should bring some signed "apps" for that important purpose. I shared my wine with those newly found friends on the deluxe bus that was used to take us up 8,000 ft. to Center City and Black Hawk. They are two historic mining towns that Colorado maintains in the original wood and mortar, the churches, opera house, homes, town hall, etc, and oh yeah, the old saloons which are now state-licensed gambling casinos. I could even have done some gold panning up in them thar hills.

I now tried to pick up the pace in covering the area from Naples to Port Charlotte. I had accounts with a variety of companies in the building industry, a

Baby Danny, 1992

Author and granddaughter, Sarah, ca. 1998

mix of activity, owners, and employees. My long days were usually planned completely with phone and personal calls, presentations, office records, driving Zeni for various needs, helping Christina get around to after class activities, and visits to friends. I looked forward to Sunday for a bit of family leisure.

Maria gave birth to Daniel in 1991. Now about to start his junior year in high school as I write, he holds a second degree black belt in karate, plays trumpet in the marching band, and pitches on the baseball team. She also gave birth to Sarah in '93. An honor student, her forte is literature, creative writing, and she has taken up Japanese on her own. Both obviously inherited a touch of grandpa there.

Always up very early, I had a heavy tray of activity and, around '92 or '93, I could feel some slowing down in my intended plans, and that meant the bank account was a bit thin from time to time. I recall a couple of times I really needed a good Thursday or Friday so I could send in some "apps" for that week, and I would begin a presentation under those anxious conditions. I recall a comment by Lee Trevino, the "Tex-Mex" great golfer of those days, speaking about golf course pressure. He said, "Pressure? I will tell you about pressure. I was a kid out there on the public links with no money or food. I bet a guy $3 dollars on the match, and I'm down 2 strokes starting the 17th hole. That's pressure." Well, similarly, I was "down," going into the close of a presentation and needed some "apps." Pressure? I think I would have rather gone through some moments of my past ("Hey, they're shootin' at us," or, "Howard, your Manila office has just been blown up.").

Upon graduating from Ft. Myers High School (currently rated 67th in the whole country by a *Washington Post* analysis) with a 4.26 GPA, Christina started at

U. of Florida and lived in the honor students' dorm the first two years. She started as a double major in graphic arts and journalism, finished with a BFA in Graphic Design. She was the editor of the school's literary magazine one year and the graphic designer another, as well as the editor of the honor student's weekly. She also worked 8-10 hours a week at *The Independent Florida Alligator,* the student-run and student-read newspaper (circ. 25,000 a day). Jumping to the present, she has been recognized for her senior designer work in the publications department of a large university and in her leisure time she has visited her country of birth twice (at which time she opened a very informative blog), visiting relatives, backpacking, and swimming with the butanding (whale sharks) in Bicol (Philippines), as well as backpacking in Bolivia, and kayaking with the whales off of Vancouver (What's with the whales? She read *Moby Dick?* She likes the Book of Jonah?)

ZENI—ADJUSTING BETTER

Mom decided to go to work. Michele was not living at home and Christina was at UF. Also, I was just getting the bills paid, so that was an important matter. Knowing much about clothes and style, she worked in women's apparel but was not busy enough in the first two stores she tried. Neither was very active, being overpriced and slightly ahead of the wave in the anticipated local growing economy. But she took a job at Montgomery Ward and as soon as she became familiar with the system, she established a nice sales record. The store manager was looking for someone to introduce and sell the newly created MWard credit card to customers and shoppers in the store, and asked Mom to work out a sales plan.

Howard and Zeni visiting Christina in Gainesville, Florida, ca. 1995

They agreed on a base and commission. She had a counter at the front door, sold bi-lingually, and worked the plan. She set some records for the country. Montgomery Ward was pleased, and a Senior VP in Chicago sent her a letter of commendation for her work. When the guys in the appliances section realized she was making more than they were, they complained to management and asked for an upward adjustment in their commissions. But management played it the other way and decreased Mom's commission. Nevertheless, she continued to be productive and her contribution to our family finances at that time was necessary and greatly appreciated.

After attending the British American Drama Academy in London, Mariana graduated from the Tisch College of Theater, NYU, performed in several Off Broadway plays, and helped develop a unique theater company, but it lacked the necessary backing. She teaches theater at a private school in NYC. She continues to seek auditions. We all admire her diligence and "never, never, never" give up spirit. With her knowledge, ability, character and attitude, she truly is a success. That important "personal best" of which the running guru spoke is with you throughout the race and your life. One might not win the race, but regardless of the outcome, cannot lose.

ANOTHER MINISTRY

In the mid-90's I volunteered to sit with hospice patients while the primary caretaker, usually a spouse, took a morning or afternoon break. After a three day training seminar I did that once or twice a week. Two patients stand out in my mind: Hans was 91 and had a disease of the bone marrow. Bedridden, he lived in a farmhouse on the outskirts of Ft. Myers. He was by himself most of the time. The hospice nurse visited daily; a family member came by a couple times a day to prepare meals. I visited twice a week for a year. We became good friends. He had left home in Europe at about 18 when the economy and wide spread famine wreaked havoc everywhere. His family was poor, and his father got him passage on a ship that was going to Canada because there was no future for him at home. He worked on farms and later moved to Michigan and worked the tulip beds, married, and later went into the flower bulb business himself. He eventually had very successful bulb farms in North Carolina and Florida.

Hans had a marvelous sense of humor and was talkative even in his condition. I would open the door and walk in. "Yo, Hans." "Yo," he would shout from the bedroom. "Oh, I thought you might be sleeping." "Oh I can sleep any time. Come on in," and so we would start another conversation which we both enjoyed. He was direct and humorous. The nurse would make her scheduled visit and they obviously had become friends and liked to joke around, like:

(The nurse enters.)

Hans: "Oh boy, oh boy. Hi honey."

She: "Now keep your hands to yourself. I almost didn't come here today."

Hans: "How come?"
Nurse: "Because you're so ugly."
He: "Yeah, but I'm working on it."

Naturally there were times when he was anxious, distressed, or unsure. Then we talked about God, Faith, Love, and I helped him to recall some relevant teachings from his childhood. Early in our friendship I read him the beautiful writing about Love, that God is Love from the First Letter of John, Chapter 4, verses 13-21. He absorbed it like a sponge and I always read it upon my departure. He would remind me if necessary. "Hey Howard, you forgot to read John."

One day I found out Hans had never tried to contact anyone from his family in his country of birth. I asked if he wanted me to call that small town in Holland and see what happened. I did, and asked the operator there if she could let me speak to someone of that name. On a second try someone scurried around to find an English-speaking relative and it worked out that a grand nephew came over from Europe to see Hans and his children, and some other relatives came over later on, connecting for the first time.

Some months later Hans was moved to the Hospice House and, at the invitation of his sons, I went there and led the prayers in his crowded room. He was in a semi-coma but could probably hear. I went back at dawn the next morning. The place was empty, still and quiet. In the dim light, I leaned over my good friend Hans and told him who I was, that Jesus loved him very much, and I was sure we would meet again. He incoherently grunted his reply and final thought to me. I probably read I John 4:13-21.

At his funeral, after the eulogy by a son, the director asked if anyone wanted to say anything. I got up and talked about the goodness of Hans and explained why I would then read 1 John Ch 4, 13-21, which I did with the family's pleasure and thanks. Later in the day when I had some quiet time at home, I came to realize I was beginning to hear the answer to "What's it all about Lord?" and yes, with the guidance of the Holy Spirit I was making a difference.

The other patient was Bill, about 81. He had heart trouble and incurable cancer. He was born in Florida, joined the Navy at about 18, and went to radio school, worked his way up to Chief Petty Officer, and kept right on going to Captain, with a wartime commission of Commodore, a real "mustang" in Navy parlance. Most of his activity in WWII was on destroyers, the "tin can Navy." We hit it off nicely, talking Navy most of the time. In fact, when I mentioned old Chief Mooney on the USS Vesole, Bill recalled him from their early radio operator days. When I would get ready to leave the nursing home, I would salute him and say, "Permission to leave your ship, sir," and he would return it with a smile, blue eyes twinkling, and quietly say, "Permission granted."

One day when I visited, he was sitting in his wheelchair in the garden with his wife. He sat there, eyes closed, with a knowing smile while his wife told me their "together" story. She met him through a mutual friend at a dance when they were about twenty. She related that the friend commented to her that Bill was so smart he was either going to be an admiral or the head of General Motors. As it happened, they were married about five weeks later. She said, "Well, I figured if that handsome devil is going to be the CEO of General Motors, or an Admiral, what are we waiting for?" All the while Bill was sitting there, his light-sensitive eyes closed, full head of white hair, with that nice, knowing, smile on his face. After Bill had retired, they bought a 38-foot sloop and sailed anywhere they chose, free spirits on the wind.

A NOSTALGIC STOP AT THE BEEHIVE

In June 1995, I attended the graduation ceremonies at St. Benedict's Prep and concurrently the 50th graduation anniversary of our class of '45. There were 26 of us sitting off to the side in suits and ties, except one. He wore a shirt with a nice mix of tan, brown and yellow leaf design. The headmaster called us to the stage one at a time, before the actual graduation ceremony started, to receive our commemorative diplomas. When he called my name, "Howard Newhard," and I walked the aisle and started up the stairs to the stage, he obviously noticed my choice of attire and added, "Aalll the way from Florida!"

One of the speakers was a bishop from Africa, Bishop Arinze, I think, before he became a cardinal, when he was my choice for Pope to follow Blessed Pope John Paul II. He thoughtfully said, "I see what the class of 1945 looked like and I see what the class of 1995 looks like. I wonder what the class of 2045 will look like?"

It was nice to be back in the old "core years" structures and environment. I recall a touch of humor by the main speaker, a Harvard Law School graduate from Philadelphia who had come up the hard way and gave an inspiring speech to the graduates. He opened with, "Every big city has that tough place where you don't want to walk at night, even if you can whistle. In Los Angeles it's called Watts. In Chicago it's called South Side. In New York it's the Bronx. In Philadelphia we call it Philadelphia."

Early in the year I received some kind of a call to start doing things and work with my hands. Those who know me well would call this a miracle. I started by cleaning the garage, painting its floor, and building wooden storage racks on both sides, plus a work bench. I put muriatic acid on the circular driveway and waterproofed it. I moved 50 wheel barrows of river rock from the circular drive to the rear of the property and planted and mulched the vacated area. On the back property line I built a 120ft x 6ft wooden fence with notched supports and painted it. I also built a picnic bench and put a motion light in the rear area. I have written "I," "I," "I" throughout the paragraph in keeping with the truthfulness of this tale, i.e., all by myself. I can't believe I did that in the summer of 1995, or any other time for that matter. I also built a bench on

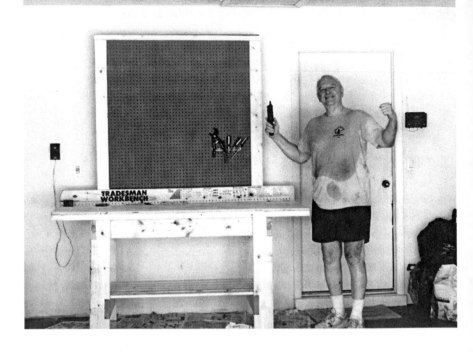

our corner for the school children waiting for their bus. On the attached plaque, which is still there, is a verse which I wrote:

> *To students who do their best each day,*
> *For God, family, country, and friends,*
> *Unsung heroes now but our future's way,*
> *In the Grand Design that never ends.*

I continued on with my work for PFC. Sometime after we drove Christina up to Gainesville to the University of Florida, I visited the Gainesville Builders Association and signed up. When I visited Christina in the future I stayed 3-4 days and called on the membership. The company I remember most from that area was a lumber and sawmill company, a bit out of town. Strictly rural, the road in from the highway was dirt and the big circular saws, conveyers, flywheels, and drive-belts were out in the open with minimal roof and overhead covering. Large mulch and sawdust piles were near the road for loading, and the sawed lumber was stacked in a large yard in the back of the property. The owners were nice folks and they liked the PFC program. They figured the best time for me to present the program to the employees was when they ate their lunch on picnic benches in the employees center, an open-air, roofed location with soda machines, wash basins, makeshift lockers and a dirt floor. With my background, I am not touched by racial constraints and have had many friends of all ethnicities; so I was a bit taken back to be in an environment where all the African-American employees sat and ate on one side of the center and the Caucasians sat on the other, as I did my presentation, with the dirt floor aisle in the middle. They knew each other, worked together, sometimes at dangerous jobs, and I assumed some were friends having worked there many years, but this situation about lunch break unfortunately kept the old ways alive. Many needed the savings and retirement plan and liked it. They didn't earn much up there in the pine woods and it fit them perfectly. I visited there many times and was able to help, especially when PFC introduced an inexpensive disability program. It was nice to know I made a difference.

I started a program in our neighborhood to collect winter clothes in September and take them over to the Guadalupe Center in Immokalee, about 50 miles away, for distribution to the poor who work on those vegetable farms. We lived on a corner, so the neighbors would just drop off a sack of clothes against our garage door. One Thanksgiving Day Michele and I joined other volunteers of the Guadalupe Center to help cook and serve 2,000 meals at Immokalee Park to the homeless and itinerant farm workers and their families. That started me on a project I feel strongly about. The large companies which own those large tracts of land and ship those vegetables all over the country pay those workers a pittance and they get "hosed" by their landlords. I was in a couple of protest marches to change the law. We all wrote to state legislators. Over the years religious, political, and entertainment figures have visited there and loudly decried the injustice and still nothing has been done. Do they teach lobbying in college now? It's such an important industry. Their motto is "In Money We Trust."

In 1997 I was 70. The good news was it was the year of our 35th wedding anniversary, and the family came together for a celebration. The bad news was that a routine blood test showed a high PSA rating, and the ultrasound and biopsy procedures concluded I had prostate cancer. Zeni, my urologist, and I agreed I would undergo a series of radiation treatments, and after a short wait, a transtitial irradiation operation, wherein they placed irradiated "seeds," the size of a grain of rice into the prostate. It was successful but of course I was "dragging" for a total of 4-5 months. I had told my customers what was happening and now I went out to pick up the action. Some had left me, but others were intact and so I was at the same old corner selling the same old apples and pencils, a bit tired, and older, but I liked the work and PFC. That December I wrote to our relatives in the Philippines (Appendix E).

The following year I had just finished a sales call on a company owner, got into the car, and became a little dizzy while feeling a mild thumping at the base of my throat. I started the engine and drove straight to the nearby emergency room of S.W. Regional Hospital. They thought I had had a heart attack and gave me a catheterization, where they put the scanning "snake" into the large artery in your leg that goes into your heart so they can watch it on the monitor screen. I was fully conscious, and the nice doctor explained to me what we were seeing.

The good news was there was no blockage. Atrial fibrillation was the answer, which I have been medicated for ever since. As we finished up I told the doctor that with all the money they made they should be able to afford a color monitor screen. He politely laughed. So I tried to get back to work. Christina showed up. We visited my general practitioner. I think having talked with her sisters, she proceeded to convince me to close it down, do some of my ministries, but no more sales work. The doctor agreed. My frame of mind at that time might have contributed to my writing of The Omega (see Appendix F).

Mom, God bless her, had become overweight, was pre-diabetic, and was having depression problems. We had not been back to the Philippines in all this time and it was a logical course of action that she should go and visit her family and friends. A measure of her unhappiness showed when she stayed for four months. Upon her return Mom, in a better frame of mind, laughingly said, "Moy was shocked that I stayed so long and asked, "Did you get a divorce?"

Mom had trouble with Acceptance. Why not? She never had any conditioning for it outside the war years. But even then she was a young girl and family-protected. Even though I had written and told her we could not keep the house because we fell behind in the mortgage payments (we had rolled it twice) it was hard to accept. We had lived there for about eleven years. For me, the garden apartment I picked while she was away was nice with a large pool and top of the line workout room and a large communal lounge with giant TV and a couple of pool tables. We were early tenants in a new development and received a bargain rental.

Michele and Chloe at diner, 2002 *Chloe as reindeer, Christmas 2004*

I did my hospice work and started my Eucharistic Ministry to the hospital. We did more things together now, and Mom had some friends with whom she went out with for shopping and movies. Sometime we would be with John and Michele. John is a nice guy, a good artist and salesman, and ex-Coast Guard sailor. Then in April 1999 Chloe was born as Mom, Donna (John's mom), and I, standing in the hall, listened intently for a baby's cry, knowing Michele was in labor behind the door. John was with her as was the nurse midwife who had delivered about 2,000 babies. Suddenly there it was and Chloe had arrived, and the three of us with arms around each other danced in the hall to the smiling reactions of the passing nurses. Chloe is a lovely girl, strawberry-blonde with hazel eyes and all those different racial genes bouncing around to make her the beauty that she is.

Mom was more herself again when helping to take care of another little baby girl. Chloe was the tonic for Mom's occasional melancholy. Michele and John were both working as hair stylists so Chloe was with us often with Zeni leading the diaper changing, feeding, and the rest. They lived in a duplex apartment near a pond with ducks, and bought an English Bull Mastiff named Angus to keep little Coco the Jack Russell terrier company. What a combination. Those two were the best of friends. Now, years later, as I move toward the end of my story, I live with Michele, John, and Chloe, along with three cats, two dogs, and a big black-and-white rabbit called Tootsie Roll. Michele boards Raven, a black Arabian mare; proving, I guess, that she retains subliminal "vibes" from the days of "Thumper," the quail hatch, and the mountain ponies of Baguio.

The next year I drove to Tampa with Mom so we could attend her U.S. Citizenship award ceremony. As a child, before the Japanese invasion of the Philippines, in December 1941, she had pledged allegiance to the Stars and Stripes and sang the national anthem and knew some American History because the Philippines, like Hawaii, was a U.S. territory then. All this was sort of an extension in time and she was happy to become a citizen, knowing the real meaning.

Over the next couple of years Chloe was with us often. Mom, as you guys know, gained more weight and became a diabetic and I took her to a clinic to review the do's and don'ts concerning eating. It did not seem to help much. The doctor was medicating her. She seemed to be more irritable and one day when Chloe, then about two, was with us, I mentioned I would help clean the kitchen and she took that to mean I was actually criticizing her for not cleaning the kitchen and she lost her temper. I tried to correct her impression and then asked if she wanted to walk over to the nearby children's playground with Chloe and me. No. She remained angry. So Chloe and I walked over to the playground for her usual happy session. When we returned to the apartment, I opened the door and walked in looking straight ahead at Chloe, who was heading for one of the bedrooms, while I was talking to Mom who was on the sofa to my left. As I walked well into the apartment, I realized that she was not answering or responding to my talking. I looked over and she was sitting on the sofa slouched backward, head to one side; her eyes were shifting from side to side and she was motionless. I grabbed the phone for 911, gave the necessary information and told them she had a stroke. I put Mom in a more comfortable position and said, "Zeni, can you hear me? Squeeze my hand, can you raise an arm? Please open your eyes!"

The EMS squad arrived a few minutes thereafter. The three of them were superb. While two started to minister to Zeni, the other asked me questions. Is she a diabetic? How long? How much does she weigh? High B/P ratings? Last reading? And so forth. All the while I was holding Chloe, and then Zeni was on her way to the hospital. Michele came over to get Chloe. I rushed to the hospital. She was on a respirator in ICU and not responding. Oh, God, my Zeni was helpless! She had a major left brain stroke and they suspected the whole right side was paralyzed.

I immediately called you all in New York and you arrived the next morning. I had her POA (Power of Attorney) for critical health decisions and the five of us went to the hospital to see Mom and have a meeting with the neurologist in attendance. Of Philippine heritage, he himself was born in the U.S.A.. He said, "I'm sorry about your Mom. Look, you know this is very serious and you don't know me. I am Dr. Gamez and we don't have much time for you to check me out, but I want you to know that I am very good." This, and our ensuing meaningful conversation, established the necessary rapport that we all wanted. He is very good. Today, he is my neurologist and has always treated us as "family." He once said Mom reminded him of his aunt. Mom was being fed intravenously and not responding much. Did we want her to stay on the respirator? Yes.

The next day they had more information. She was responding but she could not talk or swallow and her whole right side was paralyzed, except for that side of her face. Sometime thereafter they took her off the respirator based on the readings, only to have a relapse. We were asked if we wanted her to go back on the respirator and we all said yes. The staff doctor asked me how about if we take her off again and it's not working out; do you want us to put her back on a third time? We all voted no, leaving that emotional crunch deep in our memory bins.

We all went in to see her several times in the next few days. Mom came off the respirator again as the vital signs improved, and remained in the hospital about 10 days before being transferring to the Shady Rest Nursing Home that I would get to know so well. It was February 2002.

To assist my narration, I will partially quote from a letter dated May 7, 2002 that I wrote to my friend Digi in response to his letter. Hearing about Zeni, he announced the situation at our St. Benedict's class reunion held at a restaurant in Spring Lake, New Jersey. All my classmates who were in attendance, about twenty, wrote a note of encouragement and prayer on the menu, to which Digi attached to his letter.

"Digi, I read your letter to Zeni. She can understand what she hears, and I know is grateful. Horse Haesler was talking with Fr. Ambrose, OSB, Class of '47 and told him of Zeni's situation. Fr Ambrose said he would ask the monks to remember Zeni in their daily Mass prayers. I told Zeni that many in the St. Benedict's community, including some "heavy lifters," were now praying for her. She understood, and smiled, liking my sense of humor. She cannot converse, but now and then can repeat a word that she hears. The problem is that the damaged part of the brain cannot form and program what is to be said. Of course I ask questions with multiple choice answers and she can head-shake yes or no as we go along in our experimental communication mode. I am now quite accomplished in the "sending" part of charades. A head shake "yes" means that she now has "got it," but of course can't say what "it" is. The progress is slow. Baby steps, if that.

"Three weeks ago she swallowed for the first time. I did not know that swallowing was such a complicated, multi-faceted action, starting with the brain. Today they will test her swallowing with special equipment so they will have a real time and permanent picture of her swallowing action. Meanwhile, she continues to be fed and medicated through a detachable tube that connects to an in-place tube that runs from outside the stomach through the stomach wall and into the stomach. This allows her to be lifted out of bed, and go to therapy on a wheeler cot. I also wheel her out into the garden that she likes so much. Her whole right side will never recover, but the left side shows some improvement, arm, leg, hand, and foot. But again it's baby steps. It's not the lack of muscular strength but brain damage that inhibits the use of the muscles and nerves. She is not depressed, smiles often, and when she struggles to say a word and it won't come, as usual, I might say, "Ay naku" (Tagalog expression meaning something like "oh my," or " doggone it"). Then, repeating, she will say, "Ay naku" and smile that lovely smile.

"You know DiGi, I thought I had seen it all, the wars, ruined countries, Hiroshima, the starving in backward countries, losing our soon-to-be-born son, helping sick and dying people in my Hospice and Eucharistic Ministry visits to hospitals, the terrorism I faced with the death threats and having my office bombed out in Manila, to say nothing of my activities with the Agency. I'm a pretty tough guy, can take the hits. Sacramentally, spiritually, and in our human hearts, Zeni and I have been one for 40 years, but now we have come to the time of the stroke and 'Zeni, can you hear me? squeeze my hand, make a sound,' to the baby step progress I described above.

"I tell you, looking at that helpless part of our oneness (she had Last Rites) was very difficult, and I am being treated for mild depression. But in the words of the great Churchill we never, never, ever, ever, give up, as I see her every day and help with the baby steps. A biblical thought that comes to mind: For those who love God, all things work for a greater good. Zeni cannot create and say a thought. She can repeat a word, is even improving on sing-a-long therapy, *but she cannot speak the thoughts she is thinking. However, we had a miracle about two weeks ago. She looked me in the eye and slowly, clearly, said, "I want you to know I go with God." Wow, those chills again.*

"Family and friends have been just great, and now you, my old buddy throughout the years, whether in touch or not, I again thank you for your love and kindness, (signed) Howie."

In September of that year my nephew, your cousin, Rob Rettino died after a long illness. My mind drifted back to when we would have family outings at the shore swimming, crabbing, the good times at their Toms River home. In later years when I was visiting, Rob and I would walk the beach together and talk of the important things of life, its meaning, salvation, and God's mercy. Further on, when he was very ill, we would talk on the phone, he in Jersey and I in Florida. He had a Bible nearby and I helped him in his efforts to become familiar with it, especially concerning Love as expressed in John's first letter.

I was honored to deliver the eulogy (see Appendix G).

Over the many months it was slow, painfully slow, as Zeni progressed. Eventually she was placed in a wheelchair every day and slowly started to use her left hand and arm to propel the chair, go to the dining room and into the activity room of her unit and watch TV, listen to conversations, and be among familiar faces, as the baby steps piled up. As she started the long road of progress in swallowing, she went from pureed food, to ground, then chopped, and finally regular food that we cut up for her, a pleasure I reserved for myself at lunchtime. I made it happen. It was the highlight of the day.

NOW TO CHURCH FOR MASS...AND THE REAL PROGRESS STARTS

Fr. Paul or Fr. Stan came over to the nursing home to celebrate Mass once a month, and now Zeni was able to attend in the chapel there and receive the Eucharist. That June we celebrated our 40th wedding anniversary in the chapel at Shady Rest. We had about forty guests, including some Brothers in Christ and wives. Father Paul said the Mass and stayed on for the festivities. The nursing home folks, all friends by now, helped to make it a success. Surely Mom's progress was stimulated, as you, my daughters, know.

Finally it was decided that she could go to Sunday Mass at Saint Cecilia's in the Shady Rest bus with the lift for the occupied wheelchair. The top administration officer there, Tara, had a license to drive the bus, and belonged to the St. Cecilia community. She was kind enough to take Zeni and myself to the church almost every Sunday, so typical of the compassion and thoughtfulness of the Shady Rest group. Mom was so happy. The nurses and aides dressed her in her Sunday finest and when I would push the chair into the church and place it in

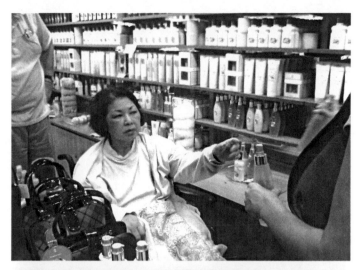

*Zeni at Bell Tower mall, shopping and having lunch with
Howard, Mari and Christina (not pictured), 2003*

the wheelchairs' space, friends would come over before Mass and hold her hand
and wish her well. During Communion a Eucharistic Minister would go to that
section to give those folks the bread and wine of Salvation, a truly joyous occasion, and she was there participating.

I then arranged for us to go out to lunch and a movie once a week, using the
county's bus system for wheelchair and other disabled people. That was a happy
highlight for my movie buff. We developed a routine. We would be picked up late
in the morning and dropped off at the Bell Tower Mall. I would push her around

to the various shops and she would look and comment (hand movement, facial expression, and head movement to answer my yes-or-no questions) and sometimes we would buy perfume, soap, whatever. Once we stopped by a silk shop where Zeni worked before Montgomery Ward, but the ownership had changed. Then we would wheel over to Albert the waiter and the chef/owners at a very nice Italian restaurant, an easy "push" to the theater. The restaurant folks always greeted the lady in the wheelchair as we became Thursday "regulars." Zeni would read the menu and point to her choice, usually a baked fish, or seafood salad. The walls were of Mediterranean motif. One section depicted grapes, a glass of wine and a loaf of bread, with a famous inscription circling it. It was in front of me and behind Zeni. I read the first few words and Zeni picked right up and finished it. She knew it by heart (like the sing-along situations). The speed of the response was most encouraging. From there it was a "roll-on" to the movie with Zeni pointing out which sidewalk she thought was best for us to travel, and where to cross the parking lot and road, more progress. After the movie we would board the bus and return to the nursing home where she would have a nap before the evening meal and I would return to the apartment.

Mom's happiest times were when Michele and Chloe would visit or when you New Yorkians would show up and we would all do the lunch and theater bit, or sit in the garden and do sing-alongs. Of course she was pleased with my daily visits but that was an everyday occurrence and you guys were special. She understood everything that was going on around her and developed a routine in her limited conditions. In the evening she was comfortable in bed watching

Zeni at Shady Rest, a few months after her first stroke.

Wheel of Fortune and Jeopardy, a standard TV setting for her by the people in attendance. As time went on we were told that Mom had reached her improvement limits and we could expect her to level out. We could accept that, knowing where she had started and the improvement made, and seeing that she was not depressed, smiled often, and was interested in watching TV, listening to other patients in the activities room, sitting in the dining room and eating with others, and was able to move her wheelchair forward using her left hand.

Auntie Luz visited the U.S. in 2004, and after some time in California came to the east coast to see relatives in New York and then here in Florida. She was very pleased that Mom was well cared for and had made progress. She stayed a week or so and returned to California for a while en route to the Philippines. About that time another speech miracle occurred. Mom and I were sitting at a table in the activity room. She reached for my hand and looked straight into my eyes and clearly said, "I love you." It was a tender moment that lasted and I got misty and she smiled and I kissed her. A few days later an attendant went to wake her from an afternoon nap to get her ready for dinner, but she would not wake up. I rushed over and Dr. Gamez told me she had a stroke right in the "fuse box," that area at the base of the skull. That she would not recover and he recommended that we place her in hospice, which, of course, was done. Fr. Stan gave her Last Rites, you guys came in the next day, and the day after that, May 26, Mom entered Eternal Life.

I recalled those two speaking miracles. "I want you to know I go with God," and "I love you." She was ready to move through the valley of the shadow and go Home.

Auntie Luz flew back from California for the funeral service at St. Cecilia's. We used the community center for the after-service get-together. You, my dear daughters, along with Michael and John, did so much to make the event a celebration of Mom's life. So many friends and relatives sent messages of condolence. My good friend and Georgetown classmate, Dick Barba's letter is Appendix H.

Some of Mom's ashes were placed in an urn which Auntie Luz took back to the Philippines to put in the family mausoleum with a commemorating wall plaque, and another urn was given to our church for the ashes to be placed in the memorial garden. My ashes will be likewise distributed.

I had been going to the Shady Rest Pavilion for 28 months, had many friends there, staff and patients, and continued with some minor volunteer work there, or sometimes just visited. I would go home to my empty apartment with few thoughts for the next day. I was ripe for a grievance period. The hospice counselor helped me some. Going to Mass and meeting with my Brothers in Christ helped me more. Michele and John and Chloe's presence was good for me, as was a trip to see my New York daughters. My doctor put me on a depression medication and later on I visited a clinical psychologist that Fr. Stan recommended. I told her that I felt like taking a big bag of books up onto a mountain somewhere and staying for a long, long, time. She used that in her analysis later and after about the fourth session she told me I would not have to see her anymore, but I should just pick up on my Eucharistic ministry again, visiting the hospital and nursing home, doing soup kitchen work, plus my usual routine of attending Mass followed by meeting with my Brothers in Christ a few times a week. I moved along on that line through the summer as the need for medication ceased, although the loneliness of it all naturally remained. That being a concern, Michele and John suggested I get a dog. "A boxer, Dad, that's a good dog for you." But it just didn't fit into my thinking. But it was Uncle Rich and Aunt Joyce who solved the problem. One day a large box was delivered by UPS. It was a computer (about which I knew nothing), but after a while I got the hang of the basics and have enjoyed using it, right up to the writing of this letter of my life to you, my dear daughters.

In the fall I was called to do something important. More and more I recalled the prayer from *Thoughts in Solitude* by Thomas Merton which begins: "My Lord God, I have no idea where I am going. I do not see the road ahead of me. I cannot know for certain where it will end. Nor do I really know myself, and the fact that I think I am following you does not mean that I am actually doing so. But I believe that the desire to please you does in fact please you. And I hope that I will have that desire in all that I am doing......." It became so clear to me to go and live in community, a simple life, and work with the poor, homeless, addicted, marginalized, and illiterate, however God wanted to use me. To me the calling meant to follow Jesus more closely, living a simple life among the poor. So I wrote to many groups. Of course my age, 77, was against me. One inner city job that I liked in Kansas City required some heavy lifting in their soup kitchen, another questioned if I would mix with a group of recent college graduates, but the Lasallians in Baltimore and the Franciscans in Philadelphia said let's talk and I drove there to do so. I liked them both, especially the inner-city Philadephia operation. They both were not deciding then, but had a yearly cycle of volunteers that started in July, after their selection was made in May. It was the same for another group for working in the Bronx, or Brooklyn. So I was frustrated and I guess a bit out of place age-wise. Fr. Stan, himself from Philadelphia, said, "Why do you want to go to an inner city environment? You are not young anymore and you don't have a safety net. We have plenty for you to do around here." And of course he was right. There have been enough ways for me to serve. Now I am doing my Extraordinary Eucharistic Ministry to nursing homes and the hospital, and delivering meals on wheels to those in need.

In my later years I have become more aware of the creations and presence of God in the world. It's all around me. Every once in a while I will watch a person actively talking on the sidewalk, in the street, a meeting hall, a church, a restaurant, gesturing and going through all the actions and sounds of lecturing, explaining, advocating, or whatever, and I marvel at what I am really observing. That is, how they express, think, gesture, modulate the voice, as I observe the wonder that is on parade, with no knowledge of the physiology of it all, except there is an "energy source" that cannot be measured, I focus on the miracle that I am witnessing, and give glory and praise to our Maker.

Similarly, living in this Florida land of sunshine, I find myself in adoration of God many times. When the angle of the sun, early or late in the day, gives that special luster and color to the palms and other trees and green growth, I am inspired. Van Gogh, and Fernando Amorsolo, that great Filipino artist, could bring that special tropical lighting, aura, and mystique into their paintings, reminding us, day or night, of the beautiful world that God has given us to walk through.

Eschatological inquiry is an integral part of the very nature of the human being. If one is not able to resolve those questions, which are prompted by that need for a solid base of hope and faith, when entering through the Valley to Eternal Life, therein lies a fear of the unknown in answering that biggest question of all times.

While aware of an increasing level of Faith over the years, there was even more fulfillment with the help of the Oblates of St. Francis De Sales, and our Brothers in Christ group. I also note that some aspect of reinforcement naturally developed as I volunteered at Hospice, and also read the works of its founder on "out of body" experiences, and other similar research.

I consider all the suffering in the world since time immemorial, and again comes the haunting refrain, "What's it all about, Lord?" I have come to know in my heart that we all suffer from time to time, some more often, others less, in the Divine Plan to achieve a greater good in Eternal Life, the goal of this Walk. In Christian thought there is a redemptive value in suffering, hence the lasting symbol of the Cross, whereupon one who is suffering and in true contrition joins Jesus toward joyful, eternal fulfillment.

Buddhist philosophy teaches that once born, suffering is inevitable, in small and large measures, physical and/or mental, caused by ignorance and attachment to secular matters. It goes on to look for a freedom from suffering, wherein enlightenment, to eliminate ignorance and attachment to the unimportant things of the world, is achieved through various degrees of meditation. "What's it all mean, Lord?" My faith senses that I will finally know when I arrive home. Faith: that yeast in the dough of immutable truth. Meanwhile, I like to consider Only the Now (see Appendix I).

Recently I was meditating on the word "holy," which means dedicated to God. Wow! That is powerful stuff. Are you holy? Am I holy? Many people would answer "yes," applying the definition. Pollsters might surprise us with the amount of affirmative responses. That does not mean humility has been cast aside. In Chapter 6, Joining the Navy, I wrote in a light vein, that truth trumps humility (TTH), but in a more serious sense, humility is a staying within one's self. De Sales said, "Humility is knowing your place and taking it," and in a similar context he said, "Do not wish to be anything but what you are, and try to be that perfectly."

Pilgrim sailing that mysterious course,
You surely don't know the way,
Reefs, strong waves, might bring remorse,
As you struggle ever a day.

The end's not near, oh, you think it is?
And soon you will be Home?
Shifting shoals you hope to miss,
Unknown and unseen in the foam

Only in Now, crossing that sea
Sailing with Faith to the end,
"What's it all about?" now you will see,
When Home and Peace and God all blend.

As I finish this story, I reflect on how it all started. She said, "Dad, you never talk about yourself." So here, my daughters, is my lasting gift to you. Thanks for the challenge. I sense we are all better in our love and understanding because of it.

Now, "Good night Zeni"…."Good night Dads,"…"Good night, Dear Daughters"…"Good night, Dad" …"Good night, Moose"…."Good night, Howie" …."Good night little man"…"Good night Howie, did you make a difference?" "Oy Vey! I could write a book."

<table>
<tr><td>18</td><td>ZENI

An Epilogue</td></tr>
</table>

Howard and Zeni on their honeymoon in Japan

When we first met she was such a happy person and took life in big chunks. Articulate, personable, and very pretty, she had modeled from time to time, and was the muse at the Philippine Military Academy graduation day celebration in Baguio, when in her junior year at Santo Tomas University. She liked her work with the airlines (although she would have preferred to work in journalism) and traveled widely. Mom also had a quick and pleasant sense of humor, which added to her personality and storytelling style. I always knew the goodness, character, and beauty in her soul, and that truth was shown to me through my faith in those times of tumultuous happenings, and so I stayed the course, and was there when she really needed me. Mom entered eternal life happy and fulfilled, as we all had told her that we loved her many times in those days in the nursing home. As she said, "I want you to know I go with God." Now, before participating in Mass 2-3 times a week, when spiritually aware in the quiet of the morning, I visit Mom in the lovely tropical setting of the memorial garden behind our church.

Did we have troubled times? Yes. Could I have been a better husband? Yes. Could I have been a better father? Yes. But then, a "been-a-better" inquiry, about most anything, always deserves a "yes" answer, if Pride with its deceitfulness is not to win the day. One reason for the "yes" appears through the mist of time from about forty years ago. We were at a husband and wife retreat in a marvelous, isolated, rural setting, sitting on a bench talking to get to know each other more and deepen our relationship. Mom asked me to open myself up more in dealing with her, to say what was on my mind more often, and to talk about myself. I admitted that did not come easily for me, but I tried.

Among many pleasing memories, I recall we were truly happy in love when we took a weekend trip to a lodge on the ridge of Tagaytay in the Philippines, that lake within the ancient volcanic crater. It was a cool February night over those tropical hills, with a clear starry sky hanging low, and a full moon stealing the show. We sat out on the balcony high on the ridge overlooking the lake, while the first two joys of our life, Maria and Mariana, were sleeping inside. We talked and snuggled as the moon drifted on. It was a touch of heaven.

Mom lost your brother to-be, Andrew, in a miscarriage at the 6th month, and she had another miscarriage between the births of Muning and Michele about 1969, and another between Michele and Christina about 1972. In addition, she had an operation for cervical cancer at Manila Doctor's Hospital about 1981. A few times in the later years, most of the sadness having gone away, she would say with a smile that God knew we could not handle seven.

There were seldom any rocks in the road in the first ten or so years, but slowly Mom would come to upsetting situations where she would shout and "lose it." This would be followed by a happy and cheerful Mom, when all would be in good order. Then Mom would find fault with many matters. She became quite demanding on me, the maids, and demanding on you, my daughters, about the various matters of school and growing up, some perhaps valid, others unfounded.

I could never reconcile Mom's increasing "ups and downs" with her usually pleasing personality and character, to times of unhappiness even depression. When it became a repeated problem, I asked her to please see a psychiatrist and seek advice. She always refused. In her mind and culture such a move was embarrassing and seldom discussed. Mom's compulsive eating and weight gain also entered into her overall health problem. Looking back from more recent years and after a bit of research, I feel, aside from the weight problem, she had bipolar syndrome. Had she gone to a psychiatrist and been told, "It's not your fault, there's a chemical imbalance in your brain which we will fix; take your medicine, and you will be all right." Ah, ifa, woulda, coulda, shoulda…could I have done more? Yes.

Not to say we didn't have our happy times along the way, but a tranquil family we were not. I guess each of us carried our burdens of various weights, sizes, and descriptions at various times. My dear daughters, no two relationships are the same, and while we all have had our commonalities in our relationships with Mom, good and otherwise, I have felt this whole matter is better served by writing this epilogue. For surely I feel a part of me went with her that day in May in 2004.

About a year ago, after seeing you guys in the New York area, I was driving back to Florida, and around Jacksonville heavy rains came and continued as I headed toward Orlando. On that stretch it increased, along with the wind. It was dark, construction and vehicle lights only. Many roads were under construction. The signs about where to turn and what not to do were barely visible in the pouring rain, as the big trucks roared along adding more confusion. Upon leaving Jacksonville, I had thoughts about checking into a motel, having driven all day. I was sleepy and struggling and fighting to keep my concentration. Suddenly I felt Mom's vivid presence in the seat next to me, where she had sat thousands of times. With the trucks thundering by, I could not look over, but I talked to her. "How are you Zeni? I love you. I will be with you one day," while peering into the storm. There was no reply as the storm, rain, thunder, and truck noise prevailed. Later, when I could look over, the seat was empty, but I knew she had been there for a minute or so. I soon found a motel and drifted into a long deep sleep. She had been there, in the car. I knew it.

That thought from Kahlil Gibran (mentioned in Chapter 9, CIA) that "the mountain is seen clearer from the plain" speaks of distance and time, and it is clear to me now, that another miracle took place, concerning Mom. One in addition to thinking, creating, and delivering " I want you to know I go with God" and "I love you." Look back to where she was in her youth and years of vitality, as described, and then continuing a nice lifestyle, having lovely children and a loving husband. Then she became ill as she was losing that lifestyle, and happened to be angry at her husband just before she had a major stroke. She showed courage from the very beginning in her new life at the nursing home. That was difficult with the slow progress and limited success.

As Mom improved a bit, in other areas like swallowing and developing some motion on the left side, she said, "I want you to know I go with God." And later, "I love you." She knew and felt that condition. I tried to imagine what it must have been like to for her to struggle to say that. What kind of mental effort was it to concoct those words and then get them on to the "speech conveyor" and deliver them? Miracles for sure, since it could not be explained why it was only those words which she spoke "from scratch."

But the third miracle, of which I now write, is that she accepted her situation. She was not on "happy pills" and she wasn't sad. This articulate, gregarious story-teller lost all signs of sadness, wow! but smiled, gestured toward a chair when I came to visit, would reach over with her left hand and pick a piece of lint from my sleeve, or smooth over some uncombed hair. She had put herself in God's hands. She was not going to worry about her condition. This proved she was walking with God. Miracles? Yes. "An event inexplicable by the laws of nature and so held to be supernatural, or an act of God." (Webster)

An amusing thought came by. Mom is now in her heavenly home and taking that life in big chunks, planning and giving parties, and sometimes coaxing St. Peter about the furniture and design of her cool abode.

Now she is Home and I in the Now, as that cute, funny, little old game, "ifa, woulda, coulda, shoulda," is no longer played, but has faded into the dusk of nothingness while Lifeletter has become its own entity.

20 APPENDICES

Appendix A: The Way It Was

"We've been through the wars together; we took our foes as they came,
And always you were the leader and ever you played the game,"
Said the Yankees to Lou Gehrig, he of "iron frame" fame.
There were similar thoughts from players and fans who really loved the game.
And across the land, whether player or fan, there was excitement about the game,
Played by boys, teens, and men of great skill; Baseball was its name.

A whole day of fun, lots of "pepper"* and "B/P,"**
and autographs for free, the way it oughta be.
It was all part of the game.
The owners of teams were men of the sport, making some money for sure,
But they loved the game, players kept to team plans,
gained an army of fans, whose loyalty was pure.
And the fans loved the game, and their heroes remained
with the team that they knew was theirs then.
Win or lose, while it mattered, their faith never shattered,
that the team was playing all for them.

Yes, the fans loved the game, and there was much more,
a whole day of fun, and the game was the core.
The players, owners, and fans made up that core,
some with no name, and others with fame, creating the soul of the game.
Always it came, like a refrain, to "get on the bus"
or "don't miss the train, cause we're goin' to the game."

---

*It was a warm-up exercise. Over in foul territories, four or five players in a line would be faced by a player with a bat in hand some 20-25 ft. away. They would use one ball, throwing it to the "batter" who would half-swing, hitting it at the line of players. The one fielding the ball would throw back to the "batter," who would hit it back to the line, and so on. The fielders in that line would often put on a show for the fans doing tricky things with the ball, like throwing it behind their back, around their necks, rolling it down their extended arms and across their shoulders, in flipping motions to each other, and then throwing it back to the batter. They had a whole routine of motions and tricks.

** B/P is batting practice. It lasted a long time. They would practice a lot of bunting, then pulling the ball along the foul line and hitting near the opposite foul line. Most could hit a long ball but there was less emphasis on the home run than today.

Today there is greed, that destroyed that fine breed,
that once took the game to its height,
It will never return, and in history they'll learn,
the soul of the game took flight.
So the "big money's" there, running that fair, focused on fortunes and fame,
and because of this, they don't even know, they've helped take the soul from
the game.
Money/profit is king and most owners bring their own style of high-power
business.
Money/profit is king and for that big ring most players will bring their kisses.

What's it all mean? It's sure a bad dream.
We know baseball it's not, and what's left will rot,
while the players keep changing their teams.
The Yankees concluded in honoring Lou, that glorious Fourth of July,
When the players and fans who loved the game listened without a dry eye,
"But higher than that we hold you, we who know you best,
knowing the way you came through every human test,
Let this be a silent token of lasting friendship's gleam,
And all that we left unspoken, your pals of the Yankee team."

No more will I hear, or I'll turn a deaf ear,
should they come and say again, to "get on the bus," or, "don't miss the train,
cause we're gonna see a game."
For it has said its goodbye and will never be the same.

Note by author: The quoted lines in the beginning and end of my poem are from the poem which was written on the silver plaque which the Yankees presented to Lou Gehrig on July 4 1939. I was there in Yankee Stadium that day with my Dad and the next day I memorized that poem from the newspaper write-up. I have carried the full poem in my memory all these years. —Howard Newhard July 4, 1989

Appendix B: Korea Lesson…In War, If You Don't Win, You Lose

After WWII, the Soviet Union stepped up its program for communist world domination (started with the Russian Revolution of 1917), by occupying various countries, including North Korea. Its growing worldwide network of espionage, psychological warfare, and guerrilla warfare was energized. The Cold War was on. Regardless, the U.S. drastically reduced its own military strength.

Following its established policy to fight its so-call Wars of Liberation using troops of its satellite countries, or insurgency movements of indoctrinated, organized, guerrillas, knowing the U.S. had armed South Korea with only light defensive weapons, and knowing the U.S. itself was militarily lighter, especially in the Northwest Pacific area, and having a veto in the U.N. Security Council, the Soviet Union had North Korea, headed by Moscow-trained Kim Il Sung, attack South Korea in full force on June 25, 1950.

General Douglas MacArthur, stationed in Tokyo as the Supreme Commander Asia Pacific (SCAP), was directed to set up a defense for South Korea and stop the advance. He was short on almost all important assets, especially well-armed, combat-ready troops. The result was the Pusan Perimeter. Our small force there had a lot of heroes, but they were nearly pushed off the peninsula before adequate help could be mustered and applied. When, later, we started to win and had the North Korea People's Army (NKPA) beaten, the Chinese Communist army entered the war from Manchuria to save their communist comrades from the "Yankee imperialists." But they could not improve on their initial gains created by their heavy ground invasion. We retook the advantage and the battle line settled to roughly the 38th parallel, the original boundary which the U.S. had agreed to with the Soviet Union in 1945 for the sole purpose of disarming the Japanese troops that had occupied Korea since 1905. Thereafter the Soviet and U.S. troops were to return home, and presumably Korea would set up its own government.

When the Chicoms entered the war in December 1950, MacArthur wanted to bomb the Manchurian railheads at Harbin, Mukden, Sinuiju and Antung, and cut off their supplies. He was not allowed to do so. How's that for backing up our fighting forces? We had been attacked by a very large army that attacked us from Manchuria and we allowed a sanctuary to be used against our guys. Similarly, our fighter pilots were forbidden to give chase to the MIG fighter planes, which were based in Manchuria.

The U.S. had about 120,000 casualties, 45,000 of which were KIA's. Millions of Korean civilians died. President Truman committed the U.S. to that war without hesitation, and rightly so. Then, when we could have won, the friends of communism in the U.N., the U.S., and around the world, worked hard to start a "peace settlement" (and save North Korea for the communists). Some in the media were influential as they harped on peace and bring the boys home, and we can all get along, and peace, and peace, oh yeah. And so the Panmunjon peace talks started, while the fighting went on another two years (July 1951-July 1953), and no armistice.

The North Koreans immediately began to talk about nonsense things at the peace table. How high will the flagpole be? Where will it be placed? How big should the table be? Who should sit there? Why does the U.S. use germ warfare? etc, etc, week after week, month after month, stalling, stalling; all the while they were militarily rebuilding and regrouping. Our high level officers who sat at the peace table were subjected to shouting and screaming about germ warfare, treatment of prisoners, etc. And the media was there parroting the lies verbatim, printing it around the world, and wittingly or unwittingly helping the enemy. Hear that déjà vu bell ringing? The situation as of now, December 2007, is that the North Korean Communist regime is in full control of every person in that country, which is very poor as it uses all it's begged, borrowed, donated, and ill gotten (counterfeiting U.S. currency) funds in a concentrated manner for military supplies, favored members of the communist party, and especially for developing a nuclear strike capability.

Our "leaders" do not know what to do. Their hands were already tied many years ago when we did not insist on unconditional surrender. Now, we have appealed to Communist China several times to help us arrange a reasonable settlement with their Communist brothers who they saved from defeat in the Korea war and would now have us believe that their little brother is an embarrassment, and they would be happy to help us.

The geopolitical strategies of the Northwest Pacific would have been entirely in favor of Korea, Japan, U.S. and the rest of the free world over the years had we fought to win and created a unified Korea. We lost the Korea War because we did not fight to win.

Having fought and won against the Japanese Empire under the policy of unconditional surrender, I know we "lost face" in Japan when we allowed North Korea and its Communist Chinese ally to "arrange" the final conditions of a cease fire. Having been in the Japanese occupation WWII, and having lived in Japan 1958-1964, and being in the Korea War 1951-1953 as a CIA case officer, and studied the matter from those viewpoints I concluded some time ago that IN WAR, IF YOU DON'T WIN, YOU LOSE. History teaches that time provides the proof for this thesis.

Appendix C: Papa Buhain's Letter of Blessing and Approval— April 2, 1962

Dear Howard,

I received your letter of March 11, 1962 and I regret very much that I was not able to answer it immediately. You know the thing you are asking me is a serious matter which I alone cannot decide and have to consult my sons and daughters before I can make a far reaching decision. My eldest son is in Okinawa participating in SEATO exercises "Tulungan" and has just arrived; hence, this delay. I hope you will be very understanding enough and patient. I assure you that I have not purposely delayed my consent.

I join you, together with my beloved wife Isabel, my daughter, Rocio, sons Moises, Vicente, Jr., Efren, another daughter, Luz, and youngest son Amado, in wishing you both all the happiness and joy in connection with your approaching marriage to my youngest daughter Zenaida. I have prayed hard to God Almighty to give you all the blessings, good luck, happiness, and blessed and sacred life of matrimony.

My only request to you in giving this consent is to take care of my daughter and learn to understand her and her shortcomings. I am quite old and in the remaining years of my life there is nothing I would treasure most than to see you both happy and living a happy and contented life. It is very reassuring and very kind of you to let me know that you "would never break any trust that you would give me and would bear it on my honor." In God's name I join you on this together with my wife and the rest of my family.

I am leaving to you both any arrangement for your approaching marriage. I would like, however, to thank you in advance for consenting to have your marriage in the Philippines and thus honoring a long established Philippine tradition. My family is also looking forward to meeting your parents which Zeni told me are coming. We assure you that we are very grateful for this and looking forward when they will arrive in the Philippines.

At the sacrifice of being redundant and repetitive, let me conclude this letter with the assurance of my blessings and prayers for the happiness of you both. In our small way we welcome you to our family. I remain, Your understanding father-in-law.

(Signed) Vicente Buhain

114 South 11 Street
Quezon City,
Philippines

April 2, 1962

Dear Howard,

I received your letter of March 11, 1962 and I regret very much that I
was not able to answer it immediately. You know the thing your are asking me
is a serious matter which I alone cannot decide and have to consult my sons
and daughters before I can make a far reaching decision. My eldest son is
in Okinawa participating in a SEATO exercise "Tulungan" and have just arrived;
hence, this delay. I hope you will be very understanding enough and patient.
I assure you that I have not purposely delayed my consent.

I join you, together with my beloved wife Isable, my daughter Rosio, sons
Moises, Vicente Jr., Efren, another daughter Luz and youngest son Amado in
wishing you both all the happiness and joy in connection with your approaching
marriage to my youngest daughter Zenaida. I have prayed hard to God Almighty
to give you all the blessings, good luck, happiness and blessed and sacred life
of matrimony.

My only request to you in giving this consent is to take care of my daughter
and learn to understand her and her shortcomings. I am very happy to know that
you are a Catholic and perhaps you understand the message I am trying to commu-
nicate to you. I am quiet old and in the remaining years of my my life there
is nothing I would treasure most than to see you both happy and living a happy
and contented life. It/very reassuring and very kind of you to let me know
that you "would never break any trust that you give to me and would bear it on
my honor." In God's name I join you on this together with my wife and the rest
of my family.

I am leaving to you both any arrangements to your approaching marriage.
I would like, however, to thank you in advance for concenting to have your
marriage in the Philippines and thus honoring a long established Pilipino
tradition. My family is also looking forward to meeting your parents which
Zeny told/are coming. We assure you that we are very grateful for this and
looking forward when they will arrive in the Philippines.

At the sacrifice of being redandant and repetitious, let me conclude this
letter with the assurrance of our blessings and prayers for/happiness for you
both. In our small way we welcome you to our family. I remain

                              You understanding father-in-law,

Appendix D: Mom's Letter to Nana and Pop-pop, 1962

15 July 1962

Dear Mama and Papa Newhard-

Do forgive us for not having written sooner. It is really surprising sometimes when little and big things can so crowd one's schedule, and you are just a little beat at the end of the day. That is certainly no excuse, but we hope that you both somehow understand.

Howie has so many wonderful friends here at Misawa, and they have been moving out of their way to make us newlyweds more settled in our home. We are still staying at Howie's former bachelor house - a very cozy, and tastefully decorated place that bespeaks my sweetheart's very good taste. He said if I wanted to do the place over, I could do so, but there is really nothing to do over since he did a very good job as it is. We are hunting for a bigger place though, because we just don't have enough space for all our stuff, and all the other things we have become richer by after our marriage.

Howie and I are oftentimes invited to dinner by his many friends here whose wives are such excellent cooks. He really has a ball then because it is a welcome respite from my very limited culinary know-how. And I have a ball myself!

We are enclosing a batch of pictures - some taken during Howie's arrival in Manila, some during the trip we made to Pagsanjan Falls (one of the tourist's attractions, a real must), some during our honeymoon, and some pictures of the wedding. We are sending you some color pictures of the wedding in about three weeks or sooner, and a little later, some more pictures in black and white. We have not yet received a lot of these pictures we plan to send, hence, the delay. Mail service between Manila and Misawa is extremely bad -- it sometimes takes two weeks for the mail to arrive.

I just received the letter you wrote to me addressed in Quezon City, Mama, recently - so that was why I was unable to answer it right away. My parent's forwarded your letter here in Misawa, and as I mentioned earlier, mail service between these two places are just awful. That was such a beautiful letter, I always read it because it makes me feel closer to you - and time and space seem immaterial. I am keeping it in my treasure box, and pray that I may be worthy of all that you wrote, and worthy of the wonderful family it has been my privilege to be a member of.

It is not difficult to please Howie because he just naturally well-tempered and has a very cheery disposition. I hope someday to get contaminated with my sweetheart's very recommendable virtues.

Today is the feast day of the Tanabata here in Japan. They are going all over it in a big way here in Misawa. The Tanabata is the Star Festival taken from a Japanese myth involving the legend of a weaver and a cow herder who were in love, and the cow herder in his passion for his lady-love, forgot all about his work, so the then king decreed that they should meet only once a year in the Milky Way. Both of them represent the two big stars. Misawa town is all-

22222

aglow with the festivities. The streets are gaily decorated with colorful lanterns that look like giant bon-bons, and tree branches. There was a parade this morning and a selection of a Miss Misawa at the beach. There were more parades and floats this afternoon that continued up to evening. The streets are naturally banned from traffic. This is a three-days celebration, and I am particularly happy for that because right now I can't walk around as much as I would want because of a slightly swollen leg. Dr. Newhard is such a good physician that my foot feels better already, and maybe tomorrow I can go out and take color pictures of the event.

Goodnight, dear Mama and Dad — our love and thoughts are always with you.

Do write us please — when you have the time. Here in Misawa, we are always starved for letters from home.

All our love,
Howard and Temi

Appendix E: Author's Advent Letter to Buhain Family in Philippines, 1997

Dear Moy, and Luz, and all the Buhain family,

In this time of Advent my thoughts are sharpened to the many years I spent in the Philippines, raising our family, and being close to you all, sharing our love, a meal, a party, a golf game, or just "hanging out" as the kids say. When I am in some quiet time and can count my blessings and good things of my life, in praise of the Lord, those days, those years and that Love shared, touches me with a mixture of fondness, sadness, gratitude and, always love. In the early years of my return to the U.S., having planned to retire and live in the Philippines, I had a lot of anger and resentment for those who had a hand in the reorganization, downscaling, and "ease-out," that left me without a job, good pension or future. It was an agony that I returned to repeatedly over the years. It was not until some years ago that I looked deeper into the teachings of Jesus that I surrendered myself completely to Him, (Totus Tuus) that I found peace with myself.

I am sorry that I have not maintained some correspondence with you…no excuses…but don't ever think I don't care.

I still work at my little business. Not too much action this year because of my cancer therapy and procedure throughout the summer, with some diminishing side effects to now. I am with a group at our church called the Brothers in Christ and do a Eucharistic ministry to hospitals and nursing homes.

For the last few years before the colder weather starts I organize some neighbors to give me cold weather clothes that I then take out to Sister Judy at the Guadalupe Center in Immokkolee, about 50 miles east of here in the vegetable growing region.. Michele joined me and one of the brothers in Christ on Thanksgiving Day when we went out there and helped cook and serve 2,000 Thanksgiving meals complete with apple and pumpkin pie to the homeless and itinerant farm workers.

We took over Immokkolee Park and it was a nice day for those people and their families. That got me on to a project I feel strongly about. The large companies that own those large tracts of land on which to grow vegetables (shipped all over the U.S.) pay those poor farm workers terrible wages. It's a horrific injustice. So we are going to try to change the law by referendum through pressuring the state legislature.

With prayers and love, May the Peace of Christmas be always with you, Howie

Appendix F: The Omega
by Howard Newhard, February 2003

It was late Spring. All day long he had trekked the wilderness, abandoning his car when the road became a trail, then a path. The twilight was blending into nightfall. Could he find a safe place, perhaps a cave? Yes, a deep cave, a cavern. But supposing all of those news reports were wrong and there was really nothing to worry about? Maybe it was all a hoax, like the Orson Welles "news" broadcast of many years ago. His father had told him that the broadcast had predicated an invasion from outer space, and many people had believed the hoax.

But no, this was real. So many astronomers, astrophysicists, and mathematicians agreed with the report. It had been all over the news reports for three months now, and not one "opposite view" report had been made. It had to be true, as reported, that a celestial body, probably from the outer limits of our galaxy, had mysteriously "slipped" its orbit. It was traveling faster than any known comets. It would hit the earth, head on, in six months. The earth would break into several parts. Some parts would gravitate toward the scorching sun and some would drift away into unbearable Cold. No one would survive.

During the past three months, while his anxiety was being nibbled away by fear, he had, of course, observed how people reacted to the repetitious report. So many people were turning to God, through whatever religion was most familiar to them. The churches, synagogues, shrines, and mosques, were always crowded. Many who had no religion, or who had ignored such thought during their lives, were now seeking God and asking friends to help them pray. He also noted that some long-standing problems and irritants within the ecumenical councils had evaporated.

Also, violence, immorality, greed, pride, and defamation of religions had disappeared from the media, TV, movies and from inter-personal relations. People were more outgoing, more helpful, and said please and thank you more often. No one was trying to gain recognition or power. An aura of humility and love prevailed. Everyone was quietly going about their daily chores, while the scientists repeatedly checked their calculations, hoping to find a mistake.

Glancing through some light brush and trees, he saw a cave that he hoped would provide adequate safety. He thought, after all they could be wrong. Maybe I could survive a brush-by or a near miss. He stopped, then asked himself, what is that just in front of the cave? Seems to be a man. He has a strange presence. Is he holding a light? The brush and twilight shadows distorted his vision. He asked, "Sir, do you live in that cave?" "No" came the reply. "I am just resting a bit, then moving on."

The young man stayed where he was and took off his back pack and laid down the rifle which he had brought along for game. Exhausted, he leaned across a boulder, saying to the man at the cave, "Later on I will go into the cave and live there. I pray that I will survive but I fear it is hopeless." The old man said, "Yes, just as in ancient times, places where people had become notoriously sinful were sometimes destroyed, along with the inhabitants" The young man responded, "Do you think that God will allow the world to be destroyed now because of its decadence and sinfulness?" "Well," the figure of shadow and light answered, "What is God's wish for his people?" The young man answered, "He wants what is best for them. He loves them unconditionally. He wants them to love him, serve him, and seek forgiveness when they offend him, so that they will have salvation and be with him in Eternity." "Is that what is happening now?" the man queried. The young man replied, "Yes, most of the people are expressing their love and asking for forgiveness and salvation." The man said, "And is all that good?" "Yes," the young man responded. The man went on, "And is the attaining of eternal happiness what the people want and what God wants for them?" Again the response was "Yes." "Then it seems that this approaching celestial body will serve the highest form of good," the man concluded.

The young man was now sitting on the boulder, looking through the trees, and into the sloping valley below, while the twilight performed its dimming magic. He said, "I can tell you are a person of great wisdom. I want to tell you what troubles me. The people on earth are made in the image and likeness of God. They are all sure of one thing, and only one thing. They are all sure that death, when their bodies cease to function, will terminate their existence on earth. Almost all people believe in a life hereafter, that is, an immortal soul."

He continued, "Now knowing that death is certain three months from now, almost everyone is loving, caring, sharing, humble and kind to each other and to God. Similarly, terminally ill people know the time they will die, and in such a case they make an effort to attain peace and reconciliation with God and those people they know."

The young man went on, "But in the everyday routine of life most people, although they know that death is certain, do not know the time it will occur. In this usual situation many act differently toward God and among each other. In recent generations we have seen violence, greed, bigotry, hatred, pride, immorality and other sins become common place. Even glorified through movies, television, and other media. It seems that many people have decided to ignore God. Many ridicule religions. Such an environment would be compounded into the future generations. They would have to sail sinful and treacherous waters without a moral compass; the devil's playground."

Resisting the fatigue that weighed on him, he focused toward his conclusion. "Knowing that death is certain and can visit at any time, what is it in the human psyche that causes this dilemma? What is driving this inability to stay focused and prepared for the most important day of their lives, the beginning of eternity? For those who are well prepared it is a day of celebration. For those who are not, it is not."

He turned to the cave saying, "What are your thoughts about this, sir? Please enlighten me." But he saw no one by the cave and the dim light was gone. He went to the cave and took a flashlight from his back pack. Night had closed in. He thought, Who was that? I didn't see him leave. Being so tired, was I in a trance?

He began to pray and after a while his firm concentration took him into contemplative prayer. He was at peace. It was comforting to be alone with his Heavenly Father. He did not fear the future, but looked forward to the beatific vision and his entry into Eternity. In this spiritual state, he apologized for having been afraid. After all, the Gospels echo with the admonition of "Be not afraid." It became clear to him that tomorrow he would return to the city and help as many as he could with their preparation. Then he gladly surrendered to the overwhelming waves of sleep that engulfed him.

Rev. 21:6: "And he said to me, 'It is done! I am the Alpha and the Omega, the beginning and the end. To the thirsty I will give water without price from the fountain of the water of life.'" (Holy Bible, RSV, 1952.)

Appendix G: Eulogy for Robert Rettino, Jr.

By Howard Newhard, September 7, 2002

The goodness of Man comes from the love we all have within us. That universal love that comes from God, for God is Love… Rob had a heart full of love.

We are not bodies with a soul. But we are souls with a human body.

The body dies but we live forever. We are on a pilgrimage to a better place; along the way sin is common. The church is not a museum of saints but a hospital of sinners. It is the love and mercy of God manifested in the life, death and resurrection of the Son Jesus that conquers all evil and sin…As you know, the direction of my life took me away from here, my home area; and so I have not seen my close relatives very often over these many years. Never the less I have some fond memories of being with Rob.

When Zeni and I lived here for about eighteen months in the mid-sixties, Maria was about two years old, Rob was about thirteen and he watched and played with her whenever he could. It was fun to be around Rob. I remember being with him crabbing or swimming at the Shore, or picnicking at my Mom and Dad's place. Days of fun and love. Rob had a sense of humor. He laughed and liked a good story.

I recall when he was much older we had occasions to walk the beach and talk of many things, including the basics and meanings of life—-eschatological concepts say the theologians—or simply, what's it all about? Rob had some understanding of that. It started with his love of God. St. Francis De Sales said, "Not only is God always in the place where we are, but God is, in a very special manner, in the depths of our spirit." In later years Rob kept a bible near his bed. And sometimes referred to it. In these years we occasionally spoke on the phone and talked of many things including Jesus and Salvation. As Scripture tells us, for those who love God, all things happen for a greater good. In those conversations I would sometimes mention a biblical writing that seemed appropriate. I have a favorite which became familiar because I read it many times to a Hospice patient I visited years ago. It is about God's Love and ours. This was meaningful for Rob. It is John 1 Ch 4, 16-19. "We have come to know and believe in the love God has for us. God is Love and he who abides in love abides in God and God in him.

Paraphrasing from John, our love is brought to perfection in this; that we should have confidence on the day of judgment; for our relation to this world is just like His. Love has no room for fear; rather perfect love casts out all fear. And since fear has to do with punishment, love is not yet perfect in one who is afraid. We, for our part, love because He first loved us.

No one on earth has ever seen God or knows the Grand design. But the thought has crossed my mind many times in my life, as I have seen various kinds of human suffering, that those who love God and suffer much are looked upon with great favor as they enter Eternal Life.

Pope John Paul II said, "In suffering there is concealed a particular power that draws a person interiorly close to Christ. Suffering more than anything else makes present the powers of Redemption. Suffering is present in the world in order to release love.

Rob suffered greatly. He placed his trust in God's mercy, and we who mourn are confident that our petition pierces the clouds and finds an answer, as we ask God to look upon his sufferings and grant him refreshment, light and peace.

Appendix H: Condolence Letter from Richard Barba

May 27, 2004

Dear Howie,

Your grief certainly does mark the measure of your love, but it is your genuine happiness for your sweetheart Zeni's entry into eternal paradise, promised by our Lord, and your acknowledgement of this moment as the blessed occasion that it is, that demonstrates clearly your absolute selflessness, and that is the single, most defining characteristic of true love. On this day God has blessed your most beloved Zeni, and you too Howie, with his own infinite and unselfish love.

As you know, St. Paul wrote, "The human eye has not seen, the human ear has not heard, nor has it ever entered into the mind, what God has in store for those who love him."* Today at last your dearest, most beloved Zeni knows.

Praise be to God,
(Signed) Dick Barba

*I Corinthians 2:9

Appendix I: Only the Now

Now and only now can I listen to God. I can't yesterday, and the uncertainty of tomorrow suggests that NOW is the time, precious time.

It seems the free will aspect in the human psyche gave us a built-in time line on which we record victories and defeats, good and evil, despair and joy, who lived when, where and how, and the beat goes on, right up to our present time, with injustice, hate, unforgiving, and bigotry, still prominent on the general scene, while the decadence of Nineveh and Gomorrah is revisited.

The Lord's Prayer asks "Thy will be done on earth as it is in heaven." Wilkie Au, in By Way of the Heart, writes "Unfortunately, many people view the will of God as rather a ten ton elephant hanging over head, ready to fall on them. Actually the word which we translate into English as 'will' comes from both Hebrew and a Greek word which means yearning. It is that yearning which lovers have for one another. Not a yearning of the mind alone or the heart alone but of the whole being. A yearning which we feel is only a glimmering of the depth of the yearning of God for us."

As St. Augustine wrote, "You made us for yourself and our hearts are restless until they come to rest in you."

The Divine Will of God caused the immaculate creation of Adam and Eve, fusing the human will into the divine will, becoming one family with God the Father before the Fall. Such was God's love for his creation of Humanity.

Was there a time-line in that earthly paradise, that extension of Heaven? What was the need for one? since total Love, Peace and Joy was in the NOW. What is Eternity, but NOW, to the infinite power.

At least for a while, we can step off this timeline. Find a quiet, tranquil place, contemplate into your inner self and listen to God, in that sanctuary that is God's alone. That's NOW, only the NOW. That's a touch of Heaven.

Appendix J: The Four Marias in Two Photos

From left to right: Maria Luz, Maria Anna, Maria Michele and Maria Christina in Baguio, Philippines, ca. 1978

From left to right: Mari, Christina, Maria and Michele in Ft. Myers, Florida, 2001

I wish to thank those who provided encouragement and other support as I moved along in writing this book. Daughters Maria, Mariana, Michele and Christina got me started. After that, I proceeded at various speeds as it all unfolded from my memory.

My friends since high school, Dick Haesler and Frank Di Girolamo helped to generate enthusiasm when I "hit a wall." My son-in-law John Schellenberg was helpful in responding to ideas and thoughts which I bounced off him from time to time, and my brother Rich Newhard and cousin Frank Eilbacher were most helpful in the final phase.

Shirley Furry is a strong editor and I am grateful for her efforts. Her insightful approach helped to crystallize my story path. I also appreciate the suggestions and proof reading done by Maria. Christina's professional and exceptional talent in book design, layout, printing preparation, and graphic arts was most welcome and appreciated.

Brother-in-Christ Brett Urban, whose book on symbolic Christianity should be out by 2010, deserves my sincere thanks for the many times he fixed the mistakes caused by my computer illiteracy.

There were times, when writing of miracles, eschatological matters, or a theological consideration, I looked back, re-read, and knew that was not me. I had help. My loving thanks, as always, to the Blessed Trinity. "In Him we live and move and have our being." Acts 17:28

901134
Bio. Sec.
Newhart

Breinigsville, PA USA
18 August 2009
222538BV00001B/208/P